Editor WILLEM L. OLTMANS, <barcode> W9-CDU-482
born and Yale-educated international journalist, writer, and lecturer, has traveled the world over in producing ON GROWTH. His research and writing in this field are continuing, and he is widely recognized for making a signal contribution to an understanding of the key issue of the twentieth century.

ON GROWTH

ON GROWTH

Willem L. Oltmans

Capricorn Books, New York

G. P. Putnam's Sons, New York

CAPRICORN BOOKS EDITION 1974

SBN: 399-11233-2
Library of Congress Catalog
Card Number: 73-82032

PRINTED IN THE UNITED STATES OF AMERICA

Preface: On Growth

This symposium about *Limits to Growth* is the result of a switch in journalistic interest. After having covered foreign affairs and international relations for twenty years, I discovered late in 1970 the Club of Rome.[1]

In those days I was representing NOS National Dutch Television in the United States. I had learned that the US and USSR were conducting semisecret negotiations about the creation of an institute for systems analysis. I contacted McGeorge Bundy, the onetime Henry Kissinger of President John F. Kennedy, who was rumored to lead the discussions with the Soviets. He introduced me, however, to Dr. Philip Handler, President of the National Academy of Sciences in Washington, D.C., who had taken over these sensitive *pourparlers*.

It was Dr. Handler who informed me about the work at the Massachusetts Institute of Technology of Professor Jay W. Forrester. Here I learned about the existence of the Club of Rome and its assignment to Forrester's system engineers at MIT[2] to study with computer models the limits of the planet as a whole.

Early in 1971, I began producing a documentary film on the information I obtained in Washington for NOS National Dutch Television. I included conversations with Dr. Handler (in Washington, D.C.), Professor Forrester (in Cambridge, Massachusetts), Dr. Aurelio Peccei (in Rome, who is founder and chairman of the Club of Rome)[3] and Dr. Djhermen M. Gvishiani[4] (in Moscow, who is vice-chairman of the state committee of the USSR Council of Ministers for Science and Technology and corresponding member of the USSR Academy of Sciences).

My film was shown September 26, 1971, in prime time on Sunday night, and apart from being a world premiere, it caused a major sensation

v

in the Netherlands. A Club of Rome sponsored exhibition was organized in Rotterdam, drawing tens of thousands of visitors, while it was opened by Queen Juliana. The Dutch edition of the MIT report, *Limits to Growth*, sold a quarter of a million copies in less than a year. During the general elections in the fall of 1972, issues raised by the Club of Rome and the Forrester-Meadows team in Cambridge, Massachusetts, turned into campaign issues.[5]

News about the plans for a US-USSR combined think tank even reached the front page of the New York *Times* a few weeks after the subject had been shown on National Dutch Television.[6] In the meantime, on October 4, 1972, twelve nations signed an agreement in London to set up a joint Institute of Applied Systems Analysis in the eighteenth-century Laxenberg Palace, ten miles from Vienna, Austria. Dr. Gvishiani was chosen chairman of the institute for a period of three years. Participating nations, besides the US and the USSR, are East and West Germany, Italy, France, England, Poland, Czechoslovakia, Bulgaria, Japan and Canada.[7]

July 6, 1972, I had a dinner meeting with Dr. Aurelio Peccei at the airport of Frankfurt. During our conversation, the plan came up to gauge, collect and publish opinions about *Limits to Growth*. Initially, I intended to gather some thirty interviews, ten at the suggestion of the Club of Rome. But soon, I decided not to limit myself to comments by economists, systems engineers, biologists or ecologists, but to look for reactions from a wider range of disciplines. Thus, the series grew to seventy conversations.

I regret that a rather large group of persons that were invited to take part in this project were unable to participate, owing to conflicting time schedules or other previously arranged commitments and want to mention in this respect, Jacques Monod, R. Buckminster Fuller, David Riesman, Barbara Ward (Lady Jackson), Bertrand de Jouvenel, John K. Galbraith (who was in China at the time), Konrad Lorenz, Hannah Arendt, Erik H. Erikson, J. Bronowski and others. On the other hand, it has to be realized that one could enlarge the group indefinitely, but a collection of conversations like this is also bound by "limits."

I am most grateful to all participants in this project, both for their most valuable help and assistance in helping me find my way in this endless labyrinth of problems and dilemmas confronting us all in this latter part of our century, and for their strenuous efforts to shape the tape-recorded interviews, correct them and make them as readable as possible for general audiences. Most interviewees felt unsatisfied about the quality of their remarks, which were intended in the first place as leisurely conversations. Professor B. F. Skinner protested altogether to having an edited version of our conversation printed in this bundle, and therefore I invited a senior editor of the magazine *Psychology Today*, Kenneth Goodall, to rewrite the text, eventually with Professor Skinner's agreement. I do not intend this book to be a scholarly, unreadable heap of scientific language. As I found that most scientists possess a treasure chest of thoughts and opinions about the *problématique* of our day, I have collected some of these, as a contribution to the worldwide discussion now under way about the finiteness of all things around us, as a further contribution to a rising consciousness that generations of today or tomorrow have no right whatsoever to leave the children of tomorrow or the days after tomorrow one huge garbage pile.

I am most grateful for their continued advice and warm interest in this project to Aurelio Peccei, Margaret Mead, Jay W. Forrester and Philip Handler, who actually helped me to discover the Club of Rome and the *Limits to Growth* study.[8]

W. L. O.
Christmas 1972

NOTES

[1]The *New York Times* described the Club of Rome on February 4, 1973, as "an elite international study group."

[2]Team leader was Professor Dennis L. Meadows.

[3]Who is also member of the board of Fiat; vice-president of Olivetti and chairman of Italconsult, Italy's foremost think tank.

[4]Son-in-law of Premier Alexei N. Kosygin.

[5]*Limits to Growth* was presented to the American public and press at the Smithsonian Institution in Washington, D.C., during a ceremony on March 2, 1972.

[6]See the New York *Times*, October 14, 1971.

[7]See the New York *Times*, October 4, 1972, report written by Richard D. Lyons from London.

[8]The author is embarked on a second series of conversations, this time in socialist nations and the Third World, likewise centered around the theme *Limits to Growth*.

Contents

Foreword: The Club of Rome

With man at the pinnacle of his knowledge and power, a profound malaise is spreading through human society. Faced with an increasingly more complex and ever-changing tangle of intertwined problems—some of them overarching all political, cultural and geographical boundaries—mankind is threatened by an unprecedented crisis.

Thirty European scientists, humanists, educators and managers met in April, 1968, at the Academy of Lincei in Rome, to discuss how this world *problématique* could be understood and met. Some of them pledged to stay together as an informal group, and to coopt people of vision and action from all continents, cultures and value systems, who shared their conviction that traditional institutions and policies are no longer able to cope with this situation or even to perceive its trends.

This group is known as the Club of Rome. Its members can number one hundred as a maximum. None of them is involved in current political decisions, nor has the club as a whole any ideological, political or national commitments, although many of its members have access to decision makers and have great stores of information and knowledge to draw upon.

The Club of Rome has two main objectives: One is to stimulate research and reflections aimed at gaining a deeper understanding of the workings of the global systems; during the first phase, this activity has been centered around the study of limits to growth, which is being discussed in this book as its main theme. The second objective is to use the insight so acquired to promote new policies and strategies inspired by a new humanism and capable of setting mankind on a saner course.

Aurelio Peccei[1]
Founder and Chairman of
the Club of Rome

NOTES

[1]See also the concluding conversation to this book.

1. U Thant

U Thant, the Asian diplomat and statesman who stood at the helm of the United Nations in New York, first in 1961 as acting secretary-general and from 1962 to 1970 as secretary-general, was born in 1909 in Pantanaw, Burma. He studied education at University College in Rangoon and became dean of the high school in Pantanaw from 1931 till 1942. After occupying various government posts, he became secretary to Prime Minister U Nu of Burma from 1949 to 1953. Before being chosen to head the world organization in New York, Dr. Thant served five years as permanent representative of Burma to the United Nations.

Dr. Thant, when you left the United Nations, you spoke upon your retirement, from where you stood, during the '70s the world would have to redirect the drift of events or face the disintegration of civilization, in other words, you want the world to do something effective now.

I made that statement in 1969 at one of the seminars conducted in one of the halls of the General Assembly of the United Nations. I felt convinced at that time, and I still feel more convinced than before, that if the international community does not concentrate its attention on the global problems, including of course the economic problems, then the human community has only ten more years left. Because I feel very strongly that the disparity between the rich and the poor countries is getting wider and wider; and this, in my view, is more explosive in the long run than the division of the world based on political ideologies. I come from a less-developed country, as everybody knows, and I am fully conscious of the magnitude of the problems confronted by these poor countries. If the developed countries do not take into consideration this aspect of the problem, I am afraid that the human community as a whole will suffer. Both the rich countries and the poor countries have to think of these problems together, and work together.

I heard Mrs. Indira Gandhi say in Stockholm, [1] *poverty is the worst polluter of all.*

Yes, I agree with her entirely. Poverty, disease and illiteracy, if I may say so. These are the cancers of mankind today. I think it is time now for the more affluent countries, the wealthier northern half of the world, to realize the full significance of this titanic problem.

You spoke of four factors, would you like to elaborate?

Well, in my view, there are four factors which are responsible for the crisis situations we are witnessing today. The first is the division of the world based on political ideologies. The second is the division of the world based on economic disparity, i.e., the difference between the north and the south, between the haves and the have-nots. In my view this division of the world is much more significant, much more important, and in the long run much more explosive, as I said a moment ago, than the division of the world based on political ideologies. The third factor is the division of the world related to the remnants of colonialism. This is also a very great factor in dividing the world, dividing the human community today. The fourth, but not the least important factor, is the division of the world based on color of the skin; in other words, the racial segregation or apartheid, as the United Nations termed it, in regard to the situation in South Africa. This discrimination on the basis of color is also a very distressing factor facing the human community today.

These are the four major factors which we have to deal with. Everybody knows that as far as the political ideologies are concerned, I am for democracy. I have been advocating democratic processes in my own country, and then as ambassador to the UN, and as Secretary-General.[2] This is my personal credo. But my conviction in the superiority of democratic processes does not blind me to the knowledge that there are hundreds of millions of people who disagree with me. I think that the division of the world based on different political ideologies is a passing phase, because all political ideologies have to coexist for a long, long time to come.

What I am most concerned about is the division of the world based on economic discrepancies. Since the end of World War II, as everybody knows, the rich countries are getting richer, the poor countries are getting poorer, and the gulf is still widening. We have to try to narrow the gap. This was one of the main purposes of the United Nations in launching the first development decade in 1961, when I took charge of the secretary-generalship of the UN. The international community launched the second development decade last year. The primary purpose is to narrow the gulf between the rich and the poor countries. Unless this problem is tackled in right earnest, with full consciousness of the gravity of the problem, particularly by the rich countries, I am not very optimistic about the future of the human situation.

The Limits to Growth *study,*[3] *sponsored by the Club of Rome*[4] *and carried out by the computers in MIT,*[5] *very much warned mankind that there is a limit to resources, a limit to economic growth and a limit to expansion. They advocate more equilibrium and more, exactly what you said, give-and-take, much closer cooperation and interdependence between the continents for the future.*

Yes, this is the fundamental basis on which the human community has to start: the spirit of give-and-take, especially the spirit of understanding on the part of the rich countries. The United Nations and its family of agencies have suggested a contribution of one percent of the gross national product on the part of the developed countries to the developing countries. This has not been met, as you know. Far from meeting this, some rich countries did not pay any attention to this. However, in this connection, I must say that most of the Scandinavian countries, as well as Canada and the Netherlands, if I am to pick and choose a few, are very conscious of the importance of this problem.

As a Dutchman, I would like to point out that Holland reached 0.78, that means the highest percentage of the gross national product in aid, while it is amazing that the United States next to Italy is the lowest, when this nation is by far the richest.[6]

* * *

Well, I don't want to comment on this *per se*, but I mentioned the Netherlands particularly because of my close study of the Netherlands' policy regarding economic aid. I must take this opportunity of expressing my appreciation to the government of the Netherlands for its understanding and the spirit of cooperation with the United Nations and the agencies in this particular respect.

In Stockholm only a hundred million dollars were proposed as an allocation to the human environment studies and fighting, the preservation of human environment for the next five years. Now, in view of the fantastic amounts of billions of dollars that still go in armaments, isn't a hundred million dollars very low in relation to the needs to preserve the environment?

Well, to this question I think Maurice Strong would be in a better position than I am to answer. But when you speak of a hundred million or X million dollars, we have to think in terms of relative priorities. Just to illustrate my point. All the participants in the Indochina war last year, according to figures available to me, were spending in the Vietnam war for one day, an equivalent to what has been spent for the United Nations for one year. This means, if the Vietnam war were to go on for another year, the expenditure incurred by all participants in that war would be equivalent to the expenditure of operating the United Nations at the present level of expenditure for another 365 years. We have to think of all expenses in relative terms. I am sure Maurice Strong[7] will feel that a hundred million dollars for five years to cope with such a gigantic task is a very low figure.

If we think of the tremendous expenses incurred by many countries on armaments, then we will realize how much economic aspects of human development have been ignored or bypassed. That is one illustration of the need for priorities on the expenditures regarding war and peace. When I say "peace," I mean both peace building and peace keeping. Of course the UN has been involved in both aspects of peace; one is peace building, another is peace keeping. This narrowing the gulf between the north and the south is one aspect of peace building. Without this essential prerequisite, there will be no peace. In other words, without social justice, not only in national societies but also in the international scene, there will be no peace. This is an important basis on which enduring peace can be built. This is the number-one problem facing humanity today.

Was it not frustrating in your life experience that you could not bring peace to some areas where [there was] consistent strife like the Near East or Southeast Asia?

Yes. I must say that in my ten years as Secretary-General of the United Nations, there have been moments of frustration as well as moments of gratification: a plus and minus. I am now devoting my whole time to writing my memoirs. But the book will not be memoirs in the strict sense of the term. It will be my reflections and analysis and evaluation of the international scene in the last decade. I am projecting myself, my personal credo and my personal philosophy, into this book.

Of course the situation in the Middle East is a case for frustration. The Vietnam war is a case for very extreme frustration on my part. The question of war in Vietnam was not brought before the General Assembly or the Security Council, for reasons known to everybody; but death and destruction and devastation of the country is unparalleled in human history. This war could have been ended earlier, in my view. There were many cases of missed opportunities, which were not seized by the parties concerned. I am going to disclose some of these important developments in my book.

As far as the Middle East is concerned, my concept and my approach to the problem is known to everybody in the United Nations.

My view of the international problems is necessarily different from the viewpoint of the member states concerned. My view may be likened to that of the view of the man from the bridge. The purpose of the UN after all is to build bridges. I regard myself as a man standing in the middle of the bridge. My view of the international situation may well be different from either end of the bridge. My assessment of the problems and my understanding of the nature of these problems may well be different from the understanding or the approach of the member states concerned.

Secondly, I am a very strong believer in the UN, as you know. The UN is the last best hope for mankind. The United Nations, like all human organizations, whether national, regional or international, must have some ground rules. The Security Council is the main organ which is responsible for the maintenance of international peace and security. When the Security Council adopts a resolution on any question, and particularly when that resolution is adopted unanimously, including the five permanent members of the Security Council, then this particular resolution must be implemented. This is the basis of my approach.

For the sake of argument, if my own country, Burma, is involved in an international dispute, and if that dispute is brought before the United Nations, and if the Security Council takes up this question, and if the Security Council decides one way or another involving some actions on the part of my government, then the government of Burma must comply with that resolution. If the government of Burma refuses to comply with the decision of the Security Council, particularly the unanimous decision of the Security Council, then as far as I am concerned, I will be on the side of the UN, not on the side of my own country.

NOTES

[1]In her speech to the World Conference on the Human Environment in Stockholm, Sweden, June 5-16, 1972. Mrs. Ghandi is Prime Minister of India.

[2]See also *Toward World Peace*: Speeches and Public Statements, 1957-1963, by U Thant, Thomas Yoseloff (New York, London, 1964). Selected by Jacob Baal-Teshuva.

[3]*Limits to Growth*: A Report for the Club of Rome's Project on the Predicament of Mankind. A Potomac Associates Book by Donella H. Meadows, Dennis L. Meadows, Jorgen Randers, William W. Behrens III, Universe Books (New York, 1972). Also in a Signet book from the New American Library pocket edition.

[4]The Club of Rome, an international group of some one hundred individuals from all continents—scientists, educators, economists, humanists, industrialists, and national and international civil servants—under the chairmanship of Dr. Aurelio Peccei (see conversation no. 70).

[5]Massachusetts Institute of Technology, Cambridge, Massachusetts.

[6]See Address to the Board of Governors by Robert S. McNamara, President, World Bank, September 25, 1972, p. 21.

[7]See conversation no. 30.

2.   *C. H. Waddington*

Professor Waddington has been Buchanan Professor of Animal Genetics at the University of Edinburgh, Scotland, since 1946. He is considered one of the greatest minds in contemporary Britain and actively participates in Club of Rome meetings. He was born in Evesham, England, in 1905.

He studied at Clifton College, Sidney Sussex College and graduated from Cambridge in natural sciences. He lectured in zoology and embryology at the Strangeways Research Laboratory at Cambridge, was traveling fellow of the Rockefeller Foundation in 1932 and 1938, visiting Einstein Professor at the State University of New York at Buffalo, and has been since 1969 president of the International Union of Biological Sciences.

Publications: *Introduction to Modern Genetics* (1939), *Organisers and Genes* (1940), *Epigenetics of Birds* (1952), *The Nature of Life* (1961), *Principles of Development and Differentiation* (1966), as well as a four-volume work, *Towards a Theoretical Biology*, Vol. I (1968), Vols. II and III (1969), and Vol. IV (1972).

It is important to get some idea of what computer simulations of complex situations can and cannot be expected to do in the present state of the art, and how far the MIT team, and others more recently associated with the Club of Rome, have actually got to date.

The procedure in setting up a computerized model of a complex system is something like this: You start by choosing, on the basis of common sense, a certain number of major components of the system which seem likely to be of importance. The MIT study chose five main variables: population, capital expenditure, natural resources, pollution, and capital investment in agriculture. Each of these is then subdivided again into a lower level of active factors; such as for population, birth rates and death rates, or in other sectors such factors as the amount of arable land available, the capital cost of bringing new lands into cultivation, and so on. Then one has to try to put into the model quantitative estimates of the strengths of interactions between the factors. For instance, what effect does pollution have on population? These interaction effects ("multipliers" in the system builders' jargon) at present usually have to be guessed, since there are only a minimal number of facts on which to base the estimates. However, the computer is flexible enough to deal with "multipliers" which change according to the actual values of the two things which are interacting. For instance, the MIT team suggested that pollution does not have a proportionate effect on death rates at all levels, but has very little effect until it reaches a fairly high level and then rapidly becomes more and more of a killer. This is a guess, based on such phenomena as, for instance, the great London smog of the winter of 1952, which was reckoned to have precipitated the death of three thousand people.

The only real check—and it is a pretty feeble one—on the validity of these guesses, is to show that the whole system produces a reasonably accurate picture of what happened to all the variables for which figures are available for some period in the past, for instance, from 1900 to 1960. Any set of interaction values which fails to do that would of course be unacceptable; but quite a lot of different values would probably produce a reasonably decent fit to the existing data, particularly since some of the factors which look like becoming very important in the future, such as high levels of pollution or the exhaustion of some natural resources, did not begin to exert any important influence until quite recently.

Having set up the model and shown that it does work at least for the past, the computer will work out for you what would happen if the same set of interactions continued into the future. The result the MIT model turned out is that by the end of the century the world begins to run out of natural resources and can no longer support such a large population, which gets dramatically, indeed catastrophically, reduced.

The MIT team then tried the effect on the behavior of their model of altering some of the numerical values they fed into it. As a continuation of their original setup would lead to an exhaustion of natural resources, an obvious step would seem to be [to] reduce the rate at which natural resources are exploited. When they changed the values in the model to correspond with such a new policy, what came up was an eventual rise in pollution, which again led to population catastrophe. So what about both reducing the rate of exploiting natural resources and increasing the efficiency of industry in relation to pollution production?

This postponed the catastrophe for a bit, but eventually led to the same type of result. In fact, the only alterations to the MIT model which gave rise to an essentially stable situation, in which the population neither rose nor fell abruptly, was one involving severe restraints on the rates of capital investment, of resource exploitation, and even of food production. To those used to everything getting continuously bigger and better, it sounds like a very cheerless prospect.

*   *   *

How seriously should these results be taken?

As *predictions* they should not be taken seriously at all. They do not pretend and were not intended to forecast what *will* happen. Their importance, which is quite real, is of a different kind, or rather of three different kinds.

In the first place, they do show types of catastrophic misfortunes which *could* take place if the world went on working according to a system which is not too drastically implausible. It will be wise for mankind to keep well in mind that catastrophes are by no means unthinkable.

Secondly, they drive home the lesson that if one does something to—makes an alteration in—a complex system, the response of the system may not be at all what was expected or intended. This is a lesson which people continually have to learn over again. The behavior of complex systems is often what the MIT team call "counterintuitive"—the damn thing just does not do what it "should" do.

An earlier study by the same group of workers at MIT was on the growth processes in cities. It has been quite a common experience, particularly in the United States, that a well-meaning authority carries out a program of slum clearance, erects a lot of new quite superior housing, and within a few years finds that the original slum area is even more overcrowded with poorer people than before. Probably one of the main factors in causing this counterintuitive behavior is that the new buildings attract a large number of people into the area, but if there are not enough jobs for them, they remain poor and let their dwellings get even more overcrowded. Understanding just why the complex systems do not behave as expected is the main purpose of trying to make models of them.

A *third* importance of the MIT world scheme is that it is a beginning of a process of exploring a variety of models to see if one can be produced which really behaves as the world itself does.

Professor, if it is true that the treasure of life, the richness of life, is stored in the diversity of genes, of living beings, if diversity is a must, is man's behavior destroying this needed richness?

We are certainly destroying it in the natural world. We are killing off many species. We are depleting the fauna and the flora in various parts of the planet and it is very important that we stop doing this. Many of the genes we need for improving crop plants or for protection against disease and so on, exist in wild species and if we eliminate all these wild species, we shall have got rid of them; and it will be very difficult to get them back again. Now, within the human species, on the whole what we're doing is not so much a genetic effect, but much more a cultural effect. We are really making it possible, I think, for people to be much more diverse than they could be in the past, because we have greater wealth and greater leisure and so on. There is less pressure simply to keep themselves alive. On the whole, people are being able to be more different, and this certainly applies to the developing parts of the world where up till now everyone has simply had to work all the daylight hours to keep themselves alive. In some of the richer parts of the world, such as in Europe, possibly the richer classes could have been a bit more diverse in the past than they can now. There is a considerable pressure for uniformity. But I think nothing like the pressure for uniformity there was in the peasant medieval civilizations, when they had to spend their whole daylight hours working in the fields and had no opportunity to do anything else much.

And Skinner's[1] approach would lead to a form of authoritarian (world) management?

It might do, but of course, Skinner is very anxious that it shouldn't do. I think Skinner is quite right in emphasizing how much we influence each other, and how much we are programmed by our upbringing and so on. But I think it's really much too early to think we could design a system of programming to produce the optimum sort of person. We have got to experiment gradually along this way. We cannot avoid influencing each other and being to some extent programmed. But I think Skinner is overemphasizing a valuable contributary element in the situation. And I think Chomsky[2] is overemphasizing the other side, that everything is totally spontaneous and wells up from the deeper levels of the spirit without any influence of other people and other things. I think they are both overemphasizing their particular points of view, both of which have something in them.

You would feel reality is in the middle?

Somewhere in the middle.

What in your opinion is molecular biology, which has been called the practicing of biochemistry without a licence?

Well, a lot of the talk about genetic engineering and advanced biological manipulations is by people who are looking fairly far ahead. It's really just as well that people should start talking about these things even ten or twenty years before they are practicable. But many of these things will not even be practicable. I don't believe that you would be able to invent a lot of better genes and synthesize the DNA, and insert it. I don't think we will be able to make a radical plan for alterations to the human genes. But it is much more possible to manipulate human eggs and sperm. It is not out of the question, to produce many identical twins, for instance. In fact it has already been done with frogs. To do it with a mammal would be much more difficult, but it may well be done with livestock, with beef cattle and pigs and so on. I should say it could be done within ten years if a large research program is invented. To do it with human beings could require another great development program. To do something on human beings, it's got to get at least ninety-nine point nine percent reliable, if not more. To do it on farm animals you would not mind if one percent of them died or did not work very well. But to do it on humans it's got to be fantastically reliable and this is an enormous program.

I don't know if you have ever come across an article by a man called Djerassi, who is the head of the Syntex Corporation, which discovered the source for making the steroids which are used for the contraceptive pills. He was considering what would be involved in making a real advance in a new type of contraceptive pill. And he points out that legislation in America requires extensive testing for toxicity and effects on embryos and testing on different species before you can come to doing it on experimental groups of humans. This testing takes a minimum of about fifteen years and costs a minimum of some tens of millions of dollars. He said that the chance of getting the money back from the result is small, and he maintained that it will not be done. The contraceptives in 1984, he said, using a fashionable date, would be essentially the same as they are now; nobody could afford to develop a really new one.

Unless the war in Vietnam is stopped.

Even if they stop the war in Vietnam, you could not cut down on this testing. But you could possibly do it in India or Brazil, or some country that has a very big population problem, and hasn't got much of a sophisticated legislation about safety. But I am mentioning this because if you think of these funny procedures like genetic engineering or producing identical twins and so on, they're going to involve the same sort of magnitude of testing and control before they can be put into human use. The only one, I think, which is quite likely to come out is the determination of the sex of your next baby.

This would have some agricultural importance, though not very much. It would have enormous importance for man. I am rather doubtful whether we shall really get population control accepted everywhere, unless people can be quite certain that the two children they do have are the sexes they want. If they want boys, and had a girl at the first time, they want to be certain the next one is a boy, otherwise they would go on till they do get a boy. It would be to the advantage of population control, if you could tell people that they could choose and be sure about what sex the next baby will be. They could get it now, but only by a rather unpleasant way. You can diagnose the sex of the fetus and abort it if it is the wrong sex. But you cannot at present do this until it is fairly old. Furthermore it is rather unpleasant to abort, and by this time the mother is already rather attached to it and does not want to get rid of it, so it is not a pleasant way of doing the job.

Is work being done on this?

Well, a little. I mean, there may be a dozen scientists in the world, possibly not more than half a dozen, working on it—infinitesimal in comparison with those working on supersonic transports.

Don't you believe that it is essential that these programs be under some sort of world body's supervision, the United Nations or WHO?[3]

Yes, I think they should be. They are bound to be under national control already, because they cost so much that they won't be done by anything but national bodies, using national funds, that is essentially taxpayers' money, with parliamentary control or whatever system of government the country has. So I don't think they can be done by private individuals. I think they should be under some sort of public control. Now, I would like to see this *world* public control.

You would be in favor of it across the border, with the socialist countries, the Soviet Union, for instance.

Yes, I would. But whether the existing international societies are really adequate to do this—the experience of the Olympic Games, for instance, to give one example—suggests that the international bodies of the moment are not very world-minded.

NOTES

[1]Harvard psychologist B.F. Skinner; see conversation no. 7.
[2]MIT linguistics professor Noam Chomsky; see conversation no. 42.
[3]World Health Organization (WHO).

3.   *Jan Tinbergen*

Professor Jan Tinbergen teaches mathematical economy and development programming at the Netherlands School of Economics at Rotterdam, the Netherlands.

He was born in The Hague, Holland, in 1903. He studied physics and mathematics at the University of Leiden. From 1945 to 1955 he was director of the Central Planning Agency in The Hague. From 1935 to 1968 he was director of the Netherlands Economic Institute at Rotterdam.

Aside from numerous honorary degrees, Professor Tinbergen received in 1967 the Erasmus Prize and in 1969, simultaneously with Professor Ragnar Frisch of Oslo, Norway, the Nobel Prize for economics.

Some of his internationally known works are: *Shaping the World Economy*, published by the Twentieth Century Fund (New York, 1962), *Lessons from the Past* (1964), and *Development Planning* (1967).

What are the plus and minus points of the MIT report Limits to Growth?

I consider a very big plus point that for the first time an attempt has been made to estimate the joint effect of a number of new phenomena, the population explosion, the exhaustion of energy and raw materials and the increasing pollution of the environment. That is a point of extreme importance. On the other hand, there are minus points, almost inevitably. The model that was used cannot be very precise, of course, especially when it comes to worldwide distribution of the various, let me say, disasters that probably may occur. So there is, I think, an outspoken need for more precise approaches and in fact, as you know, as a follow up of the MIT report already a number of other projects have been started.

Projects such as? . . .

First of all, as a consequence of what I just said, we in the Netherlands under the guidance of Professor H. Linnemann, want to make an attempt to disaggregate the model. That is to say, that we are considering six different regions, or about that number, of the earth while at the same time disaggregating the manufacturing industry and other sectors of the economy. In that respect, therefore, we hope to come along with a refined model, which in some respects may be more reliable.

To mention an example, it seems proper to assume that part of the problem can be solved by natural reactions of the price mechanism. We can expect that polluting industries will become more expensive, because they have to invest in rather important new equipment in order to avoid pollution. A specialist from Unilever and other researchers in the United States and Japan have calculated, for instance, that if one were to spend about three percent of the national income on those needed installations, that in all probability one could keep pollution below the critical level. For the rest, of course, it remains a big problem, which to some extent, in fact, the market mechanism will solve. It depends on what sort of substitution—or let me say, on what willingness—there is for the consumer to shift from one product to another. Also the same applies to managers: Can they change their processes in such a way that they use less energy instead of ever more, that they try to avoid using exhausted or almost exhausted materials and so on. The program requires the cooperation of numerous very different people, as you will understand. We plan to have—and we have already—subgroups working in the physical field, in the chemical field, in the biological field.

All in the Netherlands?

Not necessarily, but quite a few of them. But we are still looking for other Western European partners in our project. We already collaborate with some experts outside the Netherlands.

How long will it take to design the new model?

We promised Dr. Aurelio Peccei[1] that we will try our best to come along with something worthwhile around the middle or towards the end of 1973.[2] But I think the question should almost be inverted. We accept that we have to have some results at that time. The question remains: How much will we be able to tell?

Professor Tinbergen, Robert S. McNamara[3] said in Stockholm that he estimated pollution control could be built in development projects at an additional cost of three percent. This raised strong voices in the developing nations that seemed unprepared to pay for our pollution problems.

I fully share the difficulties—or let me say the concern—of the developing countries. I am of the opinion that if anything, there should be a better distribution of incomes among all countries.

Does this apply within countries and within continents?

Both, indeed. This means that we will go on arguing in favor of a more forceful development policy for the developing countries. It implies that the rich countries will have to pay the larger part of these new investments. Moreover, there are, happily enough, also some positive aspects to the matter. If, for instance, we are imposing on our new industry certain conditions because of the pollution—we already have—then this will raise our prices and at the same time enhance the competitive situation of natural products. If one takes into account that—especially in the field of synthetics—there are many polluting industries, then in that respect the position in the world market of the poor countries will become better. There are many different aspects. In our project, we will tackle especially this problem. This is also why we brought in six geographical areas, making a distinction between developing countries and developed countries.

Some of your areas of study are in the developing world then?

Yes, because we continue, as the Meadows team[4] did, to try and look at the world at large. We think that since they did not specify areas, you don't know anything about what the position of the developing countries will be. This is one aspect of which our team is very much aware and which has got to be solved because the development problem and the approach by the Club of Rome are intimately connected.

Limits to Growth *advocates less exponential growth, a calmer economy. Less of a race for profit only. But how could the developing world make the progress it badly needs to combat poverty without making our mistakes or those of Japan?*

The production of the developing countries has to go on rising. It means that a large part of the deceleration that is needed will have to be done in the rich countries. As you know, since the citizens of the poor countries are using per capita only a very small part of the critical resources, it stands to reason that if restrictions are needed—and they will probably be needed—then it will first of all be for the developed countries to apply these.

High priority should still be given to the necessities of the poor countries to improve their position—or let me say, to provide themselves with the prime necessities of life. One aspect, of course, we have to stress for all countries—that is the population aspect. There will be a need for almost all parts of the world to slow down, and rather drastically slow down, population growth. Quite recently some encouraging observations have been made. We found for instance that in some East Asian countries the birth rates are already going down, although their average income per capita is no more than three hundred dollars per annum. Formerly, it was generally assumed that one had to reach a level of one thousand dollars per annum before that sort of wisdom arose. Here we can now be a little more hopeful. But the population check should take place, I think, most of all in the European countries, which are rather overpopulated. You have seen the Blueprint for Britain. I would not agree with everything in it. In some respects it is too utopian, but I do agree with their idea, that we have to count in the future on populations that go down. I think that the time may even come—but that in a much longer perspective—that for the whole world this will be the best policy. But that is a question of a century from now.

If resources will be going down, where does aggression come in?

You are touching on a very important subject. But also on one where, of course, it is very difficult to give an opinion. One aspect of aggression, according to Konrad Lorenz,[5] is crowding. If I am saying that the populations of some of the rich countries have to go down, I am thinking in particular of the Netherlands, where crowding is a very important phenomenon. It is already contributing to irritation we can observe around us.

And how to achieve a better distribution of wealth?

You are quite right that apart from overcrowding a tremendous problem will be created by the distribution of ever scarcer raw materials. We cannot say anything here yet for certain, since it also depends on the further elaboration of our models. But there remains a possibility that at a certain moment commodity agreements will have to be concluded, not only for agricultural products, but also for copper, silver and those metals. Aluminum might be somewhat less of a problem, because there is still a lot of bauxite. All this certainly will be a new aspect of great importance and will depend to a large extent on the wisdom of the Western and socialist blocs to solve it by peaceful means.

Barry Commoner[6] suggested in Stockholm that we go back to the rubber tree.

I would even go a step further. I think that in fact one of the greatest problems that we are facing is that we have to make a choice in agriculture. There are quite clearly two main currents: One is what I for short-ness' sake call the Green Revolution—applying ever more fertilizer, water and so on; and the other, so-called natural-cycle-agriculture—which is now coming to the fore and may well be one of the solutions. In fact, the most important problem we have to solve in the long run is how we can switch the economics from the economies based on exhaustible materials to one based on the flow of sunlight coming in and which is heavily underutilized.

I think this is the big problem, that especially in agriculture will show up. And some of these alternative agricultural methods do use more of this flow of sun energy; so one of the subgroups that we have at work is to inform us about what the possibilities here are.

For the second Club of Rome report?

If you like, yes.

NOTES

[1]See conversation no. 70.

[2]Professor Linnemann, leader of the Dutch Club of Rome World Project II, informed the author that the report is estimated to be ready for publication by June, 1974, prior to the World Population Conference in August 1974.

[3]President of the World Bank in Washington, D.C., who addressed the World Conference on the Human Environment in Stockholm, Sweden, June 5-16, 1972.

[4]Professor Daniel L. Meadows left MIT in the fall of 1972 to take charge of a new faculty of system analysis at Dartmouth College, Hanover, New Hampshire, and told the author that he is setting up an entire new department with a staff of fifteen instructors and professors.

[5]Konrad Lorenz is the father of modern ethnology and works at the Max Planck Institute, Seewiessen, Germany.

[6]See conversation no. 26.

4. *Margaret Mead*

Dr. Margaret Mead is curator of ethnology at the American Museum of Natural History in New York City. She teaches anthropology at Columbia University.

Mrs. Mead was born in Philadelphia, Pennsylvania, in 1901. She went to Barnard College and graduated from Columbia University in 1929. She became famous for her books on various expeditions to Samoa (1925-26), the Manus Tribe, the Admiralty Islands, and New Guinea (1929), and for her studies of American Indians in 1931 and a lengthy stay on the island of Bali, Indonesia (then the Netherlands East Indies) from 1931-1938. Over the years she revisited the tribes and primitive peoples she had studied in the thirties and published numerous books: *Coming of Age in Samoa* (1928), *Growing up in New Guinea* (1930), *The Changing Culture of the Indian Tribe* (1932), *Sex and Temperament in Three Primitive Societies* (1935), *Male and Female* (1949). More recent publications are *Culture and Commitment: A Study of the Generation Gap*, Doubleday (1970), and *Blackberry Winter: My Earlier Years*, William Morrow (1972).

Dr. Mead, what is your impression of Limits to Growth?

I'm very much in favor of simulations, and I think the only way that we can handle these large-scale problems that are too dangerous to experiment with or that are on such a scale we can't make any living experiments is by simulation. I have been advocating for a long time that we make a model of the entire planet and recognize facts in the areas of which we have no knowledge and then try to work on the areas of which we do have knowledge in terms of the inclusion of the unknown, so that from the point of view of using such models, I'm thoroughly sympathic.

I think that without computer models we have very little chance of handling the complexity of the problem that we are going to be facing.

Of course you are aware that what a computer states depends on what has been put into it.

Of course it does. Obviously the computer doesn't do the thinking, but you can put into a computer a complexity of data that it is impossible for a single human mind to deal with, and I think that if we had reached the degree of technological interdependence in the world that we have reached now without computers—and without television-computers on the one hand and television on the other—we would have very little chance of handling the crisis that we are in.

The problem is the way in which your simulations are then interpreted and presented to people and the Limits of Growth study has. It has a great many technical difficulties because there are no hard data in it of any kind. It doesn't include, for instance, any human values. It doesn't include in the model the effect of its own existence. Now any adequate model of change has to include the effect of any result that comes out of the model, and I don't think that has been correctly and adequately done; so it includes possible corrective devices, corrective steps of one sort and another and the way they may negate each other.

Nor has it provided adequately for the change in values which would be the result of believing any of the interpretations that are made of it. And I also object to the word growth, as applied to nations and as applied to any economic activities.

You mean, you can't say growth is wrong?

No, I don't think it ought to be called growth at all. The amplification of the gross national product, I don't call growth. I don't think it is a biological activity, and I don't talk about, and I don't believe in talking about a nation in its youth and in its maturity as if a nation had grown like an organ. A nation gets bigger, but that is not growth in the same sense as when a living organism grows.

A tree.

A tree . . . or human being. Now so that using a living organism as a metaphor for either a nation or an economy I think is a mistake. When you say to the American people that we must have limits on growth—Americans feel that growth is good. All people feel that growth is good. They will rebel against the idea. I don't know any people in the world that don't think that growth in the sense of a child is born and grows or a tree is planted and grows, is good.

What word should have been used?

Limits on expansion. The expansion of technology; limits on unbridled consumption. I mean there are plenty of metaphors for setting limits to materialism.

Society should be geared to social need, not personal greed?

That's a perfectly good statement, you see! You have to say different things to people in each country.

In each continent?

In each country. To Americans one can say: Your ancestors started out as poor people, looking for a little warmth and a little freedom. A little freedom for a religion or politics or a little security and well-being for their children.

And your ancestors came here and they worked very hard and they began to find on earth the kind of security that they thought only existed in heaven. They began to identify material well-being with spiritual well-being and began to identify having a good bathroom with somehow having a better spiritual life. And so we built up this tremendous standard of luxury for every individual. We didn't think it was luxury; we began thinking these things were necessities. When the automobile was invented, it was seen as something that frees the average man. That he could buy a Ford car. It gave to each individual a freedom that they never had before. That's what we thought. And now we realize that the automobile-civilization that we've built is a prison, and it not only endangers the atmosphere of the whole country and endangers our cities and endangers life, but it imprisons people because people without a car can't go anywhere.

So we're beginning to realize that we have built a kind of economy which imprisons us, uses an enormous amount of energy and irreplaceable resources of the world, places a great drain on the rest of the world—as exploiting the people of the rest of the world—and is even making a section of our own population poor, ill-fed and unhappy. We've got a system that isn't working, a system that has got to be changed. The doctrines that everything could be solved by economic growth, which was preached after World War II, and that the disparities between the rich and the poor nations could be corrected by technical assistance are now both proving to be wrong. We have to change them and we have to reorganize our life-style.

To say that we are seeking an equilibrium society is not, I think, the way to say it. It is true that we need to establish a better balance between population and resources and technology and to be certain that we are not: (1) endangering the world through nuclear war and other forms of scientific warfare; (2) that we are not endangering the planets, atmosphere and oceans; (3) that we are not using up irreplaceable resources; and (4) that we are not exemplifying a life-style that does these things.

The first three deal with survival really, and it isn't any good talking about a good life-style if the human race is not going to be here. But so we deal first with survival, with preventing the fatal and irreversible change and then with a life-style that is human.

But Dr. Mead, how do we—how do you bring that about? Who will bring it about? Will we live with a Spanish type of dictatorship? Will we—you know, as Skinner[1] says—stop making a fetish out of freedom and dignity?[2]

And let him run the world?

Skinner?

Well, I think the real question about Skinner is: Who programs Skinner? And if you ask that question, you look at his whole position.

But then, when the resources get further depleted, don't you expect a question to arise over who will have the resources and who will decide?

Just think yourself back now and suppose you lived in a little Greek city-state of which there were over 250 in Attica. Each one of them sharing resources and spoils. They trade and fight with each other. It raised the question: Who can ever possibly produce any kind of order in which there would not be warfare between those 250 city-states. And yet we've managed to build a society containing 200 million and 400 million people, where one town is not putting down the next town, killing its men and carrying off its women. Go back in history and see yourself standing and looking at what was happening and being certain that nothing could ever come out of it.

This question about who is going to do it we don't know yet, that's what we've got to invent. But the real problem I think is to be very certain what the situation is. I think understanding is endangered by irrelevant arguments—you know, arguments as to whether the population is or is not going to reach 7 billion in the year 2000.

Now, whatever it is going to reach, it is too many, so experts should stop argumenting about details. These are the arguments between Commoner[3] and Ehrlich,[4] which is, again, a piece of nonsense, because if we didn't have as much population, we wouldn't have as much trouble. True. And if we did have the population without the technology, we wouldn't have as much trouble. True. And so what! We've got the population, we've got the technology; the technology has broken the chain of the relationship to nature and endangers the planet; the population continually puts pressure on the use of the technology. They are both right.

Should there be a moratorium on science?

I don't think so. I think what we need is more good science and especially more good social science. Some real understanding of human behavior that isn't based on experimenting on pigeons and rats.

But Dr. Mead, do you think—since we are going to have these skylabs around us, with Russians and Americans together on it—will we migrate to other planets?[5]

We cannot migrate to other planets at the present, you know. No, we want to be here. There's not much use about talking about the time when we might migrate to other planets, because the danger is the next twenty-five years. Yes, we have got to change, tip the balance of population, so that we stop this headlong exponential growth of population. And we've got to stop our amplifying consumption. We've got to balance our technologies. But when you say equilibrium, people think of something static. Even if you say dynamic equilibrium, they just think of something that sort of bounces back and forth and back into place. And that is never going to capture the imagination of the human race that they have just to stay where they are.

Will that be the new needed vision?

That will be no vision. But if you say you're going to be free now from this terrific burden of the search for material things, that we can begin to build cities where people can live again like human beings, that we can stop this separating people up in their artificial little boxes, all built for families with minor children—where there's no place for the old and no place for the adolescents and no place for the unmarried and no place for the poor—and begin to build communities again, where people can have a joy in each other. All these things are cheap. They don't pollute, they don't put an undue burden on human resources. They don't endanger the atmosphere.

But how about Asia? The Third World?

Well, we could free them from want right this minute. You know. We have the means to feed people now. Hunger is sheer maldistribution, and it is improving, you know. This recent deal between the U.S. and Russia illustrated this—where Russia needs food, and they are going to buy it from us. And when we had unemployment and hunger in Seattle, it was the Japanese that sent the first ship, you know, which is a fantastic thing. It is a horrible comment on the US, but it is also a comment on the necessary interdependence of the world.

How do we get this needed vision within twenty-five years?

Well, we have to work on it. The question one asks now, you know, is we've gotten so used to the idea that we need a new motorcar, we get together a team of people and tell them to invent it. We need an atom bomb, we shut up a lot of people in a Manhattan project and say: "Invent it."

Now changes in social organization don't proceed that way. You don't sit down with just a group of bright people and invent the change. Everyone has to take part in it. If social change is going to be really meaningful. You have to have the active enthusiasm of at least a proportion of the population.

That is how Mao did it. Whatever he wanted to achieve, he did achieve in China a total reorganization of society.

Yes, and that is what we need. We need a total reorganization of society. We can't do it in one country the way it is done in another. And furthermore, Mao[6] is the only leader, you know, a great leader who survived, who did not make his changes primarily through the use of mass media. All the other great figures of the 1930s and '40s depended on radio: Hitler, Mussolini, Churchill, Roosevelt, all of them. Now, what we don't know yet is what the part of television is going to be. We don't know how we can use television. Even with satellites and all the possibilities of television.

That the Russians are afraid of.

The fact that the Russians are afraid of [it] is a compliment to television. The fact that India has gone ahead with their special form of satellite is also a compliment to television. All of these things are what is happening next. They are the things that we need to watch very hard. We need to have material, what they called *software*. For the satellites. When the whole satellite system goes into effect.

We have the technical means, we can take the pictures that will show what is happening to the world. We can build beautiful photographic models of endangering the atmosphere. We can show the picture of the earth seen from the moon and show how small it is and how isolated and how much in need of care and cherishing. The vision of the earth, seen from the moon, I think, was worth every cent we ever put on going to the moon, because it gave us a new sense of proportion. It was a thing that touched us extraordinarily and sparked these things that are happening today, the movement to protect the environment. We have the technical means. If you people who are concerned with the mass media will use them, you see.

I've sat in New Guinea and listened to the children talk, who heard over the radio the details of Glenn's[7] flight and knew when the lights were turned out in Perth and know what a sputnik[8] is and understand what a sputnik is.

In New Guinea?

In New Guinea.

So you've seen an enormous metamorphosis in the past thirty years?

Yes. So I've seen people come from the stone age into the present. I know where we came from and I've seen peoples move so fast, which is one reason I have more faith and hope than most people have that it can be done.

And in that respect the Club of Rome did a pioneering thing, because they put the entire planet into one model.

That gives us a start. What we had before, was the US making models of the Soviet Union, the Soviet Union were making models of the US, and both of them ignoring China, as if it wasn't there; no one was thinking about the whole. At least the Club of Rome has got the whole planet in.

NOTES

[1]Professor B.F. Skinner; see conversation no. 7.

[2]Commenting on his latest work, *Beyond Freedom and Dignity*, Dr. Skinner told *Time* magazine (September 20, 1971, p. 47), "My book is an effort to demonstrate how things go bad when you make a fetish out of individual freedom and dignity. If you insist that individual rights are the *summum bonum*, then the whole structure of society falls down." See also, conversation no. 7.

[3]Professor Barry Commoner; see conversation no. 26.

[4]Professor Paul R. Ehrlich; see conversation no. 13.

[5]See also, conversation no. 60, with Professor Freeman Dyson.

[6]Mao Tse-tung, founder of the Chinese People's Republic.

[7]John Glenn, the first US astronaut.

[8]Soviet spacecraft.

5.   *Arnold J. Toynbee*

British historian Arnold J. Toynbee was born in London in 1889. He studied at Winchester College and graduated from Balliol College at Oxford University.

During World War I, he joined the department of political intelligence of the Foreign Office. From 1919 to 1924 he taught Byzantine and modern Greek language, literature and history at London University. From 1925 until his official retirement in 1955, Professor Toynbee was director of studies at the Royal Institute of International Affairs and research professor of international history at the University of London.

A Journey to China was published in 1931. *The World and the West* (1953), *The Economy of the Western Hemisphere* (1962),

Man's Concern with Death (1968), and *Experiences* (1969) are among his best-known works.

I think reaching the moon was a useless expenditure. It was perhaps a valuable demonstration of the simple fact that for practical purposes the habitat of mankind and of all other forms of life, which Teilhard de Chardin[1] called the biosphere, is nothing but a thin envelope of air, soil and water round the surface of a single planet, in which we happen to exist. It is strictly limited. Its contents, too, are limited. For this reason, the perpetual, infinite growth of the numbers and the wealth of the human race is an impossibility. This objective is not attainable for the human race.

All human creatures are greedy, but the Western minority has consecrated greed and has made it into a deliberate objective. This first began when the Americas were discovered. That gave the Western peoples a false impression, an impression of infinite space and wealth at Western man's disposal. Then, secondly, at the end of the eighteenth century the mechanization of industry through the harvesting of steam power again gave us an impression that we had opened up an infinite source of production. In our time, the mechanization of man's activities has gone to extraordinary extremes, but now we have suddenly realized that the biosphere is finite and that it sets absolutely insuperable limits to material expansion. These limits will be reached in the near future by increased technical power and by increased population.

As far as human beings recognize this simple fact, *Limits to Growth* ought to have a revolutionary effect on our attitude to life's objectives and ideals. This will be a very painful and difficult reversal to Western man's attitudes and aims during the last five hundred years of human history. Meanwhile the non-Western majority of the human race has been envying the West and trying to imitate it. It will be very difficult to persuade them to stop their efforts to develop—especially because it is just these poorest and technically most backward peoples that increase in numbers the fastest and are under the greatest pressure to increase their production. As I see it, the question is: Will the human race as a whole be able to reverse its attitudes and aims before we run into a catastrophe.

Limits to Growth is a very able book. It is a very skillful presenting of the necessary mathematical information for people like me, who are not mathematically inclined. Ordinary people can understand these data. The mathematical expression of facts is necessary in order to understand facts. I hope this book will be widely read and will be taken to heart and acted upon.

But, did the MIT report overlook exponential growth in technology?

Technology can be used for many different purposes. At present, it is chiefly used for two opposite purposes: destruction in war and maximum production of material wealth. If we were to abolish war, and to concentrate wholly on production of wealth, I think exponential growth of technology might delay a catastrophe for a certain time. I cannot guess for how long. It will only be a question of delay. Inevitably these limits will be reached sooner or later.

Dr. Margaret Mead has said to me: "We need a new vision but I don't know what vision." [2]

I think there is an old vision, though it is not very old compared to the age of the human race. I am thinking of the vision of the founders of the great religions. I am thinking of—putting the names in a chronological order—the Buddha[3] in India, Lao Tse[4] in China, Jesus[5] in Palestine and one Westerner, Saint Francis of Assisi.[6] Just one Westerner! But Saint Francis is very important for us because he was a Westerner. He is an example that we ought to pay attention to and try to follow.

These religious founders disagreed with each other in their pictures of what is the nature of the universe, the nature of spiritual life, the nature of ultimate spiritual reality. But they all agreed in their ethical precepts. They all agreed that the pursuit of material wealth is a wrong aim. We should aim only at the minimum wealth needed to maintain life; and our main aim should be spiritual. They all said with one voice that if we made material wealth our paramount aim, this would lead to disaster. They all spoke in favor of unselfishness and of love for other people as the key to happiness and to success in human affairs. They all personally renounced material wealth and power. The Buddha was the son of a king of a small kingdom. He gave it up, voluntarily. He didn't have to, he did. Saint Francis was the son of one of the earliest successful Western businessmen. His father was a wholesale cloth merchant.

Forerunner of Aurelio Peccei[7]

Indeed, in point of professional success, but *not* in point of insight. And Saint Francis's father wanted Saint Francis to take over and inherit the family business, to look after the family business. Saint Francis rejected this. He marries Lady Poverty instead. Unfortunately we fellow Westerns of Saint Francis, we have paid lip service to Saint Francis, we have called him a saint, which indeed he was, but the person we have followed actually is not Saint Francis, but his father, Pietro Bernardone, not Francesco Bernardone. Pietro is the prototype of the modern successful Western businessman, of Dr. Peccei, for instance. Except that Aurelio Peccei has different ideals, very different ideals.

Now, what we have to do, to try to do, is to make a spiritual revolution. This is not something entirely new. It was the vision of Saint Francis of Assisi, the vision of Jesus, the vision of the Buddha, the vision of Lao Tse.

As you know, this Taoist Chinese school of philosophy believed in the minimum development of material wealth and the maximum development of spiritual life. They were the antithesis of the Confucians, who were rather materialistic-minded. I think the people who preached self-denial and renunciation of material wealth are going to prove to be the most practical of our advisers, because, by following their way of life, you and I could go on living in the biosphere as long as the biosphere is habitable. We should not be using up or contaminating the resources of the biosphere. If we follow Saint Francis's father's advice, we shall destroy the biosphere and destroy ourselves and, with ourselves, all other forms of life which are dependent on ourselves.

How do you see chances for children of today, in 1972, with the year 2000 approaching fast?

I have two great-granddaughters who, if they live to my age—I am now eighty-three—they could be alive in the year 2050. Now, you and I cannot conceive what the world will be like in 2050, and I feel anxious about these poor little children who have been brought into the world without their permission having been asked. Their parents do not know any more than you and I know what kind of a world they are going to have to live into. I think we have no time to lose. I think my children's generation, my grandchildren's generation, my great-grandchildren's generation have got quickly, at once, without waiting, to change their aim in life, to think a long way ahead, to think in the disinterested way that the Buddha and Jesus and Saint Francis and Lao Tse all preached. To think in terms of the next two thousand million years, to think in terms of maintaining the human race in existence. This is very difficult for us, not to think of our own immediate advantage but to subordinate that to a more distant future. But we can at least think in terms of children whom we have already brought into the world. We do feel responsibility for them. And if we think in terms of children who will be alive in 2050, like these two great-grandchildren of mine, then we ought at once to follow a very different aim and to take very different action from the present. This will be extremely painful and difficult for us, but surely it is not impossible. It involves really a kind of conversion, as Margaret Mead was saying.

Dr. Toynbee, are you familiar with Skinner's theories in Freedom and Dignity, *that man is programmed by his milieu?* [8]

Yes. I read his book, with respect—he is a very able man—but also with disagreement. I do think that it is quite true that the environment has an enormous influence on us. I think one of the early Jesuit fathers said, give me a child during its first seven years and I shall have conditioned him for life. However, the child who has been conditioned can break away from the conditioning. I think a human being, because he is conscious, self-conscious, has a certain power of choice, a certain degree of freedom. This question of the reality of free will has been disputed ever since the time of Pelagius[9] and Saint Augustine.[10] I myself believe that while we are partly conditioned, we also partly have free will. So, I don't agree with Skinner. Skinner is an extremist, isn't he?

You know the Hindi doctrine of Karma. Karma, I think, is a Sanskrit[11] word. The literal meaning is "action." The technical meaning of Karma is the cumulative effects of our past actions for good or evil, either in a single life or, if you believe in reincarnation, in a series of lives. According to the theory of Karma, a human being has a kind of moral credit and debit account, he is always adding to each column, the credit column or the debit column. Sometimes he is "in the red," sometimes his balance is positive, but it is always an open account. I think this is much nearer to the truth than Skinner's theory. We are conditioned by our heritage of Karma, enormously conditioned. We do not enter the world as completely free agents, but we are partly free. We can change our Karma. We can make it worse or we can make it better, to some degree. And this is the important point: Our freedom to change our Karma to some degree.

But Professor, how do we bring into harmony, into equilibrium, your view of an Alexander[12] *at the helm of the globe and individual freedom for seven billion people? Can we maintain this freedom, and our individual growth? Or do we have to become computerized, puppets of a great Alexander who rules the whole world?*

I think everything creative, everything good in human life, comes out of individual freedom, individual action, free action. Everything bad comes out of this, too; for this is the source of energy, and for good or for evil. I think, as I have said, that the cooperation of human beings is the most difficult thing in human life. Technology is easy, artistic achievement is easy, social cooperation for good objectives is very difficult. Therefore, I think that as so often happened in the past, when some drastic social change needs to be carried out in a very short time, or the alternative is some supreme disaster, there is a choice of evils. Either we have to run into disaster or we have for a time to have a kind of dictatorship.

The Romans had a very interesting system. They had a constitution with popularly elected magistrates. These temporarily abdicated and appointed a dictator with full powers. When the dictator had dealt with the crisis—if he did deal with it—he abdicated and the magistrates came back. Now, I don't like this at all. I would far rather achieve what is necessary by wholly democratic methods, but I think it is probable that we haven't the time to do this, so we might need a temporary dictatorship. This is extremely dangerous, because the big question is, will it be temporary?

Julius Caesar[13] and the Emperor Augustus[14] claimed that they were temporarily taking the dictatorial part to deal with a crisis, but these dictatorial powers were never given up by their successors. This is a danger. But all of human life is a choice between evils. This is the lesser evil. I do feel that some minimum of global government to abolish war, to cope with pollution, is absolutely necessary. Here is a very simple point. The world is divided theoretically into about a hundred and forty separate local territorial sovereignties. The air and the water, which in places are polluted, are theoretically divided, but you cannot really divide the ocean or the air into local sovereign patches. To prevent pollution in them you have to have some global worldwide action by what is, in effect, a world government. If that has to be dictatorial to begin with, this, to my mind, is a lesser evil than destruction, which will be the end of everything. We might have to have a temporary dictatorship, and this could be an evil, but at least the human race would survive, and while there's iife there's hope. Within the next two thousand years we might be able to get rid of the dictatorship, whereas if we destroy ourselves, well, everything is gone.

Thinking of your great-granddaughter, do you feel education responds sufficiently to the enormous changes in the human environment?

Unfortunately the modern response to the great increase in the amount of information, of potential knowledge, has been specialization, cutting up knowledge of the universe into compartments, in the way we have cut up the biosphere into local sovereign states. Education now consists far too much in specialization. I'm afraid that Britain has gone further in this than almost any other country. Further than the United States, where at most universities there is a first year, a freshman's year, in which students are compelled to study widely. Now this compartmentalization of knowledge is very unfavorable to education, unfavorable for fitting people for life, or for saving human life in the world into which we are moving, because for this purpose we need to have a comprehensive view of reality. I have been much criticized by fellow historians, as you know, for refusing to be just a specialist and trying to be a generalist. They say that I am an amateur, not a true historian.

That is exactly what Aurelio Peccei says, "we need generalists." He hammers on this.

Yes, the trouble is now that the popular form, the conventional form of education is specialization. Generalization is left to amateurs, even to charlatans. What we want is for our best people to become generalists. I think in France there is a good tradition, what the French rather ironically call *oeuvres de vulgarisation*. You will notice that the very best French savants put their very best work into these so-called *oeuvres de vulgarisation*, beginning with people like Renan. Some of his best works are what nowadays the specialists would not consider really serious research at all. They are really very serious research. They are the essence of education for ordinary people. The public we should aim at is the nonspecialized intelligent public. This is the public that can move the world, can change the world. They should not be compelled to find their education somewhere in specialization, either humanistic or scientific. They should be enabled to have a comprehensive education—an education in understanding the universe as it actually is—the universe in which we have to live.

Limits to Growth and its shock effect, do you think it a good thing at this juncture, when something has to be done now? Like Margaret Mead said in Culture and Commitment, *her last sentence: "The future is now."* [15]

Yes, that is very good, "the future is now." The chief shock effect will be on people of the middle-aged generation in the United States, people who survived the economic slump of 1929 and of the early thirties and who put their treasure in economic growth and material success and whose children have turned against them. This is very upsetting for these parents. The parents brought up the children in luxury and the children repudiated it all rather in the way as Saint Francis had repudiated his father's wealth. The shock effect is the greatest on them.

On the other hand, on the hippies the shock effect will not be so great. I like to point out that Saint Francis himself was a hippy. When his father objected to his marrying the Lady Poverty at a certain stage, Saint Francis stripped himself naked. This is a hippy gesture. He threw his fine clothes at his father's face, and the bishop who witnessed this scene took Saint Francis and put him underneath the bishop's cloak. This was a marvelous act of the bishop's, because Francis's father was a really important constituent of that bishop, and the bishop defied Francis's father. This was very brave and much to the credit of the bishop.

But my point is that though Saint Francis started as a hippy, he did not end as a hippy. He ended by putting himself under discipline and doing something very constructive. Now, he was not an organizer, not an administrator, and he understood this when suddenly his new order of friars became popular. He abdicated from being the head of it. He put himself, as an ordinary friar, under the discipline of another friar, and a very contentious figure, Brother Elias, really founded the order. He was an administrator; he had the gift. Saint Francis did not have this gift and he knew he did not have it. He was out for his own individual salvation, for the imitation of Christ, like the Netherlander in the fifteenth century, the author of the *Imitatio Christi*. . . .

His name was Thomas à Kempis. [16] *Perhaps the entire hippy and drug movement is a kind of forerunner to turning back towards Francesco of Assisi's mentality. The crazy race towards more productivity for profit only must be dropped.*

Only for profit, yes. Now, this is what we have to get rid of.

But in the Soviet Union there seems to develop the same race. The waiter in a Moscow hotel wants to buy my jeans.

Unfortunately. You may say that we have to change our objective, change our ideal. Change from Saint Francis's father to Saint Francis.

NOTES

[1]Père Pierre Teilhard de Chardin (1881-1955), French paleontologist and philosopher.
[2]See conversation no. 4.
[3]"The Enlightened One," who flourished in India about the sixth century B.C.
[4]Chinese philosopher, supposed founder of Taoism, born in 604 B.C.
[5]Founder of the Christian religion, born 6 B.C.
[6]Italian friar (1181?-1226), founder Francescan order.
[7]Chairman of the Club of Rome. See conversation no. 70.
[8]See conversation no. 7, with Harvard psychologist B.F. Skinner.
[9]British monk (about A.D. 400-418 his ideas flourished) who denied originalism and maintained the freedom of the will and its power to attain righteousness.
[10]Leader of the early Christian church (A.D. 354-430).
[11]Ancient classical literary language of India.
[12]Conqueror of the Greek city-states and the Persian empire from Asia Minor and Egypt to India (356-323 B.C.).
[13]Roman general, statesman, and historian (100-44 B.C.).
[14]First Roman emperor and successor to Julius Caesar (63 B.C.-A.D. 14).
[15]*Culture and Commitment: A Study of the Generation Gap*, Natural History Press/Doubleday (New York, 1970), p. 97.
[16]Writer on religious affairs (1380?-1471).

6. *Albert Szent-Györgyi*

Professor Szent-Györgyi was born in Budapest, Hungary, in 1893. He studied first at the University of Budapest and completed his doctorate in 1927 from Cambridge University, England. He started research as a medical student in histology, then turned to physiology, pharmacology, bacteriology, physical chemistry and chemistry. Eventually he took up wave mechanics and cancer research, studying the basic mechanisms of regulation.

After teaching in England, the Netherlands and Hungary, Professor Szent-Györgyi came in 1947 to the United States and was appointed director of the Institute for Muscle Research at the Marine Biological Laboratory at Woods Hole, Massachusetts, where he still works. After numerous honorary degrees, memberships and other achievements, Professor Szent-Györgyi received in 1937 the Nobel Prize in medicine for elucidation and discovery of the catalytic function of C_4-dicarboxylic acids and the isolation of Vitamin C.

In 1947 appeared *The Nature of Life, A Study in Muscle*, in 1960 *Introduction to a Submolecular Biology*, in 1962 *Science, Ethics and Politics*, in 1968 *Bioelectronics*, in 1970 *The Crazy Ape*, as well as *Fifteen Minutes to Zero*.

In the Crazy Ape *you wrote that man seemed bent on bringing about the Kingdom of the Cockroaches.*[1]

There are certain rules, half physical rules, rules made by physicists, by their experience. The one rule is that what can happen will happen. There are two thousand bombs ready to be fired. Nuclear bombs, each of which will destroy the entire world, because if one is fired, all of them will be fired. There are some two thousand buttons. If one button is pressed, all of mankind will be wiped out. For every button there are four fingers to press it. There are four people sitting next to it. So there are four thousand people on whom man's fate depends. We do not know who they are. Therefore, statistically the probability is that one of these groups of four people will press the button sooner or later.

35

By accident or by going crazy. As you know, people can be quite irrational at times. Two years ago, the animal house of my laboratory,[2] where I do my experiments, was destroyed by vandals. There was no sense in that either.

How many animals were in your laboratory?

A few hundred.

They were killed?

They were killed, yes. They were thrown into the sea.

You have repeatedly complained that since World War II the United States has spent a trillion dollars on arms and war.

A trillion dollars! Can you imagine such a sum of money? I cannot. How much safety could that money have given America. Now we are very unsafe. Everybody is unsafe, not only in America. If we had spent that one trillion dollars on feeding the children of the world, America would now be the country loved by everybody and the United States would be quite safe. Instead we are now very unsafe.

According to where we presently stand, there are fifteen tons of TNT[3] for every single human being. So we actually sit on a keg of fifteen tons of TNT. Both here and in Russia the military leaders think that we will be really safe only when we sit on thirty tons of TNT, not fifteen. We improve our missiles and we design new submarines. The Soviet Union too makes more missiles and submarines. Then of course, someday, thirty tons will be not enough and they must have sixty tons of TNT to sit on for every human being alive.

Are the scientists not responsible for this state of affairs?

Sometimes I give lectures to students. There are always some who get up and say, "Why don't you scientists stop war? If all scientists would say we do not work any longer for war, there would be no war." I reply, "Why pick on us? If all students would say we do not accept the draft, if all workmen would say, we will not work for war industry and all taxpayers would refuse to support war, there would be peace." In other words, everybody is responsible. As it stands now, the political scoundrels, who are thinking only of the next election and nothing else, are willing to kill the whole world for it.

You once quoted a Hungarian poem: "If you are among brigands and you are silent, you are a brigand yourself." [4] *That is then actually what we all are doing?*

Yes, that is what the Netherlands does. What Scandinavia does. But governments should get together and say, "Stop that, we do not intend to be killed by you." But Richard Nixon just laughs. Why does not Holland say, "We break diplomatic relations with those who endanger our life." It took three billion years to develop man. Why life endangered by a handful of insane? Man seems to be unfit to make a livable world. We are clever enough to construct supersonic airplanes and rockets to the moon, but we are not fit to engineer a human society. Man will get what he wants, what he seems to be looking for.

Follow the dinosaurs?

Yes, that is what I expect.

If man's brain was not developed by nature to search for truth, but to search for food and the brain is an organ of survival, how to program man, as Skinner seems to envisage? [5]

We cannot program man. He searches safety, but only the wrong kind—short-range safety. My brain is made only for short-range not for long-range thinking. The long-range safety would be not to build bombs. Man is not fit to build a stable society, such as we ought to be building. The globe has become too small. Only one group can live on it. It is very simple. The force of weapons has increased ten million fold. At the same time distances have decreased a thousand fold, that is already a billion fold difference. So we can wipe out all mankind, and that is what we will do. You cannot have the distance and the globe shrinking and the power of weapons growing. They are now too big for this little globe and they are in the hands of a few political schemers.

But could it be that they are all afraid of using them?

Till an accident happens.

How do you envision the future, especially for children?

There is no future. I do not like to discuss the environment, since I am not an expert. I am a chemist. But Paul Ehrlich[6] is a good friend of mine. He has written about it. He showed that if we go on at our present rate, all the planet's resources will be exhausted in no time.

But some believe new sources of energy can be tapped from sunlight.

Sunlight, no. The energy problem can be solved by hydrogen fusion. That would give an endless amount of energy. That would give us energy but would not make metals, nor would it give us food. Nor does it solve our problem that we don't know what to do with our brain. Every problem has two solutions: a technical solution and an intellectual or moral solution. Without the moral solution the technical solution is worth nothing. Till now, mankind has learned by making mistakes. That is how people learn. Now, we cannot learn anymore by mistakes, because if we were to make the mistake of an atomic war, all mankind will be wiped out. We cannot learn from mistakes anymore. We just seem to go on making more and more mistakes without learning.

You seem to be without hope.

Indeed, I am not very hopeful. Of course, it is preposterous to say mankind must disappear. Perhaps it will not. I do not know. No one knows. But as a scientist looking at the trends and looking at the statistics, I say it will disappear if he does not learn to think in global terms.

But that is what the Club of Rome is advocating.

Yes, that is very fine. But what will Richard Nixon do at the same time? He has ordered thousands of acres of crop land destroyed every single day in Vietnam, with enormous bulldozers, they call them Roman ploughs. They continue to erase thousands and thousands of acres of crop land every single day, while the Club of Rome is making calculations that we will have not enough food.

How to stop Nixon?

We cannot stop him because people are stupid and they like what he does. Churchill once called democracy not a good system but there was no better. That is still the situation. Any system is good if the people are good. We like what Nixon does and that is why we have him.

Are you totally pessimistic?

There is a little chance that there is a break. There is now a generation gap. The young people clearly see that this world of ours is idiotic. They do not have a plan what to do, but they reject this world.

You have noticed this in students?

Not students. I see that in hippies. The hippy movement rejects the world, because it is senseless. They cannot accept it. If you do come into this world with a normal brain, you cannot accept it. What can they do? Reject it. One of the troubles of our society is that it is a geriatric, gerontocratia of old people. And it is a rule that after forty the brain cannot take in new ideas. Everybody knows that you cannot teach new tricks to old dogs.

But that is not true. Kant[7] wrote his first book when he was forty-four.

Yes, but he had thought about these problems when he was young. He just put down on paper what he had thought of as a young man. You cannot change that. I am a very active scientist, because as a young man I have learned that science was beautiful. I lived for it. Now I realize that science is harmful, but I seem to be unable to stop working, because as a young man I learned it that way.

But you could not do harm with your cancer research.

Oh yes, one can. If I were really to solve the problem of cancer, if we would know how to stop cancer, we could also make cancer chemically. At once, the Pentagon would produce the matter by the ton in self-defense. There is nothing that cannot be abused. It depends on moral and ethical considerations, and our modern rulers seem to have none.

NOTES

[1]*The Crazy Ape*, Grosset & Dunlap (New York, 1970), p. 11.
[2]Professor Szent-Györgyi is Director of the Institute for Muscle Research at the Marine Biological Laboratory at Woods Hole, Massachusetts.

[3]Trinitrotoluene.
[4]See interview with Robert Reinhild, the New York *Times*, February 20, 1970, "Biologist Doubts Man's Survival in a World Run by 'Idiots' Too Old to Change."
[5]See conversation no. 7.
[6]See conversation no. 13.
[7]Immanuel Kant, German philosopher (1724-1804).

7.   B. F. Skinner

Professor B. F. Skinner was born in 1904 at Susquehanna, Pennsylvania. He went to Hamilton College and began to study psychology at Harvard University in 1928.

After various research and teaching posts Skinner returned to Harvard in 1947 and was named Edgar Pierce Professor in Psychology in 1950. He is now ranked among the most influential psychologists of our time. His latest work, *Beyond Freedom and Dignity*, has stirred a major controversy in the academic world.[1]

Professor Skinner's novel *Walden Two* is for the first time since its appearance in 1948 on the bestseller list. Other published works: *The Behavior of Organisms* (1938), *Science and Human Behavior* (1953), *Verbal Behavior* (1957), *Schedules of Reinforcement* (1957), and *Technology of Teaching* (1968).

Professor Skinner was the sole person out of seventy interviewees who did not understand the author's intention to publish the conversation in its original form. He refused permission to print the verbatim text. After negotiations he did allow, however, the senior editor of the magazine *Psychology Today*, Kenneth Goodall, to rewrite the text in its present form.

In addition, the author invited Mr. Goodall for a brief interview on the basis of his own research and first comprehensive survey of applied behavior analysis and application of Skinnerian psychology. Goodall is preparing a book on this subject to appear in 1974. Also see Goodall's article, 'Shapers at Work,'' *Psychology Today,* November, 1972.

B. F. Skinner, the Harvard psychology professor whose experiments with rats and pigeons opened new territory in behavioral science, has become increasingly concerned in recent years with the human condition and the problem of human survival. First in his utopian novel *Walden Two* (1948) and later in *Science and Human Behavior* (1953), he wrote of the need to redesign cultures so that human beings might live more rewarding lives. By 1971, when he published *Beyond Freedom and Dignity,* he saw the redesign of cultures as an imperative for survival. It was with this book that Skinner gained a wide audience. Most of the things he said in this book he had said before; but this time a growing number of people, alarmed by the triple threat of pollution, overpopulation and war, were ready to listen.

The burden of *Beyond Freedom and Dignity* was that man, in order to survive, must develop an elaborate behavioral technology based on the principles of operant psychology that Skinner himself had outlined in his first book, *The Behavior of Organisms.* This technology, now in the early stages of development, would allow man to control his own behavior much more precisely than he has been able to do. As Skinner sees it, two main barriers, both of which are remnants of eighteenth-century rationalist philosophy, stand in the way of a behavioral utopia: man's futile desire for freedom from control and his blind faith in human dignity. Man can never be free, Skinner says, for the operant psychologist's scientific analysis of man's behavior has shown that all his acts are controlled almost exclusively by his physical and social environment. Dignity, too, is an illusion, since man can take no credit for his own behavior.

Skinner's book outraged many readers, and no wonder. His pronouncements, like those of Darwin[2] and Freud,[3] represent a view of man that is radically different from man's traditional self-image—and much less flattering. Darwin told us that we are descended from apes; Freud, that we are ruled by animal passions; now Skinner would have us believe that we are no more in control of our lives than are the rats in a Skinner box.

While this view might lead lesser men to despair, for Skinner it "offers exciting possibilities," as he wrote in *Beyond Freedom and Dignity*. "It is hard to imagine a world in which people live together without quarreling, maintain themselves by producing the food, shelter and clothing they need, enjoy themselves and contribute to the enjoyment of others in art, music, literature, and games, consume only a reasonable part of the resources of the world and add as little as possible to its pollution, bear no more children than can be raised decently, continue to explore the world around them and discover better ways of dealing with it, and come to know themselves accurately and, therefore, manage themselves effectively," he stated. "Yet all this is possible"—through the science and technology of behaviorism.

A year after the publication of *Beyond Freedom and Dignity*, Skinner discussed his ideas in an interview with the author of this book, Willem L. Oltmans. The psychologist, asked to define his concept of freedom, told Oltmans that the historical struggle for freedom has been a struggle to free oneself from punishment or aversive treatment at the hands of rulers, employers and others in positions of control. The struggle to a great extent has been successful. As a result, we are less subject to the more obvious forms of aversive control; we have greater opportunity to do the things we want to do, and when we do these things we say that we feel free. But it is a mistake to suppose that we *are* free. "We are just as much controlled when we do what we want to do as when we do what we have to do," Skinner said. "I am simply insisting that we examine the reasons why we do not resist the kinds of control which do not make us feel unfree."

Although scientific investigation shows that almost all our actions are products of our environmental histories, the relationship is difficult to understand, Skinner said. "We all believe that we initiate our own behavior. I don't think that is true. I think we behave in the first place because of our genetic endowment and secondly because of what has happened to us as people during our lives. Now that means, of course, that these conditions can be changed, and we can change them." The world as a whole must be redesigned, he said, to induce people to behave in ways that ensure a future for the human race. "If we do not change the environment and hence change human behavior, then we will have no future."

Skinner intimated to Oltmans that his book was intended to frighten men and nations into taking action. "A scare technique, a Cassandra-type of prediction" is necessary, he said. "We have to frighten people into doing something. I don't like to do it that way. I wish we could offer a picture of a beautiful future for which man would naturally work for pleasure. But I'm afraid it has to be the other way around, and we have to make perfectly clear the horrible future that men will work to avoid."

For Skinner, "survival is the only value." It no longer is a question of whether any one culture is going to survive, he said. "We must take mankind as a whole into account." But survival is a difficult value that "can only function if you understand the conditions which must be met in order to survive and then somehow make sure that human behavior will have the properties it needs in order to meet those conditions."

The Club of Rome's model of the planet's future is a very important step, Skinner said. "Any clarification of the future is a step in the direction of dealing with it properly." Skinner said that his only objection—certainly a crucial one for him—is that the model "tends to concentrate on physical and biological technology and not on the behavioral technology that will be needed." The model has not taken into account the role of the environment in the determination of human behavior. As Skinner pointed out, "We know how to solve the problem of population through birth-control methods. But there is one step further: how to get people to use them; how to get people to give up the pride they take in a large family; how to avoid being laughed at because you have only two or three children. These are behavioral problems, and they are not going to be solved by any number of methods of contraception."

Rising expectations and overpopulation are severe threats, Skinner said. "There's no question that the world cannot support its total population at a level of affluence similar to that which now prevails in a few countries. Can you imagine, say by the year 2000, a billion Chinese driving sports cars over millions of miles of superhighways? Unless there is some miraculous discovery in new sources of energy, that simply is not possible." But if a few countries remain so much more affluent than others, there will always be a war because "if people do not have what they need they will want to take it away from others who have." To avoid that kind of world, "the affluent countries must simplify their lives; the very basic process of human behavior that has led to affluence must somehow be deliberately reversed." To do that, he said, will require "a great deal of very careful behavioral engineering, because it is not natural for man to give up the things that please him most."

Oltmans asked Skinner who would have the power to redesign a culture in this way—a benevolent dictator? Skinner replied that the change must not be dictated but must come in the culture itself. "A culture must somehow redesign itself so that no one can emerge in a position of power such as the phrase 'benevolent dictator' suggests," he said. "We must have a culture in which those who have control—power, money, weapons and so on—can act only in certain limited ways.''

But who should take the lead, Oltmans asked—the behavioral psychologist? ''All the behaviorist could do would be to make recommendations,'' Skinner said, just as a structural engineer gives advice on how to build bridges but not where to build them or how many to build. The behaviorist ''can recommend methods, but he himself is not going to make the decisions. No engineer has the power to induce people to behave in this way or that way. He will tell those who have the power what to do to make sure the desired product comes about.''

Skinner assured Oltmans that it would be possible at this juncture to put the behavioral variable into the Club of Rome model. The technology is developing rapidly, he said. ''We are learning a great deal now about the relations between behavior and the environment, and we are designing better techniques in such fields as psychotherapy, education, industry and so on. We are making great progress in education today; we're teaching children who have been branded unteachable by creating better environments for them.''

In the search for limits to growth the behavioral factor is of paramount importance, Skinner said, because ''in one way or another the very characteristics of human behavior, which have brought us where we are today, are causing the trouble we are facing.'' As a matter of fact, Skinner said, ''the only possible limit to growth which we have to look forward to would be that which comes about from our scientific analysis of human behavior and the policy-making which takes that analysis into account.''

Interview with Kenneth Goodall

You are completing the first full-scale study of the development and application of behavioral technology based on the principles of Skinnerian psychology. How advanced is this technology?

In some areas, such as the teaching of children, it is quite advanced, especially when you take into account the fact that its development has been almost haphazard, with none of the official and sustained support of the kind that put a man on the moon.

How and where has the development taken place?

B. F. Skinner started it all, both through his direct influence on two or three of his graduate students at Harvard and indirectly through a few other young researchers who were impressed by the principles he outlined in *The Behavior of Organisms* in 1938. For animal experimenters it would have been a natural step to proceed from the analysis of the behaviors of rats and pigeons to the more complex behaviors of the human animal. But it took nearly twenty years after Skinner published his book for the experimenters to take that big step. Skinner blames the delay on outworn notions about man's inherent freedom and dignity, and I tend to agree with him. It is a fine and noble sentiment to argue for the dignity of prisoners, say, but the term "dignity" is not functional. What is dignity for me may not be dignity for you.

But who is to define "dignity" for you, or for me?

The behavioral technicians are finding ways to spell out the meaning for each of us in behavioral terms. They could list eight or ten major items that constitute "freedom" and "dignity" for me, and they could measure the frequency with which these items occur. Sleeping late might be an important element of my freedom, for instance; in prison this freedom might well be taken away from me every morning. The difference between the number of mornings I sleep late in prison and the number of mornings I sleep late out of prison would be a behavioral measure of the extent to which I had lost this one freedom. Of course, the technicians' definition of my freedom is limited to the specific behaviors that make me feel free. Unlike prison wardens or even do-good liberals, they have to consult me before they can define my freedom. To answer your question, the behaviorists can put individual freedom into behavioral terms; they can measure it and manipulate it; but they can't define it—only the individual can do that, through his own actions. And the definition may change from day to day, even from minute to minute.

Who are some of the outstanding technicians, and where have they made their greatest accomplishments?

Most of the accomplishments have been the result of team efforts. In fact, Skinner's doctrine—that a person's achievements are almost entirely a product of his physical and social environment and that therefore the individual deserves little or none of the credit—emphasizes the necessity of team work and pretty well kills the great-man theory of scientific development. The applied-behavior analysts—the behavioral technicians —apparently accept this doctrine in their own lives. They tend to cluster in groups at major centers of activity, each working on specific problems but all interacting. In addition to Harvard, clusters have formed at Southern Illinois University, the University of Washington in Seattle, the University of Kansas and a few other places.

The Kansas group—Donald Baer, B. L. Hopkins, Barbara Etzel, James Sherman, Vance Hall, Todd Risley, Montrose Wolf, Don Bushell —has been incredibly productive in the last seven years. Their work has centered on the learning problems of children, both normal and disturbed; but they have worked with adults as well. Learning problems, of course, include social interactions as well as academic achievement, even such seemingly elementary tasks as learning to tie one's shoes. For a three-year-old it isn't elementary, but the Kansas group has found a way to get three-year-olds to learn this task in less than an hour's time and virtually without any errors. They have helped reshape the lives of slow learners in ghetto schools, retarded and autistic and brain-damaged children, potential criminals, persons with speech impairments, and all kinds of institutionalized persons. They have also worked with the parents and families of these persons to ensure that the gains they have made will continue.

Will this kind of therapeutic work likely be the behavioral technicians' main contribution to human welfare?

It is probably too early to tell, but I'm inclined to believe that their major contribution will be in establishing the basis for a new social contract. The United States Constitution guarantees certain rights, and our various laws have established some more or less mutually agreed on limits to these rights. But until now we have had no way to define and measure precisely the extent to which each individual either has or does not have them. Behavioral technology gives us a way to do this. It is also developing an instrument to guarantee an equitable distribution—the behavioral contract. If behavioral contracting were instituted on a large scale, prisoners, for instance, would sign contracts with the warden and the state spelling out in precise terms the elements of their dignity, the limits of their freedom and, perhaps most important, the exact behaviors that will gain for them an exit from behind bars. Their release would not depend on the whims of a parole board but on the fulfillment of the terms of a contract which they have helped write. In the same way, we could have behavioral contracts with our employers and even with our elected officials. A president who was elected on an end-the-war platform would be under contract to end the war; if he didn't, he would go on probation and might eventually be removed from office through a process that would have been spelled out in advance. Perhaps the last example is a bit far out, but obviously something must be done to make our elected officials responsible to the people who elected them.

You are saying, in effect, that behavioral technology has within it the makings of a political revolution, a social revolution.

Exactly. And that is one good reason why I believe it is important for the Club of Rome to follow Skinner's advice about putting the behavioral dimension into the model of the planet's future.

NOTES

[1]See also *Time* magazine cover story, September 20, 1971.
[2]Charles Darwin (1809-82), British naturalist. The body of his biological doctrine maintained the species derived by descent, with variation, from present forms, through the natural selection of those best adapted to survive on the struggle for existence.
[3]Sigmund Freud (1856-1939), Austrian neurologist and founder of psychoanalysis.

8. *Paul A. Samuelson*

Professor Paul A. Samuelson was born in Gary, Indiana, in 1915. He graduated from the University of Chicago in 1935. Since 1940 he has been connected with the Massachusetts Institute of Technology, where he is at present a professor of economics.

In 1970, Professor Samuelson was awarded the Nobel Prize in economic science.

There are two different viewpoints from which a study like *Limits to Growth* can be appraised. First, there is the viewpoint of the plain man in the street. One can ask: Does a book like *World Dynamics*[1] or *Limits to Growth* help the good cause of mankind? And since the man in the street is not a specialist in demography, engineering technology, or economics, then having the authority of a Forrester and of an MIT computer can serve the useful purpose of alerting the man in the street to a real problem, the problem that an affluent society uses up irreplaceable resources at a tremendous rate, and that the world is going faster at this moment than ever before in its history. If not in the year 2000 or in the year 2073, nonetheless, sometime ahead catastrophic problems will descend upon humanity unless we use our conscious intelligence to do something about it. From the standpoint then of the plain man in the street, I must judge the Forrester-Meadows to be a good thing.

But there is a second viewpoint from which one can appraise works like these—from the viewpoint of experts in the area. Such men have spent decades in measuring, reporting and analyzing data. I have in mind people like Simon Kuznets, Nobel laureate for 1971 in economics. One may ask: What new data does the Club of Rome group marshal, what new data do they analyze, what new methods of analysis do they bring to the data that will widen the understanding of the experts in the field? Now, a prophet is sometimes said to be dishonored in his own country; and so it may be that when more background information is available, I shall change my opinion. But up until now there has been a paucity of new data in the Forrester-Meadows studies. Indeed, they are surprisingly superficial on the factual side.

What about their methods of analysis? In the past Professor Forrester has been a pioneer in analysis of complex systems. We salute him for this. But now we have, all over the world—from Pontryagin in Russia, Bellman in California, Wold in Sweden, Phillips in New Zealand —elaborated methods for tackling stochastic-optimal-control problems. A jury of informed experts finds no seminal breakthroughs of analysis in the Club of Rome and *World Dynamics* studies.

A number of scholars have begun to analyze their equations to test them against the patterns of empirical experience. This is the normal method of science. Nobody rests on his laurels. No man's reputation is sacrosanct. Each nominated new hypothesis must be subjected to careful scrutiny by one's peers. This work has just begun. I would think it premature to render any final decision. But let me, objectively as I can, summarize what seem to be the first indications from such careful auditings.

First, are the results of the Forrester methodology *robust* under changes in the assumptions, or will the results be changed sensitively if certain of the assumed relationships are altered? I have before me a study from the University of California, in which the author summarizes his provisional results as follows: "The results of Forrester's world model are shown to be very sensitive to changes in assumptions." By the way, the author is Robert Boyd. He is not an economist; he is from the zoology department at the University of California at Davis, California. I have also had the privilege of seeing a provisional manuscript by Professor William Nordhaus[2] of Yale University, a distinguished younger economist. He happens to be a graduate Ph.D. from the MIT department of economics, so you must discount my partiality toward him.

Dr. Nordhaus finds out that our knowledge of the laws of diminishing returns, factual knowledge, has not been added to by the material that appears explicity in the Forrester and Meadows books. The fundamental omission by the Meadows and Forrester models is that they pay too little attention to the effect of scarcity on price and use. When resources begin to be short and the bottlenecks of supply begin to slow down the rates of growth, as in the Forrester simulation runs, then in the actual real world their specific prices will rise. Men in England used to be able to burn timber in order to melt iron. The forests of England as they became decimated would not permanently permit that. And so there was a substitution from timber to coal. This is where T. Robert Malthus[3] made his great mistake in his 1798 prophecy of population disaster ahead. Malthus did not foresee the wonders of industrial revolution. And those wonders of industrial revolution are not over.

I have been reading the J. D. Bernal lectures, given in London by one of the world's most distinguished physicists and astrophysicists, Professor Dyson[4] from the Institute for Advanced Studies. He takes a long look forward to a time when we shall develop through biological engineering new organisms that will process and recycle raw materials, that will do the mining and scavenging for the human race. As Dr. Kneese of Resources for the Future (Washington, D.C.) pointed out, the gloomy simulations by the computer of the Club of Rome group suggest that a great number of us will be dying in the future from cancer induced by asbestos. Indeed, it is true that asbestos is conducive to the creation of cancer. But, asks Kneese, who believes that the brakes that stop our automobiles in the century to come will still be made of asbestos when the hospitals are full of its victims? There are innumerable new substances which will become cheapest and safest under new circumstances of scarcity. Processes of substitution and of taxing pollution—to put the burden where it must be—are processes which naturally occur to the economist and perhaps do not naturally occur to the engineer. All these are glossed over and largely omitted in these particular studies. The result is that a jury of experts in this area would be justified in saying that the moment of catastrophe is as likely to take place in the year 2373 as in 2273 as in 2173 or 2073.

Now, let me bring these casual thoughts to a close. These days cynics say, in order to sell sometimes you must oversell. Perhaps the jury of future experts will bring in as its final verdict: "The Club of Rome studies represent overselling. In that broad range between complacency and hysteria, they err on the side of hysteria."

Nonetheless we may leave the austere court of science and move to the forum of men of affairs: statesmen, the man in the street, the vulgar public. It may be that in order to convince public opinion on the need to do something about ecology and not just talk about it, the overselling of a Forrester, of a Meadows, of the Club of Rome, of biological scientists like the distinguished Paul Ehrlich[5] of Stanford University—all these may still be found to earn a gold star for good performance in that court of final judgment.

NOTES

[1]See conversation no. 34 for bibliography of Jay W. Forrester's work.

[2]See conversation no. 19.

[3]Thomas R. Malthus (1766-1834), British political economist who contended that population tended to increase faster than the means of subsistence and should, therefore, be checked by social and moral restraints.

[4]See conversation no. 60.

[5]See conversation no. 13.

9. *John R. Platt*

Professor John R. Platt is professor of physics and research biophysicist at the University of Michigan in Ann Arbor, Michigan. I met with him for this interview at the Center for Advanced Study in Behavioral Sciences at Stamford University in California where he was in December, 1972, engaged in research work.

John R. Platt was born in Jacksonville, Florida, in 1918. He obtained his Ph.D. in physics at the University of Michigan in 1941. After numerous teaching posts he returned to Ann Arbor as a professor in physics in 1966. Professor Platt also regularly attends meetings of the Club of Rome.

Among some of his best known books are *The Excitement of Science* (1962), *The Step to Man* (1966), *Perception and Change: Projections for the Future* (1970), and *On Social Transformation* (1972).

Professor Platt, The Limits to Growth, *how did it go over with you from a behavioral scientist's point of view?*

My feeling for many years has been that we have a problem in society which few people have appreciated until very recently. The problem is that we are now passing through a great world transformation. It is unique. It is the first time and the only time in the history of the human race that we are passing through a transformation of this scale. It is such a great transformation that it is far greater than ten industrial revolutions and Protestant reformations all rolled into one and all taking place within a period of twenty years.

Do you think the model of Forrester is a step into the direction of learning to manage the planet?

Yes, I would agree with that.

* * *

From the angle of behavioral science, is it not a model of figures rather than of social interaction?

Well, many things are necessary to be done in parallel. We have to do simultaneously: consciousness raising, the education of the world, the industrial development of underdeveloped countries, behavioral studies and forecasting. We have to do in parallel a thousand things. Human society is at least as complicated as an automobile. A typical General Motors automobile has fifteen thousand parts, each of which had to be designed and they had to fit together. Society is at least as complicated. We must have designers and students, architects who work on the fifteen thousand aspects of society in parallel, and they must fit together. From this point of view *The Limits to Growth* is just a coarse first step in attempting to see the total global structure, and what its consequences are for the future, and how many things we have to adjust if we are going to survive.

How to reshape what Marshall McLuhan calls the ground? [1]

This revolution of the last thirty years is already producing enormous changes. It is going to change every human institution out of all recognition. In fact, we now see these changes before our eyes. The changes of the farm, the bank, the industry, the army, the police, the legal system, the nation-state, the international system, the family, the school—every one of these is in the midst of enormous ferment. Did I say the church? That, too. Everything is in enormous ferment.

To give an example, take the changes in the family. One now reads almost every day or every week in paperback books or magazines, how the family must change, how we must find ways of group living, or get away from the limitations of the nuclear family, or find ways of communal living. I'm not sure that all of these articles will actually lead to communal living, but in this area here, around San Francisco, last summer there were estimated to be forty thousand people living in communes. There is no way to count them because they disappear as soon as you try to count them. But it is estimated that they represent about five percent of all the people between age eighteen and age thirty. This is a significant fraction. It is not a majority, but it is a sizable group which is experimenting with new patterns of family living, with new moral values and with new ways of living in harmony with the environment. Some of the experimenters are living on farms, others are living in the city or in apartment houses simply sharing the rent. Sometimes they have sexual freedom, but other groups are living like early Christians, where they have communal meals and they try to love one another as the early Christians did. The point is that this is experimentation, and it is experimentation by a wide range of groups all the way from hippies or professors to businessmen. If you look at this movement, you'll find it is not limited to the younger people by any means. It is changing our ideas of what a family is and what a family ought to be and of how free and easy people might be in a new society.

And Skinner's "freedom" in a new society. How will we reach the "step to man"? [2]

I see Skinner's work as making possible new forms of group living, in which we don't punish each other, but rather, as Skinner says, we reinforce each other, reward each other by the glance of the eyes, the affection of the voice. It is the old Christian idea of "love your neighbor" or "love your enemy." That's the most powerful method of changing your neighbor's behavior or your enemy's behavior.

Do you think this "reinforcement approach" is an important contribution to a new way?

Oh, yes. We must find new ways in a number of these areas of human relationship, must find new reinforcements, because our old ways will destroy us if we continue past this plateau we are now approaching around the globe. The old ways of economic growth, of expansionism, when new nations are all trying to grow all over the world, will simply make them collide with one another. This leads to destruction. The old ways of unlimited births had great survival value once, because life was hard and disease was everywhere. But now suddenly we have limited disease, have limited death, and now we see that we must limit births also. This means new psychological rewards, new reinforcements for new patterns of personal behavior if we are going to survive.

How do you see the role of the individual in the future society? Toynbee spoke of "benevolent dictatorship" to manage the world.

I am not a believer in dictatorship, either benevolent or otherwise. Dictatorships were an old pattern that sometimes "worked" for nations that were each following an expansionist policy; but in a total world society, in a global society, we must think not in terms of central authorities or dictatorships but of *networks* just as in the human brain. There is no dictator-cell in the human brain.

But there is authority.

In the human brain?

No, but in that network of human living there must be a form of authority.

There is no "authority" in the blood supply. There is a chain of feedback loops which regulate the valves, they open and close, they regulate the adrenalin, the blood pressure. There is a whole chain of interacting loops of feedback stabilization of the organism. In our body we have a blood-supply loop, we have a nervous-system loop, we have a lymph-system loop (you know, the lymph nodes, like those in the armpits which supply this necessary fluid). We have many, many chemical loops of enzymes and antibodies and digestive processes.

In the same way I think that in a world which is well organized there will be no single dictator that dictates to the rest. There will be no single professor or group of professors, to do all the planning. There will be no single government in a single city. What we see instead, already, are these networks growing all over the world. One sees a network of science or of nongovernmental organizations. The Club of Rome is an example. This is a group of businessmen and internationalists and scientists who are *concerned*. They are not dictating to anybody, they're only trying to educate each other and those who are willing to listen. Another network is the network of communication satellites through which we can all watch, say, the Olympic Games. This unifies the whole world emotionally, when we have an event like the terrorist murders, at the games. The whole world has responded to this, just as the US responded to the television network coverage of the death and funeral of John F. Kennedy, or as we responded to the landings on the moon. It becomes a collective human experience. Now, where is the dictator? There is no dictator in this. This is a network—a shared network of pooled communications.

Another network consists of the great international corporations. These corporations are spreading across the world, not only IBM and General Motors, but also Toyota and Volkswagen and Royal Dutch Shell. In some ways they are wicked, because they are bigger than small countries and so their policies dominate small countries. But in other ways they are the only powers in the world which are strong enough economically to resist the militaristic aims of governments and which have a major concern for peace. The result is that we begin to have a feedback which is now for the first time moving towards establishing a global pattern of international trade, of international agreement, of cooperation rather than international hostility.

We should move or we have to move towards a planetary dialogue in all directions.

Yes, but what I am emphasizing is that there is no central dictator, there will be no single city. It won't be the United Nations in New York, it won't be Washington or London or Moscow or Tokyo, it will be a *network*—a network of trade, networks of communications, a network of science, networks of tourism—networks which have their own feedback all around the world, just like the blood system and the nervous system in the human body.

And the role of the "biofeedback" revolution, the technique of teaching a person to recognize and then control his own internal body?

Well, some aspects of the so-called biofeedback revolution are exaggerated and some of them are faddist, but other components are useful medically and psychologically. It is useful to know that you can control your own blood pressure, let us say, if you wish to. These reinforcement methods permit us to control our own overeating, or permit us to control our smoking. I know dozens, even hundreds of people who have reduced weight or stopped smoking, essentially by new reinforcement methods coupled with publicity and with a little help from their friends. As a result, we now begin to feel that we are not the victims of our own bodies. We are not controlled by some vicious animal within us which is running against our will; but rather we see that we can be a self-controlled unity. Our bodies and minds are not as separate as we have supposed. This is a healthful and hopeful development, I think. The sense of self-management is the beginning of the sense of world management. If the human race is to feel that it is at home on the globe and that it is designing its own destiny and responding to its own creativity, it must start with the individual, so he is designing his own destiny and responding to his own creativity.

Let me say that this comes back to the question you were pressing on me earlier. What is the role of the individual in this social or world system? Obviously there are many types of society which might develop in the future and probably might be stable; that is, they might learn to manage the threat of war and so on. One type of society might be like ancient Egypt or ancient Sparta—say, a very rigid society, in which the individual is tightly controlled by the group. I think another type of society though, might also become stable, namely a society of maximum diversity in which our technological abundance—even with some limit on our energy consumption or consumption of natural resources—can make possible enormous diversity by comparison with any society in the past. The first reward of technological achievement is a kind of narrow abundance, millions of Volkswagens and nothing else. But the second reward of technological achievement is an easy diversity.

So, once upon a time there were one or two companies that controlled all phonograph records. But now with LP records, there are hundreds. The result is that you can now get on records a diversity of nightclub entertainment, of dirty jokes, along with great songs of the past, great speech and poetry and music of the past, all the way back to Monteverdi.[3] All the music of the past is now simultaneously present in phonograph records put out by different companies. The rush of the folksingers with their impact on the young, their contributions to the civil rights movement and the Black Power movement and the antiwar movement, came about through records, because of the diversity which has been made possible by technology.

Today I think that in the US and probably in Western Europe, there is more diversity in clothes—in the length of skirts, for example, or whether women wear skirts at all, pants, shorts or mini—much more diversity in clothes, in types of housing, in styles of life, in vehicles, transportation, in forms of communication, books, music, the arts, in types of architecture, than there has ever been in the world before, more freedom for individual taste and choice. The result is that each man can carve out his own individual niche in this with his own taste in music, clothes, style of life, books, relation to his family, travel and so on. And I see this kind of diversity as being typical of the kind of pluralist society that is now being made possible by the new abundance, and I see it as a desirable type of society for the future.

You have said that in order to meet the present crisis, you feel that a large-scale mobilization of scientists would be necessary.[4]

Yes, I think we have to regard this human crisis, this global crisis of transformation today, as being as serious as a war and as urgent as a war. In wartime, for example, scientists in World War II were able to develop atomic energy, and sonar and radar and antisubmarine warfare, not on a "crash" basis of doing something within a week or within a month, yet at the same time not on a long-term peacetime schedule of doing basic science for thirty years. Rather, they worked on projects that would produce large-scale results within a year, or within three years or so.

In the same way, I think our global crisis today has a time scale of the order of five or ten years in which we must begin to solve some of these problems if they are not to kill us. In order to survive, we must make better peace-keeping stabilization mechanisms. We must begin to limit population. We must control pollution. We must limit our consumption of natural resources. I think scientists need to contribute to solving many of these problems, because they are technical. I do not mean just in the physical and engineering sciences. We need also mobilization of our brains and knowledge in the social sciences including behavioral technology. We need urgent studies on small-group structure, on feedback mechanisms in organizations, on ombudsmen, participatory democracy, new experiments in group living and family living, even new religious and philosophical restructuring. Every field needs the contributions of scientists as well as the contributions of politicians and the businessmen and of every citizen.

There you are, the power is with the politicians to bridge the gap.

Well, I don't agree on that. I think the politicians have much less power than we suppose. We are too hypnotized by newspaper headlines. The newspapers are somewhat lazy, and because they have their regular journalists in Washington and in London and so forth, they report what government organizations hand them. But the real action may be in Skinner's lab at Harvard, or in dozens of other labs of research and innovation.

How much does Nixon know about Skinner?

I don't think it makes any difference.

But he's the one who goes to Brezhnev[5] and Mao.

Yes, but as I say, I think that's only a small part of what's happening with the human race. We are in the midst of a great collective flood of change, a great waterfall, in which Nixon or Washington is only a small ripple on top.

But there is not a single scientist in Congress.

That's true.

So how can you get these congressmen to do the things that are necessary, that the scientists feel are necessary.

Well, you write a book like Rachel Carson did, *Silent Spring*, and within ten years the result is that the public is aroused and Washington has banned DDT[6] and we are getting rid of other pollutants. If you write an effective book and if this—

—like the Club of Rome—

Yes—and if what the book says is congruent with the way things are, that is, if this book describes reality, then people realize, "Ah, that's how it is," and the people are mobilized and the politicians follow. Paul Ehrlich writes a book, *The Population Bomb*,[7] and organizes a little society called Zero Population Growth. And when this is added to the many other population analysts who are building up the pressure within five years, ten years, the effect is everywhere. Ralph Nader writes a book on automobile manufacturers and auto safety, and within five years you have a total change in outlook and law and action. This initiation of the calalytic steps does not come from Washington; Washington follows. There is a little time delay in these governmental responses, but the time delay is shorter now than it has ever been. The time delay in the United States is in the range of four to ten years.

The whole crisis needs a deadline in fact.

We probably need to shorten the time delay still more, but the point is that we are now in the most responsive society in history. The problem is that we don't know whether this response will be fast enough. But one must not say there's no change; and one must also not say that the initiative comes from the politicians. Politicians follow.

* * *

NOTES

[1]See conversation no. 12.

[2]*The Step to Man* by John R. Platt, John Wiley & Sons, Inc. (New York, 1966). A striking collection of visionary essays on the evolving social and intellectual nature of man.

[3]Claudio Monteverdi, Italian composer of opera, mass, psalms, and a magnificat (1567-1643).

[4]*Biology and the History of the Future*, a conversation among John Cage, Carl-Goeran Heden, Margaret Mead, John Papaioannou, John Platt, Ruth Sager, and Gunther Stent, presented by C. H. Waddington, Edinburgh University Press (Edinburgh, 1972), p. 15.

[5]Leonid Brezhnev. Soviet Communist Party leader.

[6]Powerful insecticide, dichlorodiphenyl-trichloroethane.

[7]See conversation no. 13.

10. *Paolo Soleri*

Paolo Soleri was born in Torino, Italy, in 1919. He studied at the University of Torino where he received his doctorate in architecture. He came in 1947 to the United States on a Frank Lloyd Wright fellowship. Since 1962 he has lived in Arizona. Two Guggenheim grants permitted Soleri to complete his studies in the field of architecture as human ecology.

Soleri created the Cosanti Foundation, a nonprofit urban research organization now established in Scottsdale, Arizona, his headquarters. Arcosanti, a self-teaching community for 3,000 in north central Arizona, is currently under construction. Arcosanti will be the first urban environment designed according to the principles of archology, the complete living system to host life, work, education, culture, leisure and health.

Soleri has published *Archology: The City in the Image of Man* (1969) and *The Sketchbooks of Paolo Soleri*.

You have seen Limits to Growth.

I have seen the book, I went through it quickly. In many ways I am more optimistic than the material of the book may imply.

What brought you to your redesigning oeuvre of urban civilization?

The conviction that urban civilization is going to pieces. I believe that life is a phenomenon of implosive character and not of explosive character. Anything that has to do with life, with life instrumentation or life development, has to present very clearly this character of implosiveness as against explosiveness. That's why I am very much sold—or somebody might have said stuck with—the idea of complexity and miniaturization.

Your future dwellings are based on miniaturization in an effort to rehumanize man?

I don't think really we can start anything by basing our actions only or purely on past experience, which starts with Adam and Eve. I think it's a syndrome that is very pervasive. Many scholars are going about their business of finding reasons or explanations for phenomena by implying that reality begins with the life of man. In reality it begins far, far before man even appears in this world, perhaps three billions years ago.

Nature as the furnace of the sun.

That was the question—the sentence was coined to present nature in the light which is not the romantic light of niceness, prettiness or arcadia. Nature is far more powerful, far more demanding and far more complex than our romantic ideas.

Cruel, too.

Nature is, because of the vastness of the phenomenon, in a way very indifferent to any formal life. Life is in a sense the encroachment of a very specific thing on the phenomenon which does not give a damn about life itself. We have to be able to find ways of keeping at bay this cruelty and this indifference by using nature at the same time. Humanizing, if it means anything, means producing more spirit by transforming more matter, in a way the transformation of matter into spirit is what life is. So unless humaneness is geared to this, humaneness does not mean very much.

If you talk about humanizing cities, where does aggression come in?

In my opinion, this theory of aggression is only relatively true and it has not been demonstrated really. If we take crowding at an animal level, we might be right in objecting to it. If we take crowding at a cultural level, that crowding is caused by the media by which culture develops. Which explains why the city has become more and more the center of civilization. It's there where the pressure of things becomes critical, where things happen or start to quicken.

By redesigning our urban dwellings, do you also take into account the redesigning of consciousness?

Consciousness has been designed in a way by the environment. We would not be what we are unless the earth had a certain diameter, moved at a certain distance from the sun. We are environmentally defined. There's no escape from that, and that's why we are unique. The position of the relationship between the earth within the solar system and what the solar system is, is defining in a very definite way the morphology of what we are. That is what you may call the nonwilled part of life.

Where the willed part of life comes in I cannot follow through with Skinner. There is something more to it than reacting to punishment or reward. I cannot explain the behavior of a person through positive reinforcement. There's more to it than that, I am quite convinced, in saying that by defining a new environment, you redefine man, as Skinner does. We are in a way what our environment is. We can only develop if the environment around us is carried into new levels of quality of performance.

Do you feel that your way of designing urban centers will also promote the collectivization of consciousness?

I am very much in agreement with Teilhard de Chardin when he says that in order to have a better person, you have to have a better society; and in order to have a better society, you have to have a better environment. The more society becomes a true cooperation of individuals, the more individuals will be personalized. There is no contradiction here.

There is some reinforcement which does go back to Skinner in a way.

When you sit down at your table to design, are thoughts of how to bring people closer together on your mind?

I am not sitting down ever to design dwellings for people. I think I'll find out the relationship which is absolutely fundamental. I am trying to illustrate this relationship. Nobody has asked me to design a city as yet. So I haven't designed it. But the materials that I've been producing are just symbols of schematic definitions and explanations of an idea. The idea stands for this methodology, that says every time you've something more lively, you have also something more complex. Every time you have something more complex, automatically—by the nature of complexity—you have something which one must miniaturize. So if you are hoping to come out with something which serves life, you have to come out with something which is automatically more complex and automatically more miniaturized.

We have been mostly talking in terms of the Western world. Would it be possible for the Third World,[1] where the real crowding is, like India, to build your kind of cities?

Not only possible, in a way it's going to be mandatory. It is true at this point where we begin to think that the amount of matter and energy available is limited. At this point we have to find ways of not punishing life by limiting growth, but by a transformation, a quantum jump into something which is quite different.

This is in a way the interiorization of more matter into what you might call new landscapes for man. What I am advocating is the interiorization of the city. Make the city into an interiorized milieu, which becomes in a way a new organism. By doing so you achieve a new economy. This economy is utterly connected and tied to this process of spiritualization. Each new organism is an interiorized universe; and organisms somehow get together and work together to produce systems which are more able to grasp and to make use of the environment. The beehive is a good example. The termite colony is a good example. There are many, many examples.

You make these beehives livable.

No. You would want to introduce the human element in these supersystems. And what's a human element? It's the mental element which displays itself in fundamentally intercultural expressions. We must do at the human level and the social and cultural level what the bee has been able to do at the biological level. This translates the beehive into the city. To be appalled by the analogy, I am afraid, is not to grasp what those supersystems are able to do for the person or for the individual. For the bee they evidently are very essential for the survival and for the development of the bee life. For mankind they are going to be essential and very positive instruments for the development of man. Keep in mind that cooperation is fundamental to life. Nobody can survive for one day without almost full cooperation from people, organizations, institutions, all sorts of routine mechanisms.

But when you inject the mental and cultural elements from, say, Calcutta, you hit an entirely different world.

Survival is one thing—if your goal is survival, then Calcutta might just be a way to go about. But survival is the basis for something much more hopeful. So to be able to define a good beehive does not mean as yet to define a good city or a good environment for persons to develop in. Those are instruments and as such might only be sufficient for a very limited kind of phenomenon. You'd keep in mind that the instrument is one thing and the creator or the musician is something else. If you want to produce music, you need some kind of device, if only the vocal chords. That does not mean that one would become a great singer or a great composer. If we want to produce a civilization, we need the instruments that are permitting production. Going back to *Limits to Growth*, I only think that this study says that it might be advocated they should be translated into a quantum jump, as I was saying. A quantum jump, where more is done with less, which is what complexity is able to do and the physical side of this is the miniaturization process.

That is archology, another one of your inventions?

That is what archology is trying to illustrate. To achieve it is something else.

*   *   *

Should archology become the ultimate instrument for human collectivization?

If there is an evil intention somewhere and this evil intention is going to develop, is going to flourish and the media can be penetrated even archology could not stop them. In fact, it might become a good instrument for evildoers. But that's a chance we have to take. But two equate to two does not make any sense, also because we ourselves are collectivized phenomenons. The billions of cells that are composing each one of us is a good example of a phantastically organized and beautifully coordinated and automized kind of universe. To reject those aspects as if they were against life is to ignore what life is preponderantly. We must go beyond that, but we cannot go beyond that by rejecting it. We must go beyond that by incorporating it into the development of life.

Would you say that what you are trying to do is to achieve a transformation of human life, both mentally as well as architecturally?

Architecturally in a sense of environment; mentally in the way this environment would be used by individuals that find themselves within that environment. The starting point is that this environment would permit the person or the group to go about the business of life in a more efficient way. That means an environment which is more responsive to the aims of people or to anyone. One can make a very good example about the frustrations that the cities of today are causing in society because they do not deliver the goods they are supposed to be delivering. The fundamental good is information. We guard any kind of gathering of interaction in life for the sake of information. We want to know. We want to know, because we want to perform and we can only perform when we know. That's why life is a gathering, is an implosion, is a cooperation. In order to know more and to act more. If the environment defeats this goal, then this environment is antilife. And this is what the metropolis today is simply trying to do, to defeat this interaction, this knowing, this finding out, this connecting, this cooperation and so on. It tends to segregate too many things, it tends to put too many obstacles to too many things until the person becomes lost and reacts violently or aggressively. The basis is instrumental. The goal is beyond the instrumental.

*   *   *

Are you hopeful that some day your ideal will come through, will be realized?

I guess so. Although the current interest might be just curiosity.

NOTES

[1]The author uses the term "Third World" rather as an abbreviation describing the developing nations and does not accept this term in the meaning it is usually given, as if there were such a thing as a third world.

11. *Carl Kaysen*

Carl Kaysen has been director of the Institute of Advanced Study at Princeton, New Jersey, since 1966.

He was born in Philadelphia, Pennsylvania, in 1920. He studied economics, first at Columbia University, and obtained a Ph.D. from Harvard in 1954.

During World War II he served in the Office of Strategic Services in Washington, D.C., with an accent on problems concerning the German war economy. After entering the Air Force he served in Europe as intelligence officer.

From 1947 to 1968 he was consultant to the Rand Corporation in Santa Monica, California. From 1953 to 1954 he acted as consultant to the Weapons System Evaluation Group in the office of the Secretary of Defense. In 1961 he worked as White House staff member to President John F. Kennedy in the office of the special assistant for national security affairs. From 1961 to 1963 he became deputy special assistant to the President for national security affairs. From 1963 to 1965 he acted as special consultant to President Lyndon B. Johnson.

Why are some of the world's top economists so critical of the MIT study Limits to Growth?

Because the model around which the argument is built, ignores some elementary economic propositions. The most important elementary economic proposition which the model ignores is that there are adjustment mechanisms through prices that when things become scarcer, that prices rise, change, that change in prices in turn includes further adjustment and demand on the one side, lessening the supply and on the other hand increasing it, calling forth new technologies, new substitutes. These adjustments have in the past led to increasing supplies of resources. The fact they are nowhere recognized or discussed makes economists suspicious of the model.

Could resources be measured at all in economic or physical terms, by *computer simulation or otherwise?*

Resources can certainly be measured in physical terms and they conventionally are. One speaks of acres of land, or tons of coal reserves and millions of oil reserves and so on. On the other hand, I think one gets a deeper insight into resources by measuring them or thinking of them in economic terms. There are acres of land which are easily accessible and easily operable. More acres of land can be added at a higher price by irrigation, or by reclamation or by swamp draining and so forth. Similarly, if one thinks of a mineral resource, there are easily available supplies, there are less available supplies—at higher prices of recovery, more is available.

I was speaking only the other day with an executive of one of the larger aluminum companies, who remarked that they were moving from bauxite, which is the most easily worked aluminum ore, to a somewhat less easily worked aluminum ore never before used but which has enormous reserves, and potential. This may mean that a ton of aluminum will cost a few more cents, but at a few more cents reserves increase, so that one of the problems of the notion of limits to growth is that the measurement of resources in physical terms obscures the important fact that they look different when measured in economics.

But more land, more of this new aluminum source, it all will need more *money. How would poor countries, the Third World, raise the money* *in order to develop new land, irrigate it, cultivate it?*

There is no other way the problems of poverty in the Third World can be solved except by general world economic growth. Without general world economic growth the problem of the Third World will get worse, not better. I think it is totally unrealistic to expect that there can be a radical redistribution of wealth and income without growth in the present. First of all, a higher standard of living in the poor countries implies by the very fact economic growth in those countries. Since they include nearly two-thirds of the world population, economic growth in those countries implies economic growth in the world as a whole. Further, economic growth in the poor countries depends very heavily on trade with and investments from the richer countries. It's again really impossible to conceive that they will be increasing trade and increasing investments when incomes in the richer countries are going down, not up.

Would you say there are signs that technology also grows exponentially?

We have a good deal of history on that. Of course, predicting the future is a chancy business. The only way we can do it is to look at the experience of the past. The area in which this has been best studied in quantitative terms is in the United States. Over the last century approximately, technology in the United States—the value of output that can be got from a given bundle of input—has been growing at about two percent per year, in other words exponentially. We have information for rather shorter periods on some European countries and on Japan. They also show exponential growth of technology in the same sense. There is a very faint indication—which I myself find too inconclusive to base a reliable judgment on—that the rate of technological growth has increased in recent years. I think one will have to wait another decade or two to see whether this is in fact the case.

Bringing this increase of technological growth into the model, the MIT planetary model, that would of course change the outcome of the results.

It would be a very fundamental change in the model. This particular model can be described rather crudely in the following way: You have quantities, population, industrial production and the like, which are growing exponentially. You have a fixed ceiling. When these quantities bump into the ceiling, they not only cannot go through it, they must bounce back with a great crash. That great crash is the downturn in world population, world wealth, a catastrophe which the MIT model predicts.

Once we introduce the exponential growth of technology, what we see is that the ceiling is also growing. The question then becomes how fast is one growing with relation to one another. Further, at this point we can then go back to examine what is the adjustment mechanism which connects, so to speak, the level of the ceiling or its rate of growing with the rate of growth of these quantities like population, industrial production, use of mineral inputs and so on.

Adjustment mechanisms are vital?

No useful economic model is complete without some account of adjustment mechanisms. The very important adjustment mechanism which is central to the whole economic idea is the mechanism of the price system. The MIT model nowhere recognizes that this mechanism comes into account.

Take a very simple reason for skepticism about the arguments that are made about the limits of mineral resources: It is not in general true that the share of minerals in the national output or the share of food in the national output, agricultural production, has been rising. Rather it has been falling over the long period. This is certainly true in the United States, where we have good lengthy-period figures. It seems to be true in Western Europe as well, though it can be that our information to this comparison is not as complete or does not stretch over a longer period of time. If the MIT thesis were correct, we would expect to see rising a relative share of output in minerals and more resources needed to supply these scarcer and scarcer minerals. We see the opposite, a gentle decline in the share of output.

Talking to Professor Nordhaus[1] at Yale, who constructed a model with Professor James Tobin of Yale, he said that the MIT model was far too complicated. He pointed to the need for a much simpler model than the MIT one.

It can be simpler in many dimensions, but I think it should be more complex in some others, in bringing in some price-adjusting mechanisms. I have not yet had a chance to see the Nordhaus-Tobin model.

You say no to the MIT model, on what grounds exactly?

Really on the ground that the basic argument that leads to the conclusion we must stop growth is simply wrong, intellectually unconvincing. Once we say the catastrophe isn't inevitably at hand, we have to ask what are the alternative choices. As I said earlier, if one looks first and foremost at the question of poverty in two-thirds of the world's population, it is impossible to see how that poverty can be alleviated without continuing economic growth.

In saying this I don't want to suggest either of two things: One, that the patterns of growth must be the same as in the past; perhaps they should change. Two, I don't want to suggest that the problems of pollution and of resource exhaustion are not real, aren't problems to which attention has to be paid; I think the problems of pollution both in the industrialized countries and in the industrializing countries are very urgent problems.

We haven't been doing the right thing about them. We are only beginning to learn what to do about them. It's quite important that we should do so. Part of the problem of pollution is to think of the choice of technology in ways which will make pollution less. Part of the problem is again to use the very simple advantages of the price mechanism and make polluters pay for the damage they inflict on society in general. If we make them pay for it, they will have strong economic incentives to minimize it. Under our present system, producing pollution, so to speak, is free; and since it is free, there are no economic incentives to avoid doing it. Similarly there is no question that there is a world population problem.

However, the discussion in the little book, *Limits to Growth*, of that problem is very shallow. There is no analysis, no distinction between desired family size and achieved family size. There is no discussion of what determines the capacity of the achieved desired family size, on the one hand, and what determines desired family size, on the other. My own judgment is that no matter what we do in the sphere of spreading knowledge of birth-control methods and pointing out to people the desirability of having smaller families—we will have to make people aware of the fact that with the higher survival rate, especially the lowering of the death rate, complete family composition will be attainable with a much smaller number of births and that the world population will increase very shortly in the next thirty years. We have to think more of ways of adapting to this increased standard than trying to wish that it didn't increase.

This striving for a global computer model in order to inventorize this planet's resources and problems, would you be basically in favor of such a thing?

Well, I think this is a question like other questions of intellectual enterprise. They are things that people have to decide for themselves. If somebody thinks this is a very good idea and feels he knows how to do it, let him go ahead and do it. My own taste would not run in that direction. I think there is such an enormous information gap in many areas that the model as such will be really very crude, therefore the conclusions that one can draw from it are very slender. Furthermore, I think there is a great deal of computer mysticism which is terribly unnecessary. Many of the main ideas in the MIT model could be dealt with without elaborate computation. Elaborate computation is important when a model contains a great deal of detailed information and when it makes a real difference when a number has one magnitude rather than another. Given both the lack of knowledge of the structure of the relations involved in the MIT model and the very, very crude quantitative dimensions, it seems to me that there is a tremendous overemphasis on the role of computation.

But it was really meant as a tiny first step—

Yes, it was meant as a tiny first step, and perhaps an interesting first step. I have been more interested than many critics in the model. Perhaps the criticism will help the model makers make a better second step—

That's why I am here.

—and that I think is always a desirable direction. There is, let me repeat, the element of computer mysticism. Calculations made by the computer are not by that fact more correct than the calculations made by the man with pencil and paper or a calculation machine. When a model gets sufficiently complicated in the sense of having a right number of equations or relations in it, it is necessary to use a computer. I think it's all a matter of judgment.

Do you see society evolve towards a planetary management on a scale like IBM or General Motors? Do you think it will be desirable to move more towards a kind of practical pragmatic management of this planet?

I cannot see that far ahead. I would guess myself that some things will be managed on a large scale and some things will be managed on a smaller scale. As an American I have a kind of a Jeffersonian prejudice to believe that things should be managed on as small a scale as possible.

A look at the current world scene does not suggest that we are moving toward more political unity, more political homogeneity with any great speed.

But could scientists influence politics toward, I would say, this most necessary kind of world management?

Let me perhaps answer this question indirectly by saying the most powerful political force in the world today seems to be nationalism, not rational calculations. I suspect we will have to contend with that for some long period of time. Very few things in the political world happen because the logical arguments show that they would be good things to do. I don't want to underprize the role of reason, in which I believe ultimately; sometimes it takes a very long time for the arguments of reason to prevail.

NOTES

[1]See conversation no. 19.

12. *Marshall McLuhan*

Herbert Marshall McLuhan was born in Edmonton, in the province of Alberta, Canada, in 1911. He studied at the University of Manitoba and obtained his Ph.D. at Cambridge, England, in 1942. After teaching at the University of Wisconsin, the University of St. Louis, and Assumption University, he came in 1946 to St. Michael's College at the University of Toronto, Canada, where he is director of the Center of Culture and Technology.

Some of his best-known books are *The Gutenberg Galaxy: The Making of Typographic Man* (1962), *Understanding Media* (1964), *The Medium Is the Message* (1967), *War and Peace in the Global Village* (1968), *Culture Is Our Business* (1970), and published recently with Barrington Nevitt, *Take Today: The Executive as Dropout* (1972).

Professor McLuhan, what do you call "ground"?

It is a term from Gestalt psychology.[1] Look at the *ground* "around" the *figure* of the automobile, or the *ground* "around" any technology. Each kind of technique, or technology, necessarily has a large *ground* of services and disservices associated with it. Now, the ordinary attention is fixed on the *figure* rather than the *ground*, on the wheel rather than the huge system of road services necessary to maintain the existence of a wheel or wheeled vehicles. With a motorcar, most people are interested in changing designs or patterns of the car. They pay only incidental attention to the huge service environment of roads, oil companies, filling stations, and other allied services of manufacturing that are the *ground* of the car.

The motorcar, when it was first introduced in the early part of the century, was thought to be a sure way of getting rid of cities, by taking us back to the country. Watching the *figure* of the car, they saw the immediate possibility of simply transporting city dwellers back into the country where they came from. An early phrase about the motorcar was: "Let's take a spin in the country." It never occurred to them that this *figure* of the car might generate a huge *ground* of new services far bigger than the figure ever was thought to be. In other words, the car created a totally new environment or *ground* of services and disservices which we have come to associate with the American way of life.

There is another weird feature of the car which is completely unnoticed. The car is the ultimate form of privacy in America. In Europe, the motorcar is a toy, a fun thing. In America, it is the ultimate den or boudoir, the main form of privacy; and therefore every American has to have a big car. He is not going to use public transit because that means going out to be with people. In North America there is a universal and hidden assumption that we go outside to be alone. That's why we do not have cafés or pubs or public entertainment, except for our "dates." When we go out with our dates, we do not go out to socialize. On the other hand, when we go home, we do not go home to be alone, we go home to be with people. There is little or no privacy in the American home. But this total situation is a hidden *ground* around another *figure*, the *figure* of the pioneer determined to conquer nature, as a commando or as a team.

By not looking at the *ground* around the automobile, you miss the message of the car. For it is the *ground* of any technology that is the *medium* that changes everybody, and it is the *medium* that is the message of the technology, not the *figure*.

You mentioned ancient Rome apropos figure *and* ground *interplay.*

The huge service surround necessary to maintain even the roads of Rome suddenly collapsed because they had become too expensive and required too much skilled labor. Roman roads were marble-surfaced for speed and smoothness. The courier system, sustained by the roads, was, in turn, a *ground* created by papyrus, which was a *figure* with its own *ground* of services, which included a further environment of a military kind. The whole Roman military system depended upon papyrus and written documents that could be moved very quickly across large territories. This kind of communication, in turn, fostered the wheel and the wheeled vehicle. But there is very little study of what sort of roads they had. It has mainly been noticed *where* they were. But the Roman road as *figure* involved a huge *ground* of services, deriving ultimately, perhaps, from papyrus.

Papyrus supplies ended when the Nile got polluted. It does not grow even today, except in the upper Nile which is relatively free of pollution. But when the papyrus plant could no longer grow in the Nile, the Romans switched to parchment, which remained the medieval form of paper. It was too scarce for the old papyrus uses, however. But the paper system necessary to maintain the huge military bureaucracy depended on a diversified but hidden *ground*, or environment.

The *figure* of paper is really the key to the *ground*; but the *ground* is not chosen for study, even though it is the *ground* that creates the changes in people. The *figure* is not the medium and it is not the cause of change. However, it is the *figure* that creates the *ground* that is the means of changing people using any technology. Yet the *figure* merely sits upon the *ground* itself, while it is the services engendered by such a technology that alter the lives of people.

In the movie industry, for example, the huge Hollywood surround of services dried up very quickly when the figures of jet and TV appeared. It was the new *figures* that eroded the whole *ground* for the film industry. Film-making for home television, rather than for movie theaters, completely decentralized services. Hollywood, but not the cinema, was finished overnight. Now that's how quickly a new *figure* can disperse or dissolve an old *ground*. It is the old *ground* that provided, and indeed, *was* the movie way of life. Hollywood itself was a new way of life which is now gone.

It is sometimes said that the motorcar is "obsolete."

This term has many meanings, and I once spent months studying "obsolescence as the matrix of innovation." Perhaps the simplest way to get at the changing role of the car is to point to the fact that the jet plane has put an entire new environment around, not just the *figure* of the car, but the *ground* of the car. The jet goes around the entire highway system, even as the highways had earlier gone around the railway system. By offering a totally new kind of transportation services, the jet threatens the highway as much as the highway threatened the railway. The jet offers a completely new time scale to travelers, creating a *ground* of services that is worldwide and on a twenty-four-hour pattern, giving access to every part of the globe. The jet has not only revolutionized the planning and conduct of all commercial activity, but of all politics and all news coverage as well. Tapes and films are flown from all parts of the world on a twenty-four-hour basis. Students, for example, can now plan their studies in completely new ways, since it is as cheap and as quick to go to distant countries to study language or archaeology as it is to take a course in the local university. Meantime, the local university has obtained grants to send its staff to all parts of the world to pursue projects of the utmost diversity. In contrast, the motorcar and its service environment takes up new functions both of utility and recreation, which are, to a considerable degree, dictated by the new time scales of jet travel.

Thus, it is not so much the car as a *figure*, as the *ground* of the car that is transformed by the new service environment of the jet. This same new service environment of the jet profoundly alters people's image of themselves and of one another, as witness the hijackers for whom the jet offers the immediate prospect of world news coverage. There is a sense in which the hijackers are the real jet set who have, as it were, intuitively grasped the meaning of this new medium as a thing that has bypassed the establishment and outmoded our legal system. Perhaps, then, it is possible to approach "obsolescence" in this way, and see it as a phasing out of some service by a new service, by the encompassing of the old *ground* by a new *ground*. This does not, however, mean extinction of the previous service, since in many cases the older service can go along side by side with the new service, as in the case of the motor car and the jet, or of handwriting and the printed word. Even the typewriter did not extinguish handwriting. There may well be more handwriting in the world today than there was before printing. But quantity is no clue to function or use.

In terms of obsolescence the printed book has been bypassed several times by new services, such as photography and film and Xerox. Whereas Gutenberg[2] made everybody a reader, Xerox makes everybody a publisher, bringing the Gutenberg technology full cycle, as it were. Yet the old uses of the printed book remain side by side with many of the new features of photo and film and Xerox. If one looks deeper, however, it is evident that when one service is enveloped by a new service, those who employ the old service are deeply affected by it. Writing for the press in the age of the print and the photo was considerably altered by these intensely realistic developments. Cinema used the book for scripting, but cinematic techniques, in turn, radically altered modes both of perception and composition.

Do the MIT global studies of man and his situation cover the ground?

It might be well to point out that these studies are carried out on "systems development" patterns which tend to concentrate on the *figure* and ignore the *ground*, or the surround, of services and disservices. Similarly, the Milton Eisenhower[3] report on violence is mainly concerned with the images of violence as they are presented in various programs in various media. Violence is accepted as a *figure* of program input, and these studies try to discover a matching *ground*, or cause, to explain this *figure*. In practice, however, the *figure* of violence has its meaning only against an altogether different *ground*, namely, the extreme mobility of contemporary human environments. Mobility, as such, erodes human identity, and the threat to identity is the proximate cause of "violence." In all cases, violence is a response to threatened identity images; and since many kinds of change can threaten identity, there are a great many kinds of violence or response to these threats. For example, the use of the car or plane, insofar as it exceeds all private or individual human power, represents an aggressive manifestation of the human ego which, on the one hand, asserts the identity of the driver or user and, on the other hand, threatens the identity or even the very existence of those in the environment of this activity. If only for that reason, speed and power incite all people to use the same means to assert and to protect their own identity. In this situation, the cyclist, for example, is an extremely violent person, asserting his threatened identity by the most extreme measure of resistance.

General systems studies have so far discovered no way of investigating the *ground* of any *figure*. For example, to study the nature of radio by establishing the number of listeners, and the kinds of programs, simply ignores the *effects* of radio, as radio, on the human psyche and nervous system. Radio as *ground*, as a world surround, transforms the relation of everybody to everybody, regardless of programming. General systems studies, like most media studies, ignore the rub of *figure* against *ground* and try to deduce the *ground* by a simple quantitative study of the *figure*, which is then relegated to the category of "content." This approach leads to hopeless confusion, since in every instance, and in the case of every medium whatever, whether of language or clothing or radio or TV, it is the user himself who is the content, and it is the user alone who constitutes the experience of that service. No matter what is on TV, if the user is a Chinese, it is going to be a Chinese program, just as surely as a movie on TV is experienced as a TV show. For the TV medium translates the movie medium into itself, rendering not a movie, but a TV image.

In this respect the systems-development people, whether at MIT or at the Rand Corporation, try to translate all *ground* into *figure* in their studies and they classify all *effects* in terms of "inputs." Their reason for doing this is related to the fact that all of these investigators are *unconsciously* alphabetic and literate men who can think of no other strategies of investigation except in terms of quantitative assumptions by means of yes-no or "two-bit" programs.[4]

The problem of Western literate man, when he confronts an African or Oriental, is his aggressive need to translate the African or Oriental into his alphabetic culture in order to dominate him. There are inherent reasons why phonetically literate man is a one-way character incapable of two-way dialogue with any other kind of culture. These reasons are discussed in *The Gutenberg Galaxy: The Making of Typographic Man*.[5] Phonetically literate man, from the Greeks to the present, has refused to study the effects of anything, since he is totally committed to inputs and content only. Inputs he considers to be the content, and anything which impedes the movement of these inputs to their target is called "noise." Today, phonetically literate man is in great trouble because of his inflexibility, and also because he is now merely one *figure* in a huge acoustic *ground* of simultaneous electric information.

When the Club of Rome made its study of the limits to growth, it committed the usual Western mistake of studying only hardware and inputs, ignoring the quality of life and the satisfactions and effects of the various ways of life. Phonetically literate man has systematically ignored the effects of phonetic literacy on himself or on others. The Japanese are about to launch a multibillion program to impose Western phonetic literacy on the whole of Japan. This program will scrub off the entire face of Japan, eroding its oral culture and its iconology and ritual. The ripping-off of the entire Japanese identity will release a fantastic flood of violence and a corporate quest for new identity on a competitive scale unimagined in human history. Phonetically literate man, from the Greeks to the present, has been consistently aggressive and at war with his environment. His need to translate his environment into phonetic, literate terms, turns him into a conqueror and a cultural bulldozer, or leveller. Since Sputnik, the sudden awareness of the planet as an art form has compelled men to program all aspects of the old "nature." When the planet went inside a manmade environment, art superseded nature for good or ill, much as the market had superseded nature in the nineteenth century. The recognition that survival now depends upon an ecological balance of all factors simultaneously, in a deep sense makes Western man "obsolete." Indeed, his own new electric environment drives him inward, even as the old Western hardware is driving the Orient outward toward nineteenth-century objectives of conquest.

NOTES

[1]A type of psychology that arose as a strong reaction against atomic psychology in all its varieties, equally hostile to behaviorism and to introspectionism; its basal contention is that mental processes and behavior cannot be analyzed without remainder, into elementary units, since wholeness and organization are features of such processes from the start.

[2]Johann Gutenberg (1400-1468), German inventor of printing from movable type.

[3]Milton Eisenhower (1899-   ), brother of former U.S. President Dwight D. Eisenhower.

[4]These hang-ups are explored and explained at some length in *Take Today: The Executive as Dropout*, Marshall McLuhan and Barrington Nevitt (Harcourt, Brace, Jovanovich Inc., 1972).

[5]University of Toronto Press, 1962.

13. Paul R. Ehrlich

Paul R. Ehrlich was born in 1932 in Philadelphia, Pennsylvania. He obtained his Ph.D. in biology at the University of Kansas. In 1966 he was appointed full professor of biological sciences at Stanford University in California.

From 1969 to 1970 he acted as president of Zero Population Growth. His book *The Population Bomb* went at the time into its twenty-second printing in its original edition. He followed this bestseller up with *How to Be a Survivor*, written with R. L. Harriman (1971). Together with his wife, Anne, he published *Population, Resources, Environment* (1970).

The data in Limits to Growth *concerning population, were they sufficient to illustrate your position on population growth?*

Well, they were highly aggregated, but they were perfectly sufficient for the purpose of the model as presented. In other words, I think a lot of the people who have reviewed the book have not bothered to look very carefully at other things the authors have said.

Skinner complained. . . .[1]

Nobody really reads his book either. With the qualifications stated by the people who did the *Limits to Growth* work, it was utterly adequate. The conclusions drawn by the study were the same as those drawn by, I think, every competent scientist who has looked at the entire world situation.

Barry Commoner[2] *called* Limits to Growth *a step backwards.*

Dr. Commoner seems not to have looked at the entire situation, I think, because his political beliefs will not permit him to accept the important role played by population growth in the environmental crisis. It is too bad that he does not have an ecologist in his group to help him avoid such errors. Perhaps he meant that *Limits to Growth* was a "step backwards" for the Commoner crusade to persuade people that population and affluence are unimportant. In that respect, I think he is correct.

Is the only way to alert mass public opinion the doomsday approach?

Well, I don't think one wants to take a doomsday or a nondoomsday approach. What you want to do is make the best possible diagnosis of what is going on. That's basically what the Meadows team[3] has done, and what I am doing. It is making a prognosis, not a matter of optimism or pessimism or doomsday or not doomsday. You look at where the trends are going and then you say, in our best estimate if we don't change our course, the trends are going this way and the results are likely to be bad.

Most of the people who say the so-called doomsday people are too pessimistic are simply people who are utterly ignorant of the fundamentals of ecology. There are many people who have gained some understanding of the demographic situation, which is simple. We teach our undergraduate students all the demography that is necessary to understand the world demographic situation in two lectures. After that the question becomes one of understanding resources, understanding ecology and (what is much more difficult, of course) understanding social and political systems. We know in general where the solutions lie as far as the physics and biology and ecology go, but what we don't know really is how to change human institutions so that corrective action will be taken in time.

How much time you think we have?

Well, it depends. If you ask how long do we have until utter catastrophe overtakes the Western world, I feel that the MIT report is too optimistic. I think it will be some time within the next twenty years, probably sooner than later, but it is hard to judge. It depends on how things go. If you ask when we should have started, of course, we should have started down the right track in the 1930s, 1940s at the latest. For instance if there had been crash programs for population control in the underdeveloped countries in the '40s, then they would not be faced today with the hideous problems of unemployment, which political scientists and sociologists cannot see any way around. To prevent rising unemployment India, for instance, will have to provide more than a hundred thousand jobs per week throughout this decade. We have enormous numbers of people coming into economies which are not able to create jobs for them, and impossible food problems and so on. We are well way past the time when we should have had crash programs to try and change our course. Another question now is if we start to change, will the built-in lag time within the system destroy us anyway. You know, we may have already gone on too far. I think that is the major question that concerns many ecologists.

And how about the gap between the rich and the poor cultures?

Well, it has been growing continuously. It's still growing and the run-of-the-mill economists' answer to this problem, both between nations and within nations, is to turn the same old crank faster. All we have to do is to keep the economy growing and growing.

That's the point of view McNamara espoused at the Stockholm Conference on Human Environment.

The idea is that economic growth will leave enough crumbs to improve the condition of the poor. But, of course, that's a game we have tried. It does not work. We have been doing that bit for the last twenty-five years or so, and we see quite clearly that the gap continues to grow. Therefore, although there is no absolute proof that it will never work, I think you will have to make the judgment that the "eternal growth" approach will not work—especially since it leads to eco-catastrophe. What we need to do is to work very rapidly to get equilibrium economies—spacemen economies, as they are called—in the over-developed nations. Then we must face the problem of redistribution of wealth. That, of course, is one of the most difficult political and social problems.

And what about the rebuilding of the environment? Where do the behavioral architects come in?

Well, the whole question, of course, is how do you change human behavior into what I would call a more survival-oriented mode.

That's what Skinner calls the aim of life: survival.

In many ways I am a Skinnerian, although many of his specific solutions are at the most impracticable. What I would take hope from is that as far as we can see, looking at other cultures, man is not necessarily an aggressive waster. The question to me is not now so much how do you change human nature—although that is an interesting question—but how do you change human institutions.

There have been suggestions for a World Population Institute.

Well, I have no objections to institutes and committees, but frankly none of these things turn me on. The institutes, commissions, academies and so on are the standard answers to establishment scientists and politicians who have been running the world for the last twenty-five years and sending it steadily on down the drain. They're the people who cannot find the way to disarm. They're the people who cannot find a way to keep the automobile from destroying the United States. They're the people who cannot figure out any way to stop a continuous exponential growth of energy use of between five and eight percent a year in the United States. In other words, when you look at the members of the American National Academy of Sciences, at the people in the American national government, the British national government, American state governments, and so on, these are the people who are unable to move off the course of oblivion. To expect to change the system by setting up more of their kind of institutions is just preposterous. We have a theory about them that is called "I am the proof." In other words, the fact that these people are at the top of the system to them is the proof that the system has to be perfect, otherwise they would not have risen to the top. They are the last people in the world whom we expect really to change it.

John R. Platt[4] talks about mobilizing the scientists to tackle the job.

I agree with John that we've got to mobilize the scientists to meet this crisis, much as we did during the second world war. But first we must mobilize the people and then the politicians.

But we are in a war condition.

The point is until the politicians and the people realize it's war condition, you are not going to mobilize the scientists. First of all, scientists are among the most conservative people in the world. They are trained to stay in their laboratories, do what the politicians tell them to and keep their mouths shut. There are rare exceptions, but with three hundred thousand or so scientists are at least two hundred and ninety-five thousand of them who have sold out completely to either industry or government.

The establishment.

Yes, of course. They are not going to mobilize anything, they have jobs. What they want to do is mobilize the space programs and try to get them moving again. You know in NASA[5] they are working very hard to continue all sorts of nonsense. You cannot expect the leadership to come from the scientists.

What is the role of the media in this?

Well, in the United States the media are of course owned lock, stock and barrel by the same people who are interested in continuing the status quo. One of the problems we have is freeing the media from the control of General Motors and so on. This is a very big problem. It may be possible but again you keep coming right back to the same thing—if you've got to change the media, you've got to change the politics. The agency which controls the media is the Federal Communications Commission, which of course is largely controlled by the people who are supposed to be regulated. The foxes are guarding the henhouse. We keep coming back to politics. The ecology is relatively simple, the demography is simpleminded beyond belief. The politics, the sociology and so on tend to be very, very complicated and difficult.

I guess you don't expect too much from the World Population Conference of '74 either.

Something good could emerge from it. It was in a sense a miracle that we had the environmental conference in Stockholm four years after the first politicians learned the word ecology. Stockholm had a sort of propaganda value, but basically it had little immediate impact. The coverage in the United States of Bobby Fischer's chess games was considerably more substantial than the coverage of the media of the environmental conference, so—

But a population conference could be a step in the right direction.

It's a step in the right direction. But it's as if somebody is bailing with a thimble while the boat is sinking. But you can say every thimbleful of water you throw overboard is a help. But if the water is coming in ten tons a minute and you are baling three, four thimblesful an hour, yes, it's a step in the right direction, but it's hard to get excited about how you are going to save yourself by doing that.

NOTES

[1]See conversation no. 7.
[2]See conversation no. 26.
[3]Team led by Professor Dennis L. Meadows, formerly of MIT, which drew up the report on global problems for the Club of Rome sponsored publication *Limits to Growth*.
[4]See conversation no. 9.
[5]National Aeronautics Space Administration.

14. Lewis Mumford

Lewis Mumford was born in 1895 in Flushing, New York. He studied education at City College of New York and at Columbia University.

Among his best-known works are *The Culture of Cities* (1938), *The Condition of Man* (1944), *The Myth of the Machine: Technics and Human Development*, Vol. I (1967), *The Pentagon of Power*, Vol. II (1970).

In 1972 Mumford received the National Medal for literature.

When John Glenn came back to earth, he said: "Let man take over." Limits to Growth *advocates just that.*

This has probably been part of my thinking from the very beginning.

In 1938, when I published *The Culture of Cities*, I took for granted that the population statistics at that time would continue. The leading West European countries were losing their old rate of growth, except for Holland. The other countries were all looking forward to having a balanced population by 1970 or 1980 at the latest, so *Limits to Growth* is no fresh idea to me. I felt that this was the very basis of the laying of the foundations of a new kind of civilization. For a century and a half we have relied on population growth to ensure industrial expansion and financial gain. We have been overpressed into doing everything too fast and quantitively too great.

But if this was your opinion in '38, how much progress do you think man has made over the past half-century in achieving this goal of a more managed industrial growth and population growth?

Insofar as the knowledge of contraceptives has been spreading, great progress has been made. This began first in France, because even the peasants in France knew how to use contraceptives during the nineteenth century. They learned from the upper classes how to limit their population. France had almost reached stability before the second world war. But just the opposite has happened with industrial growth. War and waste on an unparalleled scale have overstimulated this kind of growth.

Don't you think that the explosion of population about three percent in Venezuela, et cetera, needs a World Population Council, a management, to make the planet livable towards the year 2000?

That is only a paper solution. The real question is, how much can be done by education within the time allotted us. You cannot control the sexual life of simple people merely by passing laws and police inspection. There has to be some other way of doing it. In the past this has usually been done by religion. Now we have no such control. That control grows weaker and weaker as time goes on. Our task is to appeal to the great masses of people on the basis of something that concerns them as much as making love and having children. It's hard to give a simple answer to this question, except in the general terms of a better all-round life.

Could you tell us what your basic concept is of what you call the "pentagon of power."

The basis of the "pentagon of power" is an unqualified commitment to power, money, and pleasure. All natural wants have limits that are soon reached. But there is no natural limit to the acquisition of power or money, whether or not any sensible social or personal use is made of it. Money plays a psychological role in modern society that is strangely like that of the recently discovered pleasure-center in the brain. A monkey with an electrode attached to his pleasure-center forgets all other life needs, even to the point of starvation, in order to prolong and intensify this pleasurable stimulus. So with our present drives to increase physical energy, political control, military power and personal power in the form of status, privilege, fame, publicity—all translatable into the abstract symbols of money. For this reason all over the world the environment is being mined, bulldozed and wrecked "for pleasure," that is money.

There are various things involved. First of all is energy itself. That is power in the fundamental sense. It's basic to all society. We're not going to do away with this basis, but we can do away with the notion that this is the only important factor in human society. The expansion of power is not the chief business of man. He needs the right quantity of power at the right place at the right time, and therefore he must have the ability to increase it or diminish it in accordance with his needs.

The myth of power has dominated all large-scale societies for five thousand years. Every nation thinks of its life in terms of increasing its power, that's to say increasing its ability to fight and overcome and exploit other nations. This is an irrational factor, obviously. Then the other part of the "pentagon of power" is the overwhelming need for inflating the organs of publicity. We do it now through radio, television and advertising. More and more of our life is spent for the sake of gaining the attention of other men through publicity. This was once the great prerogative of kings. Their palaces and monuments were advertising devices, to show how powerful they were. If you are a president or a dictator, a bandleader or a television star your image appears every day in every place because of the fact we now have worldwide communication. The common man has fallen for this as well. Crimes are undoubtedly being committed by people who merely want to get attention for themselves—

—*Like Oswald*[1] *and Bremer?*[2]

—right down to the latest fanatic who has killed somebody just to get into the newspapers, even if he's going to be caught and executed.

You speak a great deal of the electronic phantasmagoria of Marshall McLuhan,[3] who thinks that "we are electronically inducing mass psychosis." You don't agree with McLuhan?

I disagree with his notion that we should submit to these things. He's a very erratic thinker, so he contradicts himself frequently. I haven't attempted to catch up with the latest McLuhan. But the McLuhan I am familiar with—and I've been familiar with him for a long time—is the McLuhan who felt that man's real life now lies outside him, in the machines that he has projected and that he should submit to this, that he should regard this as his destiny. I take just the opposite point of view.

You accord an entirely different importance to the individuality of man then.

I think the most important part of man's nature, the fundamental fact about all living organisms is that they are autonomous, they are self-governing, they have their own method of growth, they have their own relationship to the environment, their life springs from within, not just from outside. It is of course affected by all that lies outside, but there's something within every organism that makes it true to itself. On my reading of what's happening we have more and more transferred our own vital activities to various pseudo-organic machines, who can perform them more efficiently but always under somebody else's control, not under our control.

Including television?

Including television, surely.

But you would not deny the disastrous influence on masses of people—and children—being glued day in, day out to television and being offered too often plain garbage.

Yes, it's a kind of suicide, this being committed to the pseudolife of mass organizations—daily suicide. Under the command of television you surrender your life to this or that organization. Then you find your life has become emptier and emptier. Without the stimulus of drugs in one form or another. And television is just the cheapest and most common drug; without this mind-killer you cannot bear life. Beneath this there's a very deep tendency to commit suicide, to abandon the effort to develop, to say that all life is worthless. That's what the whole avant-garde is now saying to us, both in literature and in painting.

Disoriented society. How to pull out of this maelstrom?

Well, the answer is that there are large numbers of healthy people still at work in it who are oriented towards life. Every time a new baby is born we have somebody who is potentially oriented to life. I can see a change already taking place. Two things are happening at the same time: One is negative, a surrender of all the traditional life-making habits and institutions to the great bureaucratic and military organizations that control our life, the "pentagon of power." On the other hand, among many of the young there is an attempt to resume autonomy, to think for themselves, to act for themselves. They do this very crudely and childishly because they are thinking about a very narrow self; they are thinking in terms of the pathetic five-year culture that they're familiar with. They don't realize that they couldn't think at all unless they were thinking with a Paleolithic invention called language, which is at least fifty thousand years old and probably much more than that. In other words, they're trying to leave the past behind, and on those terms they can have no future. Real life always involves keeping the past and future working together, within the mind. The past cannot be denied or totally effaced any more than the genes. The past exists in our genes. We cannot wipe out our genes. They're there with us for good and bad, and that's true of history as well.

Mr. Mumford, you don't believe in this notion of a global village?

Yes and no. Long before McLuhan, I said that for certain purposes "the whole planet is a city."[4] Not a village, but a city, a vehicle for the highest and widest forms of communication. But open only to a highly cultivated and disciplined minority, today represented largely by scientists. Just the opposite of the limited village. You cannot communicate with anybody whose language you don't speak. You cannot even do that by images, because shaking the head from left to right means yes in Turkish and up and down means yes in most European cultures.

Only for certain narrow purposes could we have a global village. The richness of life has never been encompassed by a village. Indeed, a global village would constitute a very primitive and a very elementary culture, lacking human qualities that even the most primitive village possesses.

You often discuss Toynbee[5] and you speak of the process of dematerialization, parallel to Limits to Growth, *to improving the quality of life at the cost of this mad race for material gain or of power.[6] What is your concept of dematerialization and how is that to be achieved?*

Well, it is a matter of limiting the demand for goods to the necessary amount, not to the amount that gives you status, not to the amount that gives you profit or power, but to the necessary amount in terms of life. I can give you a very simple illustration from what goes on in any American suburb. Most suburbanites measure their prosperity by the size of their lawns. If they can acquire as much as an acre, they spend eight hours every week going back and forth on their kiddycars mowing this lawn. Just a grass wasteland. We have the same amount of space here. Instead of a wide lawn, I have reduced it to the smallest possible amount, I can mow that land with a hand mower in an hour and a quarter. Actually I can run this entire acre and keep it order without outside help. We have various kinds of raspberry bushes and currant bushes and an asparagus bed and a vegetable garden. In other words, we can enjoy all the richness of this environment through spending the same number of hours that the suburbanite spends on keeping his lawn in order. In that sense he belongs to the power culture. His lawn gives him status. He does not have a single useful thing growing there, whereas I belong to the human culture, which enjoys an enormous amount of variety and which does not involve more work. The suburbanite has to use up oil and gas in order to keep his lawn going. I only have to use up the sun's energy through food. This is one way to answer the problem of what are we going to do about the demand for energy. The answer is you can reduce the demand for energy by the right kind of planning. I don't require extra gasoline to do any of the operations here.

You speak of a vast amount of valuable knowledge becoming relegated to a mountainous rubbish heap, and you mention an overproduction of books.[7]

This is a mental pollution, of course, and we should have been aware of this a long time ago. We have invented a system which demands greater and greater growth in every department that promises profit. We talk about the gross national product and the necessity for increasing that every year. This goes on in every field, and plainly it goes on in the production of books. If you don't produce books and papers, you cannot get promotion in a university.

That is overkill.

Of course it's overkill. It's overkill of the mind as well, because nobody in another fifty years will be able to find his way among this mountain of books.

Limits to Growth *used computers. Would you say computers are socially disruptive?*

None of our inventions is by itself socially disruptive. It's the absurd use we make of them that's disruptive. The superstitious notion today is that if you feed certain data to a computer and the computer gives you an answer, that answer acquires a godlike authority, which the same knowledge did not have when it came directly from a human being. This is the kind of machine worship which I regard as a new form of idolatry, a mating of the Mechanical Calf with the Golden Calf.

You call automation a self-inflicted impotence.

Yes, because we surrender the most precious power of all, the power of using all the attributes of mind, memory, feeling, intuition, organs, anticipations, as well as abstract thought. We surrender all this to a very elegant but limited apparatus, which operates fast and accurate, but which lacks many vital human dimensions. True, there are certain forms of drudgery that the computers avoid. That was why the computer was first invented, to perform astronomical calculations that would take hundreds of years to do by ordinary human means. That's a legitimate use of the computer. But no computer is a substitute for the full organism—all our machines are facets or fragments of a human organism. The human organism has a much richer range than any machine will ever be able to simulate. Each machine is only a part of whole man.

As Barbara Ward has said, "they don't blush and they don't feel." [8]

Yes, and that was said before by Erwin Schrödinger, the physicist, in his book *What Is Life?* He said that the world of science is a world without color, without feeling, without emotion, without things that are characteristic of any kind of organism.

But cybernetics—computerized direction of the planet and its masses of people—do you think computers could assist like they did the Club of Rome in creating a catalogue of the planet, or could we do without them?

Yes, I definitely think their use is limited. Because our problems really aren't technological ones. Our problems are psychological and moral ones. This involves the building up of inner controls that we have abandoned. It involves a change of mind, a change of our way of life so that it would be fantastic, it sounds fantastic to any sufficiently cultivated person that anybody should spend eight hours or even three hours or even one hour every day in the year before a television set. It should be used when you need it, when something in your life demands it. Just as when one puts on a record in order to hear a particular kind of music. But to have to do that every day in order to survive would be nonsense.

Like some people who look eighty percent of their free time at television.

Which means eighty percent of their time is spent in not actively living.

In The Pentagon of Power *you quoted Emerson[9] using the laconic metaphor of the earthworm becoming a man.[10] Man does not progress by increasing rate of growth or becoming simply a bigger earthworm. But we are having these vast numbers of earthworms born still. Do you think we need a new Jesus or Marx, do you need a new religion, what does man need to save himself?*

I don't think that religions can be manufactured. I think we are increasingly dominated by a religion which we don't recognize as such. We are under the myth and the religion of the machine. This is a very ancient religion. The dreams and wishes that technology embodies today can all be found in the Egyptian and Sumerian and Babylonian epics. Germ warfare in the Bible, too, practiced by God on the Egyptians. Everything that the gods in these earlier religions did is now being done by man, who therefore foolishly thinks that he is God. What he forgets is that there are two sides to God. The one side of God is called the Devil, the forces of destruction. The creative and constructive forces are the other side. Usually we ignore this unknown power which is housed in us, for it works through both means. I don't believe in saviors. I don't believe that anybody can create a religion. If religion were created today, it would be something like Christian Science or McLuhanism. It wouldn't be a real religion at all. If the world is to be saved, every man, woman and child will have to play a part.

Would you agree with Skinner that the main purpose of life in our day is survival?

No, the main purpose of life has always been creativity. Survival will happen if we turn ourselves to creative acts, if we live our lives in a fashion that will persuade us to make the necessary sacrifices. We do not have to persuade a real artist not to live like a stockbroker. He is so much more interested in the work he is doing that he'll often live on bread and water, live in a very modest way, the way that Cézanne[11] did, spurning physical goods which are necessary for the great tycoons or the generals in the Pentagon. People who have a creative life can live on very meager rations and often do. Not that poverty is desirable in itself, but if you are sufficiently absorbed in your work, you don't give a damn for how much money is coming in or how much publicity you get from it.

That's Paolo Soleri[12] from top to foot. How can we promote the young to take this road towards creativity as a absolute necessity for life?

First of all by paying attention to them. By turning our attention away from all the noncreative modes of life that we've submitted to. A great deal of our life is deadly routine. This applies to more than the worker in the factory. There is nothing sacred about mass production. We may do much better for ourselves by a much lower standard of production in which the work itself is of interest to the people who are doing it. I regard the assembly line as an old-fashioned form of technology, not as the technology of the future at all.

Workers in the factories in Detroit are totally bored and irritated.

There is resentment and sabotage, we hear from Detroit, because if you cannot live creatively, you will live destructively. You will try to destroy everything that's hurting or laming you. This is the point to be remembered. Like Captain Ahab taking revenge on the white whale.

Mr. Mumford, what role could the media journalists play in helping to turn towards a more positive way of living?

Well, by paying more attention to it. There are two kinds of things that interest newspaper editors and magazine editors. One is the exciting things that seem to catch the public eye because they are unusual. The other is the things that are really important. That news is often not known for a long time. People didn't realize when the great discoveries of the late nineteenth century were being made in physics that their world was changing. If there had been really good journalists at that time, they would have done what the managing editor of the New York *Times* did back in the early 1920s when Einstein announced his second theory of relativity. Van Anda, who was managing editor of the *Times* then, put that whole story on the front page of the *Times* and devoted two or three extra pages to Einstein's discovery. That was the real news, and not news in the old-fashioned sense. In the old-fashioned sense, if somebody had murdered or raped a woman, that would have been the front-page news.

They become scarcer, like certain breeds of animals.

You know what Harold Ross, the editor of the *New Yorker*, did when he was faced with the John Hersey's story of Hiroshima, something that no ordinary editor would dare to do. Without telling the advertising department he threw out every bit of advertising in order to print the story of Hiroshima complete in a month's issue of the *New Yorker*. That is great editing. You cannot do it every day, but you should be able to do it when the occasion calls you.

NOTES

[1]Lee Harvey Oswald, accused assassin of former President John F. Kennedy.
[2]Arthur Bremer, attempted assassin of former Governor of Alabama, George Wallace.
[3]See conversation no. 12.
[4]See *The Pentagon of Power*, pp. 293-300.
[5]See conversation no. 5.
[6]See *The Pentagon of Power*, pp. 427, 428, 433.
[7]See *The Pentagon of Power*, pp. 181, 182.
[8]See *Only One Earth: The Care and Maintenance of a Small Planet*, by Barbara Ward

and René Dubos (Pelican, 1972), p. 36. "And the computer is yet to be invented that also smells, tastes, sees and touches, thus adding to its capacity for abstract thinking all the emotional richness and complexity of a total human response."

[9]Ralph Waldo Emerson, U.S. essayist and poet (1803-1882).

[10]See *The Pentagon of Power*, p. 202.

[11]Paul Cézanne, French impressionist painter (1839-1906).

[12]See conversation no. 10.

15. Leonard M. Ross/ Peter Passell

Professors Leonard M. Ross and Peter Passell were interviewed simultaneously since they coauthored (with Marc Roberts, another Columbia University economics professor) a devastating critique of *Limits to Growth*, as well as Jay W. Forrester's two books, *World Dynamics* and *Urban Dynamics*, in the April 2, 1972, New York *Times Book Review*.

Leonard M. Ross was born in Los Angeles, California, in 1945. Both he and his colleague Peter Passell studied at Yale University in New Haven, Connecticut. Ross went to Yale Law School, while his friend Passell got a Ph.D. in economics at Yale in 1970. Professor Ross is completing his economics degree at Yale as well. They both teach at Columbia University. Together they recently published *Affluence and Its Enemies*, The Viking Press (New York, 1973).

Professor Ross, you have been one of the critics of Limits to Growth, *in the New York* Times, *for instance.*

Professor Ross: Our basic feeling was that it was a bold and ambitious attempt but one with very negative consequences. We thought it so far fell short of decent standards of scholarly inquiry that it deserved reworking rather than republication.

Yes, but you speak of a public-relations stunt. From my knowledge of the people involved they have been very seriously trying to create a first planetary model.

What we criticized was the decision to issue a very orchestrated barrage of publicity about the results without even presenting the underlying data for scientific criticism. The normal procedure in any serious scientific study is for a period of professional criticism and review. After that worldwide publicity may well be appropriate. Our criticism was not so much of the publicity, but of the decision that the publicity was more important than the underlying study.

In the Netherlands funds for a special public-relations effort were not necessary at all. The report was handed directly to the media, and it had an immediate and terrific impact on public opinion.[1] But what is your objection to the kind of simulation model that Forrester and Meadows used?

Well, we have no objection to simulation as a technique. It has proved very valuable both in the physical sciences and, with rather severe limitations, in the economic sciences. Our objection was not to the idea of simulation but to a twin set of assumptions that underlay every computer run in the *Limits* model. The bad things in the model, the things that place stresses on the environment—pollution, population growth and so on—are all assumed to be growing exponentially. On the other hand, the things that could relieve those stresses, the good things—technological progress of the right sort—are assumed not to be growing exponentially. *Limits* makes the assumption, that the maximum potential improvement in antipollution techniques would reduce pollution per unit of product by seventy-five percent. That's a once-and-for-all reduction. After that reduction is made, things can never get any better. Once you make that assumption, it follows as a pure mathematical fact that eventually something growing exponentially will overwhelm something which can only grow by a fixed multiple and can grow no longer. And so built into that assumption is the conclusion—the collapse of the world system.

All that could be justified if the assumption were correct. But the assumption that the maximum improvement in pollution techniques is seventy-five percent is simply nonsense. It has no basis in fact, and no facts were offered to support it. For many kinds of pollution the technology now existing can reduce pollution by much more than seventy-five percent—what's lacking is not a mysterious and speculative breakthrough but simply a political decision.

Now that does not mean that the right political decision is in any sense guaranteed. We share the *Limits'* team's concern—and a lot of their pessimism—about the pace of political action on pollution. But it's one thing to say that mankind must make a political decision to stop pollution and it's another thing to say that it must make a political decision to stop production. The last is non sequitur. The first is absolutely correct. If that were the only message in *Limits*, we would applaud it.

But what you are against is this non sequitur?

Yes, the assumption that those problems will necessarily be exaggerated by the growth of production, and that they would necessarily be solved by the stoppage of production. It seems to us that the growth itself—

What you call from a growth- to a service-economy?

Well, that's really a side argument. It's one that the *Limits* authors only got into very tangentially. The suggestion has been made—I think more explicitly by other people than by the *Limits* authors—

Professor Samuelson also talks about a services economy.

Yes, that growth in the future will be more oriented toward services than industrial goods. I think that both as a prediction and as a description, that has a good deal more validity for the developed world than for the underdeveloped world. What someone who is sleeping on a sidewalk in Calcutta needs is not necessarily growth of services but more food and a roof over his head. That's going to require some industrial production, and the only real hope of alleviating the desperate poverty of most of the world's billions involves a stage of substantially expanding industrial production. We quite agree with the *Limits* authors that industrial production can produce terrible stresses, and that urgent political action is needed to deal with those stresses. But that is very different from saying that political action is needed to shut down the machine entirely.

* * *

But they stress equilibrium.

They speak of zero growth as their goal. They talk about distribution from the rich nations to the poor. We very much agree with that goal but see no reason to think it will happen. Studies have been done of Britain under the Labour government, of the United States under the New Deal, showing that even these supposed social revolutions produced precisely no movement in distribution of income. Twenty years of Labour government according to recent studies by Titmuss and his associates— twenty years of Labour government which saw the growth and maturation of the welfare state—produced a net change of zero in the relative distribution of income among classes. The same is true of the United States under the New Deal. So with those kinds of precedents from the most progressive social movements in the Western World we see very little reason to think that suddenly Americans will reduce their standard of living to five hundred dollars per capita so that the Indians can increase theirs to two hundred dollars per capita. Regardless of the merits of the proposal that's just not the way the world has ever worked.

Do you feel that Limits to Growth *overstates the finite sources of energy without taking into account possible new discoveries?*

We certainly have no basis for predicting the future. There is a clear possibility that the development of nuclear fusion will open up a vast and perhaps enormously cheap supply of power. There is also a clear possibility that it might not. We don't dismiss the problems of the pollution caused by conventional fuels and their eventual depletion. But we see no basis for the kind of undoubting projection of current energy sources into the future. The world has never worked like that in the past. At least historically something else has always turned up.

Are there indications that technology also grows exponentially?

That's the implication of the best of studies that have been done today. Tobin and Nordhaus[2] at Yale have estimated the production function in modern times, and they find an exponential growth in technology and in the productivity of energy sources. Any econometric estimate, including those by Tobin and Nordhaus, has its dangers as a basis for predicting twenty or fifty years into the future, but better sound econometrics than the kind of mindless projection than the *Limits* authors engage in.

Robert S. McNamara said in the 1972 Stockholm World Conference on Human Environment that the developed world could pay up to two or three percent in helping poor countries to combat pollution.

I am all for redistribution and a vastly more generous attitude on the part of the developed nations to the underdeveloped nations. But the target of one percent of the GNP as a foreign-aid objective has never been met, and we are falling further and further away from it in the United States. So I see no reason to think that a new study or a new call for urgency would suddenly prompt a degree of generosity that we have never seen in the past.

But how else to get politicians to act than by methods of publicity?

Again, our objection is not really to the publicity, but to the uses to which the publicity urge is directed. If the publicity were simply directed against pollution or for redistributing income or aiding the less-developed countries, we of course wouldn't quarrel. But the publicity of *Limits to Growth* is directed to the worst of nonsolutions—to throwing a monkey wrench into machinery which, if anything, contains the eventual salvation of world poverty.

Comparing the Forrester[3] and the Meadows models, you have said that Forrester at least left some hope in his global model.

Forrester, using the same methodology but a slightly different set of arbitrary assumptions, reached a conclusion which was not as desperate. I think that both sets of conclusions are so fluid in their assumptions as to be worthless.

But how then to improve this existing planetary model like the Tinbergen[4] group is doing in the Netherlands with Professor Hans Linnemann as team leader, working on the Club of Rome's second world project?

Tinbergen, of course, is one of the world's most distinguished economists. I am not familiar with the model, but I am sure it would be an entirely different enterprise than Forrester-Meadows.

Professor Passel: My major objection is that the project is an exercise in deductive logic. All the conclusions are built in the assumptions, so we get an enormous mass of pseudoscience to arrive at the conclusion that was made very transparently from the first.

You call that fixing the wheel.

Yes, exactly. If you start out with the assumption of exponential growth of bad things and, as they constantly say, linear growth of good things, eventually the bad things are going to overtake the good things, so the collapse is inevitable.

So it is a faulty conclusion that the outcome will be unfavorable.

Exactly. I personally am not sure what was on the minds of the people involved in the project: whether they understood what they were doing and out of ideological commitment wanted to publicize the danger they believed in; or whether they naively believed they were being scientific.

It does demonstrate the failure of economists to make their points clear outside their fields. Forrester, who is the father of the project, obviously is a very brilliant man; he proved that in other fields. The kind of errors that were made in *World Dynamics*—and, in fact, in Forrester's other books—are trivial by economists' standards, the sorts of mistakes that earn graduate students C's on term papers. The project really has its tragic aspect. A lot of talented dedicated people were wasting their time.

The MIT team lacked collaborators with a basic scientific approach to economics?

Yes, surely. What they lacked were some people who understood simple introductory economics, the kind of economics you learn as a major in undergraduate studies in the United States.

But that won't be sufficient?

Surely sufficient to see the basic errors. There are a couple of places in *Limits* where I think anyone who is familiar with the intermediate level of price theory would catch the error. Particularly this business of trying to talk about allocation of scarce resources without reference to prices. It's a sort of eighteenth-century approach to the problem.

How to improve, to enlarge upon the initial model? Because a world planetary model is needed.

Well, if anything, we don't want to enlarge on the model. We want to simplify the structure of the model. Perhaps computers are not even necessary. What we want to do is have more substantial economic input and less systems-analysis input. The kind of work I am referring to would be the Nordhaus and Tobin paper, which is a much more conservative attempt to look at what's happening to the world resource base today and what will happen to it the next fifty or sixty years—a major input of economic theory and a minor input of econometrics and model building. The bulk of the work ought to be a careful construction of the problem. Not a long series of estimates of numbers which are very difficult to estimate and the arbitrary construction of models where misspecification entirely destroys the meaning of the project. That strikes me as the most efficient approach to the problem. It's not if it is not a problem. It surely is a problem. Just as Meadows and Forrester suggest, we might find ourselves in a hundred years with a tremendously reduced resource base. It is surely very useful to know if there are "limits to growth."

It seems to an outsider like me, flying in from the other side of the ocean, that it could be extremely interesting to see the Nordhaus-Tobin and the Forrester-Meadows teams get together and build a new model.

Well, it might be arrogance on my part, but I don't know the Forrester people have much to offer. I don't think that their particular kind of skills have much place in the analysis of a problem which is essentially economic. They may have done a service at least to bring the problem to the public attention. But Forrester's skills are in systems engineering not economics. And for the near future I am pessimistic about the value of applying systems analysis to most areas of social science.

NOTES

[1] In the Netherlands *Limits to Growth* sold in Dutch translation a record number of a quarter-million copies within the year, another world record.

[2] See conversation no. 19.

[3] See conversation no. 34.

[4] See conversation no. 3.

16. Alexander King

Dr. Alexander King has been director-general for scientific affairs of the Organization for Economic Cooperation and Development (OECD) in Paris since 1961.

He was born in Glasgow, Scotland, in 1909. He studied chemistry at the Imperial College of Science in London and at the University of Munich. During World War II he acted as deputy scientific adviser to the minister of production. From 1943 to 1947 he was head of the United Kingdom Scientific Mission in Washington, D.C., and Scientific Councillor of the UK embassy in the United States. From 1947 to 1950 Dr. King was head of the Cabinet Scientific Secretariat in London.

In 1968 he became a founding member of the Club of Rome.

What have been the reactions of scientists at the OECD and in the United Nations circles on Limits to Growth?

Very varied and mainly reticent. Like the general public the scientists are very divided on this. Naturally as a vested interest the scientists tend to think that the "technological fix" will be able to solve everything, but they are becoming more and more convinced that the time factor is important. You see, we are agreed now that science policy must be articulated with economic policy and social policy. But as the development process takes about ten to fifteen years to develop from a new discovery as a concept, into an industrial product or into a new social innovation, this means if science is directed to problems of today, it will be fifteen years too late. It will remain as a kind of trouble shooting, rather than a creative impulse. Therefore, the importance of *Limits to Growth* to the scientist, which is just beginning to soak in, is that he must plan ahead much more and he must look with the economists and the politicians to the more distant problems, otherwise his results will be *depassé*. Nevertheless, to my mind as well as many of my colleagues, the technical factors have been understated a bit in *Limits to Growth*.

It is possible to do more, but everything depends on the availability of abundant energy.

Tinbergen[1] said there is a need for more precise approaches in the model.

Of course there is. No one thinks this model is perfect; not even the authors. I think what is so astonishing, apart from the emotional reaction of the economists, which indicates it was high time they were stirred up, is that so many people feel that this new approach, a pioneer approach, the first research in a new field, should provide all the answers. This is contrary to the whole pattern of scientific development—it is an emotional, not a scientific reaction. It opens a door, that's all, but that is an enormous thing. The subsequent approach will be that Tinbergen and his team, and many others, will gradually give us much more information, much more certainty, will bring it down to terms which can lead to political actions.

When talking to B. F. Skinner[2] on his controversial book Beyond Freedom and Dignity, *he said that eighty to ninety percent of the reviews had been devastating because people could not read. Does this apply to* Limits to Growth?

Undoubtedly. So many of the bad reviews I've read—and I must confess that some of the good reviews are equally in terms of obvious preconceptions without necessarily having read it. For example, the book itself says again and again that it is not futurology, that it is not predicting the future; it is merely saying what will happen if we don't change. And yet so many of the reviewers say that predictions never come true, changes always intervene to ensure that they don't. Well, that is the objective of the book; so they obviously haven't read it.

How do the Third World scientists you are familiar with and how do the East Europeans, the socialist countries react?

This is an enormously interesting problem. Clearly, not only the scientists but any thinking person in the underdeveloped countries will initially react badly because it indicates a situation which places the Third World countries in a more precarious position than is generally recognized. And they must react against that. It can appear as a kind of blatant neocolonialism, the reaction of the rich man who has dirtied his nest and wants to consolidate his own position and wants to stop everything else at the same time. But my experience, particularly after the discussions the Club had at Rio de Janeiro, was that the Latin American scientists as representing underdeveloped countries change their position after a time. They realize that there are basic facts that must be faced up to. And hence, we are enormously happy in the Club of Rome that the Latin Americans will deepen the study with financial support from Canada, which the Club has obtained for them, will in fact look at this from their own point of view. This is an enormous advance.

You talk about Rio. In the June 5-16, 1972, World Conference on the Human Environment in Stockholm, Brazil took a position that it would not allow ecological concerns to prejudice its economic growth.

That is certainly a natural tendency and a very understandable one. In a big empty country it is very difficult to give priority to the longtime future, to weight ecological damage against the short term, terribly desirable economic advantages. This is the inevitable schizophrenia which all the individuals and all countries have between our immediate interest and our more secure long-term interests.

Dr. King, do you feel that the environment problems are entering now the political consciousness of the world?

The environment problems, yes. I think from the discussions we have had—particularly Aurelio Peccei[3] and I with the political leaders and others—that the body politic is becoming very well aware of the total problem. The environmental problems as such, the pollution problems, receive most attention. Perhaps partly because they are the easiest part of this complex which we call the *problématique*. They are problems which can be solved technically and economically at not too enormous costs. That is the most hopeful side. But whether the politicians will really face up and act on the longer-term socioeconomic, depletion and industrial problems, whether this will really lead to the beginning of the end of the economy of consumption and waste, I don't yet know.

Are you hopeful?

Yes, I am hopeful, but whether there is enough time, I don't know.

You have worked a lot with Aurelio Peccei as initiator of the Club of Rome. Professor William Thompson of York University,[4] Toronto, Canada, recently remarked in Harper's *magazine, "Peccei is the example of the multinational manager in search for a new concentric order."[5] What is your impression of him?*

I have known and worked with Aurelio for many years. In fact, the whole concept of the Club of Rome arose from discussions which started in this room here between the two of us.[6] To my mind, he is a unique person. He is not typical, unfortunately, because the average tycoon or multinational firm bureaucrat is inevitably tied up rather exclusively with company business. Nevertheless, I agree that the multinational firms with their worldwide operations do see things more globally and therefore one would expect more understanding, a little more longer-term thinking from here.

But Peccei is exceptional in that he puts this whole concept of the world difficulties before everything, and I think he is one of the most devoted people I have ever known in my life. He lives this, and his motivation, to my mind, is as pure as that of anyone I ever have met. He is enormously hardworking. He devotes a great deal of his time to these things. He has a truly world vision. He is certainly not in any way representing multinational business, nor is he representing the industrialized countries. He is one of these few rare world spirits whom we want to cultivate, but it is not easy.

He once told me, "How could I do anything else, when I look at my children and grandchildren?"

Yes. All world citizens might take that point of view but don't. That's the difference between Peccei and the rest; his concern is for the future of humanity.

NOTES

[1]See conversation no. 3.
[2]See conversation no. 7.
[3]Chairman of the Club of Rome, see conversation no. 70.
[4]See conversation no. 68.
[5]William Irwin Thompson, "The Individual as Institution," *Harper's* magazine, September 1972, p. 55.
[6]Dr. King's office at OECD headquarters in Paris, Rue André Pascal 2.

17. Dennis Gabor

Dennis Gabor was born in Budapest, Hungary, in 1900. In 1933 he came to England, and since 1967 he has been senior research fellow in electronics at Imperial College in London. In 1971 he was awarded the Nobel Prize for physics for his invention of holography.

In 1964 he published *Inventing the Future*, in 1970 *Innovation: Scientific, Technological and Social*, and his latest book is titled: *The Mature Society* (1972).

Professor Gabor takes an active part in Club of Rome meetings and programs.

You feel Limits to Growth *was a publication that was needed?*

It certainly was a publication that was needed. The most interesting thing about it is the unbelievably violent reaction which this has aroused, especially from economists. Economists just don't know any other means of running our free society than with continual growth. If there are limits to it, then, of course, the dangers are very great. Arnold Toynbee has written: "We cannot be sure that even in England parliamentary democracy is going to survive the fearful ordeal of having to revert to the stable way of life, on the material plane." You see, this is the danger. Our free society is running into such trouble that some people do not see any other way than totalitarianism.

In my book[1] I try to show that there may be a way. Of course, we have to sacrifice certain freedoms. The freedom, for instance, of the stock exchange, to produce a slump at any time, and of the freedom of trade unions, to hold an entire country to ransom. This sort of freedom we cannot retain. But, at the same time, we must retain essential freedoms. I would like to retain the freedom of the entrepreneur to innovate, and the freedom of the author to write what he likes. I wonder if the second can exist without the first. Think of it, that in the USSR, where there is no economic freedom, Alexander Solzhenitsyn cannot publish a single line.

Do you believe in the perfectibility of man?

Yes, I do believe in the perfectibility of man.[2] Only unfortunately it goes very, very slowly. There is no doubt that there is some progress. We are more advanced, for instance, than the Romans. During the Roman empire or even the Renaissance, murder was considered an inevitable occurrence and a very natural means of getting rid of your enemies.

The great question is, of course, how to come to terms with the "zero-growth society." You write that in our society hope has become synonymous with growth.[3] But do you keep hope alive in a "zero-growth society," or, to use your expression, how can one "engineer" hope?

We professional people and intellectuals can rise in status, rise in wisdom, rise in recognition by our peers during our life. It simply does not exist for common man. The workman enters his factory, say, at the age of sixteen or eighteen, and often he has the same standard wages until the day when he leaves. His only hope is that by the growth of society and by the fight of his trade union that he will get a bigger piece of a bigger cake. Nowadays this means only getting a bigger piece of the same cake. In the last years we have had a foretaste of what will happen in a "zero-growth society," because growth has slowed down somewhat. In the three countries in which I live, the United States, England and Italy, class warfare has intensified. People are taking it away from each other. They cannot take it out of a growing common pool. Economic growth will have to stop sometime. The approach of this will be terribly painful. Our free society possesses absolutely no mechanisms for slowing down.

You believe in "the perfectibility of man." You believe in "the growth of man to improve himself," but at the same time you quote Freud as having said, "mental health is the absence of inner conflicts." You even write, "we must have respect for this deep pessimism but we must rid ourselves of it."[4] How?

Good health is a little more than the absence of inner conflicts. And I believe that hope is more than the absence of despair. Society can be stationary, but the individual can improve with age, improve in knowledge, know the world and be at peace with it. This is not very easy, if you think of all the intellectuals who hate our world so much that they think that first of all one must smash it up.

Somerset Maugham[5] wrote in his memoirs: "How the Gods must have chuckled, when they added Hope to the evils with which they filled Pandora's box, for they knew very well that this was the cruelest evil of them all, since it is Hope that lures mankind to endure its misery to the end."[6]

This is really an impressive passage. But I would still prefer a mankind which endures its miseries hopefully to one which despairs.

It is too pessimistic for you?

It's much too pessimistic. Somerset Maugham was of course a great cynic. I have often wondered that—preacher of hope as I am—I have such a liking for cynics as Maugham, Evelyn Waugh,[7] Anatole France[8] or the early Aldous Huxley.[9]

You were saying something about how scientists and enlightened industrialists could influence a better outcome for mankind.

Yes, this is perhaps the most important point. I rather differ from other futurologists in that I am unashamedly *normative*. I believe in giving directions, and addressing them to men of action. I have worked myself for twenty-four years in industry. Industry has cornered not only some of the best technological talent in the world, but also some of the best clear-headed and energetic people in the world. This is a force which must be our ally in this great transformation which is coming. I believe in private enterprise but not on the basis of competitive waste.

First of all we must fight pollution. It is not a big problem. Some environmentalists have exaggerated the problem. The example of London shows that one can make the air clear and the water clear without a too costly effort. The second problem is waste. We are wasting the resources of the world in a terrible, irresponsible way. So long as copper is cheap, so long as tin is cheap, we use them regardless of the future shortage. But the most important thing is of course to provide in time for abundant power, by substituting atomic energy for oil and coal and synthetic oil for natural oil. We must do this while oil is still gushing out of the earth. Nature has laid it up for hundreds of millions of years and we are wasting it in something on the order of a century. This is where technology can help, and this is why I would like to mobilize the whole of science and technology to provide inventions, innovations, which are not at the moment profitable but which will be indispensable if we are ever to approach a reasonable equilibrium.

But how can the scientists and the clear-headed minds of this world influence the politicians to take the decisions necessary?

Here I am not quite as pessimistic as some people. Of course the politicians are not fiends. The politicians are in a straightjacket. They must please their voters, who are usually much lower intellectually and sometimes also possess a lower ethical standard. Don't be shocked, what I say to you is a simple fact. The British Labour government has put through three laws which in my opinion are ethically progressive against public majority; the laws on homosexuality, abortion and the death penalty. At least eighty percent of public opinion was for retaining the death penalty. It was the same with the Common Market. The Common Market would undoubtedly have failed in a plebiscite.

But how to mobilize the scientists to have much greater impact on United Nations or some other form of world management?

First of all, the scientists must speak with one voice. At the moment scientists are not a hundred percent agreed regarding the results of Forrester and Meadows. First of all, they must agree and if they were to speak with one voice, I believe that they will be heard.

The ingenuity with which the Apollo program[10] was organized could be applied by some clear-headed minds in other fields. Do not think of the engineer only as a gadget-maker who works with pieces of metal. There is now developing a considerable science of systems dynamics, in ordinary language called "software science." We are now dealing with very complicated systems quantitatively, which we knew before only intuitively and imperfectly. Scientists may be listened to especially after some initial successes in organizing social projects. The condition *sine qua non* is that there shall be basic agreement among themselves.

But may I inject here that Skinner[11] and Chomsky[12] live in the same town, Cambridge, Massachusetts. Chomsky hacks Skinner to pieces in the New York Review of Books.[13] *When I asked Skinner whether he discussed his views with Chomsky, he had not. Chomsky told me later he only reviewed Skinner's book because he was asked to. He would not want to discuss it with Skinner, since "it was all nonsense what*

Skinner wrote anyway." They live in the same town. They disagree violently. Now why don't they get together? If scientists are unable to meet with each other in Cambridge, how to get order in the community of world scientists?

Both Chomsky and Skinner are of course "soft" scientists. I have been really talking of the "hard" scientists—of physicists, chemists, biochemists, pharmacologists and the like.

But talking about scientists, shouldn't we unite both soft- and hardware scientists?

I wish we could, but as you see clearly, it will be very difficult. For us, "hard" scientists, it is of course a little ridiculous that, for instance, any psychologist who has some little idea of his own immediately forms his own school. We haven't got schools or parties in the hard sciences, and perhaps in time we shall be able to penetrate the soft sciences, too. Economics is now a hardening science.

Talking about science—science in combination with nationalism has created a situation, you wrote, in which total war could wipe out civilization. We talked earlier about hope. How hopeful are you that with these first planetary models of Meadows and Forrester that kind of nationalism can be wiped out so that there can be hope for a good reason.

I am very hopeful in this respect. I am even more hopeful than when I wrote my last book, in which I said that to a nuclear war between America and Russia in this century I would give the probability nil. I was not so hopeful about China, but what I have learned since then about China has made me more optimistic. It's evident that so long as Mao's teachings will prevail, China will not try to annihilate the rest of us. China appears to work towards a sort of intermediate technological level. It does not want to become an industrial superpower and a consumer society. Here I really see something of the "wisdom of the East," about which I am normally rather doubtful. I honestly don't think we need to reckon with the possibility of biological warfare in this century.

Can we really eliminate strife? Is not strife a necessity for man? Is not excitement as much a necessity as daily food?

I am afraid this is the case. But the excitement which we now get from industrial disputes might get into such a serious crisis that the majority of people will ask for a strong government, which of course is just another name for dictatorship.

Moving back towards fascism?

Indeed, it might move us towards fascism. I have seen that movement in our time in Germany, thirty years ago. I am afraid there are signs also in other countries, for instance, here in Italy, where, as you know, fascism has been growing, though not yet to a dangerous extent. But in a free society some sort of strife must remain, excitement must remain, only let us hope that it can be kept down to a level at which one can live with it.

Don't you think television is providing a lot of strife in the worst sense of the word?

Indeed, in the worst sense of the word, by presenting violence as a matter of fact. But nevertheless, on the whole, my opinion is this: that television has a sort of cathartic effect on ninety-five percent of the people; about five percent of them try to emulate the violence, in other words, while ninety-five percent are satisfied by vicarious violence.

Yes, but it needs only one assassin to kill.

I am afraid the five percent are a really serious danger. It is something like five percent on the one end of the intellectual scale who move the world forward and the five percent at the lower end, the moronic criminals (and sometimes not even moronic), who are endangering it.

Yet, one bullet could still bring down the world.

Yes, it could, indeed.

NOTES

[1]*The Mature Society, a View of the Future*, Praeger Publishers (New York, 1972).
[2]*Ibid.*, p. 6.
[3]*Ibid.*, pp. 159-62.
[4]*Ibid.*, p. 85.
[5]William Somerset Maugham (1874-1965), British novelist, dramatist, and short-story writer.
[6]*A Writer's Notebook*, William Heineman Ltd. (London, 1949), pp. 6, 7.
[7]Evelyn Waugh (1903-66), British novelist.
[8]Anatole France (1844-1924), French novelist and essayist.
[9]Aldous Leonard Huxley (1894-1963), British novelist and essayist.

[10]United States space-research program.
[11]See conversation no. 7.
[12]Noam Chomsky, MIT linguistics professor, see conversation no. 42.
[13]"The Case Against B. F. Skinner," December 30, 1971.

18.   Robert Jungk

Journalist Robert Jungk was born in Berlin in 1913. He acquired his Ph.D. in modern history at Zurich University. In 1950 he became an American citizen. At present he lives in Salzburg, Austria.

Some of his best-known books are *The Big Machine, Tomorrow Is Already Here* (1954), and *Brighter Than a Thousand Suns* (1957).

We will have to have translators. Very often scientists don't understand each other. I see myself as a translator, as a mediator between scientists and politicians, because I have lived in the political community for a long time. And not only do we need translators, we even need in our universities departments where scientists and specialists learn to talk to each other or to the public or to the politicians. We have a fantastic tower of Babel nowadays, where people don't talk the same languages anymore.

Sung Tse said already, "They don't know themselves and they don't know their enemy." That's the problem of the world today. No one speaks the same language.

We have to get this communication working. I think it can be done. What I am most interested in is helping to bridge the gap between the scientists and the people, the intellectuals and the people, the simple people.

I feel that there exists a new separation between haves and have-nots. The have-nots are not the people only who are poor in material goods. The have-nots are the ones who never can express their own ideas and their own thoughts, who are condemned to an eternal life of receptivity and passivity. If you deny to a man the possibility to express himself, to elaborate on his own ideas—to "invent the future" (to quote Gabor), not leave the invention of the future to a few planners and intellectuals but give him a chance to take part in the invention of his future, because the future belongs to all of us—then he won't be interested.

Is it a matter of schooling, of education?

No. I was very much interested in the research on creativity. If you talk to people who researched creativity, there is a very interesting thing they have discovered. A lack of information is very bad. A lack of experience, lack of education, is terrible in most fields. But in creativity lack of education is an asset. The less information, the less education you have, the more naive you are, the more original you can be.

A French diplomat returning from Peking has reported that he found in New York too much information and in Peking too little; thus, following your theory, the Chinese would be more creative than Americans.

The Chinese did find new ways, because nobody told them things had to be done. That's what we are being told from our early beginning, from a very early image.

Programmed—

From the beginning of our life, we are told that's how it ought to be, that's how it is. Instead every new human being coming into the world should discover the world and create the world out of his own imagination, out of his own knowledge, out of his own experience.

We are being programmed by the environment?

Skinner[1] wants us to go on to be programmed. I think we should develop our program ourselves. I have started future-creating-workshops. I get together with the uneducated, with young workers, with young peasants, with men from the street, in Germany, in Austria. I did this, for instance, in Vienna with groups of young workers. I asked them, now

I want you to invent the future, your own future. I asked them, what are your different ideas? What do you want? What do you criticize in education? What do you criticize in your working environment? What do you criticize about the environment, the big environment? This is how it works.

These people come up with negative lists, for instance, they tell me what they don't like in their work. I compile a long list, about a hundred different points of criticism. Then I ask them choose two or three things they would like to change immediately, what burns them most. Somebody will say, the repetitive character of work. The fact that he cannot be interested in the work. The fact that he is being told what to do instead of doing it himself.

Then I say, "Okay, have you any ideas how to change the repetitive character of work, have you any ideas how to develop the initiative of your work, on the shopfloor?" Then they turn up with ideas. They come up with the most different ideas. They develop them. They say, for instance, we could set up our own projects, what we want to produce. We could discuss this with the production managers, but we are never asked. They always only tell us. I let them invent during a kind of brainstorming session. I apply the techniques of brainstorming. I'm interested in social invention. These people then come up with ideas and then—this is the second stage of what I am doing in the future workshop. Then comes the most important stage. They come up with new ideas and then I bring in experts or politicians. In Vienna I had a Minister of Public Industry or Minister of Education. The people, who had just "invented" a new form of schooling, a new form of work, they were confronted with the decision-makers. The decision-makers usually do say it cannot be done, it is too difficult or it costs too much, or there are such and such obstacles. I said, "All right, now you have a confrontation between dream and reality. You two sit together and develop strategies how your dreams could become true." And then the exciting thing happened, I have seen it again and again, that people who are not interested in politics, who couldn't affect any decisions, sit together with the decisionmakers and discuss possibilities to overcome the obstacles to get something new going. Thus, I do two things: First of all, I introduce the people who really represent ninety-nine pecent of the people of the world into the decision process because I am using their imagination. I get them to learn, so they become educated. What they do is their baby.

* * *

This was creativity, social creativity. What is your second major interest?

My second interest is very closely related to this. I feel that most of our future research lacks imagination. I try to get the artists and the people who are, so to say, specialists in imagination into work of the future. Not only scientists. Scientists follow logical paths, but artists who employ intuitions, visions.

Paolo Soleri.[2]

Exactly. Artists have a heightened sensitivity. I try to introduce the artist's way of thinking into future concepts. I feel that the role of the artist in society is not to introduce reality like in socialist realism, but to bring their special qualities of intuition and vision, of seeing quality instead of quantity, into life. In fact, I am starting next year in Salzburg an Institute for the Future of the Arts, where the people will get together. First, we will start a documentation center. Then I will get seminars rolling and in the end I'll do research. I want to apply the artist in society as a work of art. The artist does not have to produce works of art, but to put his special gifts to work for society on the whole.

The second phase is the democratization of future research, of future planning, by introducing more imagination and especially artistic imagination into that and a kind of a counterpoint to the logical, scientific and technological imagination, which was used too far. Man has more dimensions than the scientific and technological ones. There's a new movement now, I mean, people around John Platt, people who talk about new science, the science which is larger than the purely logical rational science, which embodies more of the things you cannot express so clearly, where you have more half thoughts and more dynamics and more flow, this is what actually is coming up.

What is your new book about?

The provisory title is *Man Plus*; the subtitle, *For a New Direction of Growth*. I am trying to explain the following. We are coming to a certain slowing down, maybe to a certain end, even, of our material development, as has been said in *Limits to Growth*. I feel there are no limits to growth. We are underdeveloped in the direction of human development and social development. I feel that a new field of progress, so to say, is a development of human faculties. I have seven fields developed in my new book. The one I've told you about is imagination. Imagination is a fantastic sort of creativity which has been buried and which we have to liberate. The second thing is the development of seeing the whole instead of the parts.

Like the model of MIT.

Yes, that is something going into that direction. The third thing is foresight instead of seeing the consequences of what you are doing. The fourth is that you begin to experiment that changes, not something terrible but something natural, to introduce flow and change and experiment into society instead of being afraid of it. The fifth is cooperation, because what we have—we call now cooperation—is really sheer competition, even if you have units—

Solidarity—

Yes, I mean really cooperation, group processes. How you can actually see the other person as your *Verstärkung*, as a strengthening of you, instead of being a competitor. Then the sixth is the entire domain of nonfinality, of play, of game, of doing things not for the benefit, not to get a result—

Creation—

No. Of game, of play of—not only free time, it is more, it is an attitude of mind. Usually we do something because it is beautiful or do something because we get something. We have a goal. I feel that the whole art of man—because he was always forced by deed, by external need—is always going to an object, to an aim. I think that one of the developments of man is doing things just for the fun of it and not having a bad conscience at the same time. And the seventh thing is what I call —the growing universe. The further you go into the heavens the further the universe recedes from you. The universe is growing all the time up to a certain point. I develop an idea of growing man. Man never will be God, but man is growing, nevertheless, all the time. Man so far has only grown to a very small percentage of his capability. Man is larger than he is thought of so far. I speak of—as I've written in an article for Unesco—"mind laboratories." These mind laboratories would have a similar pioneering role as the physics, biology and chemical laboratories in the nineteenth and twentieth centuries. In the mind laboratories you would have a cooperation of anthropologists, sociologists, psychologists, ideologists, pharmacologists. It is a kind of prospective anthropology which is why I'm so interested in Edgar Morin,[3] because he tries something into this direction. I feel these mind laboratories will have a similar impact on the development of mankind, as the natural science laboratories in ages of the past.

How much sympathy and Begriff [understanding (Ger.)] do you find in the scientific community for mind laboratories?

I launched this idea in the social-science magazine of UNESCO. The difficulty is this: A new generation of young scientists is growing up, who are much less discipline-oriented and much more generalist-oriented. You probably know of *Notes on a Counterculture* by Rossack, which carries an important point. Rossack talks about the myth of objectivity. The fact that science actually tries to dissect everything and does not see the whole—

What McLuhan[4] calls "compartmentalization"—

Exactly. This is why I feel we have a fantastic development now among younger scientists. They will be the ones who will be able to execute mind laboratories—

Because they are generalists—

They are generalists, and they are not so proud of their own discipline. For instance, one group in Heidelberg is working on complex phenomena, rather than on single phenomena. They look at complexities, and this is the way to look at things. So if you ask how scientists received my ideas, I feel I am in excellent contact with younger scientists, because they understand this. The older ones still think that precision counts, what we call *Fliegenbeinen Ausreiss-soziology*—when you count the legs of flies instead of seeing the whole. The younger ones don't count the legs of flies anymore. They see the big problems and they see how they are interrelated, how they change, most of all how they are dynamic. The central idea to everything I undertake is this: I've been to physics laboratories, to biology laboratories, to chemical laboratories—in all these laboratories it is no more the single atom, the single molecule, it is a process, a dynamic process, that is being studied. There are no atoms, there is a burst of energy which you can photograph as atoms. There is a dynamic process going on. The other way of conception is to limit it, to see that really.

Now, I think in social science it's similar. We have had a static conception of political and social reality, and we are developing a dynamic view. Science is based on data. When you read the data, they are all thousands of corpses of reality, particles of reality. When you read a book, the events have moved beyond the book, so what has to be changed is the concept of what is reality, what are data. You have to look, to monitor the flow of things, the dynamic of things, rather than all this running behind history and running behind the events.

That's the approach of the Club of Rome.

Yes, exactly. We get this dynamic concept into the whole thing. What I am critical of in the approach of MIT is that it still has too few factors, it is still too limited. It is as if man was only a skeleton of man. You don't see the flesh. I see the bones of history in the report of MIT. I see the big lines, but I don't see the flesh. I don't see the breath. I don't see the contour, life. This has very much to do with our rigid, old methods of perception, with our rigid, old methods of seeing things. We want to put them down. Faust says, Goethe says, you write it down and then you can carry it home. Nothing of the kind. You carry home a corpse, something dead, and what is alive goes on. We somehow have to hitch onto that alive thing, that's why I was so interested in McLuhan, because you have in the electronic media, you are, so to say, watching the process while it's happening.

Is it not a shadow of what is happening—what you see on TV—and thus fake?

No, it's incomplete. It's two-dimensional. It's not three- and not four-dimensional. You know what I mean, it's just an *Ahnung* [a vague idea, a notion (Ger.)]?

Is it not dangerous to live by Ahnung?

Yes and no. If you see them as *Ahnung* only and if you see that the complete picture is a combination of the single plus what you yourself add to it.

That is how you might interpret the mechanics of watching television.
But I was talking about the far majority of the TV audience.

You are quite right, there are large misconceptions. One of the dangers
in the Club of Rome approach is the following: *Limits to Growth* becomes
now—and it was certainly not intended by either Aurelio Peccei[5] or by
Meadows[6] as such—a kind of technocratic ideology. There arrived a VIP,
who announced the world is in danger. We have to do something fast.
We have to decree what should be done, and people will have to conform. We have to save the world and we have not enough time to discuss
it all. What I am afraid of is that the whole idea of the Club of Rome
becomes a kind of a technocratic ideology justifying a few powerful
people who try to impose their ideas and their picture of development
onto living and *widerspruchsvoll* [full of contradictory ideas (Ger.)], a
reality which is full of *Widerspruch*.

Frankly, I am afraid of Forrester. I have seen Forrester. He is a
Stalinist[7] type. He's a type of man who is actually very cold, very inhuman, who actually tries to impose his pattern on reality. He was very
cool. Most of the things he has said about, let us say, that slums should
be continued, instead of building new quarters for people. He insists one
should first raise productivity. But this is extremely dangerous.

Therefore, I am so interested to tie in people. If you don't ask people,
if you don't take in what the people want to do, if you really impose
ideas on them, if you impose planning on them, you really will prepare
revolutions and explosions of an unknown, a never-experienced violence.
I am really firmly convinced—and I speak from the experience I had
with my "future workshops"—that people are much more reasonable,
that they are much more inventive than we trust them to be. If we do
show the patience, if we do take the time to talk to them. The intellectuals don't have patience. That was my main trouble with Oppenheimer.[8]
Oppenheimer had a fantastic mind. He was a special kind of man, but
he had no humility. He had no patience. He had no possibility to talk
to simple people and to understand them. If we enter into the crisis,
which has been delineated in the report of the Club of Rome, then we
need the ideas of everybody. We have to enlarge our basis of creativity
and originality, and we also have to have the people with us instead
of imposing ideas on them. This is where I think in a different direction.

For me, the most important sentences in *Limits to Growth* are the last
in the book, where it is said, "We have to think of man, what is going
to happen to man, how man could change and should change." You
probably know it by heart, this very last sentence in the report. That's

actually where we should continue our work. We should go from there into this field and that's what I try to do. I try to work on the development of man. That's why my new man is called "Man Plus." We have not to take man only as an elite of man but really include everybody. And I would say if we could have a project "Every Man," like we had a Project Apollo, which actually exploits the treasures which are buried in the common man, then we make a fantastic discovery. That's what I'm trying to fight for.

To unearth common man: You compare to drilling for oil—

It is very hard to go through this whole Pantzer [armor (Ger.)], man's fears and depressions, not ever having been asked to. It's like drilling. You have to drill through a crust, and only if you have the patience to drill through it, then you hit the sources, the living creativity which had been buried from the early ages on.

That's what Mao Tse-tung has been doing in China.

He is trying to do that, yes—

Everybody participates in decisions.

The only thing is, then again, doesn't he force people too much to crowd that in a certain language which is again being dogmatic? The terrible thing is that everyone wants to build his own monument. I am afraid that Mao Tse-tung also wants to build his monument, in his language, in his teaching, in his little book. If he would be open enough to throw away the language and say let the people express themselves as they express themselves, if he would be able to do away with all the pictures and all the images. We all are afraid to die, and unless we get new time dimensions—to look beyond our death and see cooperation with following generations—it is not important what we have done or how we made our mark, but that we are only part of this flow of people going through the ages, then we would be really achieving something. There is this egoism in people, that everything has to happen in a lifetime. That's ridiculous. Important things happen very slowly, and we should think beyond our lifetime. Maybe something we start now will be finished or may be continued only in thirty years from now and in fifty years from now or even finished in two hundred years from now.

But everyone still feels he has to build his monument, within his own lifetime. That's actually what makes him dogmatic, what makes him hard, what makes him limited, and inhuman.

NOTES

[1] See conversation no. 7.
[2] See conversation no. 10.
[3] See conversation no. 58.
[4] See conversation no. 12.
[5] See conversation no. 70.
[6] Daniel L. Meadows of the MIT *Limits to Growth* team.
[7] Josef Stalin (1879-1953), Soviet dictator, General-Secretary of the Soviet Communist Party.
[8] J. Robert Oppenheimer (1904-62), US nuclear physicist.

19. *William D. Nordhaus*

Professor Nordhaus was born in Albuquerque, New Mexico, in 1941. He studied economics at Yale University and obtained his Ph.D. at the Massachusetts Institute of Technology. At present he is associate professor of economics at Yale University and staff member of the Cowles Foundation for Research in Economics, as well as on the staff of the National Bureau of Economic Research.

Professor Nordhaus published *Invention, Growth and Welfare: A Theoretical Treatment of Technological Change* (1969).

Why are economists in the United States—contrary to, for instance, Tinbergen[1] in Rotterdam—hacking The Limits to Growth *so ferociously to pieces?*

I think the contribution of the MIT team (Forrester, Meadows, *et al.*) is that they attempted to make explicit and quantitative what has been impressionistic and qualitative in the public's mind up to now. They are really the first ones to set out a global model (as in *World Dynamics*)[2] and make quantitative predictions. They predict that by the year 2050, the standard of living will be lower than it is now. By the year 2070, we will get either a pollution catastrophe or everybody will starve. More than anything else, it is the concreteness that upset and disturbed the public.

Here is where economists have had a violent allergic reaction. It is not that social scientists deny that population, pollution, and resources are important problems. These are clearly among the most difficult issues of theory and policy in political economy. It is the *approach* rather than the subject of *Limits* that has been criticized. A close look at the model has led many competent independent analysts to conclude that the underlying assumptions are founded in pure fantasy. *World Dynamics* did not refer to a single scientific study. Rather it is the computer saying that in the year 2050 the world is going to come to an end, and the computer somehow lends a dignity that would be lacking if someone just said that in a hundred years we will all be dead. Nobody would listen to a foolish man, but we worship at the temple of the foolish computer.

An analogy might be helpful. In this country we have the serious medical problem of cancer. Everyone recognizes that this is an extremely serious medical problem. I compare the *Limits to Growth* group to a group of people who suddenly claim to come up with the cure to cancer. When one asks them, "How do you know it is curable?" they reply, "Well, we have some research going, we'll let you know about it. We have a computer. We put a model of the disease in the computer, and the computer says that cancer and heart disease will be wiped out within fifty years, you can see the computer output right here." Then one asks them for information. "We don't have any data, we didn't do any research really, we just have a theoretical model." Where did they get the model? "We just thought about the problem."

This is the scientific approach behind *World Dynamics* and the *Limits to Growth*, but it is an approach quite at variance with Western traditions of scientific inquiry. The methodology that was used by the MIT team is that when you have a situation that you are trying to evaluate, you sit down in an armchair without any knowledge of the situation except what common sense tells you. Let me give a crucial specific example in both the Forrester and Meadows books. It is assumed that as per capita income or per capita consumption rises, the rate of population growth increases. There is then an iron law: The only long-run state is one with everybody on the borderline of starvation. This iron law has been known, and periodically rediscovered, since the time of Malthus. It has been rediscovered again by the *Limits* people. They have been aptly called the new Malthusians.

The point is that almost every empirical study that has ever been made found exactly the contrary, that in fact population growth *declines* with affluence. Now, if in fact population growth declines with affluence, not the other way around, then the results of both the Forrester and, I think, the Meadows model are completely different. Population stabilization or decline—such as the US is approaching—will alleviate all the growth pains in the *Limits* model. Unfortunately, Forrester's hypothetical model did not in fact refer to empirical studies that have been done in the different fields. As a result, the conclusions of the model are unsupported by empirical evidence.

The point is that over the last few hundred years there's developed a methodology in scientific research. In medical research you do experiments, you do controlled experiments usually with animal subjects before you claim that a cure for a certain disease has been found. In the social sciences you discuss the matter before you proclaim a theory to be true about the world. It is customary to look at some data, to look at the experience of the countries involved. Forrester did not do that in his study. There was no attempt to try to verify it, and as a result, it is not at all clear what this model refers to. It could refer to an ant colony. It could refer to life on Mars. It could refer to fruit fly populations in the Amazon. But until any of these have either been verified or refuted, the model refers to nothing.

Let's now look at some particular shortcomings of the model. I am going to be referring mainly to *World Dynamics* because that is the only model which has been made generally available. There are three basic problems. The first one I've referred to already, is the problem of population. Forrester assumes that population growth rises with affluence, while in fact it declines. In his model if you change only that assumption, then the results are entirely different.

Really entirely different?

Absolutely different. For example, in some work I did in a review of his book, I used a simplified version of his model. His model is very complicated. It's virtually impossible to understand—I'll talk about that in a second. I used a simplified model to try to perform some sensitivity analysis to see whether, if you changed a few of the assumptions toward greater realism (as in the case of population growth), the results change. And the one thing that came out loud and clear is that if, instead of population growth at a very rapid rate, it grows something like either zero population growth, or a small decline of population growth, then in fact you have a greater affluence than we have ever seen before and greater economic growth than has ever been possible.

A second assumption in the Forrester model is the assumption that there is no technological change.

No exponential growth in technology—

Forrester shows no technological growth at all. How much output can you get per unit input? Inputs being labor, capital, land, and natural resources. Past studies by John Kendrick and Edward Denison find something like the following: For the last hundred years the amount of output you get per unit input has been rising between one and a half and three percent. In the Forrester and the Meadows study, it is assumed that if input stays the same, there is no way you can increase output. There are no inventions. Nobody invents the computer. Nobody invents fission processes for energy. Nobody invents more efficient engines. There is no solar energy. There are no jet planes. There are no tape recorders.

But it was established that technology increases slower than population or economic growth.

We cannot really say for sure what the critical rate of growth of technology is that will make the system viable. That's the first thing. Another is that we must recognize that there are some bad aspects as well as some good aspects about technological change. Many people feel, for example, that a lot of environmental problems today are due to certain kinds of technological change. Especially those that have occurred in the chemical industries, like the growth of new inorganic fertilizers. Technology is not an unmixed blessing. Most people feel that when you net out the costs from the gains, the technological change is a plus. I suppose all you have to do is to go and travel around the world to see the difference between high and low technology and see what material benefits and costs that has brought forth.

There is a third area that I have found of particular concern and that is Forrester's view that human society is completely mechanistic, that people and institutions show no kind of adaptive behavior. When economists talk about adaptive behavior, they think of the use of the price system. For example, in Forrester's book you run out of natural resources. What happens to utilization of natural resources? Nothing happens. Prices don't go up; people don't get upset; firms don't try to economize, or recycle resources. People are just dumb lemmings and they just keep going over the cliff one after another without a thought. Just as there are no prices in the model, there is no political system in the model either. Prices can certainly fail us, as they have up to now for our atmospheric resources. Perhaps we can rely on our political system to help us out. But there is no political system in the *Limits* which is going to be of any use.

The Soviets have the same problem.

The problem of clear air and clean water is one which we've known about for many years. We cannot expect the price system to solve it for us, because these are public goods. On the other hand, if resources are appropriable (either by the state in a socialist society or by individuals in a private-property society), I think there is less cause for concern. For appropriable resources like coal and ores and oil, the storm signals of increased scarcity manifest themselves in the form of increases in price. We see these signals in areas of natural resources today, with price rises which are very large. The whole point about adaptive behavior in economic systems and political systems is that it allows the system to respond to scarcities in one area by moving to substituting plentiful materials and plentiful resources.

The reason this is so terribly important stems from another assumption in the *Limits* model, namely that there is a fixed pool of natural resources in the world. In the Forrester model there are four hundred years' worth of natural resources at the present consumption rate. In fact, there are not four hundred years of certain things. Natural gas is something that is extremely scarce right now. Petroleum is something that will probably run out long before four hundred years if we continue to use it at the current rate. But on the other hand, there are other materials which are virtually infinite in supply, like basic materials for several of the fusion processes; or like the inputs for some plastics. We are going to run out of something else long before we run out of energy if the fusion processes come along. This is an example of the misplaced concreteness in *Limits to Growth*.

Do you think there is a leeway for some economists like you to get together with the MIT team and look at some of these trends together? Why couldn't the Forrester model still be the basis for further study, as Tinbergen is doing in Rotterdam? Or could the work be carried out without a model of that kind?

You asked a number of questions. If you ask me whether there is room for collaboration between ecologists and economists and scientists and engineers, I certainly think there is and there has been a lot of collaboration in the past. If you are asking me, Is the Forrester model or the Meadows model the model that I would use to analyze the world economy, even as a first approximate, the answer is definitely not. Do I think systems analysis is the right way? If you mean by systems analysis building a quantitative, economic, social, political, demographic model, certainly that is what we have been building all along. But if you mean, Am I going to build a model in which I make assumptions without looking at data, a model in which I posit relations without talking to knowledgeable experts, a model with one hundred equations none of which have been confirmed by any empirical study, a model in which I am seriously going to predict what will happen a hundred or two hundred years from now, I think the answer to all those questions is no.

What has been your way of studying these problems?

Some time ago in fact, James Tobin[3] and I worried about the problems of population, natural resources and economic welfare. We had a couple of models of this problem in which we tried to analyze such things as the factor of population growth, the role of fewer natural resources, the importance of a slower pace of technological change on future growth of consumption, all for the United States. This was only a very preliminary exercise. For the most part they were one or two equation models. We had data for the United States from which we fitted the functions that we used, and we did quite a bit of sensitivity analysis as to the proper form of the function. But the basic difference was that these were extremely small models, because one of the things you learn when you use these models is that when you use, as Forrester did, a model with forty-three nonlinear relations and a number of other variables, that you don't have a prayer of understanding what you've built.

I think that the experience in economics has been that although big models look fancy and impress people, they're very difficult to build, very difficult to coordinate, and they don't really predict well. So as a methodological principle, I like to stay with simple models, so that I can understand what's going on. The second thing that I think is terribly important is that we continue to apply some of the work that has been going on in traditional economics and ecology to the global perspective. One of my objections to the work of the MIT team was their complete disregard of all past science. The new Malthusians profess to protect the earth and environment from the ravages of modern technology and desire to return to more traditional patterns of living. It is ironic that in returning to traditional economic standards they eschew the precious scientific tradition which has been so carefully established over the past four centuries.

NOTES

[1] See conversation no. 3.
[2] See bibliography, conversation no. 34.
[3] A colleague of Dr. Nordhaus at Yale University.

20. *Sicco L. Mansholt*

Sicco Leendert Mansholt was born in Ulrum, in the Netherlands, in 1908. He studied tropical agriculture at Deventer and worked on tea estates in Java, the former Netherlands East Indies, from 1934 to 1936. He became minister of agriculture in the first cabinet after the Netherlands was liberated in 1945 and presented in 1953 his by now famous Mansholt Plan for Agriculture within the context of the European Economic Market. From 1958 to 1967 he was vice-president of the European Common Market. January 1, 1973, he resigned as interim president of the EEC. He ranks among Europe's leading statesmen.

Do you believe a multinational world management will be achieved in the foreseeable future?

I do not see that as yet happening. Not in the near future, at least. The one organization on a global scale up till now, the United Nations, is no doubt of very great importance, but it has hardly any political or real power at all. For many years I have suggested that a democratic, world assembly, responsible to mankind as a whole, should be founded. It could function within the United Nations framework, somewhat comparable to the commission of the European Community, be independent, have a mandate from the General Assembly and be empowered to take executive decisions. That would mean some real power. In that way, such a UN commission could perhaps tackle some real urgent and serious problems before us, such as pollution, population and rampant economic growth. We would need such solutions most urgently. Do I see it in the near future happening? Certainly not. Perhaps mankind will not be ripe for practical steps until some near catastrophic situation threatens it.

You have expressed amazement that an Italian industrialist like Aurelio Peccei[1] took the initiative to have computers figure out what to do in the world.

It is no doubt a shame that we leave these most urgent matters to be solved by a private organization like the Club of Rome, and that nations have not reached the wisdom of realizing that it has become imperative to begin to organize the planet as a whole. But when I take into consideration the present attitudes of governments, of politicians, and also, when one observes the utter weakness of the United Nations, we cannot expect positive changes of any importance in the immediate future.

Is not European unity progressing at an extremely slow rate as well?

Yes. That is a great difficulty. Do we have the time to make such slow progress, that is the question. In my opinion the time element will be of the utmost importance. When we watch a development that takes fifteen years to make even a very beginning of a European monetary union. We are just on the way of mapping out a European social policy. Things are moving irritatingly slow.

But problems seem to be piling up at a terrific speed, also in technology.

Yes. If it would take man another twenty or thirty years to make a first beginning of starting an effective world organization, this would be in my opinion far too late. We would have to begin now, but no one seems to be ready for it.

You said somewhere that Marx already warned that capitalism would collapse, since it was to produce goods no one could afford to buy. The planet is running out of resources. Perhaps, both capitalism and communism or socialism will all collapse from quite another cause: hunger.

Certainly, the first resource we are running out of is food. The second disaster will be the destruction of an ecological balance. The third is linked up with the environment, and will represent the running out of energy. We will be running out of energy, out of thermal and nuclear problems. Over the next fifteen or twenty years this planet has to meet its greatest difficulties, but it seems quite unprepared to squarely face them.

Peasants in Denmark will vote to enter the European Economic Community, only because they realize they will get better prices for their exports, hardly because they are conscious of the need of a united Europe.

Of course, the sole *raison d'être* for selling their cheese and butter is to cash in better prices. Indeed, they probably were not motivated by the creation of a strong united Europe and, I admit, it is not a very good start.

It would be absolutely possible to create a better quality of life in Europe. We have the organization. We have the power. If the political will would arise, we could do it. But instead, I notice a trend into the opposite direction. Decision-making powers are slackening more and more. I see symptoms of a reappearance of nationalism, which clearly reflects in decision-making processes.

Will socialism bring necessary changes?

What do we mean by the word "socialism"? I cannot see that socialism, as it is dealt with in the Soviet Union for instance, will help us
a great deal. I am a democrat, as you know. I very well realize the
inner weakness of democratic socialism. It lacks decision-making power.
It lacks the possibility of manipulating action. We absolutely will have
to create a new socialism in which everyone is engaged. We cannot any
longer function properly with governments or ruling institutions that
decide over the heads of the people.

*Governments should be truly inspired by the groundswell of the masses.
People should be in a position to truly influence politicians, the representatives of the people. Mankind strove for this kind of thing since the
days of Methuselah.*

The only solution to meet the problems of the future would be to convince all and everyone that man is meeting the greatest challenge of all
times. To deeply convince each man of his individual responsibility for
the survival of mankind.

In my opinion our present system of production and consumption,
based on a capitalistic society, will not be able to solve these deadly
serious problems. It can only be done when the workers in the enterprise
themselves are fully responsible for the aims and objectives of the production process, and are actively engaged in it. Man needs the total
reform and redesigning of our society. In some respects, this could be
achieved by a much greater decentralization of present institutions, a
decentralization in which regions would have much greater power to meet
and deal with these questions. Every housewife, every worker, every
employee in offices or companies should be made aware of his ultimate
responsibility. And should be fully cognizant of the dangerous situation
on this planet.

When we could achieve a socialism, where not industry or capital is
deciding what should be produced, but production will be based on con-
census and the common interest of society at large, we could lead ourselves constructively out of the present impasse. I do not think that you
should feel that by simply stopping material growth, we will solve any
of these problems. I think it will not be possible to turn back material
growth over the next decade.

*   *   *

Robert S. McNamara advocates continued economic growth in order to assist the Third World in raising their standard of living.

That is not true. We do not need growth. Without growth per capita, that means growth in material-consumption per capita, we can better survive and are, too, in a position to help the eighty percent poor in the world. There is an absolute end to material growth. It will be impossible for the developing nations ever to reach the standards of living now prevailing in Europe or North America. In order not to widen the gap between the eighty percent poor people in the world and the rich nations, we have got to stop our material growth. If we would really make some of our wealth available for the developing nations, we could assist them very well in raising their possibilities for a better life. You know as well as I do that we make at present next to nothing available from our wealth to the really poor nations.

Recently, I met in the Netherlands with a group of working youngsters, laborers in their early twenties. I asked them whether they would be prepared to share a larger part of our wealth with the developing nations. And quite rightly they replied that they certainly were ready to share with the poor in the Third World, but objected to do so under present conditions and the western capitalistic system.

G. D. van Gelswijk,[2] an agricultural laborer from Lisse who replied to you, on your question, also asked you why it was that you, entertaining such progressive ideas, were working at the top of this capitalistic system, as chairman of the European Economic Commission.

That is very simple. There is more I can do to achieve these ideals from within the system than as an onlooker or a critic from the outside.

NOTES

[1]See conversation no. 70.
[2]Member of the board of the Dutch union of working youth, NVV Jongeren Contact.

21. *Ernest Mandel*

Born in Belgium in 1923, Ernest Mandel is one of Europe's outstanding Marxist economists. In his recently published book *Decline of the Dollar, a Marxist View of the Monetary Crisis*, Monad Press (New York, 1972), he analyzes the deepening crisis of the international monetary system.

Mandel studied in Brussels, Paris and Berlin. He obtained a Ph.D. in philosophy at the Free University of Berlin. He teaches at the Free University of Brussels. He is also a member of the United Secretariat of the Troskyist Fourth International.

What is your impression of Limits to Growth?

An impression of satisfaction and an impression of irritation. Satisfaction because these gentlemen, who have nothing to do with Marxism[1] and come from a bourgeois background, have now discovered with a hundred and twenty-five years' delay—compared to Marx[2]—that anarchic, unplanned, unconscious, runaway growth can threaten not only the foundation of material wealth but the very physical conditions for the survival of human civilization. It can threaten not only the conditions for the survival of human civilization but even the physical conditions for the survival of the human race. Marx understood this from practically the beginning of his theoretical analysis; as a young man he already wrote that capitalism threatened to transform forces of production into forces of destruction. One of the most striking passages in Volume I of *Capital*, his main book, is that the development of capitalism constantly undermines and threatens to destroy the two springs of wealth: human labor and nature. We now see that capitalist economists and academic scientists end up by understanding this, too. That is a reason for satisfaction.

The reason for irritation is that they still have not understood the basic mechanism which leads to these results. Therefore, the conclusions which they draw from their analysis, the solutions which they propose, are partially inadequate and partially worse than the ills they try to cure. What is the fundamental reason for this destructive potential of capitalist economic growth? It is the contradiction between partial economic rationality and global socioeconomic irrationality, embedded in the generalized market economy, which is the basis of the capitalist system.

What is rational from a capitalist point of view? Everything which increases profit of independent firms. There is of course an element of rationality in this mechanism. It would be foolish to deny that it enables firms to combine economic resources in a way which makes possible to measure costs and global results, but global only from the point of view of the firm in question. Why is this only partial economic rationality? Because any firm which wants to reduce costs or maximize profit or maximize growth can do so only by combining and comparing inputs and outputs with the measuring rod of money. Anything which has no money-price or which does not produce a monetary reward is therefore, by definition, eliminated from the analysis.

This eliminates "free goods" and human values, air, water, beauty, landscapes, solidarity, realization or mutilation of individual talent, etc., from any "cost-benefit" comparison because all of them have no price. Therefore, they can not be measured in terms of costs. On the other hand, an increasing number of costs under modern capitalism become socialized. Firms do not pay for them because the community pays for them. Sickness, consequences of certain working or living conditions, education, preconditions for certain types of work, unemployment created by layoffs—society pays most of all of these costs, not the employer.

Therefore, from the employer's point of view, it is perfectly rational to take decisions which lead to increased waste of free goods and human values to an increase in social costs. From a global social point of view, it is of course irrational "to save," for instance, one million dollars by laying off workers, if this layoff costs society two million dollars without counting human misery. But from the point of view of the individual firm, it is perfectly rational.

At the basis of this contradiction between partial economic rationality and global social-economic irrationality lies the question of human goals: What is the ultimate goal of economic activity? Marxists feel the answer to be obvious: The goal of economic activity should be to increase human happiness, to bring the maximum amount of happiness to the maximum amount of people, to enable as harmonious as possible a development of human capacities in all individuals.

But capitalist economists and all the institutions of Western society immediately put up a real stop signal and shout: No, no, no. Happiness, human development, personality, this is not measurable, this you cannot quantify. On the contrary we are able to spell out a lot of abstractions and arbitrary abstractions as income in figures. That income you can quantify. Profit you can quantify. Resources measurable in money-prices you can quantify. So you have to say: The goal of economic activity is to maximize income, irrespective and independent of consequences on happiness or unhappiness, on development or mutilation of human talents.

There you are at the bottom of what is wrong with capitalism, and of the reasons why capitalist economic growth threatens human survival. With the present scientific and technological potential of mankind, it just becomes absurd and irrational to continue to measure the resources of mankind only with the goal of maximizing income, especially maximizing income of those who control the economic system, i.e., maximizing profits.

That's what Heinrich Böll[3] recently said when he asked himself the question, What kind and how many kinds of violence are hidden in and behind a profit society? Here you are. Violence, which profit society encourages—that's exactly what you discuss here.

The word violence would be too limited. It is the sum total of all injustice, compulsion, frustration, inequality, waste of all the bad, unsocial, inhuman, immoral results of a society based on competition, on the individual's struggle for life—which are the basic ills which cause in the last analysis the tremendous waste of resources, human and material resources, revealed today by the ecological crisis.

Mr. Mansholt[4] asked at a meeting of Dutch union for young workers (twenty to twenty-six years) whether they were prepared to share the wealth of this part of the world with the Third World. They replied, "We are, but not as long as this capitalist system prevails." Mansholt then was asked why he was still working at the top of the system. He replied, "That's the only way I can do something, from within."

I don't agree. I don't agree because I think that the irrationality of this system is so big, so monstrous and so all-encompassing that you cannot change it from within. When you try to reform that system from inside, the only thing in which you will succeed is substituting new contradictions, new forms of waste, new forms of injustice for others. I'll just give you just one example: The big ecological crisis has created much discussion among economists. One suggestion made by apologists of the capitalist system is the following one: As many of these wrong decisions, on technology and on investments, which have led to the ecological crisis, are caused by free goods, well, let us eliminate free goods. If air will have a price, if water will have a price, well then, the waste of these resources will be eliminated.

You see the monstrous consequences. We will have to pay a price even to be able to breathe, while the expectation that this will solve the pollution problem is not even true. Because under the present economic conditions, the power of the big monopolies is such that they can transfer any of the additional costs which would be imposed on them for air pollution onto the consumers. It would be the mass of the people who would finally pay for their wrong decisions. This would not eliminate these wrong decisions.

You recently debated with Mansholt. What do you think of him?

He does the best he can, as a social-democrat, a liberal reformer. He is a nice person. I prefer him, of course, to conservatives, to reactionaries or to fascists. It's a "lesser evil" for society and for the working class movement to be administered by such persons than by reactionaries, but they cannot solve anything.

The balance-sheet of his agricultural policy in the Common Market is a strong confirmation to what I said. The global irrationality of the economic system in which we live can be clearly expressed by this terrible thing which happened in agriculture in the last seven, eight years —because we were forced to continue to act within a market economy, to calculate in monetary prices, monetary incomes and monetary investments.

First, we had a campaign to destroy butter, because there was allegedly too much butter—two hundred and fifty thousand tons unsalable butter in the Common Market. Then came a campaign to kill a quarter of a million cows, because there were allegedly too many cows, which produced too much butter. This was already an obscenity in a world where there is so much hunger that you destroy food in the Northern hemisphere on the pretext that there is locally too much to be sold with a profit. But after a few years these wise administrators made a shocking and unforeseen discovery: If you have less cows, you'll have less calves; and if you have less calves, you will have less meat. Now they have discovered that there is a deficit of one million tons of meat (beef and veal) in Western Europe and beef prices jump up and up. Wouldn't it have been a thousand times more rational just to measure in physical terms the need for meat and butter consumption of the people in Europe,

to ensure to the peasants a permanent income independently of price fluc-
tuations; to give away to the "Third World" any part of the production
which could not be consumed by people here? Even from a purely
economic point of view, this solution would have implied less waste than
the cyclical repetition of overproduction and underproduction, collapsing
prices and skyrocketing prices, which Mr. Mansholt introduced into the
Common Market over the past years. Not because he wanted it, but
because he was forced to do so as an administrator of this capitalist
market economy.

*Herbert Marcuse[5] cites you in regard to the question of workers and
the permanent revolution.[6] In what way can workers in this part of the
world influence a more rational social engineering of our society?*

Everything depends in last analysis on the working class. The working
class is the only class in a society which could organize society in a
fundamentally different way from the way it is organized today. I say
could. I don't say necessarily *will*. Otherwise I wouldn't be in the
revolutionary movement which I am in. I believe that workers have to
be educated, organized, helped along on that road. They are the sole
force which has the material and social potential to reorganize production
and consumption on a radically different basis from the one in which
it is organized in the market economy—a basis which Marx called that
of associated producers.

The mass of the producers and the consumers of society should decide
in advance, consciously, deliberately, democratically and in a well-
informed way, what are the priorities for which the economic resources
should be used and the way in which they should be combined. This
would eliminate ninety-five percent of all those processes which have
led to the ecological crisis. Only through such an economy, a socialist
planned economy on a democratic basis of self-management, one can
basically do away with anarchistic, cancerous growth, and replace it by
what I would call planned domesticated growth, a growth which has been
put under the control of mankind, on the basis of a certain number of
priority goals of mankind.

*Is the expansion of technology the principal cause of the present crisis
in environment or the dangerous situation on the planet?*

No, I don't think so. Technology has been a tremendous help to mankind to make life easier and to make possible a socialist society, a society of equals, and of free human beings. What was wrong with technology was its diversion in an irrational way because of private-profit interests. I would say there has been an increase in the destructive consequences of technology essentially during the last thirty, forty years, and this has happened only as the result of a few—what now obviously appear to be irrational—developments in technology. It is wrong to say that all development of technology increases dangers to the environment.

You seem to reason along the line of Barry Commoner.[7]

Yes, I think Commoner and a few other ecologists have made a great contribution to a better understanding of this problem, and are getting away from what I would call mystical and irrational formulas. Everything started with the irresponsible *uses* of technology—uses of technology not linked to correct calculations or evaluations of human welfare, but irresponsibly subordinated only to a certain number of powerful private interests. I will give two examples:

One is the development of the automobile. There were many different forms of automobiles possible. The specific form which has been chosen could have been developed in such a way as not to create all the pollution which we have known. It was developed in an irresponsible way as the result of decisions taken by key monopolies in the USA, powerfully supported by the government.

A second example is the example, which Commoner gives, of the substitution of detergents for soap. This concerns the development of the chemical industry in the last thirty years. Here the Marxist economist joins hands with the biologists or ecologists. Commoner states that the chemical industry has created a real ecological nightmare, with its flow of "new products" currently introduced before their long-term effects on the environment can be measured.

The Marxist economist explains why. The main form of monopolistic surplus profits which we have today is technological rents, technological surplus profits. One *has* to throw constantly new products on the market in order to enjoy such surplus profits. The time during which you enjoy them is limited. These profits generally do not last more than five or six years. Commoner explains that it takes more than six years to study the consequences of the new products for the environment. There you have in a nutshell the relationship between the nature of capitalism, the drive for profit, and the ecological crisis.

How do you view the next twenty years for man?

I think the end of the twentieth century will be decisive for the history of mankind. We are now faced—for several decades already—with this big choice which the classical Marxists incorporated in the formula: socialism or barbarism. In the past this was supposed to be a propaganda formula. We have witnessed the Second World War. We have witnessed Auschwitz.[8] We have witnessed Hiroshima.[9] We live under the nuclear-cloud threat. We now live, too, under the threat of ecologic catastrophe, which the Meadows report brought correctly to the consciousness of people, irrespective of the fact whether the calculations are correct, whether they are too pessimistic. We thoroughly understand that this dilemma, socialism or barbarism, has become very concrete. The outcome will be decided probably before the end of this century.

Mankind can no longer afford the luxury of free enterprise on a worldwide scale, that's to say the free, irresponsible use of material resources. A worldwide planned socialist economy has to replace it. This must be introduced under conditions of increased democracy and increased freedom for the individual. That is my conviction. It has to be done under these circumstances, because there is no mastermind, no "organization team" and no computer which can dictate to three billion human beings what they have to do. You can only solve this problem if you place them under such conditions that they discuss and decide among themselves on what rational things should be done. First, what are the key priorities and how hard you accept to work to realize them. Any decision imposed by compulsion will collapse.

NOTES

[1]The doctrine that the state throughout history has been a device for the exploitation of the masses by a dominant class, that class struggle has been the main agency of historical change, and that the capitalist state contained from the beginning the seeds of its own destruction and will inevitably, after a transitional period known as the dictatorship of the proletariat, be superseded by a socialist order and a classless society.

[2]Karl Marx (1818-83), German founder of modern socialism and communism.

[3]German novelist and writer, Nobel Prize winner in 1972.

[4]See conversation no. 20.

[5]See conversation no. 48.

[6]Ernest Mandel, "Workers and Permanent Revolution," *Counterrevolution and Revolt*, Beacon Press (Boston, 1972), p. 6.

[7]See conversation no. 26.

[8]Nazi concentration camp.

[9]First use of nuclear bomb in history over Japan by the United States (August 15, 1945).

22. *Edmund Carpenter*

Professor Edmund Carpenter teaches anthropology at the New School for Social Research in New York City. He has done field work in the Arctic, Borneo, Siberia and New Guinea. His two most recent books are *Eskimo Realities*, and *Oh, What a Blow That Phantom Gave Me!*

Would you say that Limits to Growth, *the concern about ecology, about population, about pollution, is a new kind of awareness that might gear humanity, as Skinner[1] says, to its main goal: survival?*

My own feeling is that we must understand exactly what is taking place before we even attempt these questions. Often the questions have been answered without any serious investigation of the problems and the processes that exist at this moment.

In the field of anthropology, the records that are now being released belong to an Alice-in-Wonderland[2] world. They have nothing to do with what is really happening. I worked both with the media in our culture and then in other cultures where electronic media are coming in. We find that if you want to destroy a culture, the strongest weapons you have, more deadly than diphtheria, are electronic media. They are cheaper than rifles and far more effective. You can wipe out a culture in no time at all with electronic media. This is exactly what's happening. The irony of it is these media turn back on us and wipe out our own culture and everything that represents Western civilization. Electronic media obliterate culture. They replace cultural environments with media environments. It's no longer Captain Cook stepping in and out of different cultures; we now step in and out of media. A simple illustration: I often placed cameras in the hands of natives and taught them how to make films.

In New Guinea?

In New Guinea, among the Eskimos and in other areas.

I always obtained the same results. I had hoped, at the beginning, that the native would use the camera in a way that reflected his culture, his perceptions and values. But this was never the case. On the contrary, what they made were *films*. The answer is that media swallow cultures. The native left his culture totally behind and stepped into the world of the camera. The films he made were indistinguishable from films we make.

If you visit Indian reservations in the United States, American Indians will often say to you: The land-agents stole our land, the traders took our furs, and now the missionaries want our souls. And they laugh. The implication is, they lost their land and furs, but they won't lose their souls. I heard an Indian say that on television. Missionaries had not stolen his soul, but television had stolen it in a way no missionary ever dreamed. Television now controlled his spirit! It gave him identity, denied him identity.

Culture becomes an automatic victim of media. The media become new environments and we step in and out of many of them in the course of a single day. There is no place left for culture. It goes. Culture is now a myth maintained by anthropologists and others, a thing of the past. Where do you find it?

What is the importance of losing culture?

To me, culture is where you have spirit in flesh. With electronic media you have just spirit, pure spirit.

How essential is culture to a man's life in your view? Or to his creative possibilities, to creating a life of his own?

I don't know, other than the fact that there seems to be everywhere in America a hunger for culture as it disappears. We suddenly sense what we have lost. Electronic media have made angels of us, not angels in a sense of having wings or being good, but spirit divorced from flesh, capable of instant transportation anywhere. The moment you pick up a telephone, you are everywhere in spirit and nowhere in space. Nixon on television is everywhere at once. This is Saint Augustine's definition of God: "a being whose borders are nowhere, whose center is everywhere." Today pure spirit takes precedence over spirit in flesh. You may be waiting in a line to have a clerk serve you, but if the phone rings, the clerk answers the phone. We accept this. No one protests.

We recognize that pure spirit is primary. But the danger is that as people become pure spirits and enter media, they can only enter without their bodies. They go in as purely ephemeral things. Young people in America, sensing this, turn back and try to rediscover their bodies. They drink wine, they want rich or spicy foods, they are interested in the land, they go barefoot, they try to put the spirit back into the flesh. But the media have no place for flesh.

The radio created Hitler.[3] *Now what are we creating with television on a worldwide scale right now?*

Radio under Hitler was just a beginning of what's happened. Today the real drug trip, the real inner trip, is television; and for many people it's primary. They regard the world outside as messy, disorderly, unrewarding, and they step into media and live in them. To them, that is *the* reality. I've done some simple tests with students. I took the movie *Patton* and showed it to a class—

General Patton?[4]

The film about General Patton. Then I had them read two books, one by A. J. Liebling, which is very uncomplimentary to Patton and points out that Patton was honored for battles he didn't fight. Then I had them read a book on Field Marshal Rommel, his opponent, who was a restrained man, concerned with the welfare of his troops and an anti-Nazi who died trying to kill Hitler.

Now, the fascinating thing was the students enjoyed all three. Not one student raised the question of historical accuracy. No one asked: Which version was true?

Then I took the old Charles Laughton movie, *Mutiny on the Bounty*. As a boy, I had loved that film. I showed it to the class and then had them read an account of the mutineers, who were murderers, rapists and alcoholics. Of the fifteen, only one survived; they murdered each other. Then I had them read an account on the administration of Australia by Captain Bligh, who turned out to be, not only an able administrator, but a pioneer in the human treatment of seamen. The students enjoyed all three and saw no need to raise the question: Which version was true?

Young people have stepped away from outer reality, the notion of historical truth or of physical reality. Their parents wanted to see a thing. They wanted to see movie stars. They wanted to see the real Joan Crawford. They wanted to hear authors read their works. They wanted to see the man to bring an image down to a thing that could be touched, seen, observed.

If they had seen a picture of the Mona Lisa, they went to the Louvre to see the original. They wanted to see the Eiffel Tower exactly as they had seen it in reproduction. Young people don't. They have no interest in this. I think this is one of the most monumental changes in human history. People have given up this primary characteristic of Western civilization in which all experience, all truth, was synchronized to a visible, observable universe. The young people don't care. They accept many universes, many realities. To them, television does not reflect the world outside. It is not supposed to. They are not at all disturbed by the fact that our news reports have nothing to do with reality. They don't expect them to. There is no longer any urge to look at the record.

What would be the influence? What shift do we observe here, supposedly caused by this stultifying addiction to television?

Right now,[5] in the United States, we are getting ready for an election, clearly a confrontation between print and television realities. McGovern[6] is saying: Cities are collapsing, the economy has reversed itself, people are dying. He is talking about a physical, historical reality, but no one will listen. Nixon[7] is putting on a superb television performance about something that exists only in television.

And nobody asks what the effects in the reality are?

No one. People are laughing at McGovern because it's a bad television performance. What a horror the thing is! Look at the reality. Look at the city. Let me ask: Have you ever, in any city in the world, seen as many walking schizophrenics as you see here?[8] Not in Calcutta, Bangkok, Rio. Here we are on the sixteenth floor and the sound level is so high, it is difficult to do a tape recording. This is the reality. The sound level in New York City has reached the point where people are going insane. You see it on the streets. If you walk five blocks, you'll see insane people shouting at cars, shouting in the paper bags, screaming down sewers, talking to themselves. I have never before seen a culture where the environment is driving people insane. Freud worried about the dangers that arise from human relations, but no one ever warned us that the sound level would reach the point where you could not think.

Nixon, of course, is not addressing himself to those questions. He is talking about an Alice-in-Wonderland world, and an entire nation is enjoying it. McGovern is a literate, rural, essentially nineteenth-century man, who believes that all he has to do is to tell people that they are sick and hungry and can be helped.

Are you aware of Skinner's theory of changing the environment in order to change, to make life more livable for individuals?

Pavlov[9] found he could get nowhere with dogs until he controlled their entire environment. Then, when he controlled the environment, the slightest change changed behavior, a discovery not lost on the Marxists.

Pavlov was immensely popular with them precisely because he taught them how to control people by controlling the entire environment. But the moment people begin to talk about controlling the environment, they leave this environment. Leave it behind and step into another environment. They step into the environment of the media. I can show you some of the most remarkable things in this city. You will see people walking the streets here with their ears plugged, listening to transistor radios. I know a man who, when he goes walking with his daughter, is electronically rigged so that each is tied into a radio system with a mike so they can talk. He's been psychoanalyzed by telephone and by radio.

Where will this power of the media lead us?

Anthropologists have never dealt with media.

You made special studies?

But these studies have been wholly unacceptable to anthropologists who are concerned with culture. To them, media have no existence. But they find nothing disturbing about putting a culture in a book.

In New Guinea we entered one village where people knew what cameras were. They had seen government movies and were interested in film. When we arrived, they were about to initiate some boys in a very sacred ceremony where woman are forbidden on penalty of death. They erected a great ceremonial structure, twenty-five feet high, to prevent anyone from looking in who was not an initiated male. Just before the ceremony began—I didn't dare ask if we could film it—they came to us and asked us if we would film it. We said we would be delighted to. Then they came to us and asked about a woman who was in our party. Was she a cameraman? I said she was the best of the three cameramen with us. So the elders met and said, "We want her to film as well." Not only did they invite her, but they stopped the ceremony to help her reload, to show her how to position the camera, to help in every way. At the end, they asked us to play back the soundtrack so they might listen to it. Then they made us promise that we would bring the movie back for them to see. They planned to erect another sacred enclosure and project the film. Then they announced there would be no more involuntary initiations and they offered to sell the most sacred things they had, the water drums. They said that with the film there would be no further need to initiate boys. Media takeover.

About a year ago I was invited to participate in an open seminar at a Canadian university on Eskimo life, and on the program were various Eskimos. I talked about what I knew and loved about Eskimo culture and the experience I had had with Eskimos in the past. Some young Eskimo men present were furious. They said, "This is not true." They then began to tell me what Eskimo culture was like as they knew it through the media, having never experienced it, you see, except through the media. They knew their art only through movies and books, through government propaganda, through the world of Walt Disney. Finally one Eskimo said, "Don't tell us who we are or what we are. That's a white man's lie. We know."

The angry American Indian today knows nothing of his own heritage. All he knows is his media image. He plays that and is exploited in a way that makes even his ancestral exploitation pale.

And the blacks in America?

They know nothing of their background except its exploitative aspects. When they encounter the great music and art of their heritage, they don't recognize it. They don't even know their own heroes. Ask blacks on a college campus who Paul Robeson[10] was and they wouldn't know. The only thing they know is the identity that they see from television and that's what they believe in and that's who they are.

Professor Carpenter, how would you sum up the impact of the electronic media on survival for the planet? I know it is a big question, but what would be the impact of television in, say, the next thirty years, when satellites school Indian villages, satellites that are programmed in the United States or elsewhere?

I am not as worried about the content of media as I am about the media themselves. To me, the real effect of television is that it separates spirit from flesh in a way that print did not do. I think there are certain very involved reasons why, with print, though you have an image divorced from flesh, nevertheless there is an urge always to refer back to the flesh, to the physical thing. With television and the other electronic media, this is not true. Today we are witnessing this shift, in which we abandon the very essence of Western civilization. The synchronization of the senses and the synchronization of all experiences, was a lockstep, in which everything was directed toward a single purpose, a single goal—it permitted the organization of large numbers of people. You could mass-produce things, have assembly lines, armies and bureaucracies. This was possible under literacy because it produced a type of person who used his sense and his mind in this highly restricted, synchronized, directed manner.

NOTES

[1] See conversation no. 7.

[2] *Alice in Wonderland, and Through the Looking Glass*, by Lewis Carroll (1832-98).

[3] Adolf Hitler (1889-1945), German Nazi dictator.

[4] George Smith Patton (1885-1945), US general and tank commander during World War II.

[5] This conversation took place in New York City, September 12, 1972.

[6] South Dakota Senator George McGovern, Democratic Party presidential candidate in the 1972 election.

[7] Richard M. Nixon, thirty-seventh President of the United States, Republican incumbent in the 1972 presidential election.

[8] Professor Carpenter's apartment overlooks New York City's Central Park.

[9] Ivan P. Pavlov (1849-1936), Russian physiologist.

[10] US black actor and singer, born 1898.

23. *Robert J. Lifton*

Robert Jay Lifton holds the Foundation Fund for Research in Psychiatry professorship at Yale University, New Haven, Connecticut. He has been particularly concerned with the relationship between individual psychology and historical change.

Professor Lifton was born in New York in 1926. He was for a number of years associated with the Harvard University Center for East Asian Studies. He spent seven years in the Far East.

Among other publications, he has written *Thought Reform and the Psychology of Totalism: A Study of Brainwashing in China* (1961), *Revolutionary Immortality: Mao Tse-tung and the Chinese Cultural Revolution* (1968), *History and Human Survival* (1970), *Death in Life, The Survivors of Hiroshima* (1968), and *Boundaries*, Random House (New York, 1970).

In your book, Boundaries, *already in the very first lines, you speak of "limitless destruction."*

The problem is I think that destruction is more limitless than creation or growth. There aren't limits to destruction. That's one of the first points I make in *Boundaries* and in my other work—namely, our quantum jump and our capacity for destruction in itself creates a new historical situation. So there are no limits to destruction.

We will have to talk about this on two levels. One is the actual physical capacity of the weaponry that we make, and that, I think, is virtually limitless. I mean, we have now the capacity to pretty much destroy all life on earth that we know; and one does not have to make some sort of absolute prediction about whether in the next nuclear war, if there is to be one, all of life will be eradicated, annihilated, or most of life will be. That used to be a parlor game in the late fifties and early sixties. The fact is we have the physical capacity for total destruction.

What I wrote about in *Boundaries* and what I've been most concerned about is the psychic state that accompanies the capacity or the way in which that new capacity affects our psychological lives. Here I would say we live on two levels. One is an apocalyptic level, and although there is a great deal of criticism among some groups about the apocalyptic thinking that goes on nowadays, my position is that one requires what I call an apocalyptic imagination to grasp the actualities of our time. One must live with an apocalyptic imagination because that's the true nature of our possibilities for destruction.

On the other hand, we have a day-to-day necessity of muddling through, of keeping things going, and of maintaining some sort of equilibrium in the world. One hopes for peace or to achieve peace. That requires day-to-day judgment of a nonapocalyptic character. There are these two levels of response to the capacity for total destruction.

How does this swinging between these two levels affect young people?

I think the very young people are very much involved in this. It is very hard to ascribe the behavior of the young to any one factor. My own feeling is—I have also written about what I call the Protean Style, the whole situation of psycho-historical dislocation.

Protean man.[1]

I think that the situation of the young and much of their behavior and their aspirations is stranded on this new set of historical forces. One very important force is one we've just been talking about: the capacity for total destruction. But along with that is—and this is what I emphasize very much—the breakdown of traditional symbolic structures which has been going on. It did not begin in the last ten or twenty years or even since World War II, but began perhaps sometime during the eighteenth century or before the breakdown of traditional cultures and has reached an intensity now which has been further accelerated by the holocaust of World War II. This is a second level of the breakdown of symbolic forms around which life has been organized so that life had a wholistic and integrated structure within a given culture. I am speaking of structures of religion, of government, of the life cycle, of marriage, of education, of all the major activities in life.

These are no longer ordained by a set of cultural symbols. Not that they were as precisely ordained as we sometimes think in premodern cultures, but nowadays there is a radical collapse of the viability of these symbols. The symbolic structures are still there. We still live in families.

Many of us go to the churches or synagogues. We vote or don't vote and have relationships to our government. But my point is we don't inwardly believe in our relationship to all these things, our capacity to really be grabbed by them internally has diminished, so that we live with a kind of residuum which is no longer vital, which no longer has vitality. That being so, the combination of that breakdown of vital symbols and this new capacity for total destruction or for annihilation of man and his history by means of his technology gives great importance to this mass-media revolution.

There are three elements, the mass media revolution is important because it spreads images rapidly, totally and almost instantaneously—images of possibility, whether they are psychological possibilities of how one should live or whether they are images about material objects that interest or tempt one, or images of other cultures—we now have the possibility of any image being available to anyone at any moment. That really is another radical shift in our psychic life.

Those three elements, to get back to your question, very much affect the way that young people behave. To me there is a great logic in radical experiments by the young, even if they at times seem destructive or overshoot themselves, even if they fail to act. Even if they fail to achieve immediate solutions, which of course are impossible to achieve. Still there is a logic behind these experiments, given those elements in our situation.

Do you feel Jean-Paul Sartre[2] is somewhat an example of this protean man?

I used him as an example of Protean Style because he is a tremendously important modern figure in the twentieth century. He is important on many levels, but I used something of his life, and his work. His autobiography *Words*[3] is an example of Protean Style. In his case, he has achieved a very creative equilibrium between continuity and protean experimentation. He has maintained an impressive continuity as an experimental writer. He stresses in his writing the absence of a fixed ego, a fixed consciousness, and rather sees consciousness or ego as a kind of flow or flux. In that sense the very content of his psychology is radically protean. In his own life, his various experiments and his responses to various groups and to the young he has shown many protean inclinations. Of course, being protean is never absolute. One always holds to certain more fixed or stable positions. That in a way permits one to be protean. In his case he had certain fairly fixed political positions and then has made protean experimentations, while holding to those political positions; but even these have altered in recent years. I see him in his life and in his works as exemplifying in many ways a Protean Style.

To get back to the third factor, the mass media and their influence. You spoke about the never-to-be-estimated damage of the spreading of half-knowledge.

I think it is happening all over. But let us get back to our general subject first, the approach of the Club of Rome and *Limits to Growth*. I heard Forrester[4] give some of their presentation in considerable detail at a conference and felt it to be a mixture of truth and misleading claims. The notion of an eco-system of the whole world, having all elements interrelated, this to me is a very profound and important approach, which I think any notion of world processes has to take into account.

On the other hand, what seems to be often half a truth in the Club of Rome approach, as exemplified by Forrester, is the set of variables that are postulated. I'm more familiar in detail with his work on the city. He set forth a series of assumptions there, which really constituted the variables that have been read to the computer that are very dubious and didn't take into account many other elements and many trends. A lot of his assumptions happen to be those in the existing order of cities. The material presented by Forrester were assumptions of those of the comfortable middle class in the city, the upper middle class more or less.

This is a great danger in computer projects. I think that we need projections of the future. We have to think of the world as an ecosystem. But I also think there is a great technicist fallacy in assuming that by a kind of technological projection of what we take to be reliable variables we can have an accurate picture of the world future. I am skeptical.

Do you think this doomsday message, this shaking of people, is damaging or useful?

It's again this issue of a half-truth. What's good about it? I wish the world could have been shaken up in a more reliable way. It may be quite true that—and many others have said it in different ways—that we are in danger of using up our resources and moving forward a precarious balance of population and resources and so on, and that we're being promiscuous and irresponsible. There is value in the fact that a fairly dramatic presentation may shake things up. But in the assumptions put forward about futurology and the nature of futurists I think there is a lot of misleading information. It is a kind of paradox, because this particular study emphasizes the danger of a false reliance on burgeoning technology and technological growth, because after all, technological growth requires all these resources and these are elements that are running low. On the other hand, the method used is technicist in that the mind imitates technology in trying to turn social science into a technicized machine-modeled discipline. There are paradoxes and contradictions that I think could be highly misleading. It is very hard to give positive or negative results in the end. Maybe they will be more positive than negative in provoking a good deal of thought and debate on this matter.

Do you think Professor Skinner[5] has a valid argument that the environment shapes the individual rather than the other way round?

My way of thinking is radically opposed to Skinner. I listened to him carefully at a public meeting in New York a few months ago and then had occasion to debate some aspects of what he said. Putting it very simply, I think behavioral theory of the kind he develops can be fairly accurate for relatively limited and relatively simple actions. It seems to me totally inaccurate for more complex human interactions. The notion that one can program a world environment in order to create the desirable human psychological responses I think is totally wrong. One always has to have a sort of dialectic—one hopes a creative and a constructive dialectic—between planning, which we desperately need, thoughtful planning, always based on values and not based upon a notion of perfecting an environment that will create perfect beings. Beings will always be imperfect. Planning on the one hand and a kind of openness, an open world, an open system, call it what you will, with a great deal of unpredictability and a great deal of disorder. It is that sort of dialectic we need rather than a notion of a totally planned and controlled and behaviorally predicted environment.

Do you feel our scientists take entirely different, sometimes opposite, values and cultures—as, for instance, in Asia—sufficiently into account by making global studies and predictions?

That would be one example. The notion of total planning and

behavioral manipulations on a world scale is wrong, no matter which culture you are in. One does not even have to resort to the stress on cultural differences in order to find it conceptionally wrong. Skinner is no doubt humanitarian in his own personal life. But his approach lends itself to an authoritarian elite determining the plans for the rest of us in a way that in the end they are totally incapable of doing.

Could you explain your vision of a new history, which boils down actually to changing boundaries, to changing limits constantly. You write repeatedly of this total loose approach of an infinite effort.

Yes, I think you convey in a sense what I do try to suggest. I see history, or man's experience in history, as a kind of continuous process. The notion that a particular moment will achieve perfection to me seems absurd. We need utopian visions in order to create some sort of positive forces in historical change. But in speaking of a new history, one way of emphasizing that idea was to describe what I call symbolic motive immortality, or taking up certain ideas and suggestions put forth by many before me in philosophy and in psychoanalysis. In psychoanalysis I refer particularly to the ideas of Otto Rank,[6] who saw all of human history as an effort to maintain a continuous sense of the human self. It sounds perhaps like a rather mystical notion, but what I take this to mean is to see all of historical processes related to man's need for continuity, or what I call "symbolic immortality," to feel himself connected to what has gone on before and what's to go on afterwards, whether it be human groups, human ideas and so on. This can be done, as I said, biologically through families or through man's works—what he creates—or his influences, through a religious notion of spirituality or a conquest of death or, more literally, of life after death, through nature, or the idea that eternal nature will go on despite the mortal limitations of human life or limitations of mortality. Or, finally, through what I call "experience of transcendence," a psychic state of great intensity in which time and death disappear.

From this standpoint, new history is a major shift in the mode or modes of symbolic immortality. One could speak of a new history in the Darwinian shift in the nineteenth century from the religious mode to the more natural mode that Darwin,[7] and others interested in the evolving idea of evolution, suggested concerning both the natural mode and the biological mode. We see a similar shift going on at present. What's quite clear to me is that old modes are being dishonored or questioned. I mean by new modes of symbolic immortality, higher values around which we seek to immortalize ourselves in symbolic ways. New modes concern the replacement of that which is being dishonored or questioned, this is much less clear. So, we have the idea of holocaust.

What you call "nuclear holocaust"— How does this doubtful concept of biological immortality affect young people?

The notion of nuclear holocaust is very strong in all adults. Not as an inevitable process, but as a possibility in our time. This idea has been holding in the human consciousness over the past three decades. The notion of continuity of symbolic immortality, living on in one's children, or living on in man's works, even the religious modes and the idea of living on in eternal nature may be questioned. We can destroy most of nature with our weaponry, most of our environment either with our weaponry or with our pollution, so in one phrase modes of symbolic immortality are virtually all threatened, not eliminated. They still exist for us, but they're under some basic doubts, psychologically speaking. That I think is one of the major reasons why we see this radical new interest in what I call "experiential transcendences" in various forms of highs. This could mean in intense psychic experiences, whether through the so-called drug revolution or through some experiments in consciousness without drugs or even in political actions. The young seek high moments and high experience. In this sense much of what goes on in the young, in their experiments and in the kinds of experiments they resort to, has to do with a questioning of those modes of symbolic immortality via the ideas of holocaust which have taken hold in our consciousness.

Does this tend to numb the psyche? Does it take out feelings?

The loss of response is possible to this situation of threatened breakdown in human continuity. It is not just a threat of death. It's the threat of an unacceptable death. It's the threat of premature death. The premature death really means a sudden putting off of one's relationship to all those elements that might symbolize one's immortality. In this sense it is turning a lot of psychological ideas on the head by speaking this way, but in any case there can be many reactions possible.

Sometimes there are many creative responses to this, as we've seen in the experiments with various radical institutions as the experiments of the young we've been talking about. Some of them are creative, some of them destructive, some of them in-between. But in other responses extreme numbing takes place, and I talk about that in my work. I'm trying to develop this in more systematized ways in more recent work, that I have not published yet. This desensitization, its origin, I think could be called a desymbolization or a loss of the symbolizing function or formative function, which is the essence of human living. In other words, numbing really occurs where you can no longer find some sort of meaningful fit or connection between self and world; where the gap, psychically speaking, becomes very great, often numbing is resorted to.

Perfecting nuclear power and weapons—could that be the in-between, or an effort to search for new limits, for new meanings?

The word limits may be confusing there and yet not entirely inappropriate either. I said there were many responses to this situation of what I am calling, to use a big phrase, "psychohistorical dislocation," the radical loss of viable relationship to symbols and symbolic forms. In all what we just discussed, holocaust plays a part. The most extreme response of a negative kind is what I call "nuclearism." That's an expression of this terrible ingenuity of man. He can actually worship the thing that threatens him with—renders the weapon a deity or God, the very agent of his potential destruction.

But of course that's not new, in a sense, because we've always seen our gods, in fact we've always recognized a god larger than the basis of the capacity to destroy. We turn around and worship the very thing we have created and attribute to it powers of creation as well, as we do to gods. The gods can both destroy and create and then we—with great fantasy, I think—build a deliberate system of safety, security, what I call "nuclearism," which involves great psychic dependency upon these weapons along with the deification. We expect them to do all kinds of things that they are simply incapable of doing.

This stems from a certain half-truth again, because to possess nuclear weapons is to hold a certain power in the world. Everybody seems to want them, although I think a number of countries happily have their second thoughts about the whole process. But on that half-truth is built a tremendous weapon—fantasy, in which one can build "security," the favorite word of the Pentagon in this country, with probably their equivalents abroad, in Russia, China, France, elsewhere. The disease is not limited to any one country in its potential for it.

The fantasy involves a notion of security and safety and even a kind of suggestion of realization or of some sort of transcendence via these weapons, because in some ways we are attached to, or connected with, these all-powerful entities. This is of course a very dangerous kind of dependency, to say the least, or, as I say in my work, it is a contemporary disease of power. It has to do with the effort to master and take hold of a situation that we feel has deteriorated or has left us helpless, to restore psychic boundaries or psychic forms of meaning.

The tendency towards "nuclearism" may, e.g., make man want to worship the idea of nuclear power even for civilian uses. I wouldn't make a blanket statement against nuclear power; I am not really qualified to make firm statements from a standpoint of engineering and power supply and so on. But one does see in sum the embrace of whatever peacetime expressions of nuclear power can offer us, a kind of uncritical embrace and a struggle against recognizing the potential dangers of nuclear power even for allegedly peacetime uses. If you read, e.g., a book like Edward Teller's *Legacy of Hiroshima*[8] (I use this as an example of the process—I am not trying to cast stones so much as exemplify the process), one sees an uncritical embrace of both the weapons and of the peacetime potential for nuclear power. This seems to me a rather impressive and dangerous example of "nuclearism."

NOTES

[1] See *Boundaries*, "The Self."

[2] French existentialist philosopher (1905-   ).

[3] George Braziller Publishers (New York, 1964).

[4] See conversation no. 34.

[5] See conversation no. 7.

[6] Otto Rank (1884-1939), psychologist, psychoanalyst, sociologist, teacher.

[7] Charles Darwin (1809-82), British naturalist; the body of his biological doctrine maintained the species derived by descent, with variation, from parent forms, through the natural selection of those best adapted to survive in the struggle for existence.

[8] See conversation no. 45.

24. *Claude Lévi-Strauss*

Born in 1908 in Belgium, anthropologist Claude Lévi-Strauss studied philosophy and law in Paris. In 1949 he became doctor of letters at the University of Paris.

From 1935 to 1938 he taught at the University of São Paulo, Brazil, where he conducted several ethnological expeditions into central Brazil. During World War II he taught at the New School for Social Research in New York and became in 1946 cultural counsellor to the French embassy in Washington, D.C. Since 1950 he has been directeur d'études at l'Ecole Pratique des Hautes Etudes in Paris. In addition to the chair of social anthropology at the Collège de France, he occupies the chair of comparative religion of nonliterate peoples. He is also director of the Laboratoire d'Anthropologie Sociale of the Collège de France and l'Ecole Pratique.

This is the Collège de France, 21st September, 1972, in the office of Professor Lévi-Strauss.

Professor, you have seen Limits to Growth?

First of all, I must say that I have read the French translation, I am not sure that the French translation is doing full justice to the book. My feeling was an extremely mixed one. Because on the one hand I am in full and complete agreement with the purpose, the aim and the spirit of the report. But the way it is presented seems to me both verbose and rather elementary. Perhaps the word is too strong, but I don't have another one right now. I would have very much preferred that the report should be limited to the figures and to the diagrams which in my opinion are both telling and frightening rather than the length of text (which expression is too diffuse and thought oversimplified) which they have placed around it.

Would you say the philosophy behind it isn't of the highest plateau?

No, it is not exactly the level of philosophy, because the philosophy is sound. It is rather the way it is expressed.

Critics have said it was presented too much as an Einstein-letter, as a doomsday message.

As far as I understand it, there have been two different kinds of criticism. Some criticism stems from economists or mathematicians, who claim that the models are oversimplified, that not enough variables are taken into account and so on. My personal feeling—of course it is the feeling of a layman, because I am not competent at all in the field of mathematics or economics—but it is that it should not be overlooked that what we have are models. *Limits to Growth* does not claim at all to represent what is taking place or what will take place. It is a model built in the laboratory, in order to better understand what is taking place in concrete reality. That is for instance exactly the kind of procedure which Karl Marx has followed when he wrote *Capital*. It is the kind of procedure which we always follow in the social and human sciences. From this point of view I think that the character of the model, the result of the book, should be well understood. I am not at all impressed by this criticism.

On the other hand, there is a second type of criticism you were alluding to a moment ago, the Doomsday message. From that point of view, my own feeling is that the *Limits* people are only too cautious and too weak. The situation is much more tragic, even much more tragic than the one they are debating. I can say, to be more frank, since it is almost twenty years now since I wrote my book *Tristes Tropiques*, I tried to express exactly the same kind of ideas, fears and warnings. Although of course *Tristes Tropiques* was not put in this rigorous shape which the Club of Rome was able to achieve. But having read the report, my only conclusion is that the situation is already a hopeless situation, that the remedies which are sketched by the report belong much more to the region of wishful thinking than to possibilities which can be really applied and really used. My own world view is that the situation is even much darker than this report makes it.

You also wrote in Tristes Tropiques, *"the world began without the human race and it will end without it."* [1] *Now, that was twenty years ago. If this is worse, then what do we tell our children?*

We should distinguish two completely different things. When I wrote this sentence, I was not thinking particularly of the ordeals and difficulties of the present world, but of the very obvious fact that if there is no eternal living species, that all living species had a start and will have an end and that of course mankind will have an end if only because the earth itself will have an end.

You mean the sun burning the earth—

Well, after some time, a very long time. It should not worry our children more than it should worry ourselves that from, say, I don't know how many billion years from now there will be no earth anymore and no mankind anymore. After all, this is only a philosophical factor which will assist us in thinking about these matters. But this has nothing to do with the fact that the path which is actually followed by the human species can, and most certainly will, lead not to its extinction, but to tragedies and catastrophes of major proportion.

Worse than Hiroshima? [2]

Well, perhaps not so sudden or not so brutal, but much worse because in a world where the human population becomes more and more numerous—we have only to look at the figures in the report to be convinced of it—life will become—if it is not already in many places—it will become unbearable only because of the sheer number of people. I don't think it is only a problem of human resources, of finding enough food to nourish I don't know how many billions of people. Even if this problem was solved—I doubt very much that it can, but even if it were solved—it would not modify in any way the fact that there is for mankind as for every living species an optimum density. And of course this density should not be too low, because if it is too low, there is no communication, and stagnation will result—

We need equilibrium—

Yes, we need an optimum degree of density and of diversity. What is taking place now, even leaving aside the matter of natural resources, is that we can see in the big urban cities and in underdeveloped countries, the overpopulated areas and so on, that people are getting so close together, if I may express myself simply, that each of them becomes a threat and hindrance to his fellow beings.

* * *

Lifton,[3] the psychiatrist, says that the old behaviors that society has been reinforcing for centuries, will destroy us if we continue this way; in other words, we have to redesign human behavior. Skinner[4] said we should redesign the environment in order to make life livable.

But can we? Can we? Isn't it entirely utopian? Is it possible to redesign human behavior? We can certainly hope that through some natural process and a kind of natural need for equilibrium—which works through ways entirely unknown to us and of which we are not conscious, are not aware—we can hope that this will spontaneously take place. But I doubt very much that we can think it beforehand and decide to do it and succeed to do it. It would be necessary to conceive a world with sufficient understanding and goodwill or a kind of supreme authority, able to rule over the entire earth, which of course would all be a wonderful effect or a bad one, I don't know, but in any case which belongs to the realm of dreams rather than to a reality which can be foreseen.

Do you have the impression that Mao Tse-tung succeeded to put some sort of programming into the eight hundred million Chinese, arranged some infrastructural social order into society?

I don't know, because I am not very posted about Chinese affairs. It's quite possible. It's also possible that many of us will not like very much to live the kind of life which is being planned in China.

Alberto Moravia[5] told me upon his return from China that the poverty was still incredible. The Zeitgeist *[spirit of the time (Ger.)] demanded Mao's rigorous mobilization of China's psychic as well as material economy. Strict programming became the only way out.*

Maybe China needed it, and probably the world will need it very soon as a whole, but it does not mean that it will make a very pleasant world. It may be a dire necessity. It is certainly not something which is to be hoped for.

Toynbee[6] said that the Roman emperors sometimes reverted to dictatorship in times of emergency and that a benevolent kind of world-management dictatorship might eventually be necessary.

But it remains that to revert to some kind of dictatorship—which will be dictatorship from the right or from the left, it does not matter, from our present point of view—but this is something we can conceive in traditional countries. But can we conceive it as it would be needed in order to bring a solution to the problem, on a world scale? Because what will probably take place, if many different countries start to be subject to a crisis of the right, if that will revert to dictatorship, that this dictatorship will crush together, with the other dictatorships. I don't see at all that this can be a way toward a general and mutual understanding.

What did you learn most from your studies with the aborigines in Latin America: humility?

Humility? No, I would not choose the word, but modesty probably. In effect, human groups which live happily because they have very limited needs which can be satisfied at the expense of a very limited amount of work, too; and the leisure time is considerable greater than it is in our modern society. Most of all where man or mankind does not consider itself as the master and ruler of the earth, but as having his limited share in a world order, which can be kept only at the cost of respecting the share which belongs to other forms of animal life and to vegetable life and so on. That is a humanism which is moderate, while our own humanism has become immoderate, and out of proportion, because it only considers mankind and sacrifices the interest of mankind, all the other interests of earthly life.

Yes, you have called man his own worst enemy. How is the rest of nature, of creation to survive?

I am afraid it will not. Except for the few vegetable or animal species which we need. We don't need mice, but we need cattle. We need wheat and corn—except if as we are doing with the so-called green revolution, we are selecting limited species which are particularly susceptible to blight and other diseases and which will in the long run cause their extinction.

Will your studies with the extinct societies help us to understand better the human mind? Because we will only survive if we finally learn how to handle the psyche.

I don't know if they will, but it is certainly the only way or the main way. There is a great difference between the human and social sciences, on the one hand, and the physical and the natural sciences, on the other. For the latter, it is possible to experiment in the laboratory, while we cannot experiment on human societies. It would be too costly. It would take too long, and there are more reasons which I don't need to dwell upon.

So we have to look for ready-made experiments, which is the only way to approach scientifically human troubles. Ready-made experiments are constituted by these societies, so-called primitive, i.e., completely different from our own, where we can go and test hypotheses. When these societies will have completely disappeared, which is not far from now, we will be limited to only one kind of human experiments, i.e., the one provided by our own societies. It would be impossible to do these comparisons and to measure the full span of human experiences and human abilities.

When you worked with Indians in Brazil, did they feel that you were actually carrying out experiments?

It is difficult to answer because it really depends. I must say that there were groups who were completely indifferent to the aim and purpose of the anthropologist and who just tolerated him as the visitor from whom they expect gifts, some kind of advantage. But I have on several occasions met so-called natives who were perfectly aware of the purpose of the anthropological fieldwork, because they were themselves interested in the life and customs—not only the anthropologist—of their own society. This has also frequently taken place during the late nineteenth century in the United States, among Indians who were perfectly aware that their culture was doomed, that if a record could be saved, if something should be saved, then they should cooperate with the anthropologist in order to save not only the objects but the belief, the customs and so on.

There is the case tested in literature of old priests, realizing that they would be perhaps the very last specimen in their tribes, and they definitely were interested that both their knowledge and the paraphernalia of their cult would be stored in museums and saved for future of their own generation. There is no simple answer to your question.

Professor Lévi-Strauss: in Stockholm[7] it was said that the way in which the Brazilian government is at present cutting down the Amazon forests is an ecological Hiroshima in itself. Will the Indians in these areas be the very first victims of ecological disaster?

I am afraid it is only too true even for the few tribes which were still relatively untouched—relatively, because there are no untouched tribes in the present world. The Brazilian Indians are certainly doomed to extinction with the new policy of roads, because these people, who live mostly by shifting cultivation, collecting wild foods and hunting, need a tremendous surface area of land in order to survive. If their freedom to roam around is being restricted, then they will disappear. But the policy is not only dangerous for the Indians. It is dangerous for the whole of mankind because we should not forget that the tropical forest is something which cannot regenerate once it has been destroyed. When it is destroyed, it is once and for all. It will never come back. If I am not mistaken a substantial amount of the oxygen which we have in the atmosphere is being generated by the Amazonian forest, so if the Amazonian forest were destroyed, the supply of oxygen of all mankind would be threatened.

How can scientists influence this situation? Brazil does not want to prejudice its economic growth at the expense of ecology.

I doubt very much that scientists will be able to do anything. It is perfectly understandable that a country like Brazil does not want to remain an underdeveloped country and is trying to take off and reach the development of a fully industrialized nation. This I can very well understand. I cannot even condemn it. It is just the tragedy of the modern world that what is taking place and what is bound to take place brings us to the verge of disaster and catastrophe.

Stendhal[8] once wrote about Napoleon[9] that the ladies at the court of Saint-Cloud were of the opinion that a great man is like an eagle: the higher he flies, the less he becomes visible and "il est puni de sa grandeur par la solitude de l'âme."[10] Looking back on your life and your work, your affection for the peoples in the last forests of the planet, how do you feel about mankind and life?

I am just sorry to have been born, to have to live in the century where I was born in. I would have very much preferred to live one century or two centuries ago or to go back to neolithic[11] time, but well, that is a biographical accident.

But people were storming the Bastille[12] those days, while Marie-Antoinette[13] ended up on the guillotine.

Well, let's say I would have preferred to live just before the French revolution, or just after.

NOTES

[1]*Tristes Tropiques, an Anthropological Study of the Primitive Societies of Brazil*, Atheneum (New York, 1971), p. 397.

[2]Destruction of Hiroshima, Japan, by an atomic bomb, ordered by President Harry S Truman (1884-1972).

[3]See conversation no. 23.

[4]See conversation no. 7.

[5]Italian writer (1907-   ).

[6]See conversation no. 5.

[7]At the World Conference on the Human Environment, June 5-16, 1972.

[8]French novelist and critic (1783-1842).

[9]Napoleon Bonaparte (1769-1821), emperor of France.

[10]*De l'Amour*, "De l'Orgueil Feminin," p. 108.

[11]Anthropological term for the latter part of the Old World Stone Age.

[12]Famous fortress in Paris, built in the fourteenth century and used as a prison until it was besieged by revolutionaries on July 14, 1789, a date now commemorated each year as France's national day.

[13]Marie-Antoinette (1755-93), Queen of France, wife of Louis XVI, executed during the Great French Revolution.

25.   Sir Julian S. Huxley

Sir Julian Sorell Huxley was born in 1887. He studied biology at Eton and Oxford University. From 1912 to 1916 he taught at the Rice Institute in Houston, Texas.

After World War II he served as executive secretary of UNESCO.

Sir Julian recalled during his conversation with the author that at the turn of the century, when he was asked to write an essay for a scholarship to Eton on the subject, "What would you do, if the government gave you a million pounds to spend?" he centered his theme around buying land and parks for conservation.

Some of Sir Julian's best-known books are *Problems of Relative Growth* (1972), *Evolution, the Modern Synthesis*, and *Soviet Genetics and World Science*. In 1971 he published *Memories*.

Sir Julian, when the Club of Rome report reached you, did you think it important?

The obvious and most important thing about it is demonstrating that population increase means more sewage, more litter, more technology and more pollution. That I think is the essential fact. They make some economic suggestions which I am not in a position to comment on, as I am not an economist. But I think the most important thing is to show the interconnection of population growth and the fact that exponential growth always leads to eventual doubling and redoubling. This is inevitably connected with pollution and damage to the environment, and its nonhuman inhabitants, plant and animal. Population increase also inevitably involves increase in the size of the cities, which in the modern world always seems to involve the creation of slum areas; and once you get slum areas with overcrowding, you tend to get violence.

You see, in animals overcrowding by itself gives rise to violence. Mice, harmless little mice, turn vicious when overcrowded; and this applies also to human beings, so long as we have the conditions persist —about which the Club of Rome is writing, about economic advance —we shall go on competing for our means of subsistence, notably as regard to nonrenewable resources. This may very likely lead to war, especially so long as we think in terms of power rather than in terms of the good life, of improving the human condition further.

There have been some critics—like my old friend Lord Zuckermann —he critizes the book on the ground that too much attention is paid to long-term problems like increase of population. But this after all is not long-term but immediate. He feels that we ought to concentrate more on trying to get rid of poverty and ill health. These are of course urgent, but I still think that at the back of them are these basic problems of population growth and resulting pollution.

But, Sir Julian, don't we need economic growth to fight starvation, chaos and crowding?

Of course, we need economic growth to keep up the standard of living;

but this becomes increasingly difficult as more people have to be dealt with. Thus, in India they are making a gallant attempt to industrialize the country, but this does not mean that the danger of overpopulation has diminished. Indeed it seems that Indian overpopulation is more serious than ever before.

As population increases there are fewer jobs on the land, so again you get a tendency to migrate to the cities. I don't know if you know India, but Calcutta to me is absolutely appalling.[1] Of course, conditions in it are aggravated by the refugee problem, but even before partition it was terrible—with hundreds of people sleeping in the streets and unable to get jobs—and all the diseases.

Another point—if you promote health facilities, there will be more people—and, furthermore, a greater proportion of elderly people. And they are past working. It is what we call a "vicious circle."

Sir Julian, in your essay on population you said: "A traditional culture, like a wild species of animal or plant, is a living thing." And then you added: "If it is destroyed, the world is poorer."[2]

Luckily, we in Europe are not going on in quite this way. After all, in Britain we have now a minister for the environment, we have strong conservation societies, national and international, and that is increasing pressure for population control.

Some people want to be very drastic about population and talk about taxing people for every child above two. I don't think we shall come to that, unless the situation has become absolutely intolerable: I don't believe that public opinion and political expediency would tolerate that now. On the other hand, one thing might be done—the government might diminish the amount of family allowance for every child after the second. Today even in this country (and still more in France) a family can live on its family allowances; indeed, the more children it has, the better life it can lead. This has got to be stopped. You must obviously help people, but if they don't do their duty as regards overlarge families, you can at least not pay them for having too many children—pay them less at any rate.

Sir Julian, do you think we will lose more of our freedom when we are getting to organize this planet like managers of a multinational company?

What sort of freedom?

I'm thinking of what Skinner[3] says in Beyond Freedom and Dignity, *that man might have to give up his individuality in exchange for a more dictatorial form of government.*

What do you mean by "individuality"? I think people will have to give up various types of enterprises, and will have to collaborate in certain other enterprises. For instance, a great deal of pollution can be avoided by recycling litter and other waste materials and by installing really efficient sewage plants; but I don't see that this interferes with our liberty. After all, liberty is always relative. We are not at liberty to do exactly what we like. I am not at liberty to go out and start firing pistols outside my house or to shout and make a disturbance—I would get arrested. And of course in this country there is liberty to protest. But when mass protests cause disorder and violence, then the police can interfere. I don't see why anybody should interfere with liberty to try to improve matters. But certainly the liberty of factory owners who release pollutants into our rivers will be diminished, but that is a very different thing.

Do you think Limits to Growth *and its mass distribution is contributing to a more conscious acceptance of the global* problématique?

How can I tell? I don't know anything about its distribution.

In the Netherlands the report sold 250,000 copies in one year. That is pretty good. But I don't know what is happening in America, Germany. Do you think the book is valuable?

In the whole, *yes*. I think that it includes rather too complicated diagrams and tables for the average reader, but of course for the professionals, sociologists, economists, these are important, indeed necessary. But it's rather stiff reading, and sometimes the argument is hard to follow. In general, I am sure that the report is highly desirable as showing the way in which the different facts interact, and of course one thing that we need to consider is what we thought of as really safe before, namely, the ocean as a whole. This has been stressed by Heyerdahl,[4] who reported on the polluted state of the Pacific, that he was crossing. The same apparently is true of the Atlantic. And recently I read that even Antarctic waters are getting polluted with various metals which have come all the way from the Arctic ice. The world's oceans are a unity. Already we are getting people poisoned by eating marine creatures contaminated with dangerous metals, like mercury, discharged into the sea by various industries, notably in Japan, but the same sort of thing is true elsewhere.

On the other hand, we must say that the campaign to preserve the environment has done much good in Britain: For instance, salmon have not returned to the Thames, but we have got back quite a number of smaller fish, not yet in the center of London, but close to it. Many other rivers are being cleaned up, but there's still a great deal to be done to purify our waters.

Population has always been your greatest worry. Are you hopeful about the future?

How can one be hopeful about population, which is increasing so fast? The only encouraging thing I can say is that the United Nations, the World Bank, the World Health Organization and Unesco have all set up committees to deal with population pressure. This is something quite new. As I record in my memoirs, already in 1931, I suggested that radio should focus more attention to the subject of birth control and population increase in general. I was put on the mat by Sir John Reith, then head of the BBC, accusing me of "polluting the ether" with such disgusting ideas. Since then, there's been a big change in our thinking (and our actions) about these problems. The trouble is that all the remedies first of all demand a great deal of popular education—about the need for family planning, for instance—also about the not expensive methods for preventing the environment from being spoilt, like proper sewage disposal, proper recycling. Remember that unless we recycle our water, we shall run short of it—then we should be a damned planet.

[*Following my interview with Sir Julian, he remarked:*]

I am most interested to hear what Toynbee said. Was he at all hopeful?

No, not too hopeful.

After all, he is a great historian. He has seen and read about so many civilizations, their growth and their decay—by invasion, or just by decay, or by war. Not unnaturally he cannot be very hopeful. How can I be very hopeful? All I can say is that the situation is more hopeful than it was because today more people are becoming aware of it.

Don't you think here is a task for the media?

Yes, I do.

Of course, there are some people who say they are getting terribly bored with these prophecies of doom. But it isn't doom if we act about remedying the dangers in the right way.

We shall have a difficult time, but I don't see that we are doomed. It's nonsense to say that the human species will die out. Our species will certainly survive. It may survive in stunted form, with not enough food and with too much pollution, but it will survive. After all, the distinguishing characteristic of man is his ability to think and plan and to communicate his ideas and transmit them to later generations. I think there are enough people with brains and goodwill to see that something decisive is achieved in all these threats to the quality of life and of nature.

NOTES

[1] Not only has Sir Julian visited Calcutta often, in this connection he would like to recommend to the reader *Something Beautiful for God*, William Collins Sons (London, 1971), the book Malcolm Muggeridge wrote about Mother Theresa of Calcutta, the Yugoslav nun who worked all her life among the Calcutta poor and dying.

[2] *On Population: Three Essays by Thomas Malthus, Julian Huxley, and Frederick Osborn*, New American Library (New York, 1960).

[3] See conversation no. 7.

[4] See conversation no. 63.

26. *Barry Commoner*

Professor Barry Commoner was born in New York City in 1917. He graduated from Columbia College in zoology and obtained a Ph.D. in biology from Harvard University in 1941. In 1947 he came to Washington University in St. Louis, Missouri, as an associate professor of plant physiology. From 1965 to 1969 he was chairman of the department of botany, and during the same years he was appointed director of the Center for the Biology of Natural Systems at the same university.

In 1966 he published *Science and Survival*. His latest work is *The Closing Circle: Nature, Man and Technology*, Alfred A. Knopf (New York, 1972).

What is your reaction to Limits to Growth?

I have studied the report and I find it very seriously flawed, scientifically. The approach that *Limits to Growth* uses is to gather data regarding the historical trends of various parameters that are involved in the world resource environmental crisis; it then projects these curves mathematically and allows them to interact in the computer. The way in which various parameters interact—*e.g.*, population growth, availability of food, technological development—is of course the substance of the computer program. And it becomes crucial to ask what mechanisms of interaction were chosen to design the computer program.

When you examine the Club of Rome report, you find only a very brief statement, asserting that the interaction among the factors was determined by discussions with leading authorities and by examining the literature. The interactions that were chosen have eliminated entirely one set of parameters, namely economic factors and social factors. Leaving those factors out has fixed the software of the computer—*i.e.*, the program—in such a way that it eliminates the possibility of altering the relationship by economic measures. To put it very simply: If economic information does not come into the computer, then the computer gives answers which do not relate to economics. That is the result of how the computer program is designed.

The approach which I have used is quite the reverse. I have looked at historical trends in pollution levels, population size and so on, and have asked, what interactions among these factors are revealed by these trends. This is described in my book *The Closing Circle*. As you know, the outcome of that study is that in a country like the United States the chief cause of the rapid rise in pollution is not the growth of population, not the growth in per capita consumption, but the change in productive technology which has been dictated by economic causes, by the desire to raise productivity and profit. This leads me to the conclusion that the chief driving force for the pollution crisis in the United States is an economic one. Therefore, the chief cure has to be sought for in the realm of economics.

This is precisely the area which the MIT design avoids in its conclusions. In other words, built into the entire mathematics of the Meadows design is the elimination of what my data indicate is the most important factor in dealing with pollution, namely the economic forces. And so, on scientific grounds, I have to conclude that the analytical technique used by Meadows has built into it an inevitable error.

It will not "close the circle." Do you believe in a computer model as a means to—

No. I think computer models are at the present time misleading because they force you to select the data in such a way as to leave out any information which cannot be put into strictly mathematical terms. It is much better for us to accumulate data and think about it than to turn the data over to the computer. In my experience a computer model built on an inadequate understanding of the theoretical basis of the problem is not only useless but misleading. The Meadows study has been a step backward. Let me explain why.

In the first place to assert that there is a limit to growth, you would not need a computer. Many ecologists, myself included, have said over and over again that if you look at the theoretical base of ecology, and the characteristics of the biosphere, it is absolutely clear that there is a limit to the growth of the exploitation of the biosphere.

Therefore, the chief conclusion of the report that there is a limit to growth is redundant. The basis for that conclusion is presumably in the computer analysis. However, the computer analysis is so wrong and so misleading that they have added to this old idea a set of misleading conclusions. And so, in a sense, I think what the Meadows study has done is really a step backward, because it takes an old idea and gives it a misleading meaning, a misleading coating.

And for people to feel that the basic issue in solving the problems of the world is to control growth is in my view wrong, although it's clear that we cannot grow forever. The question that has to be asked is, What is the reason for our present difficulty? If we want people to act, they have to understand why they are in trouble and what needs to be done about it.

There is no evidence that the reason for our present environmental difficulties is that we have come up to the limit of growth. In other words, if as we all know, there is a limit to the growth of production—let's say in the United States—clearly you could be in environmental trouble if we had grown to the point where we were near that limit. But that is not the reason for the environmental troubles in the United States. For example, why have we got into trouble with power production?

Let me go back. Power production is going up very fast, and it's a major cause of pollution. One of the reasons is that we have shifted production from metals like steel to aluminum. Aluminum production requires a great deal more electricity. Now why have we shifted from steel to aluminum? Because we are running out of steel? No, because there is more profit in making aluminum than in steel, and in our competitive society production shifts over to where there is more profit.

The point I am making is that the reason for our trouble is not that we are approaching the growth limit. The reason for the trouble is that we have developed technologies which are insanely counterecological. I rather imagine that if we took all the food in the world and divided it equitably among the people of the world, nobody would starve—which tells us right away that the reason for starvation is not that there isn't enough food, it is that we don't distribute food in an equitable way. It becomes an economic and political issue.

Therefore, I regard the MIT report as a step backward, because it takes what is an abstract and generally accepted notion—that there is a limit—and in a false way applies it to the immediate situation. And I think it gives people a misleading idea as to why they are in the trouble that they are in now. I also think that it is very unfortunate that the Club of Rome decided to give the report the kind of political push which it did, resulting in many people accepting the ideas without having the opportunity to look at the scientific background.

You see also a political danger because you have mentioned in the Herald Tribune *that the environmental crisis is the world's most dangerous political issue today.*[1]

Yes, I think that the history of the Club of Rome report is an example of what I meant by the environmental issue becoming a dangerous political issue. It seems to me that if on the basis of this study you come to the conclusion that the only way to solve the environmental crisis is to cut down on consumption and population, you are very near to the next step which is exemplified by the *Blueprint for Survival* in England, which lays out an authoritarian regime for Britain, dictating where people shall live, what shall be built and so on. In other words a highly organized—orchestrated, as they say—regime. Obviously it is necessary to decide what things should be done, but what is so politically dangerous is that the scheme is put forward for enormously rigorous control over the life of the country without saying one word about who is in control. In my view that kind of approach lays the ecology concept open to, shall we say, fascist use.

Do you feel that for a proper rational use of US resources, socialization in the classical Marxist sense of the nation's economy is essential, what Peter L. Berger[2] has called "a hidden agenda for socialism"?

The main lesson from the environmental crisis is that the biosphere represents essential productive capital, both in industrial and in agricultural production. It is also clear that the biosphere is necessarily, a socially owned good. It makes little sense to divide up the air or the water and assign it to private ownership. We are now confronted with what I regard to be a fairly important new idea, which I emphasized in one of the chapters of my book. For the first time it has become clear that all present economic theories, whether capitalist or socialist, have neglected a major factor of production, the biosphere. In a sense both socialist and capitalist theories are therefore missing this important constituent. When you turn around and incorporate this new constituent into these two theories, what I find is that the concept of private-enterprise economics clashes violently with ecological imperatives. Clearly it makes little sense to organize ownership on a private basis when not only the human organization of production in the classical Marxist sense is socialized but when part of the capital, the biosphere, is socially owned.

In other words, as I said in *The Closing Circle*, private enterprise, free enterprise, may be free, but it is not wholly private, because every private enterprise is using a social good, the biosphere. Thus, a system of production which is based on social ownership of the means of production would appear to be more suitable than one of private ownership. In that sense, the classical Marxist concept of socialized ownership of the means of production, namely socialism, appears to fit in better with the needs of the biosphere than one involving private ownership.

People always say, "Why is it that the Soviet Union has pollution?" The reason is that in the Soviet Union just as in the United States, the biosphere was ignored as an essential productive factor. While in the US, managers looked for more profit; in the USSR, the managers tried to fulfill the production quotas. But it appears that often they fulfilled their productive plans without worrying about the consequent pollution.

Now that in both countries the need for preventing environmental pollution has become clear, I think that it may be easier to do it in the Soviet Union than it is in the United States. In the US it is already clear that there is a serious clash between the industrialist's desire for profit, the worker's desire for a job and the people's desire for clean environment. In many places the pressures for cutting down industrial pollution has cost people jobs. The clash between the desire for profit and what the workers want is likely to be intensified as we attempt to clean up the environment.

How come to action?

As I describe in detail in both my books, the issues here are not scientific. They are political, they are value judgments. You have to judge between the value that you get from a nuclear power plant and the hazard from the radioactivity. Now, that is not a scientific question. For that you don't have to be a Ph.D. You don't need to have any particular profession for that. What you need is an understanding of the facts and a human conscience.

Now, as far as I am concerned, everyone in the world has the right to exercise their conscience. I think that what prevents most people from making the decisions on these matters is that they don't have the necessary facts. And in my view the role of the scientist, the professional, is to see to it that the people of the world have the necessary facts. I am willing to rest on the people's decision. I am not willing to rest on the decisions of Mr. Peccei[3] and his friends among the prime ministers. They are not, in my view, given the right to lead the conscience of the world.

What we have to recognize is that we are faced with a new political situation. We have neglected an important aspect of our lives, which is now being reintroduced into our thinking. I think that the judgments ought to be made on the basis of worldwide popular understanding and opinion. You may say, well, how are people going to act? I don't know how they are going to act. People invent ways of acting once they understand the situation.

In the debate that I had with Peccei, I pointed out that he put his faith on prime ministers and scientists and I put my faith on the wisdom of ordinary people. And we'll see who is right.

But Peccei also puts faith in journalists and media. Would you add to the group of people that could be of help to arouse human consciousness, journalists?

Yes, of course that is true. In the United States it has been very evident. We have a movement among scientists—the Scientist Institute for Public Information—for bringing this information to the public. We get enormous help from the news media and journalists. The political issue here is whether you trust the people or feel that you have got to manipulate the opinion of politicians. I would rather trust the people.

NOTES

¹"Man's debt to nature must be paid in more than recycled beer cans." *International Herald Tribune*, June 5, 1972, p. 8.
²Professor of sociology, Rutgers University, New Jersey, quoted from his discussion of Bertrand de Jouvenal's *The Ethics of Redistribution*, Harper & Row (New York, 1952), in *Fortune* magazine, October, 1972, p. 154.
³See conversation no. 70.

27. *Edward Goldsmith*

Edward Goldsmith has been editor of the British *Ecologist* since its founding in 1970.

He was born in Paris in 1928. He studied political science and economics at Magdalen College at Oxford University. He coauthored the *Blueprint for Survival*, published in January, 1972, a historic document signed by thirty-three foremost British scientists and men of knowledge.

The Blueprint for Survival[1] *appeared almost at the same time as* Limits to Growth. *Were they competing documents?*

No, I think they are complementary. The Club of Rome study provides a very sophisticated analysis of the world situation and hints at the sort of changes required to stabilize our society. We provided a similar but far more rudimentary analysis, but on the other hand, accentuated the requisite program of change.

From your writing I concluded that a well-orchestrated change on numerous fronts is required. In what way do you feel Blueprint for Survival *and* Limits to Growth *are contributing to that goal?*

Change must occur on all fronts and must be orchestrated nationally and internationally. However, political action is unlikely to be taken unless the changes proposed are "politically feasible," which simply means that they can be implemented by politicians without their losing votes. In other words, it is public opinion that must first be changed. The changes required are so radical that they involve just about all the basic values that we in our industrial society cherish most dearly. Needless to say, this cannot be done overnight. Both the *Limits to Growth* and *Blueprint for Survival* have attracted a lot of attention. They have been translated into about fifteen languages. In many schools and universities they are already being used as standard texts. They have also been influential at the political level. Mr. Mansholt,[2] for instance, told me that the Dutch government had been very much influenced by both of these reports. In New Zealand there is a new party called the Values Party, which has adopted a document called *Blueprint for New Zealand*, which is basically the *Blueprint for Survival* adapted for local requirements. I think they have made a contribution, but as I said before, one does not change a value system overnight.

Do you consider that present expansion in the developed countries is occurring at the expense of the Third World?

Undoubtedly. Economic growth is only possible in Western Europe and elsewhere if we can hoodwink the Third World to provide us with food and raw materials in exchange for on the whole useless manufactured goods. We in this country import every year 1.7 million tons of high-protein concentrate for our cattle from countries that badly need the protein for their own largely underfed populations. At the same time the Third World is being hoodwinked into believing that they can solve their problems by also indulging in economic growth.

But to build hospitals in India they need economic growth to be able to afford these expenses.

New hospitals are irrelevant to India's problems. India is not suffering from a lack of hospitals but from an ever-widening gap between population and food supply, as well as from countless social and material problems caused by the massive urbanization that is presently taking place as a direct result of the economic growth, however limited, that has already occurred.

The gap is only growing wider?

Indeed, it is. The population, which is already over 500 million, will have doubled by the end of the century unless it is brought to an end by famine, war or disease. What is certain is that it will not be halted by current birth-control programs. There is simply no evidence for supposing that technological devices such as the pill or the IUD have any significant effect on reducing population levels. In America there has been a reduction in the birth rate which appears to be largely the result of changing attitudes. As far as producing more food is concerned, industrialization of agriculture cannot conceivably do more than achieve this over a very short period and at considerable social and ecological costs. Even Norman Borlaug, who was given the Nobel Peace Prize for his key work on hybrid cereals and who is regarded as the father of the Green Revolution, admits that all he has succeeded in doing is putting off starvation for a decade or two. I am afraid that one has to face the unpleasant fact that man is not as ingenious as he thinks and that the basic problems of man cannot be solved by science, technology and industry.

Perhaps we aim too high?

No, it is not a question of aiming too high but of aiming in the wrong direction. Our industrial society is geared to achieving a materialist paradise in which all the ills we are supposed to have suffered from since the beginning of our tenancy of this planet, such as drudgery, unemployment, poverty, disease, famine, etc., would have been eliminated. The achievement of this paradise is known as progress, which consists basically of substituting man-made artifacts for the normal processes of nature, or what Max Nicholson[3] calls the "technosphere" for the "biosphere."

Unfortunately, the technosphere is very crude by nature's standards. It requires far more resources than the biosphere and hence generates far more waste products. Also, it is controlled by human manipulation rather than being self-regulating, which means that it is far more vulnerable or unstable. The artifacts we introduce, such as pesticides and fertilizers, are far simpler than the controls used by nature to achieve the same ends. This makes them more unstable as complexity ensures stability. Whereas the various parts of the biosphere tend towards overall stability, the technosphere is designed to satisfy petty short-term human requirements regardless of long-term consequences. For all these reasons the substitution which we call progress must and can only bring about a systematic deterioration of the world we live in.

Jan Tinbergen[4] feels that the Blueprint for Survival *was too utopian.*

I presume he means by that that the changes proposed are unlikely to be implemented by today's politicians, they are not politically feasible. This is absolutely true; but I do not regard this as a defect except perhaps from the purely tactical point of view. The ecosphere is a vast organization. Like all organizations, it is hierarchically arranged, and at each echelon behavior is subjected to a new set of constraints. These constraints are cumulative. Thus, a biological organism must obey all sorts of biological constraints, but first of all be subjected to chemical and physical ones.

No society can survive which defies biological constraints. For instance, a society in which there is the death penalty for eating or drinking could not survive. This is the mistake made by the famous American religious sect, the Shakers. They were destined to become extinct because they banned sexual intercourse. Similarly, if our politicians impose upon us a society that openly defies biological, chemical and physical laws, it cannot conceivably survive for very long, no more than the Shakers could. Yet this is precisely the situation we are in today. If what is ecologically necessary is not politically acceptable, then one has to change one's standards of political acceptability and not vice versa.

John R. Platt[5] *said actually we are at war, we need to recruit scientists like we did in the Second World War.*

It is true that we are facing a far greater emergency than we faced in 1940. If we are to avoid the worst calamities, we must treat it as an emergency. However, this is not simply a question of recruiting scientists on an emergency basis. I do not think that scientific research is going to contribute all that much to solving the problem. We are not looking for new inventions; after all, if you were given a magic wand and told you could conjure up any new device you wanted, so long as its functioning did not defy basic laws such as the law of thermodynamics, what device would you ask for? There is no human artifact that would enable us to solve the problems.

It may be argued that scientists are required to monitor pollution levels, but this is pure fantasy. The task of monitoring the five hundred thousand pollutants in our environment and the three thousand new ones that appear every year and determining their effect in different combinations on the countless different forms of life that inhabit this planet is quite beyond our means. It is unlikely that the planet could support the weight of the white mice required to carry out the experiments. In any case, we do not need better documentation of the degradation of life on this planet but action to halt the process. As Robert Allen[6] says, "If you jump out of an airplane, you are better off with a parachute than an altimeter."

Barry Commoner[7] *called the* Blueprint for Survival *a step back to fascism because who will police the changes necessary?*

I think that authoritarianism in a society must to a large extent increase with instability and tension. The *Blueprint for Survival* is designed to ensure a transition to a way of life some variant of which will be inevitable if man as a species survives the next century. Its object is to reduce instability and tension to the very minimum in this extremely difficult period through which we will be passing.

Barry Commoner is irresponsible. However, this is not surprising as he is generally irresponsible in many of the things he is saying at the moment. His favorite themes, for instance, are that the world is not over-populated and there is no justification for population-control measures. This is particularly grotesque at a moment when a large part of the population of Asia is threatened with starvation, not in ten years' time but right now. For example, 250,000 Indians reportedly starved to death two weeks ago as a result of the recent drought.

Barry Commoner also maintains that the only way to stop population from growing any further is to allow the nonindustrialized countries to develop so that they can achieve the Western standard of living. The principle being that in industrialized countries the growth rate of population has diminished. Barry Commoner knows perfectly well that the limited resources of our planet as well as its even more limited capacity to absorb further waste products makes it totally inconceivable that the whole world will ever be able to achieve the "Western standard of living." Even if it did, there is no guarantee that a drop in the birth rate would follow, since this is largely culturally determined, and nobody knows how Asian and African countries will be affected by industrialization.

Barry Commoner has a remarkable genius for coming to the diametrically wrong conclusions on the basis of the best possible information.

Jay W. Forrester[8] is now completing a model of the United States. You are designing a computer model of Britain. Are you cooperating with MIT?

No. Our plan is to introduce social factors into the model, and as soon as you do this, you meet all sorts of objections. We now have a team of people who have worked together for three years, who see things in much the same way and who can achieve a high degree of cooperation on a project of this sort.

Ninety percent of the scientists that ever lived, live today. What is your opinion about the communication between scientists?

It is very poor. I have noticed this at all the scientific conferences I have attended. The basic reason is that they don't agree on general principles. Many of them have never considered general principles. Many of the terms they use have never even been defined. Some of them go so far as to say that a definition is not required. People talk gaily of economics, life, behavior, consciousness, mind, etc., without really knowing what these terms mean. Until one gets one's general principles correct, no single terminology is possible and clearly a single terminology is required for the sciences. It is quite ridiculous that science should be divided into a host of watertight compartments. The world we are trying to understand is not divided in this manner at all. It developed as a single process and is made up of closely interrelated parts. It can only be described in a single terminology.

In other words, scientists don't understand each other because they don't know what people from other disciplines are saying?

They can't understand what is going on in other compartments—the subject matter of other disciplines—because they know nothing about these at all. But at the same time they don't understand what is going on in their own little compartment because this is constantly being influenced by what is going on in the other compartments.

In small self-regulating communities, observed by anthropologists, there is no assertion of individualism. Certain individual aspirations may have to be repressed or modified for the benefit of the community. How to turn back our super-consumer society to one or two children, one automobile, maybe no automobile, back to the bicycle, who knows? Will we first need a disaster?

You are really asking two questions: The first thing is the problem of individualism. You can see for yourself, if you live in a small village in Europe, that public opinion is much stronger than in a big town. Therefore, there are constraints on your behavior, which are imposed by public opinion, and to that extent individualism is reduced. Why should individualism be so important? I don't see it. Creative? What sort of things are we creating? You'll see that the art forms or music of primitive societies are very elegant. It may well be that primitive societies don't have Beethovens and Mozarts, but they don't have Hitlers and Mussolinis either. What you lose on the roundabouts, you gain on the swings.

One of the basic principles of industrial society is consumer sovereignty. People want something, therefore they must get it. This principle has to be completely rejected. People will simply never have all they think they want because things just won't be available. Do we need a disaster to make them realize this? To get really rapid change, you probably do need a disaster as there is a tremendous amount of inertia built into our society at every level: government, industrialists, trade unions, individuals themselves. On the other hand, attitudes are changing fast, especially among youth in industrialized countries.

What in your view can the media do, what can journalism and television do to speed things up?

It is a question of priorities. Most newspapers are simply businesses. They publish things only if they are likely to increase their readership or their advertising revenue. Some newspapers are concerned with political issues first and foremost. In other words, they feel they have a mission. We could do with a lot of newspapers with this feeling of a mission. They must realize that the issues at present separating different political parties are totally irrelevant to the future of man on this planet. Our politicians are like children fighting over chocolates when there is a time bomb in the cellar. First they must remove the time bomb. They must take up the ecological issue, which is the only one that matters today.

What tactics can be used to persuade people?

Since people are interested in politics and politics has always been news, the ecological movement must become political. This way it will attract far more attention. This has already happened in New Zealand, as I have mentioned. At the present election in France there is an environmental candidate in Alsace. It will almost certainly happen in Britain very shortly. This I think is the direction in which our efforts should lie.

NOTES

[1] Warned that to avoid a world environmental catastrophe, Britain too should stop building roads, tax the use of power and raw materials and eventually cut her population by half. See three-part series by Anthony Lewis, New York *Times*, January 28, 31, February 4, 1972.

[2] At the time of the interview, President of the European Economic Community in Brussels, Belgium. See conversation no. 20.

[3] Head of Nature Conservancy in London, England, and author of *The Environmental Revolution*.

[4] See conversation no. 3.

[5] See conversation no. 9.

[6] Deputy editor, *The Ecologist*, London.

[7] See conversation no. 26.

[8] See conversation no. 34.

28. *Roger Revelle*

Professor Roger Revelle has been director of the Center for Population Studies at Harvard University, Cambridge, Massachusetts, since 1964.

He was born in Seattle, Washington, in 1909. He studied oceanography at the University of California.

In a recent talk I had with Dr. Philip Handler, president of the National Academy of Science, in Washington, D.C., he stressed the population question as the most serious problem of the planet today.

I would say that the two most fundamental events of our time are the very rapid growth of the earth's population that started after World War II and the other equally remarkable event, the urbanization of the human population, the gathering together, the aggregation in cities. Whereas at the beginning of the twentieth century, seventy years ago, there were less than a quarter of the world's people in cities, by the end of our century this proportion will certainly increase to over fifty percent; maybe even as much as sixty percent of the earth's population will be living in cities and towns. These two related events are certainly the most remarkable change in the human condition that has occurred for a very long time.

Most natural scientists adopt the Malthusian view of population, i.e., that human beings will multiply in numbers, by an exponential increase, up to the limits set by the food supply or by some other natural resource. It is for this reason that they feel that the present rates of population growth are very disturbing.

The first thing we have to ask ourselves is what are the conceivable limits of the numbers of people that the earth could support? With our present technology and agriculture, let's say that the primary problem is food supply, although, of course, there are other problems too. If we look at the potential food supply alone, it's probably true that the earth could support close to thirty times the present population, in terms of food. It would be possible to feed that many people on a physiologically adequate but not very satisfying diet. What we mean by this is that supposing that each person requires in terms of primary plant food, food produced by plants, somewhere between 2,000 and 3,000 kilogram calories a day—that kind of food production is certainly foreseeable from the presently cultivatable, not necessarily cultivated but cultivatable land. The total amount of land that we now cultivate is about three and a half thousand million acres. This quantity of land can probably be expanded to eight thousand million acres. Not that it would be a good thing to do, but it is something that could be done.

Why is it not a good thing to do?

Because most of the land that isn't now cultivated would be difficult and expensive to cultivate.

It would need enormous investments.

That's right, quite large investments.

And insecticides and fertilizers. It would contaminate the earth even further.

Yes, that's right. And water, large quantities of water. With the present rate of population growth it would take something like a hundred and fifty years before we get up to thirty times the present population. The earth's population is now doubling about once every thirty years. At this rate the population would go up eight times in ninety years, sixteen times in a hundred and twenty years or thirty-two times in a hundred and fifty years. As far as we can see, this would be—with our present agricultural technology and methods of food production—about the limit the planet could support.

One can argue, and people do argue, that the technology of food production is improving. We won't have to depend upon agriculture for the indefinite future, provided we have enough energy. This brings us to the more fundamental problem. Is there enough energy available? The total amount of energy locked in fossil fuels is probably limited at presently foreseeable rates of energy utilization to at most a few hundred years. By fossil fuels I mean, coal, oil and natural gas. Oil shales and tar sands are another form of concentrated organic matter in sedimentary rocks. As long as we depend on this kind of energy source, the available energy will last only a few hundred years. Both from the standpoint of food supply and from the standpoint of energy from fossil fuels—organic matter in the rocks—one can see a very definite limit.

The other two things that people worry about are the supply of other kinds of natural resources such as iron, aluminum, copper, zinc, chromium, lead, helium and mercury, and pollution. If the most of the future people in the world live at a so-called standard of living comparable to that of Western Europe or the United States, the waste products of civilization would be so great that we would drown in our own filth.

When we use a kind of mechanistic or deterministic model, it can be demonstrated that if populations continue to grow with a doubling time of thirty to thirty-five years, eventually there will be a limit. Eventually the growth of population will be limited by food supply, or by energy, or by other natural resources, or by pollution. This is essentially the thesis of the people who wrote the report *Limits to Growth*, and of Professor Forrester, who developed the more fundamental model, *World Dynamics*.[1]

It seems to me that one has to ask several very serious questions about this particular set of models of the earth. First, and I guess the most important question, is this: Is there any historical evidence—from what we know about human behavior—to believe that in fact Malthus was right, that the human population does keep on growing up to the limits of the food supply? The Malthusian "principle on population" is a mechanistic notion. It says that human beings do not act in their own interest, that human beings are automata, that they don't have any freedom of action and that they are helpless in the face of their own biology and their own environment.

There is very little historical evidence that this is so. On the contrary, there is lots of evidence that in fact people do control their own fertility, control their own population growth, if they see a reason to do so. It is not very well understood just what are the forces or what are the conditions which cause them to do this. Nevertheless, the historical evidence is that they do it. To take the most recent piece of historical evidence, in many of the so-called developed countries, not all, but many, including most of the socialist countries of Eastern Europe, the Russian and Ukrainian part of the Soviet Union, northern Italy, the Scandinavian countries, the United States, and Japan, the birth rate has come down very fast over the last thirty to forty years. The birth rate in the United States now is probably just about at the replacement rate, which means that each woman is having just enough children to reproduce herself. Putting this in American terms it means she will be having about 2.1 or 2.2 children. More than half of those are boys. (There are three to five percent more boys born than there are girls.) Very few children in the rich countries die before they grow up and become able to reproduce. About two percent of the children who are born die before the age of one, and less than another one percent before they are able to reproduce themselves. So, somewhere around 2.2 live births per woman is what the demographers call a net replacement rate of one. And this is just about the number of children that in fact women in the United States are now having. Take the present fertility rate and spread it over the reproductive lifetime of women in the United States, that's the way it would turn out. The birth rate has been dropping very fast for the last seven or eight years, both among the whites and among the Negroes in the United States.

I think it is not unlikely that in all the developed countries we will find within the next ten years that women are not having enough children to replace themselves. Why this is so is not understood, but there are several possible explanations. Perhaps the most general is that the psychic, economic and social benefits that children bring to people, to potential parents, are not as great as they used to be. In the United States, a hundred and seventy years ago, the average woman had seven children. The number of children per woman has been coming down throughout the last hundred and seventy years. It reached a low point in the 1930s and went up again with the baby boom in the 1950s, but now it's coming down again.

Many people will say that this is all very well, but most of the world's population doesn't live in the developed countries, the rich, affluent countries, but in poor countries. And in the poor countries the birth rates have not yet come down, whereas the death rates are just about as low in the poor countries as in the rich ones. What has caused the enormous growth of population in the Third World is the fact that the birth rates have not come down but death rates have. For example in India, in Pakistan, and in Bangladesh, the average life expectance in 1920 was between twenty and twenty-five years. That means that a baby at birth could look forward to an expectation of life of about twenty-two or twenty-three years. It does not mean that the average person who survived for just a few years of life only lived twenty-two or twenty-three years. About half of the children died before the age of ten.

Now the life expectancy in India, Bangladesh and Pakistan is about fifty years. It's even higher in South America. It's lower in Africa, but in the Third World as a whole there's been maybe an increase of two and a half times in life expectancy during the last fifty years. Little decline in birth rates has occurred during this period, and that's what has caused the so-called population explosions, the enormously rapid rate of population growth. The average woman in a developing country gives birth to four or five children, often six or seven children. These infants are surviving now, not all of them, but eighty percent of them survive beyond adolescence. In the developed world, the average woman has a little over two children, but nearly all children survive and grow up.

Venezuela has a population-growth rate of over three percent, and yet it has a high income. Also Brazil and Mexico. Their per capita incomes are going up quite rapidly, even though the population is also going up very fast. Is there an explanation?

The explanation probably is that a great many people in Brazil and Mexico are not sharing in the apparent prosperity of the country as a whole. These countries have what used to be called two-nation societies, societies in which the poor remain poor, while the rich get richer.

The gap grows wider—

—there is a modern sector in which people are getting rich and a traditional sector in which people are in some ways worse off than they were before. That seems to be true for Mexico and Brazil; it is certainly true for Venezuela.

Now there is another country, which is perhaps the most important of all from the standpoint of population, and that is China.

About one out of every four people on earth is a Chinese. Very little is known about this enormous country. They have had only one census in modern times. This was in 1953. We don't really know what the Chinese birth rate is, what the death rate is or how these rates have been changing. We don't even know how many people there are in China. It may be perhaps a hundred or two hundred million people more than we think. There aren't many statistics. The Chinese have never been very much interested in statistics. They neither gather them nor publish them. The best thing we can do with China is to have a sort of impressionistic view of it.

* * *

The Limits to Growth *study was meant as a contribution to study how to achieve equilibrium after an era of sheer unlimited expansion and growth.*

Yes, there is no question about the fact that we have to arrive at a steady-state world. I mean, the world cannot possibly continue its exponential growth. The nature of exponential growth is that sooner or later things blow up. My principal criticism of the *Limits to Growth* is that the authors assume that exponential growth is bound to continue until a catastrophe stops it. It is not bound to continue at all. Exponential growth usually occurs only during a transition period. We are living now in one of the great transitions of human history. Toynbee has said that we live at the hinge of history. We are changing from one kind of world to another. The kind of world that has to exist in the future—not that ought to exist but has to exist—must be a more or less steady-state world.

The question is what kind of a steady-state world is it going to be? One possibility is a world with a population of around twelve billion people, ten to twelve billion people, with adequate food supply for all, resources adequate for all, a good life in material terms for everyone, and pollution under control. The extreme alternative to this is another kind of steady-state world in which we have somewhere between fifty and a hundred billion people, in which the death rate has risen to match the birth rate, in which most people never get enough to eat (which is the reason why the death rate would have risen to match the birth rate), in which poverty is almost a universal human condition, and the future is essentially hopeless, because we will have used up most of the natural resources. Mankind will live in a very limited way; most people will have just a bare existence under quite unpleasant conditions.

The real problem is what kind of a steady-state world do we aim for. But *Limits to Growth* says something worse than this: They say that the future course of events is a continuing rise and then a collapse, not a gradual approach to a steady-state, no matter how bad, but an overshooting of the use of resources, an overshooting of population, production and economic growth and then a rapid and catastrophic decline of production, population and available resources.

The argument hangs on the kind of model one builds. The model MIT built depends on continuation of exponential change. But first, exponential change cannot continue; and second, it need not continue. Instead of continuing exponential growth, one can equally well expect an S-shaped curve with growth slowing down as it approaches a limit. The economy and the population grow less and less rapidly rather than grow-ing faster and faster, and then collapsing. We are now down here . . . going up like this . . . but eventually growth can slow down and taper off.

They tried to prove that a breaking point will occur unless we do some-thing fast—unless we change the curves, change the trends.

Their main point is that unless we start doing something right now, we will end up with this collapse. What I would argue is that they put things in the wrong priority. In order to bring the birth rate down, in order to create the conditions in which people see their own interest in having smaller families, we need a continuation of economic develop-ment, particularly in the developing countries. In my opinion, it is essen-tially impossible, on the basis of experience to date, to expect people in these countries to behave in a way that will stabilize population, bring population to a stationary level, unless they have sufficient economic development so that they see some reason for doing so. It's a very easy solution on the part of us Westerners, on the part of the rich countries, to say to the people of the poor countries, you cannot possibly develop, because the resources are not available, because there would be too much pollution.

If people are going to limit their own fertility, and if we are all going to come to a point where we live in a stable, peaceful, relatively happy world, we must have more worldwide economic and social development. The question is: Are resources sufficient and can pollution be controlled? Is it possible to have economic growth without too much pollution? I think that we have to search a good deal deeper than the *Limits to Growth* people have looked.

NOTES

[1]See conversation no. 34, bibliography.

29. Edward T. Hall

Professor Edward T. Hall was born in Webster Groves, Missouri, in 1914. He studied anthropology at the University of Denver, the University of Arizona and obtained in 1942 a Ph.D. at Columbia University.

In 1946 he was appointed chairman of the department of anthropology at the University of Denver. From 1959 to 1963 he was director of the communications research project at the Washington school of psychiatry, became professor of anthropology at the Illinois Institute of Technology in 1963, and since 1967 he has been professor of anthropology at the college of arts and sciences and professor of organization theory at the graduate school of management at Northwestern University at Evanston, Illinois.

His two best-known books are *The Hidden Dimension* (1966) and *The Silent Language* (1969).

You have written in The Silent Language *that all living beings have a physical boundary that separates them from the external environment, beginning with the bacteria and ending with man himself. You stressed that every organism has a detectable limit where it begins and where it ends.*[1] Limits to Growth *is an effort to figure out the limits of man's capabilities to explore, to destroy the environment, to deplete resources, in other words an effort to start the management of the globe in a rational way.*

Certainly, the planet too, has a detectable limit. In *The Silent Language*, I was thinking about intercultural relations, not about the globe as a whole. Quite clearly one should say that you begin with the bacteria and you end with the earth. My reason for talking about bacteria and man in the same sentence was that people forget that they are first, last and always living biological organisms. That they must ultimately obey the laws of the universe. And if you violate the laws of the universe you do so at your own risk. The problem that man is facing right now is that he inevitably confuses his extensions with the thing that is being extended, in other words, extensions with reality. So that you have to keep bringing man back to the point where he begins to experience himself as a living thing. We wouldn't do the things that we do to the environment if we had not lost some of our humanness.

In regard to *Limits to Growth*, quite clearly the idea of establishing what the limits are is not only valid but essential. Unfortunately these studies have been criticized because the number of relationships which are actually involved are more complex than the ones which were taken into account. As far as I know, the people of MIT will be the first ones to admit as much. But you have to start somewhere. Nevertheless, we should also look inside man's head, because it is a much better computer than anything yet designed.

Man has developed his territoriality to an almost unbelievable extent. We treat space somewhat as we treat sex: We do not talk about it. While man is fleeing into space, it seems to me that you want him to rediscover himself, his humanness.

You have a very good point there. We can escape into space. We can also play with things, big toys. There is nothing wrong with that. But human beings are complex. As you suggested, they sometimes use these toys to evade the basic human issues which are here on the earth. Yet this is not always so. One of the byproducts of going to the moon was that for the first time men saw the earth and realized how small it is. Which brings us again back to the point which we were talking about earlier, that the earth is really limited. It is hard for human beings to realize that the system that we are dealing with is not limitless, that it is delicate and fragile and that we have to treat it with extreme care. In one sense it is like a flower. I mean that it has to be cultivated with care and a great deal of affection. Unfortunately we haven't reached that point as yet. Let's hope that we do before we destroy the earth's ecosystem.

You know the famous saying by Thomas Wolfe, "The surest cure for vanity is loneliness." Nobody would deny this value of being able to be alone, but man has less and less a chance to be alone ever.

This is the subject for an entire book. My book, *The Hidden Dimension*, deals with one corner of this very complicated subject. Quite clearly people need to be alone at times. However, the *way* in which people like to be alone varies, a matter which is not widely understood. For an upper-class Englishman, for instance, in order to be alone, all he does is simply stop talking and the people in his household are supposed to know that he does not want to be bothered. If he is a German, on the other hand, he goes behind a door, a very thick door, even a double door and he closes it. The German needs those doors and he needs those walls to screen out the sound.

I have called these two types of people screen-dependent and screen-independent. Some people have to have screens. They are brought up that way. Your own countrymen have the same thing. Which brings up the problem with the new architecture and the buildings being built today. They are too cheap (not solid). The sounds penetrate the walls and people are no longer alone in their own homes. This can be serious and stressful. A countryman of yours, Dr. Fiedeldÿ Dop, has studied children brought up in these new apartments where the parents don't allow them to play with blocks, because when the blocks fall down, the people underneath would be disturbed. They can't roughhouse or make noise. This way the children don't develop. They cannot play the way children should be able to play. It's because of the design of the houses. Does it pay to save a few *guilders* on the houses but destroy the people in them? How does this happen? Fiedeldÿ Dop has discovered the relationship of learning to use of the muscles is close. If children can't crawl on the floor, can't climb, can't exercise, then these children have trouble learning.

But the being-alone thing is complex. First, it is cultural. For the Arab countries, a man who wants to be alone is thought to be crazy. If an Arab goes to his room and closes the door, other people begin to think about calling a psychiatrist. There is an Arab saying that paradise without people is hell. Once when I was questioning Arabs on their use of space, I would ask, "Where do you go to be alone?" They would reply, "Who wants to be alone?" Or they say, "Who wants to be crazy?" So it depends upon your culture and who you are.

I think of something Nietzsche[2] once said, "We have art in order not to die of the truth." You attach great importance to artists. As a matter of fact, you wrote that the history of art is ten times as long as the history of writing.[3] You hold there is much to be learned from the way artists perceive the world.

Again, this is not a simple idea. The first cave painting is art. Art dates back at least forty thousand years, while the earliest writing began about four or five thousand years ago. I cannot imagine a world without art. I cannot imagine myself living without art. The reasons I have art is because I enjoy it, and besides, I learned so much from my paintings.

Rembrandt[4] was a revolutionary painter in his time. Because perception has to do with a man's experience of space, I studied Rembrandt along with other artists. You can observe the actual way in which the retina sees from studying Rembrandt's paintings. As you undoubtedly know, there are usually one or two or three places in his painting that are very sharp and clear. If you fix your eye on one of those places and then find the right distance from the painting, the sharpness fades at precisely the rate as the sharpness of the eye fades as it leaves the center and approaches the periphery. When the viewer looks at Rembrandt's painting right, they are three dimensional. They look real. To do this, pick the sharp place and then don't move your eye. It is as though the subject was in the room with you. Rembrandt, as you can tell from this, was deeply interested with how man sees. Whereas the painters of his time were much more controlled by convention.

Take Mondriaan.[5] You get a very different picture. One would think that a Mondriaan work is just a series of lines, but there is more to it than that. Mondriaan is helping to map the visual part of the brain. We know this because of recent work on the visual cortex. Most of all it sees edges. Imagine what it would be like not to be able to see edges. If you cannot see an edge, you will bump into things, fall over curbs, over cliffs, you couldn't distinguish objects from each other. The visual cortex of the brain structures these edges so that they are magnified as it were so that man can detect the slightest movement in nature. What Mondriaan did without knowing about the brain was to emphasize the edges.

Picasso[6] is another of my favorites. He really started something. We now have a cartoon strip in the United States, Miss Peach, that is drawn with the eyes on the side of the face and nobody notices it. It looks so natural. Picasso was just ahead of his time. Just look at his paintings and his drawings, you can tell in many cases how he was feeling when he was working. He is so clear and so natural and so much at ease that he is like a skier who has been skiing all of his life. The skis are not separate from him, they are part of him. He is not doing this consciously anymore. He is doing it just the way we talk, completely naturally.

You have written that there are different sensory worlds between races and cultures, Americans and Arabs, different touch, different emotions.[7]

In organizing this planet like Limits to Growth *intends to do, how to improve the model in dealing with entirely different cultures across the globe? How could this be brought into the study of organizing global management?*

This is the problem which faces the educator today. How do you deal with the child who is different? We've discovered that they are almost all different. That's the question that faces the town planner. People with different sensory needs are beginning to occupy the same towns. The problem that you raise is, How do you design for the different kinds of people?

How can the systems-dynamics people bring variables into their model, assisted by anthropologists? As it stands now, professional jealousies of scientists seem to outweigh a combined effort for planetary research.

I don't know what can be done about academicians.

You should be in the model.

We clearly should be in the model. We should be working with these people at MIT.

Tinbergen,[8] in Holland, is working now on a second model. But you people are the ones that should definitely come in most urgently.

Tinbergen, for instance, would be one of the first ones to bring in to the model, because Forrester and the MIT computer people will understand Tinbergen's system. They are simple systems and human systems in the first place, and Tinbergen is a beautiful scientist. His work is impeccable.

I was speaking of the economist Tinbergen.

No, I mean Nico Tinbergen, the ethologist. He was originally also Dutch, wasn't he? He deals with systems, with living systems. And if we could get the ethologists working with the systems people for us, and then bring in the anthropologists, the sociologists and so on.

Is that the way it should be done?

* * *

I would suggest that we operate in stages. One always starts with the thing one can do, then you move on to the thing which is a little more complicated, a little more difficult. We need two things: ideas and people. Who can put them together? It is really difficult to say which is more important, because right now the cliché is king. I'll leave it at that.

Yes, but the world is ruled by politicians and would-be statesmen. How can the scientists, the knowledgeable people, start to have influence? Because this planet needs management of knowledge, not nonsensical propaganda or flat lies by politicians in order to get votes.

Now we are talking about the future and McLuhan's[9] extensions of man. The extension is the enemy of comprehensive thinking. Somehow we are going to have to overcome the linear functions of extensions and to get back to the comprehensive sort of thing. This is the basic revolution. We are in the process of moving from a linear type of thinking to a comprehensive type of thinking.

It is your opinion that most of the asocial behavior that we see around us does not necessarily spring from malice, but from ignorance. We have to redesign the entire educational system, it needs revolutionary changes.

True, the schools need to be revamped and in many cases torn down and rebuilt and furnished with new ideas. That will take time. However, we could begin with those scientists who are building bridges to other disciplines. Maybe they would bring some of the others along with them. I mean, we start with people who are making connections, putting things together, willing to go outside of their field. In my case, I must have dealt at one time or another in my life with almost a dozen different fields.

NOTES

[1] *The Silent Language*, p. 146.
[2] Friedrich Wilhelm Nietzsche (1844-1900), German philosopher.
[3] *The Hidden Dimension*, p. 81.
[4] Rembrandt Harmensz van Rijn (1606-69), Dutch painter and etcher.
[5] Piet Mondriaan (1872-1944), Dutch painter.
[6] Pablo Picasso (1881-1973), Spanish painter and sculptor.
[7] *The Hidden Dimension*, p. 3.
[8] See conversation no. 3.
[9] See conversation no. 12.

30. Maurice F. Strong

Maurice F. Strong was appointed secretary-general of the United Nations Conference on the Human Environment (UNCHE) in November, 1970. Prior to this appointment he was president of the Canadian Development Agency and had extensive experience in the field of business and public affairs.

Mr. Strong was born in Oak Lake, Manitoba, Canada, in 1929. He was educated in Canada and served as visiting professor at York University in Toronto.

He was adviser to the government of Canada on various economic and international matters until 1966, when he became director general of the External Aid Office of the government of Canada with the rank of deputy minister.

Maurice Strong was a driving force behind the World Conference on the Environment held in Stockholm, Sweden, June 5-16, 1972, and contributed considerably to its success.

Would you agree with Limits to Growth *that the most urgent problem now is managing growth globally?*

This really is at the heart of the problem that man faces at this point. In my view not only because of some of the reasons elicited in the book *Limits to Growth* but probably for even more profound reasons than that, reasons that man has come to an important juncture in his own development for the first time in the history of the evolution of the human race. The future of mankind is now dependent upon the actions which man himself takes.

Don't you feel that it is absolutely essential to obtain commitments from governments as to their responsibilities to the environment?

I believe that *Limits to Growth* is important, really, in the way in which it makes us think about these problems more than in any of the specific conclusions to which it points. *Limits to Growth* has made its major contribution by the very fact that it has made men and particularly leaders address themselves to the fundamental problem of how man is going to manage the world's first high-technology civilization and the proliferation of complex interdependencies that technology has produced. It has made us realize in very simple terms that this physical system of interdependencies upon which man depends is in fact global and that it has to be seen as global, that it has to be dealt with and managed as a global unit.

And contrast this with the actual institutions through which man is attempting to manage the processes of his own development, which are clearly sectoral, clearly national, clearly inadequate to the task of global management. In larger terms, the fact that *Limits to Growth* has made people look at these problems is one of its major contributions. The *Limits to Growth* idea supports the whole concept of Stockholm,[1] that is, the growing need for man to acquire the economic and social and political instruments to deal with new interdependencies.

The second area in which I believe *Limits to Growth* has made an important contribution is in the area of methodology and the fact that this study is based on the very simple premise that these newly discovered interdependencies are complicated. It's very difficult without using the latest technological tools—the computer, for example, and computer modeling techniques—to really understand how these interdependencies are operating, how the causes and effects, which are separated very often by dimensions of space and time, and go beyond our normal abilities to measure and to judge how they really do react on each other and use this to determine the course of our own future evolution. The architects of *Limits to Growth* themselves are the first to acknowledge how primitive the beginning they have made was.

You realize Tinbergen[2] and Professor Hans Linneman are now working with a Dutch-Swedish team on a second World Project model for the Club of Rome in the Netherlands?

Indeed. This again is an enlargement of the original model of Forrester and Dennis Meadows, a model, which I have had the pleasure of following right from the beginning. I found it most intriguing and extremely interesting and helpful. Even the people who have created this model have acknowledged that it was just a beginning.

From your experience at the 1972 Stockholm conference, would you say that the developing nations need Japan's warning: Don't do what we

did, don't grow unplanned, don't have this mad, out-of-proportion explo-
sion of technological and economic growth without planning?

I think we at Stockholm began to address ourselves with some of the very, very deep and important long-range questions that studies like *Limits to Growth* point out. That is, how do we create a kind of balance in our approach to global growth? How do we create a situation in which the two-thirds of the people of the world who do command a large part of the world's territory, a large part of the world's natural resources, how these people could be brought into the mainstream of the technological civilization. And in doing so, how could they acquire their fair share of the kind of higher dimensions of life that it makes possible?

Clearly that is not happening today. Clearly what is happening is that the very technology which is giving man both this new power for creative growth and at the same time this new powerful potential for self-destruction, that this power is largely in the hands of the highly industrialized nations. Since this command of technology, of scientific knowledge, is the main source of power in today's world, we will have to find a much better way of using and sharing that power. We will have to find a much more rational basis for the use of the world's resources.

Do you truly believe in the redistribution of wealth and resources in a more honest way with developing nations?

I think that what we have to recognize is that this will not come about because of any world master plan or any creation of any supranational instruments. If *Limits to Growth* is correct about the growing scarcity of resources, then this will place in the hands of the developing countries, who command many of these natural resources, new levers which they would be able to use in their negotiations with rich countries. Oil is a very good example. The oil-producing countries have banded together through OPEC and have demonstrated the fact that the leverage which they have with the consuming countries by supplying a commodity of growing scarcity is very considerable indeed.

I like to see myself as an idealist; I believe, therefore, that the world is not going to be remade through simple processes of supranationalism and the assumption that everybody is going to embrace suddenly idealistic conceptions of man's relationship with his fellow man. I believe it will happen by a realization first and foremost that the new interdependencies created by the high-technology civilization simply require us to cooperate, to share more, to care more about each other, to work more together than we have ever done before. This will have to be done for our mutual survival. That is the basic common denominator. Secondly, the growing scarcity of natural resources and the growing problems of the rich countries do create a new possibility of leverage for the developing world. This can be used in a creative, constructive manner to give them some of the bargaining power that will help to redress the tremendous imbalance that now exists.

None of the rich nations have even reached one percent yet in assistance to the developing nations.

We have to recognize that some of the traditional approaches to foreign aid have got to be substantially modified. If we look at our own national societies, charity has never been a durable basis for the relationship between rich and poor. In our national societies we quickly replaced original programs based on pure give-away or even tied give-away programs with a much more objective and impersonal system for the redistribution of wealth. The equalization of opportunity and foreign-aid programs represents only the primitive beginning of the extension of this process into international life.

As such, we are going to have to move into a system in international life that corresponds to the kind of systems many nations have created internally, where there are more impersonal and objective mechanisms for the redistribution of wealth and the equalization of opportunity. We have to look upon aid programs as the beginning of that evolution. This is why I believe so strongly that the political and economic leverage which the developing world can muster is one of the keys to a more balanced development pattern around the world, one of the keys to their achieving a fair share of the world's opportunities and resources.

I don't mean this leads necessarily to open conflict. But remember again, back in our national societies, it was only when the poor acquired through the vote and through other means, through social and political action—only when they acquired the knowledge of their own power and learned how to use it—that they really gained any permanent improvement in their lot in society. This is true for all societies. Only when the poor nations acquire a better understanding of their own intrinsic possibilities, potentials, their own understanding not only of their own power but their own responsibilities as well, will they be able to come to the bargaining table with the industrialized countries and maximize those advantages across that bargaining table. It's only through these processes that we are going to get a better distribution of the world's opportunities and resources.

How is Earth Watch working after Stockholm? That's your baby.

Yes. Earth Watch is just in its beginning stages. Earth Watch will knit together a large number of institutions that exist around the world today. These are institutions and centers of expertise that will help throw up the kind of data, the kind of information, the kind of evaluations that will permit not only the world decision-makers but also the people who are affected by these decisions to understand the important consequences for mankind about the decisions that are going to be taken. Stockholm gives us the mandate to create Earth Watch. The 1972-73 General Assembly of the United Nations provided us with the resources that will make the work possible.

You said minutes ago, "I am an idealist." You ran away at the age of thirteen, worked for a while as a trapper and climbed very rapidly to president of one of the biggest corporations in Canada, and now you are doing this work, purely humanitarian, in the interest of all mankind. What motivated you to throw away your powerful position in the financial world and work for mankind?

First of all, I would have to say that I am doing what I am now doing for the most selfish of reasons, because I happen to enjoy it. I get satisfaction out of dealing with issues that I think are important issues. I made an analysis when I was in the business world. I looked around and came to the conclusion that purely success in material terms, purely success in economic terms, is not satisfying for society as a whole, is not satisfying except for certain individuals. The job of helping so many subtotal societies is more challenging work, is a more thrilling job. In the final analysis, perhaps, this is even a more useful job than the job of managing one little segment of society which happens to be devoted solely to the pursuit of material gain. I have to say that I am doing what I am doing because I like it, and probably that is as selfish a thing as I could say.

Let's hope you also set an example for some of the other tycoons around the world to follow your example by enlarging material gains to social gains, to gains for the benefit of all mankind. I wish more industrialists would follow your example.

Thank you. Really, I have been influenced very strongly by the example of others. I can say that there are many people I know in the business world who feel the same way and who envy me because I have had an opportunity to express these interests, an opportunity that really is denied to other people. I am very lucky in this sense. But, you know, look at it very simplistically: I have five children. At some point in one's life one looks at the future and says, What can you really leave for your children that is useful and durable? If you think of it only in terms of big bank accounts or big trust funds, it's really building your house on sand. If this is what you leave them, at the same time you hand them over to a society in which material things are simply going to be gradually or maybe even quickly enveloped in a great morass of social decay and degeneration. We cannot any longer assume that we are taking care of our families by simply leaving them fat bank accounts. We have got to leave future generations a more vital, a more dynamic society.

NOTES

[1]World Conference on the Human Environment, June 5-16, 1972.
[2]See conversation no. 3.

31. *Carl R. Rogers*

Carl Ransom Rogers was born in Oak Park, Illinois, in 1902. He received his Ph.D. in psychology from Columbia University in 1928.

He first worked with children in the Society for Prevention of Cruelty to Children in Rochester, New York. Then he taught psychology and psychiatry at the Universities of Chicago and Wisconsin. Subsequently he came to La Jolla, California, where he was connected at first with the Western Behavioral Sciences Institute and is now with the Center of Studies of the Person.

Professor Rogers ranks among the great psychologists of our day. In 1931 he published *Measuring Personality Adjustment in Children*; in 1951, the by now classic study *Client-Centered Therapy*; and in 1961, *On Becoming a Person*. His latest works are *Freedom to Learn* (1969) and *On Encounter Groups* (1970).

Professor Carl Rogers' house in San Diego, California,
6 October, 1972

I understand from your past that your initial love for nature, biology, agriculture, indicates that you would have sympathy for an endeavor like that of the Club of Rome. Your own love for the planet would come in here.

Yes. I feel that the planet is in great danger at this point. It is true that I feel that my love of nature and my love for nature as revealed in persons would both cause me to be very much interested in the question of how we might preserve this earth from destruction.

Your main interest lies with the individual. How to save the individual, because you would expect this world to be more and more controlled, more and more programmed. That's actually what Skinner says. We are victims of this environment. We need to redesign the environment. You believe that there is still a place for the individual even when space keeps shrinking?

Yes, I think that if we become more and more programmed, there's someone who is going to do the programming. This is the thing that Skinner does not like to talk about. Someone would have to do the programming. In other words, you've got to have some people who are free to make the plans to control all the rest of us. I feel that that road does lead to the destruction of individuality. I do prize the individual person, because the individual person is the reservoir of creativity. I feel that our efforts ought to be to release the individual to be his own freest, purest self, rather than our efforts being devoted to controlling him.

As a part of my belief in nature I think that the human species is by nature social. Not every species is social. The cat family is not very social. They are naturally loners for the most part. But the human being —coming as he does from the apes—is naturally social. So I believe—if individuals can truly be themselves, can be aware of what's going on within themselves and aware of their interpersonal relationships—they prefer harmony to discord, prefer constructive action to destructive action.

Yes, but the space for human beings is becoming smaller, shrinks—seven billion people in the year 2000. What institutional and organizational means for authority would be useful or possible to program behavior? I understand that you feel that our final behavior—you said some-where—will not be controlled, but the inclination to behave a certain way will be controlled. You don't believe that you can program behavior, do you?

I think that you can program behavior for a time or within limits, but that the free human spirit breaks through it. This is what I think occurs in Russia and in other places. But to return first to your main question, I agree that physical space is shrinking as we increase speeds. The actual physical space for each individual is shrinking as we let population zoom out of control. Those things are desperately serious problems.

My experience with individuals and with small groups—with small antagonistic groups—gives me some optimism. Individuals can communicate with each other at a deeper level and then can begin to resolve the problems that they are facing. What are we going to do about population? What are we going to do about pollution?

Pollution is a good example. I feel that the American people have at some fairly deep level made the choice that they are going to do something about pollution. It may take decades. They may even fail, but I think that the beginning has been made. The *decision* has been made.

In regard to the population explosion, it is uncertain as to whether the people in general have really come to a decision. I think they have in some countries. Probably India has faced up to the fact that it must control population. Much depends on the decisions that are made at a very deep level within the whole population.

How to influence the decision-makers? How to make people more aware that there is an emergency, that we are in a state of war?

I like your second phrase much better. Not how do we control the decision-makers, but how do we encourage them to make rational decisions. I like to engage in a little fantasy. So far, our relationships between nations have always been on a very formal basis. If you are the envoy of one country, you have been instructed by your government as to just what position to take. You cannot deviate from that. I am instructed by my government. I cannot deviate from that position. That approach guarantees there will be no real solution of the problems.

I have had a fantasy that if we, at the same time that there is a diplomatic conference—like the conference in Paris at the present time between the warring forces about Vietnam—if along with the formal diplomatic delegation, another group was chosen of equally prominent citizens on both sides who had no obligation to speak for their government, but who would simply be speaking for themselves, then I think those two groups would find that gradually they would move toward a common ground of agreement and perhaps that that common ground of agreement could then be interpreted or passed on to the far more rigid diplomats and governments.

I don't care how antagonistic they might be at the start, if they met with a psychologist who was trained in facilitating communication. I feel there is no question but that citizens of North Vietnam meeting with citizens representing the Vietcong and citizens representing the United States and citizens of South Vietnam could come to some kind of resolution.

Would we not probably also need psychologists to improve communication between politicians and their own electorate? Because the amount of lies and untruths that are now being spoken in order to get throngs of electorates behind false assumptions and false presentations just for votes is absolutely shocking and self-defeating. Could psychologists not interfere first at their homeground?

I would certainly hope that might be true. I only know of one or two politicians who are really attempting that. There is one in the state legislature in California who is trying to communicate *honestly* with his constituents. But by and large, without knowing other countries well enough to pass judgment, I feel that hypocrisy has grown to such gigantic proportions in this country that it would take tremendous skill to change the situation. First of all, it would take a willingness on the part of the politicians really to communicate with the people and to receive the communications of people in return. I am not sure that this willingness exists.

What role could the behaviorists and the psychologists play to promote the speeding up of a change in the politicians?

I think we are doing that in various ways. For example, there was a most promising attempt at holding what I would think of as encounter groups or human-relations laboratories with members of the state department, ambassadors and their staffs. They were enthusiastic about it. They wished to take it to the host countries so that they could begin similar groups between the American representatives and the representatives of the country to whom they were sent.

Later the whole project was wiped out for lack of funds.

This was one small start. But there will be more starts. My only question is, Will they occur in time? We have done a great deal on a very small scale. The accomplishments have been exciting in relieving racial tension through improving communication between black groups and the establishment, between Mexican groups and the establishment. I don't think it's hopeless. The behavioral scientists are at the same point as the Wright brothers when they first took off in their flimsy little plane. No one would believe it. No one felt that it had any significance. The public was not yet ready to buy the idea. I feel we have made a number of small flights like that, but so far the public as a whole does not have the confidence in the behavioral scientists that it has in the physical scientists, for example.

Professor Rogers, how about the communication between the rich Western world and the rest of the world? Where to start building real bridges with Chinese, Indians, Africans and Latin Americans, as you would say, based on being what you are?

My experience there leads me to be optimistic, when groups are not bound by some rigid control of instructions. I have dealt with groups in France, I have dealt with groups in Japan, in Australia, in other countries. In every case, to be sure, the customs were different, the traditions were different. Yet if individuals are permitted to talk beyond those customs and traditions, freely, and with someone to help each side understand the other, then you begin to get deeper personal communication. It is very similar in each of the cultures with which I am familiar.

Starting from, let's say, individual freedom as a principle—twenty years ago or eighteen years ago you had a discussion, a dialogue with your colleague at Harvard, Skinner. Looking back, do you feel the world is moving towards a Skinnerian view or a Rogerian view? What is happening?

I feel that academic psychology in this country is clearly moving in a Skinnerian direction. There is no question in my mind about that. On the other hand, I do not believe that the Skinnerian point of view is very attractive to sophisticated foreign countries. I believe that more and more voices are coming out on the side of the human individual in what I think is the deepest force in psychology, the humanistic trend. I think Freudianism is dead, though its funeral has been long delayed. I think that behaviorism, the Skinnerian point of view, has a great deal of appeal to the American culture, because it fits in with our love for technology. Here is a technology by which we can control behavior, so that must be the best way. But I actually think that time is on the side of the trend to a belief in the individual.

You, I understand, prize the privilege of being alone very much in your life, and call it your most fruitful period.[1] Is there sufficient room to be alone in our modern world with the growth of population and acceleration of directives and the intensification of programming our lives? Students in Holland cannot study anymore what they want. They cannot choose. They have been told at times to break off their studies altogether because there were too many in certain fields. Where is the hope for the individual?

I suppose my answer to that is a very radical one. I think that most of the established institutions in our society are strangling the hope of the future. I believe this is true of education. I believe this is true of the church. I believe this is true of marriage if you regard it as an institution. That is why I titled my recent book *Becoming Partners*, not necessarily becoming married. I think government is perhaps—especially in this country—the most powerful of all in strangling the hope of the future.

This is where I place my reliance on young people, because one of the primary values that they hold is the value of being themselves, being genuine. They are no longer willing to say, "Well, of course I have to accept a nine-to-five job, working for this corporation and do it the rest of my life." They are not willing to say that. Nor are they willing even to say, "Yes, I must serve my country in the draft even though

I don't believe in war." More and more of them are saying, "No, I will not do that. I have my life to live. I will not be bound by institutions." Some of the best students are leaving our universities not because they couldn't get through but because they refuse to submit to this programming that we are prescribing. Exactly what will come from that—I am really not a prophet—I am not certain. It will be something freer, looser, more communicative, more real. That I do think.

Gabriel Marcel[2] spoke of our possessions that devour us. "How other than to program the mass" of people or the young and turn the tide away from this mad race for material gain?

I don't believe that the place of the psychologist is as a missionary to turn the tide away from material things. I think that tide is already appearing and the psychologists had better understand that, just as they should understand that the tide is turning away from rigidity in education. I believe that young people are accustomed to using material things and use them very casually, without much thought. Yet when it comes to a choice between material possessions and being themselves, the trend is toward the latter. I don't believe that the young are going to fall back into being stockbrokers and suburbanites. To be sure, some will. That's to be expected. But I think we are seeing a real turning in the tide of the goals of young people in this nation.

What role can you people play in improving a planetary model in order to study what is needed to be done to achieve survival? Do you see a role at all?

First of all, I would like to be a little more clear as to your question.

This is the question: The model was made by system-analysts. Some economists have objections. A second model is being prepared. I wonder where do the psychologists and behaviorists come in? Could they come in, and should they come in, and are you behind the effort of studying this, and are you also in favor of using computers in this study? Do you use them yourself in your study of behavior of groups?

I think that behavioral scientists, including psychologists, should have a very real part to play in developing the factors that enter into any model of what this planet is going to be like. I think it has been shown time and again that psychological factors are far more important than the factors that often are given great credence. Why does the stock market go up and down? Even the economists have come to admit that to a very large extent it is due to psychological factors, that economic factors may point one way and the stock market go another way. The same is true in many other fields.

The discontent and even the despair of people at their own impotence is a much larger factor in politics than any of the politicians have recognized. Large segments of the population feel it is hopeless to try to influence the outcome of things. "I am totally impotent in regard to my government." That means the seeds of a revolution. It may not mean a violent revolution. I hope very much that it will not be. But it could be a revolution in thinking and in the way of *being* that will profoundly influence politics in the future.

Then, as to the use of computers, I am not an expert in that field. I don't use them myself. I have respect for what they are able to accomplish, if they are entirely regarded as servants and tools of the human mind and not given some mystical weight because they are so complex. It is highly unlikely that any perfect computer model will ever be designed.

Professor Rogers, how hopeful are you about the future of our planet?

I have been asked that a number of times. I have to divide my answer. I work mostly at the present time with small groups. But I worked most of my professional life with individuals. All that experience makes me thoroughly optimistic. The human organism is a constructive organism. When given a free choice and knowing all the circumstances, it seems almost inevitably to choose a creative and constructive pathway. If we are talking about the human being, about the human being as he comes together in small groups, I am a thoroughgoing optimist. I even feel, as I tried to indicate before, that we have the beginning knowledge of how to deal with much larger groups and entities. But whether that knowledge will come into play in time, I don't know. That's why in regard to our culture and in regard to the planet as a whole I have a very fifty-fifty feeling. We may destroy ourselves, or we may manage to rescue ourselves in time. Human nature has a great record, especially in democratic societies, of rescuing itself at the *last* possible moment. That may happen in regard to the globe. But I am not a bright-eyed optimist in regard to the globe as a whole.

NOTES

[1]*On Becoming a Person, a Therapist's View of Psychotherapy*, Houghton Mifflin Company (Boston, 1961), p. 15.

[2]Gabriel Marcel (1889-   ), French philosopher.

32. *Ivan D. Illich*

Born in Vienna in 1926, Ivan Illich is director of the Center for Intercultural Documentation (CIDOC) in Cuernavaca, Mexico.

Ivan Illich studied in Vienna, Salzburg and Rome. He was ordained a priest and later named a monsignor. He voluntarily renounced his priestly functions and now heads the Cuernavaca center.

Among some of his best-known books are *Celebration of Awareness* (1970) and *Deschooling Society* (1971).

A recent study at Harvard by Christopher Jencks and others established that inequality in schools was not a major cause of economic inequality among adults. In other words, to fight poverty in rich nations (the study dealt with the US), fundamental changes should be made in economic institutions rather than ask schools to solve these problems.

I have never claimed that inequality in schools is a major cause of economic inequality among adults. My main attention is directed toward the ritual rather than the causative effects of schools. For this see the chapter "The Ritual of Progress" in my book *Deschooling Society*. Like any compulsory mythopoetic ritual, the process of schooling hides from those who participate in it the divergence between the myth in which they believe and the social structure to which they are subservient. Schools foster the myth of equality and inevitably introject in its devotees a sense of belonging to a given age and grade-class. Fostering the equality of opportunities or shares in social products is among the chief goals, adopted by all societies which are committed to schooling. They all prescribe for their citizens a compulsory competition in climbing an open-ended ladder of educational consumption. The higher anybody climbs on this ladder—and the more he has supposedly "learnt to learn"—the more costly it becomes for the community to continue his studies for another year. All societies which have adopted initiation through schooling, create a pyramid of certified classes or educational consumers. The early dropout, who is identified as the educational nonconsumer, becomes an economic untouchable. The adoption of schooling is therefore equivalent to the legitimation of a society in which people are classed according to their institutional capitalization of "education." As long as they believe in the value of standardized "education," "manipulation," "social conditioning" or "socialization," they are blinded to the contradiction between myth and socioeconomic structure.

Of course, schools (1) reflect, (2) reinforce and (3) reproduce the particular class society in which they have been established. They do this independently of what happens between teachers and pupils, entirely by virtue of what I have called their "hidden curriculum."[1] But more importantly, those who believe in the universal necessity of specialized, institutionalized education are blinded by the process of schooling to the inevitable class characteristics of any expanding industrial society.

William I. Thompson[2] of York University feels that your study De-schooling Society is more aimed at changing the authority of schools or teachers as ersatz parents, rather than dealing head-on with changing or rather upgrading consciousness towards reality.

I do not know Thompson's criticism. It is precisely an unfettered view of reality which concerns me.

I concentrated on schools because among the various industrial production systems, the educational system provided the best paradigm to unmask illusions which we hold about other agencies. This is so because until recently they served as the sacred cows of industrial society. I argued that if it were possible to focus on illusions about education, it would be equally possible to push illusions about transport, housing or medicine out of the blind spot of industrialized imagination.

By 1970 at CIDOC[3] we had been able to show that:

(1) Universal education through compulsory schooling is not feasible.

(2) Alternate devices for the production of universal education are more feasible and less tolerable. New educational systems, now on the verge of replacing traditional schools in many areas, are potentially more effective in manipulating, conditioning and capitalizing people than the traditional school systems of the last forty years. They are also more reliable in conditioning people for life in a capitalist economy. They are therefore more attractive for the management of our societies, more seductive for the population and more insidiously destructive of fundamental human values.

(3) A society committed to high levels of shared learning (in opposition to high levels of planned conditioning) must set pedagogical limits on fundamental parameters of industrial growth.

This analysis of schooling led us to recognize the mass production of education as a paradigm for other industrial enterprises: each producing a service commodity, each organized as a public utility, and each defining its output as a basic necessity. At first our attention was drawn to compulsory insurance of professional health care and to systems of public transport, which also tend to become compulsory once traffic rolls above a certain speed. We found that the industrialization of any service agency has destructive side effects that are analogous to the unwanted secondary results well known from the overproduction of goods. We had thus to face a set of inescapable limits to the growth of the service sector corresponding to the limits inherent in the industrial production of artifacts. We concluded that limits to growth are well formulated only if they apply both to goods and to services when these are produced in an industrial mode.

Far from dealing primarily with changing the authority of schools or teachers as ersatz parents, I have consistently used the paradigm of schools to upgrade a new consciousness about the contradictions of any form of compulsory consumption of industrial outputs.

Jean Piaget[4] and B. F. Skinner[5] seem to deeply disagree about the programming of children: Piaget rejects Skinner's controls as means of conditioning the child for the future. Piaget maintains that background and environment will to a large extent determine the pace at which the child learns: Progress should not be too fast; all children pass through phases of understanding; developing abilities should be constantly used and tested or the intellectual growth will be stunted.

Educational psychologists usually focus on the process of initiating young humans into the society within which we live. My concern was to underline the obvious: It is impossible to condition people for a human life in an inhuman society. My main concern is not with new "education" but with the need for negative design-criteria which abound in a world in which people can effectively learn.

I am increasingly more concerned with proposing the concept of a multidimensional balance of human life which can serve as a framework for evaluating man's relation to his tools. I believe that in several of many dimensions of this balance it is possible to identify a natural scale. When an enterprise grows beyond a certain point on this scale, it first frustrates the end for the achievement of which it was originally designed, and then rapidly becomes a threat to society itself. These scales must be identified, and the parameters of human endeavors within which human life remains viable must be explored. I believe that educational psychology can provide us with guidelines for identifying some of these scales, and thereby with concepts which can become useful to outlaw forms of organization, production or tools which render the psychological environment impenetrable, secret and forbidding.

While Aurelio Peccei[6] and the Club of Rome are making efforts to transform the top of society, to make leaders and scientists see that the planet is in danger owing to limits to growth, could it be said that your work is aimed at efforts to make revolutionary changes at the very foundation of bourgeois society?

Peccei, Forrester, Meadows have rendered a very major service by their efforts to enlighten a large number of people about inevitable limits to growth in the production of goods. They have rendered the obvious evident, I would hope to complement their insight, by underlining that analogous inherent limits to growth exist also in the service sector.

In my opinion the specifically ecological limits to growth in the goods sector constitute only a subset in a broader set of multidimensional limits to the overall institutionalization of values. Society can be destroyed when further growth renders the milieu hostile, when it extinguishes the free use of the natural ability of society's members, when it isolates people from each other and locks them into a man-made shell, when it undermines the texture of community by promoting extreme social polarization and splintering specialization, or when cancerous acceleration forces social change at a rate that rules out legal, cultural and political precedents as guides to consentive procedures in the present. Tools with these effects cannot be tolerated. At this point of its growth, it becomes irrelevant if an enterprise is nominally owned by individuals, corporations or states, because no management can make such an enterprise serve a social purpose.

How do you view the future in the next two decades? Especially in view of the seemingly ever-growing gap between rich and poor people and rich and poor nations?

I believe that only the demythologization of science, the restoration of ordinary language and the recuperation of basic procedures can help us to bound institutional growth. This can be achieved only by an inversion of present political goals; these are usually oriented towards increasing the total output of a social system and with the more equal distribution of the product. This concern with distributive justice must be complemented with insight into the need for participatory justice; an equal claim to society's outputs must be complemented by concern with an equal distribution over controls of the new energies which we now can muster, even if this should lead to the realization that participatory justice demands a society with very radically limited energy consumption. In my next book, *Tools for Conviviality*, I try to deal with this problem.

NOTES

[1]See "Alternative to Schooling," *Saturday Review*, June 19, 1971.
[2]See conversation no. 68.
[3]Center for Intercultural Documentation, Cuernavaca, Mexico.
[4]Swiss psychologist, among those working at the Institut J. J. Rousseau in Geneva, Switzerland.
[5]See conversation no. 7.
[6]See conversation no. 70.

33. Erza J. Mishan

Professor Erza Mishan is reader in economics at the London School of Economics.

He was born in 1917 in Manchester, England. His books include *Welfare Economics: An Assessment* (1969), *Welfare Economics, Ten Introductory Essays* (1969), *Twenty-one Popular Economic Fallacies* (1969) and *The Cost of Economic Growth*, Pelican (New York, 1967).

What is your reaction to the publication of Limits to Growth?

One could predict that the report by MIT would not be welcomed by most economists. This is because very few among them have seriously questioned the notion of sustained economic growth as a legitimate aim of social policy. The accent since the war has always been on increasing rates of economic growth. Indeed, generalizing from the response to the *Blueprint for Survival* in the United States, the sort of denunciation it will invoke can be anticipated.

First of all, ritual scorn will be poured on doomsdayers. Prophets of the world catastrophe reaching back to ancient Egypt will be unearthed. Yet, will Malthus be dismissed as a false prophet? Economists will hasten to remind us that as traditional resources become exhausted, new materials are sure to come into being and new technology should enable us continuously to raise real standards, at least in the West. For the boundaries of science, he will say, widen today more rapidly than in any other period in history. Economists will insist that the model of MIT is far too simple to express reality, and that it makes no provision for the resource and ingenuity of man. Yet, the book is sure to make an impact as did the *Blueprint*,[1] which preceded it by a couple of months.

The model used by Forrester[2] and Meadows is relatively complex in structure. The mathematical equations describing the links between the variables cannot of course be laid bare in a popular account. And the general reader has to be content with some simple illustrations, verbal and diagrammatic, of the nature of the interconnections and, later on in the book, with descriptions and graphs (not as clearly drawn as they might be) of the time paths that emerge from the computer in response to altering initial assumptions and parameters. What the most serious critic will want to examine, however, is not only the information fed into the model but the structure of the equation system. Do changes in the structure of the equation system make significant differences to the results?

For all that, a beginning has been made, a global model has been made explicit and is therefore open to modification and to further experiment and refinement. Certainly it would be salutary for growth men and antigrowth men to have some clear ideas of the magnitude of the technical achievements that are needed over time, if positive growth rates are to be maintained.

You have written that technological conditions of production are not chosen with a view to enhancing man's experience of life, social sciences are not involved. "They seem to evolve solely in response to requirements of industrial efficiency and profit seeking.[3] *The process is generated accidentally." How to reverse this trend? How to bring in the social factors, the interests of the mass of people?*

I do not know how to reverse the trend, quite frankly. What I am saying is fairly clear though. Consider, for example, air pollution: There's been a study by Lave and Seskin, which seems to show that for certain age groups such diseases as asthma, bronchitis, and emphysema, double, as we move from low-pollution areas to high-pollution areas. This does create employment among medical men, and of course it provides opportunities for increased research. This seems to me typical of the way science approaches a problem. It first undertakes some innovation which turns out to have unforeseen consequences, good and bad. The bad consequences find a welcome place in the system, because people are employed to do research on it. Thus, when I say that there is no overall benign Being concerned continuously to the pros and cons of each innovation, that is what I mean. The system proceeds more or less blindly in this sort of way, guided only by its immediate commercial prospects.

Economic growth renders many things obsolete, one of them is economic theory. How to adjust economic thinking to the fast-changing patterns on the planet in relation to population, pollution, ecology—is economic theory running behind the facts and realities of our situation?

Yes, economic theory always does lag behind. I am sure that goes for other sciences as well. But younger people are becoming interested in ecology today. Their original training was in economics. Now they are starting to tackle a number of other problems, and the problems they can tackle are usually those concerned directly with the environment or ecology. Resources for the Future is a well-known organization in America, which has a number of very competent economists working for it, who are interested not only in producing models, but making quantative estimates. Their concern is with the conservation of natural resources and environment.

They have not tackled the broader social consequences. I suppose the reason is that they are intangible in many ways. It requires quite a lot of speculation on social questions. And the kind of questions even sociologists address themselves to are often very narrow indeed. In the nature of things I don't think they can consider many of the long-run social consequences. For example, people are today discussing this question of pornography, and the possible effects of television violence, often sadistic violence, on young people or even grown-ups. The kind of studies that are done by sociologists are so narrow in scope, merely trying to discover if seeing these things has any immediate effects on these people: if, for example, watching violence leads immediately to more crime, or watching sexual promiscuity leads to more sexual promiscuity. Statistically I don't think the results are very valuable. But even so they don't address themselves to the right questions, such as what are the ultimate effects on people's character. For the kind of life we are after will depend ultimately on people's values, and on how they feel about each other.

The question I ask myself is, if you watch television programs and see people just being abused and subjected to violence by other people with no moral at the end of it—a bad guy just getting away with his violence or getting away with his sexual promiscuity—will not young people come to take these things perhaps as a social norm, as an acceptable part of life, and try to model themselves accordingly? What kind of a future is that going to lead to? These are the sort of questions in my mind, but I cannot see sociologists measuring anything that will enable us to answer them.

* * *

In your book you spoke of teenagers between thirteen and seventeen, spending some seven hundred dollars in luxury items on the way to their dolce vita.[4] *What role could economists—or sociologists and psychologists, if you want—play to change the worsening trends, so that people will shift priorities and behave more realistically?*

This is really like the game about the hen and the egg. Because in order to change the environment and then be changed by it, people themselves have to take the initiative. The environment does not change by itself. People must first change the environment. And in this country, which is supposed to have some sort of democratic institutions, the environment can only change if the majority of people are in favor of such changes in the first place. So it follows that you've got first to have a change of heart arising from some new insight or some new awareness by many people before this is going to come about. Obviously once you change the environment, then you also change the people. As Winston Churchill once said, we shape the buildings and then the buildings shape us. It's that kind of process.

But aren't we controlled now in a so-called free democratic society? Controlled by teachers, professors, civil servants, governments. We are controlled from top to bottom. The control has to change in order to change—

I agree with you in a sense. We are subjected already to a number of political and institutional constraints. Madison Avenue[5] is very strong indeed. Vested interests are very strong. Vested material and intellectual interests are strong. This we know, and yet the only hope of radical change coming about is the recognition that masses of people will become convinced that the existing sort of life, a by-product of economic growth, is not the life they want. They want a new set of options to choose from, and once they believe that this is indeed feasible, we can start changing the environment in earnest.

Professor Mishan, would you think it feasible to run the planet earth as a big corporation?

Yes, for some people it is already on the way to being run as a giant corporation.

*   *   *

But if that's so, spending some two hundred billion dollars a year, on military budgets for the world as a whole—no efficient management would allow that kind of waste.

No, of course not. If you had a universal government this waste would not exist. But it does not need imagination to understand the fear with which countries, now heavily armed, watch one another. Any small weapons advance in one country has been matched by the other. Indeed, each country seeks to anticipate what weapons the other countries will invent in order to have some weapon to counteract it. In fact, it is the arms race between nations which endows economic growth with a good part of its current rationale. If it were not for the arms race, and the arguments about the spin-off from industrial and technological growth, the political possibility of slowing down growth deliberately in the attempt to reach a stable state would be much easier.

Yes, but do you envisage at all a possibility of managing the planet on a global scale?

Not in the near future, no. I don't see that. My position is pessimistic. If you ask me how long the civilized world is going to last, I would guess that it may last ten or fifteen years. If it lasts much longer, it will be something of a miracle. Yet at the same time, I believe man has free will, and sometimes miracles happen. So I plug along, hoping for the best, though expecting the worst.

Will we ever bridge the gap between the rich and the poor countries? If we aim at a global-scale management, which seems unavoidable in the long run, how to manage it when there are such tremendous gaps between the rich and the poor countries?

You're taking it rather out of my depth here. I was concerned very largely with affluent societies, and arguing that further economic growth for them serves no wholesome purpose. It has just become a bad habit or, as you might say, you just cannot stop the machine. Now you're asking me what we do about all these poor countries, and here I hate really to stick my neck out, because I happen to believe that these countries should have followed the path suggested by Gandhi;[6] that is to say, they should use small technology, intermediate technology, and aim at a modest but fairly satisfactory material standard. But they haven't gone that way. A small group in each of these countries have their eyes all the time on the West, and they hope to bring their countries up to that standard. Well, this, in the nature of things, seems to me impossible. Certainly impossible within a few years, because it seems clear that if all these countries could within a few years have material standards comparable with those of the United States, the world would not last more than another ten or twenty years. The rate of consumption of resources and the rate of pollution would be enormous.

Every Chinese having two automobiles in his garage—

Yes, something like that. If you ask me what is the ideal in some sense, and you don't ask me how it's going to be realized, simply supposing one had an all-powerful dictator ruling the whole world—

Toynbee[7] spoke in those terms earlier.

Well, that's the only way one can talk sensibly sometimes, because one gets continually mixed up with what is feasible or immediately realizable, what can happen in the more remote future when, we imagine, there are fewer constraints.

If there were to be a benevolent dictatorship over the whole world, then the first thing to do, obviously, would be to make every effort to reduce population growth; to stabilize total population and, possibly, to reduce it. And the second thing, of course, would be to distribute the world's wealth a little more evenly, in which case certainly we couldn't maintain standards of living in America as they are now.

NOTES

[1] See conversation no. 27.
[2] See conversation no. 34.
[3] *The Costs of Economic Growth*, p. 185.
[4] *Ibid.*, p. 195.
[5] An American expression pertaining to modern sales techniques dreamt up in offices along Madison Avenue in New York City, where most of these advertising firms are located.
[6] Mahatma Gandhi (1869-1948), Hindu religious and political leader and social reformer, Father of India.
[7] See conversation no. 5.

34. Jay W. Forrester

Professor Forrester teaches at the Alfred P. Sloan School of Management at the Massachusetts Institute of Technology in Cambridge, Massachusetts.

Jay W. Forrester was born in Anselmo, Nebraska, in 1918. He majored in education. In 1940 he cofounded the servomechanisms laboratory at MIT. He founded the Digital Computer Laboratory there and became professor at the Alfred P. Sloan School of Management. He has written extensively on digital computers and the dynamics of economic behavior. A team basing its research on the work of Forrester, led by Dennis L. Meadows, prepared the by now world famous *Limits to Growth* report for the Club of Rome, published in 1972.

A complete list of Professor Forrester's work is produced as an appendix to this conversation.

Professor Skinner[1] complained that ninety percent of the reviews of his book, Beyond Freedom and Dignity, *were based on misunderstanding or on an unwillingness to face the issues he raised. Perhaps the mental models through which people perceived his book were inappropriate. How have the reactions been to your* World Dynamics *and* The Limits to Growth *by Meadows?*[2]

I feel much the same. In fact, after reading the reviews of Skinner's book, I saw such a similarity to the reviews of *World Dynamics* and *The Limits to Growth* that I was sure it would be necessary to read his book even to determine the central message. When faced with a book that violates the conventional wisdom or that uses an unfamiliar methodology, a reviewer often distorts a book or even reverses its meaning. The nature of the reviewing process must be understood in this connection. Those with negative reactions rush into print much more quickly than those with positive reactions. Furthermore, a reviewer usually feels an obligation to differ with an author; otherwise he would not seem to be making an intellectual input himself. I think in the reactions to *World Dynamics* and *The Limits to Growth* we will see the same trends that occurred with the earlier system-dynamics books. The first reviews are negative. Then thoughtful people interested in the subject begin to dig more deeply and to examine the issues. After the first rush of negative reviews, a very different tone begins to develop. Even in the very short history of these two recent books, a change in reaction is occurring.

How would you describe system dynamics, which is the methodology behind the two books? Where has system dynamics come from?

We have been developing system dynamics at MIT since 1956. It arises from the confluence of three earlier lines of endeavor—the classical or descriptive approach to social systems, the theory of feedback structures and dynamic behavior, and the development of computers.

The first background thread, the descriptive approach to social behavior, underlies the liberal arts and the classical approach to education. It is the method of the historian and social commentator—to report, evaluate, and predict. In its most formal manifestation the classical method of description and verbal analysis appears in the case-study approach to education as used in schools of law and medicine and as popularized by the Harvard Business School in the case-study method of management education. This classical tradition, which uses description, analysis, argument, and intuitive judgment, is now the basis for all political decisions, for the passing of all laws, and for the making of all management decisions.

The classical decision-making procedure has great strengths, but also great weaknesses. Its strength arises from the direct human observation of forces, pressures, and reactions within our social systems. Each person has a rich store of information from observing men and institutions. Each person filters his observations through discussion of pressures, human reactions, and assumed consequences. Each has a rich body of acquired knowledge on the separate facets and components of social systems. For the most part these observations are correct at the elementary level of the individual pressures and responses in the system.

But the classical approach to social systems has two serious weaknesses: As one weakness, the classical tradition gives little guidance in separating the important information from a tremendous body of irrelevant information; as another weakness, the classical tradition supplies no methodology for interrelating and interlinking a given set of assumptions and arriving with certainty at the consequences implied by the assumptions.

So, the classical process of managing social systems has available a tremendous store of valid information about the parts of the system, but no adequate way to select the significant information from the excess of information, and no way to be certain of the consequences that follow from selected information about individual pressures and human reactions. Consequently, the classical tradition subjects people to information overloading and to a high degree of internal contradiction because different people draw different conclusions from the same input facts. Often the accepted conclusions are inconsistent with the accepted assumptions and these discrepancies go undetected because the systems are so complex that the human mind is unable to properly relate the multiplicity of causes to the wide variety of possible consequences.

The second thread forming the background of system dynamics has been under formal theoretical development for a hundred years. I refer to a field that is variously called cybernetics, or servomechanisms, or feedback-system theory. Feedback theory deals with closed-loop behavior in which a control action (decision) alters the state of a system (the levels in system dynamics) and sets up new information conditions for the guidance of future decisions. Every decision, whether public or private, whether conscious or unconscious, is made in the context of such a feedback-loop structure. All the processes of growth, goal-seeking, equilibrium, oscillation, and decay are generated by the interplay of forces within feedback loops.

The first professional paper on feedback dynamics of which I am aware was presented in 1867 before the Royal Society in London by Clerk Maxwell, better known for his discovery of Maxwell's equations for the propagation of radio waves through space. His paper, "On Governors," presented a mathematical analysis of the stability and behavior of the fly-ball governor as used on James Watt's steam engines. The Bell Telephone Laboratories revived and extended feedback theory in the development of feedback amplifiers for use in transcontinental telephony. During World War II the concepts were refined and applied to military equipment. More recently, extensions of the theory have guided the design of chemical plants, oil refineries, and control systems for aircraft and space satellites. We have continued the development of the principles as they apply to very nonlinear, multiple-loop systems containing both positive and negative feedback.

The principles that emerge from feedback theory guide the sorting and the organizing of the information that is available from the classical tradition of direct observation of real life. The principles from feedback theory tell us what items of information from the morass of direct observations might be relevant in producing a given observed mode of real-life behavior. The feedback system principles become a screen for separating important data from the useless. Furthermore, the system principles provide a guide to how the selected information is to be structured into an interactive system. The principles of structure and behavior from feedback theory help us escape from the information overload that is inherent in the classical traditions of descriptive analysis. But one would still be left with more information and with greater structural complexity than the human mind can handle.

The third background development, the high-speed electronic computer, solves the problem of how to draw correct dynamic conclusions from a given set of assumptions. The computer is given a simulation model, which is a statement of the motivational assumptions and information flows for each point in the system and a specification of how the forces interact at each local point in the system. The computer then simulates, or traces through step-by-step, what will happen as the separate elements of the system impinge on one another.

So, from the classical tradition comes too much information, from the feedback theory comes guidance for sorting and structuring that information, and from the development of computers comes the ability to analyze the consequences of structured observations about social systems.

In a television interview, Dr. Djhermen M. Gvishiani[3] of the Soviet Union indicated to me that the significance of computers has been exaggerated, that we must take sociological and psychological aspects into consideration and these cannot be represented in computers.

I agree that the press and many others overemphasize the computer aspect of our work. The most important input to a system dynamics model is the descriptive information and our perceptions about the influences and responses at different points in a social system. The second major conceptual input comes from the feedback-system principles that allow one to select from the excess of descriptive information and to organize the relationships that have been chosen. The computer is necessary as an economical tool but is not a part of the conceptual or theoretical structure of system dynamics.

My only disagreement with Dr. Gvishiani would be if he thinks that psychological and sociological aspects cannot be put in a computer-simulation model. One can incorporate any relationships that can be described. Any of the so-called intangibles can be represented in a model. One must establish a scale of measurement (that is arbitrary); he must relate the scale to actual situations; and he must try to be consistent in the way the scale is used. By forcing the past intangibles to become future tangibles, we become more precise. Thought and discussion becomes more orderly and more penetrating. The psychological and sociological aspects of our systems are of overwhelming importance. They can and must be included in formal models.

You speak of social systems as being multi-loop feedback systems. It is not clear what you mean by a closed loop that connects an action to its effect.

A feedback loop exists wherever the surrounding state of the system determines action that affects the system state. This is an absolutely sweeping definition that encompasses everything that changes through time. One can structure the dynamics of a simple swinging pendulum as a feedback process in which the position of the pendulum determines acceleration that determines velocity that determines position. One can examine the processes of evolution as continuous adjustment between a species and its environment in which biological change alters the suitability of the species to its circumstances and sets up new pressures for favoring those members of the species that fit best. Management and political decisions are made in the context of a feedback structure where the decisions are intended to change the surrounding socioeconomic circumstances and the changed circumstances present an ensemble of new information that becomes the basis for future decisions.

But the closed-loop viewpoint is in sharp contrast to the way most people think of cause-and-effect relationships. Most people see not the whole circular process, but only a unidirectional fragment of the entire process. Ordinary discussions and debates focus on how action A will cause result R, without continuing into a consideration of how result R will lead to a new pattern of action A. Most articles in the public press also focus on the simple unidirectional viewpoint and obscure the true circular dynamic structure that is causing social change.

Perhaps a simple example will help. If one fills a water glass from a faucet, he usually thinks of the flow of water as filling the glass, and the description stops at that unidirectional stage without identifying the remainder of the closed-loop causal structure. But it is equally true that the water in the glass is turning off the faucet. The person watches the water and closes the faucet as the proper water level is reached. The entire system is one in which the flow of water fills the glass but, just as correctly, the water in the glass controls the flow.

The process is circular and closed-loop; action alters the state of the system and the new state modifies the action. All dynamic behavior is generated by these closed-feedback loops. There are two distinct kinds of feedback loops: Positive feedback loops produce all the processes of growth; negative feedback loops produce goal-seeking, equilibrium, and fluctuation.

Several people interviewed for this book have said, "We don't need computers to deal with such matters."

In one sense that is true; in another and much more important sense it is entirely untrue. It would be fair to say that we have never discovered anything in fifteen years of analyzing social systems that someone could not honestly say he already knew and had already stated. But on every major issue there is a split opinion. People take each side of every question. On important issues, the division of opinion is apt to be in the forty percent to sixty percent range, with no assurance that the majority will prove to be right. But with such controversy, it is almost impossible to imagine coming up with an answer that has never been articulated before. The confusion arises because for each correct statement, there has been someone, whose credentials are just as good, who has claimed the opposite.

When the controversy over sheer use of computer simulation models is resolved, we will find that formal models reduce the controversy over the substance of the social issues. The reduction of controversy will take place at two levels. First, the method forces a focus on the underlying assumptions without simultaneous consideration of the implied consequences of those assumptions. The basic assumptions must be faced in their own right, without involving a prejudgment of whether or not they will lead to the desired conclusions. In the classical method of political debate, assumptions and consequences are hopelessly intertwined. One tends to start with an outcome to which he is committed and then to argue for a set of assumptions about present circumstances that appear to lead to the desired outcome. Separate assumptions are not explicitly stated and are not individually debated to resolve differences of opinion.

Usually, when assumptions are explicitly stated, as they must be in a computer model, much of the disagreement evaporates. Often it is only lack of clarity and semantic difficulties that lie behind the argument.

At the second level, the classical procedure of debate produces endless disagreement over what consequences would occur in the future from an accepted set of present assumptions. This level of conflict can be entirely eliminated between those who accept the system-dynamics methods because there is no doubt about the computer producing the consequences of the assumptions and relationships given to it.

During my interviews on the subject of The Limits to Growth *I was surprised that people in certain disciplines—I am thinking of economics —who should be working on the same kind of planetary models as you, would show reluctance to enter into contact with those of you in system dynamics.*

You are probably drawing unjustified generalities from a few individuals. Your comment is not typical of all economists. Our work has in the past drawn in relevant people representing many kinds of viewpoints. The *Limits to Growth* work was in very broad contact with many kinds of people in many different disciplines to provide information inputs to the various aspects of our work. I am now myself beginning a new program that will deal with social and economic change at the national level with a particular focus on the United States. It is already evident that we will get excellent cooperation in this from people in all areas of endeavor. Some individuals will avoid contact and participation, but that is not typical of people generally or any profession in particular.

But in my interview with William Nordhaus,[4] an economist at Yale, he mentioned having written a review of your World Dynamics *in which he asserts that your book contains assumptions that are quite contrary to empirical data that is available. Have you read that review?*

Yes. The Nordhaus review has not been published, but it has been circulated on a private basis very widely in Europe and North America. The review is an example of the errors and fallacies that can be created by someone who does not understand a new field, but sets himself up as an instant expert. The review alleges three major and three minor errors in *World Dynamics*. In fact, a careful analysis of the review shows that every point rests on gross error by the reviewer or on his misreading the *World Dynamics* book—things like mistaking a function for its derivative, reading the wrong units of measure for a variable, creating variables that are not in the book and then attributing them to the book, and misusing the real-world data when he brings it to a comparison with superficially similar but quite different concepts in the model. The review shows how poorly a classical, static training in traditional economics prepares a person for understanding the nature and the behavior of nonlinear, multiple-loop feedback structures of which our social systems are composed.

I have written an analysis of and reply to that book review; it is available to anyone that requests it. In fact, my reply shows that the data presented by the reviewer strongly support the assumptions in *World Dynamics* when the errors in the review are corrected.

One criticism of World Dynamics *has been that resources should have been measured in economic and not in physical terms and that the model is misleading because it does not include a pricing system.*

Those who suggest that the solution to shortage lies in the price system are speaking from a short-term view and are thinking about relative and not about absolute shortages. They are probably speaking from the tradition of the economist's profession where everything tends to be converted into money terms before it is discussed. But there is nothing in a pricing mechanism that generates physical space or generates resources that don't already exist in the earth's crust. Pricing is a way of redirecting effort and of determining who uses the remaining short supplies. Those who can afford the high prices will continue to use resources after others who can no longer afford the high prices have been excluded from the market. The price mechanism is by no means a solution to the issues raised in *World Dynamics*.

Realistic doubts about the significance of the price mechanism are stated by Professor Wallich of Yale in *Fortune*:[5] "We know, of course, that the prices of most natural resources today do not reflect expectations of future shortages. . . . We cannot be sure whether, given the prospect of shortages at some future time, the price system would in fact respond with sufficient foresight. Various factors besides human fallibility suggest that it might not."

He then moves from resources to one of the clearly limited aspects of the environment, namely, land: "The economics and politics of land represent a special aspect of the natural-resource problem. Land is broadly fixed in supply. . . . Here again, the price system does not offer complete assurance of being able to take care of the situation. . . . A good deal of evidence has accumulated that the price system, if not intrinsically inappropriate, is at least substantially inefficient in dealing with regional crowding. It appears that population movement responds to rising rents and rising congestion only with very long time lags.'' Here we see a recognition of the importance of long delays. We see a suggestion that prices, far from generating supply, can only operate to determine who consumes when availability falls short of need.

To put the matter another way, I look upon prices as intermediary variables that determine who shall receive allocations of a short resource. Many people have argued that higher cost will cause people to make use of lower-quality resources and that the process will extend supply by a greater use of capital, energy, and manpower. That is true and the concept is incorporated in my *World Dynamics* model. It is also incorporated in *The Limits to Growth* model, not as a price system, but through a physical extraction-efficiency system. One must realize that the falling quality of resources implies a higher effort for extraction and this implies a real, as distinguished from a monetary, inflation. The rising price implies a falling productivity. It means, therefore, a lower standard of living, because it means more effort put into producing the same unit of goods. A great deal more can be done in handling allocations—I don't mean that the treatment has been complete or final, but only that such issues have not been overlooked.

Some people have implied that the growth-and-collapse modes shown in the books occur because price and financial processes are implicit rather than explicit in the highly aggregated models. I believe that the effect of adding prices and financial flows will be in the opposite direction. New modes of system instability will become possible in the model as the additional system levels and interactions are added between money and material. When the full behavior of the socioeconomic system becomes clear, I believe it will become evident that the price and monetary system is subject to at least as much mismanagement as the physical, demographic, and physical-capital aspects, and that the price and financial flows, rather than insuring a trouble-free transition, introduces additional hazards along the road from growth to equilibrium.

Some readers of World Dynamics *feel that growth in technology has been neglected.*

That reaction to the book I simply did not anticipate. Otherwise, the nature of the handling of technological change could have been more completely explained. It would have seemed to me as quite unlikely, considering the years that I have been involved in science and technology, for people to believe I was not aware of the rapid pace of scientific advancement. The issue is not dealt with in detail in *World Dynamics*, but it is explicitly stated on page 53: "Capital includes buildings, roads and factories. It also includes education and the results of scientific research, for the latter are not represented elsewhere in the model system and the investment in them decays at about the same rate as for physical capital."

The point here involves the proper use of aggregation of variables into a model of reasonably simple structure. One can aggregate into a single variable those things that have similar dynamic behavior. Research and technological change have a dynamic behavior very much like that of physical capital accumulation. Both have, under circumstances that favor growth, a positive feedback character. Capital produces more capital; knowledge is the basis for producing still more knowledge. Both decay. The major fraction of our technological know-how resides in the heads of people and must be rebuilt in every human generation by an expensive investment in education. The time constants of obsolescence and disappearance of that knowledge are similar to the time constants for physical capital. Furthermore, the significant use of each is the same; knowledge and physical capital both raise the standard of living, increase the efficiency of capital accumulation, and increase the yield of agriculture. These are the three uses of the combined capital-knowledge variable in the *World Dynamics* model. So, capital and scientific knowledge are aggregated together because they are generated in a similar way, they have a similar life, and they are used for the same purpose.

Several people have criticized the publication of The Limits to Growth *book without the prior publication of details of the computer model from which the results were obtained.*

That was an unexpected result of funding and organizational difficulties. However, the criticism is only partly justified. First, the draft of *The Limits to Growth* model was made available in the spring of 1972 at the time of the appearance of the book to several research groups that wanted to examine it in detail, had a group of people to assign to the task, and were equipped with access to a computer to work with the model. Second, the message in *The Limits to Growth* is essentially that of *World Dynamics*, and the model details for *World Dynamics* have been available from the first. The rather large book with details and justification of *The Limits to Growth* model will be out in 1973.

This brings us to the question of values and priorities. Some believe the poor nations will have quite different opinions on growth from the rich nations.

Your question implies that the rich nations would favor the end of exponential growth while the poor nations would not. But there is no unanimity of view in the developed countries, and I believe there will likewise be no single view in the underdeveloped countries. In fact, the terminology may need to be changed from developed and underdeveloped to "overextended" and "equilibrium" countries. The less-developed countries may be better able to sustain their traditional goals and values than are the developed (overextended) countries.

I believe we will see two schools of thought in the less-developed countries. Political leaders who have been educated in the developed countries and who have adopted the academic and political values of the industrialized nations will favor growth until the growth-generated pressures overshadow their future and their political credibility. But the traditionalists and the philosophers in those countries may see that the past values are more in keeping with the long-term future and will favor holding onto the past rather than going in quick succession through two upheavals in values—to growth and back to equilibrium—merely to return to a society more like their own past than like the industrialized pattern.

The less-developed countries may adopt a more rational view than the developed countries—as one reason, they have more time to act. We should be very cautious in jumping to conclusions about how other groups will react; we have discovered in our earlier work that social and political groups respond quite differently from expectations. Sometimes the groups who may appear to be the most immediately and detrimentally affected are the very groups that have the greatest incentive to act wisely for the long run and show the greatest ability to look beyond the short term.

We may find that the assumed dedication of underdeveloped countries to economic growth is largely in the minds of economists, government bureaucrats, and businessmen in the developed countries who have been trying to push their own values and goals onto the less-developed countries. As those growth values are cast into doubt and are shown to be of only transient advantage, it is entirely possible that the less-developed countries will turn against those whom they begin to perceive as holding out false hopes and values. Because the economic-growth ethic has not been as pervasively adopted in the underdeveloped as in the developed countries, we may find that the trauma of coming to terms with the future is less severe for the poor countries than for the rich countries.

One of the criticisms of your World Dynamics *has been that to move into zero growth would be a destructive solution to our present problems.*

Some critics of the recent world studies seem to think that we are recommending the impossible, that we are suggesting that growth can be stopped immediately. Maybe the reaction is based on some of the computer runs that show what would happen if action were taken now. But, of course, major changes in values and in political policies do not occur rapidly. The computer runs are intended to show that even immediate action leads to great stress and that delayed action will lead to greater stress in the world social system. Time is short, but there is still time for choice and time to argue, accept, and implement policies that will be more favorable than continuing as at present.

We face two great dilemmas: Continuation of growth will be more destructive of present human values and institutions than will an expeditious slowing of growth; but to stop growth will create its own set of pressures—less severe than letting growth go unchecked but still substantial. There seem to be no pressure-free utopias in sight, but there are many alternatives from which to choose between possible futures. The challenge is to examine the nature of the alternatives and to choose the set of pressures that will lead us into a viable and sustainable future.

The message from *World Dynamics* and *The Limits to Growth* is: Ignoring pressures today will lead to still greater pressures tomorrow. If we take action as soon as possible, those actions may be difficult and may generate short-term controversies and pressures, but such action can reduce the pressures that we will otherwise face in the relatively near future. The issue is not one of evading pressures. Instead, the decision is in terms of which pressures, when, and for what purpose.

Dr. Carl Kaysen[6] of the Institute for Advanced Study feels that the growth mechanisms lie much deeper in our social order than shown in the models by you and Dennis Meadows.

The depth perceived in a system-dynamics model is very much a reflection of what the reader wants to see. If he wishes to perceive the least possible content, he arrives at a very different conclusion than if he wants to perceive the greatest possible content. In a highly aggregated model there is bound to be room for differing interpretations. It is possible that the different interpretations are both correct, depending on what the individual is doing with the model. The world models in their present high degree of aggregation do not explicitly show the full detail of psychological and sociological forces that connect physical variables to human responses. The system-dynamics methodology can readily accept the full scope of any psychological, moral, sociological, or value structures that one wants to include. To do so will be important in future modeling of world and national dynamics. But in *World Dynamics* the desire to focus on only the major intersectoral forces between population, capital, food, resources, and pollution meant that for simplicity many intervening variables like prices and psychological reactions were properly subsumed into the more tangible variables from which they are generated and into which they have their effect.

Have you ever included the more intangible variables in models?

Yes, we know it can be done. One example was a model of the dynamics of corporate growth, only summary descriptions of which have been published. That model incorporated some 250 variables that interact in causing the growth and crises of a new technically based corporation. That corporate model contains the psychological and leadership characteristics of the company founders, generates the way the traditions and history of the organization itself influences goals and objectives, and deals with the sociology and psychology of the corporate resource-allocating process. But such a model is extremely complex and detailed; it lacks the simplicity and clarity necessary in a book like *World Dynamics* if the model is to be understood by the average reader in the time he has available. Furthermore, we must keep in mind that the mental models now being used for national and world decision-making are probably no more comprehensive than those presented in *World Dynamics* and *The Limits to Growth*.

Should the world models be expanded to include social and psychological influences?

A model of considerably greater complexity is eventually desirable. Partly this will be to verify the adequacy of simpler models; partly the adding of omitted variables will allow the model to generate additional modes of behavior that may be possible in actual social systems. There are additional kinds of stresses and additional modes of population equilibrium and collapse that the simpler models cannot represent. But including the additional variables probably will not change the major message of the two books.

And that message is? . . .

Present world values and the resulting growth trends in population and industrialization cannot continue for more than a few decades. Many different pressures can reshape the future. Some routes to the future are much more favorable than others. The harder we strive to continue the present policies, the higher will counteracting pressures from the natural and social environment rise. We still have time to make choices that will influence the future. Unlike those who have put a "doomsday" label on the two books, I see them as messages of hope. We can have a better future than that which blind devotion to past values and traditions portends.

But since there is an urgency, can you train sufficient system-dynamics specialists to do the vast amount of research and teaching that are needed?

There is a great urgency, but the training and research will be delayed for a time by the high degree of controversy that now exists around the work and the issues raised. The controversy is probably unavoidable because it is part of a transitional period between a past certainty that the old traditions were satisfactory and the new modes of thought, education, analysis, and social-system design about which you have been asking. At present it is not likely that one could organize the kind of financial support necessary to establish the faculty development needed to create an entirely new educational system from the secondary grades up. I think the doubts will disappear. Then it will be possible to get on with the task. Now is a period we must go through. Any substantial break with past tradition unavoidably produces a controversy while the new ideas become accepted.

How hopeful are you that this can be achieved in a relatively short time? Could the Chinese or the Soviets be drawn into your approach like the Japanese have been, for instance?

I receive mail and letters from practically every country. The mail from outside the United States totals as much as from inside. The letters bring in questions, comments, requests for speeches, and proposals from people to come here to study from every kind of country, the socialist countries included. There is a very widespread knowledge of what we are doing. The ideas have not yet penetrated deeply but have traveled widely. People everywhere are beginning to think much more actively about systems that affect the future of society.

Looking at responses around the world since the publication of World Dynamics *and* The Limits to Growth, *one finds an enormous amount of discussion of the issues that have been raised. Are you hopeful that the reactions will reach enough people to create a corps of leaders who can analyze the future prospects of mankind and can alter present attitudes and policies?*

The issues are so substantial and the new directions must be so different from the old that leadership alone will not be sufficient. There must also be widespread public understanding and support. To achieve such, our educational system must become much more effective in conveying an understanding of how the socioeconomic-technical-environmental system functions. I believe that the concepts imbedded in what we call system dynamics will make that possible.

System dynamics is a way of interrelating, on a common basis, the different intellectual disciplines and the different facets of existence, so that one can put into a single structure the technological, economic, ethical, psychological, political and natural aspects of our existence. One can relate all on a par to one another to see how they interact to produce social and economic change. The problems of the world are not being generated from the issues that lie within any single intellectual discipline or any single subsector of our surroundings. The problems and stresses are being generated by the interactions between the many subsectors. Nowhere in our educational system and nowhere in our political system are these interactions adequately dealt with—not in the United Nations, not in governments, and not in corporations.

A complete revolution in our understanding of the world about us is in the offing. This new understanding will be developed on a common foundation of dynamic behavior that can be applied to any field or combination of fields. In this new kind of education a student will focus on structures that reappear in many different fields. There are dynamic structures in physics that reappear in management, politics, and ecology. When a structure and its possible behavior is understood, one understands it whether that structure is found in medicine, or in corporate policy, or in demography. These are ideas the teaching of which can begin at the junior high school level.

The world needs a modern version of the "Renaissance man," meaning individuals who are able to move between intellectual disciplines, understand each of many fields, and grasp their significant interrelationships. Unnecessarily, educators have abandoned the hope of ever achieving again the kind of man who could penetrate the apparent complexities of the multiple facets of human affairs. But we should not despair of finding a new fundamental foundation underlying the proliferation of academic diversity. That is now in sight. It will be possible to build bridges of common dynamic structures and behavior between the liberal arts, science, biology, and social affairs.

NOTES

[1] See conversation no. 7.
[2] See bibliography, conversation no. 34.
[3] Vice Chairman of the State Committee of the USSR Council of Ministers for Science and Technology and corresponding member of the USSR Academy of Sciences.
[4] See conversation no. 19.
[5] October, 1972.
[6] See conversation no. 11.

Bibliography of System Dynamics Publications

Forrester, Jay W. *Industrial Dynamics*. Cambridge, Mass.: MIT Press, 1961.

The first book on system dynamics illustrates use of the methodology through analysis of the problems of an industrial firm.

————. *Principles of Systems*. Cambridge, Mass.: Wright-Allen Press, 1968.

Basic introductory text on the philosophy and methodology of system dynamics.

————. *Urban Dynamics*. Cambridge, Mass.: MIT Press, 1969.

An application of system dynamics to urban problems.

————. *World Dynamics*. Cambridge, Mass.: Wright-Allen Press, 1971.

Presents Professor Forrester's preliminary global model on which the Club of Rome's later research reported in *The Limits To Growth* is based.

Forrester, Nathan B. *The Life Cycle of Economic Development*. Cambridge, Mass.: Wright-Allen Press, 1972.

Presents a system dynamics model of national economic development.

Meadows and Meadows, ed. *Toward Global Equilibrium: Collected Papers*. Cambridge, Mass.: Wright-Allen Press, 1973.

Collects thirteen papers describing individual research on issues evolving from the Club of Rome's study.

Meadows et al. *Dynamics of Growth in a Finite World*. Cambridge, Mass.: Wright-Allen Press, forthcoming, 1973.

The technical report of the Club of Rome project describing the complete model, purpose, and methodology.

Meadows, Dennis L. *Dynamics of Commodity Production Cycles*. Cambridge, Mass.: Wright-Allen Press, 1970.

Presents a general dynamic model of long-term commodity production cycles.

Meadows et al. *The Limits to Growth*. New York: Universe Books for Potomac Associates, 1972.
The general report of the Club of Rome project describing the exponential growth trends that dominate the global society.

35. *Gunnar Myrdal*

Gunnar Karl Myrdal was born at Gustafs, Sweden, in 1898. He studied at the University of Stockholm and is professor of international economics at the same school. He is also director of the Swedish Institute for International Economic Studies and chairman of the board of the Stockholm International Peace Research Institute (SIPRI).

Professor Myrdal has published among other works *An American Dilemma* (1944), *An International Economy* (1956), *Beyond the Welfare State* (1960), *Challenge to Affluence* (1963), and *Asian Drama*, three volumes (1968).

During the 1972 Stockholm conference on the environment, you warned that man should finally recognize and prepare for limits to growth.

It is a very much more complicated problem than most people think, including your Dutch friend, Sicco Mansholt.[1] All this loose talk about planetary and global solutions is humbug. When we see the lack of equality throughout the world, when we see the Americans using up forty percent of all the material we have, talking about global problems and solutions is absolute nonsense.

* * *

Perhaps, but you did sound a serious warning for limits.

Sure there are limits, but nobody knows much about them. All so-called facts are highly controversial. What I am particularly against is to deal with these so-called limits as if it was a fixed global issue without in any way entering the much more urgent question of equality between nations and within countries themselves.

You advocate centrally imposed and enforced planning of all human and economic activity. But how to do that?

That's exactly what I am trying to make clear. We are faced with a most serious administrative problem. And there is the political question of course. But I have written a variety of articles on these problems. I am happy to be quoted from my written works. I am explaining these things again in a book I am finishing at the moment, which will be called *Critical Essays on Economics.*

Yes, but I flew to Stockholm, not to blindly copy words you have already composed at an earlier date. Let's add a personal touch.

All right. I will tell you what I think of abstract models. In recent decades, there has been a strenuous and strained effort by the majority of my economist colleagues to emulate what they conceive of as the methods of the natural scientists by constructing utterly simplified models, often given a quick mathematical dressing. This kind of model building has been recently spreading rapidly in the other social sciences too, where in turn, the researchers apparently seek to emulate the economists.

It should be clear, however, that this adoption of the form does not really make the social sciences more "scientific," if that form is not adequate to social reality, and therefore, not usable for the analysis of it. It is on the basis of having reached down to the bottom of reality that it has been possible for the natural scientists to make often fundamental discoveries at their writing desks by simply applying mathematical reasoning to ascertained facts and relationships. Fashion changes in a cyclical way in our field of study. The pendulum has swung lately to abstract model building not only in the United States but also in the rest of the world.

I foresee, however, that ten or fifteen years from now the institutional approach will again be the new vogue. The recent attempts to emulate the methods, or rather the form, of the simpler natural sciences, will be recognized as largely a temporary aberration into superficiality and irrelevance. My reason for venturing this forecast is that the study of social facts and relationships really must concern much more complex, differing and fluid matters than those represented by parameters and variables in highly abstract models, where behavior, accounted for only in terms of aggregate and averages, is left unexplained.

To this I have several things to add in order not to be misunderstood. I have certainly, per se, no criticism to raise against models. All scientific research must be generalizing and thus simplifying. Important is only that the selection of factors to be included should be done according to the criterion of relevance.

When builders of abstract economic models characterize their approach as "quantitative" in contradistinction to the institutional approach, which they are inclined to call "qualitative," this is, of course, a misnomer. Quantifying knowledge is a self-evident aim of research, and the institutional economist, as the more censorious researcher, is apt to press harder for empirical data. If he often has fewer figures to present than the conventional economists, particularly in regard to underdeveloped countries, this is because he is more critical in ascertaining them.

My third point is an admission. In spite of the very common absence of a thorough scrutiny of the underlying abstract assumptions and of the concepts used, it is a fact that econometric models even of the marco-type referring to an entire country often do reach relevant conclusions and are more useful than in the time when Alfred Marshall denounced that method as unrealistic.

In developed countries the statistical material is now more complete and reliable. Although I am not sure that the statistics used by the MIT team for *Limits to Growth* were factual and correct.

Since Limits to Growth *aims at a global calculation, and two-thirds of the planet can be considered as in a developing stage—to put it mildly —how reliable would you say were the inputs in regard to the Third World at large?*

First of all, our knowledge about conditions in these underdeveloped lands is still extremely scant. I fear that much of the assembled data and mountains of figures have either no meaning at all in analyzing economic realities, while the inadequacies in the conceptual categories utilized must have contributed at the same time to extraordinary deficiencies on the level of primary observations. Even in developed lands we have now become aware that concepts of gross national product or income and its growth are, to say the least, flimsy. They take not into consideration the factor of distribution. There is a vast lack of clarity about what is supposed to be growing, or whether it is real growth in any sense or merely accounting for costs caused by various undesirable developments. The absolute or relative uselessness of conspicious, private or public consumption and investment is almost never taken into account. In underdeveloped countries, the absence of effective markets over a wide field of their economies and many other conceptual difficulties, peculiar to these countries, are additional factors. For these reasons, and also because of extreme weakness in the operation of statistical services, the figures confidently quoted in literature about national income or product must be deemed almost valueless certainly where developing lands are concerned.

Let me say this: The archetype of a theoretical growth model is the one where aggregate output is related to physical investment by capital-output ratio. Designed originally as a theoretical tool in dealing with problems of economic stagnation and instability in developed countries, this one-factor model was applied to utterly different development problems of underdeveloped nations.

The capital/output approach had gained popularity after the war among economists because of several studies in Western countries that purported to show a close relationship between physical investment and economic growth. In fact, for a while the capital/output ratio came to be regarded as akin to the constants that have made it possible to advance knowledge of the physical universe by purely abstract mathematical reasoning.

In recent years, however, more intensive studies of economic growth in some highly developed Western lands revealed that even there, only part of it could be explained by the amount of investment in physical capital. While estimates of the unexplained residual vary widely, they generally support the view that it is considerably bigger than that part of economic growth which can be explained by capital investment.

Would you say the use of computers in the Forrester-Meadows method used in the report issued by the Club of Rome is a promising one?

For the planet as a whole, I do not think it is a very useful method, the computer method. Because, as I stressed before, our problems are not global in the simple sense as used by the MIT people. Of course, we should not underestimate the great advantages of modern data machines in studying all our crises and enigmas. But then the questions and problems should be clearly defined. They should be clear cut. They should not contain words which are uncertain or even entirely wrong. One will never get more from this magic box than one puts in. The one thing I am dead set against is the naïve belief in being able to solve problems on silly assumptions, wrong assumptions, and get anywhere with wrong concepts or utterly bad material.

Do you believe natural scientists are willing and prepared to exert more pressure on policy makers and public opinion on behalf of a wiser use of the environment?

I hope they will do it. Of course, all scientists should do so.

International labor unions are now exploring ways to neutralize the power of global employers. In other words, get rid of individual profit-seeking decisions in exchange for the interests of society and man as a whole, including the environment.

I have not studied this field sufficiently and in detail. In theory the answer should of course be that one could have the same control by a world government as we have on the national level from our governments and parliaments.

Marx warned that the more useless production is created, the more useless people are around.

I think it a silly notion, that we will end up with too much idle laborers. We need so many people to work with and care for the old, for children, for health problems and so forth.

But certainly workers in modern industrial plants get sick and tired from the work they are ordered to carry out.

Yes, that's right. Of course, there is a lot of pleasure in work. What is happening, however, is that both demands for wages and technology are bringing about pressures on workers in modern industry in quite another style. It has got to be changed. Volvo[2] is, for instance, taking away the assembly line.

Actually we are at last finding out that there is no antagonism between the egalitarian reforms of the modern welfare state and economic growth. A few decades ago most economists—and some even today—adhered to the theory that equalization would cost money, not only to higher income strata but also nationally in terms of economic growth. But welfare reforms have actually been productive. The fact that economic growth has not been slowing down but, if anything, been speeding up in this era of radical social reform, for instance in Sweden, confirms in a broad sense those conclusions. Redistributional reforms have raised the income of the needy and have generally not even lowered income or the rise of income in upper classes. Generally speaking, the relative distribution of income and in particular of wealth, has not changed much in spite of increasing progressive taxation and expensive redistributional reforms in favor of the lower-income strata. We see now that a great number of reforms—for instance, the move toward nationalization of medical care and child welfare—have had particularly strong effects on raising productivity. A most important element in the development of the modern welfare state is, moreover, the broadening of opportunities for youths in the field of education. The old inegalitarian society had its firm basis in the upper-class monopoly of all higher education. This monopoly is now rapidly on the way to becoming broken in all the rich democratic welfare states. This development is straight in line with the interests of raising productivity in the new technological era. This political, social and economic process seems to be going on at an accelerating speed in all of the rich countries.

From your writings I would say you are neither optimistic nor pessimistic but very much follow a road of the middle geared towards realism.

That is not middle of the road. Optimism like pessimism are biases. Realism is the real thing. It does not carry defeatism either, because when things look dim, you have to possess the courage to help change the world. The basis for every scientist should be like this. Why on earth would I work on my books, when I could have a pleasant life with wine and plenty. I continue to work and write because I possess the faith which is the basis of all scholarly study. In the end knowledge is a liberating force. Illusions, particularly opportunistic illusions, are always dangerous. That is the faith a scholar possesses.

* * *

But in order to be creative, one has to have faith in mankind.

Exactly, that is what I was trying to explain to you. That is the faith of all scholarly work.

NOTES

[1] See conversation no. 20.
[2] Swedish automobile factory.

36. *Alva Myrdal*

Mrs. Alva Myrdal, the wife of Professor Gunnar Myrdal, is cabinet minister in charge of church affairs and disarmament since 1967.

She was born in Uppsala, Sweden, in 1902. She studied in Stockholm, London, Leipzig and Geneva. From 1949 to 1950, Mrs. Myrdal was principal director of the department of social sciences at UNESCO. Since 1962 she has been Swedish chief delegate to the disarmament conference in Geneva. From 1962 to 1970 she was member of the upper house of the Swedish Parliament.

Aside from publishing a number of books written together with Gunnar Myrdal, Mrs. Myrdal wrote *Nation and Family* (1941), *Postwar Planning* (1944), *Our Responsibilities for the Poor Peoples* (1961) and *Disarmament—Reality or Utopia?* (1965).

As a delegate to the disarmament conference in Geneva, you warned that in eighteen months the globe had to support once more sixty atomic tests; three in China, five in France, sixteen in the United States and several dozen in the Soviet Union.[1]

That's just one development that has to stop. There are only five powers who really are the sinners. I don't think that the hazard is too great. However, they are conducting these weapons tests in order to improve their nuclear weapons to an ever higher capacity of killing. This means of course that they are competitive. They are also monopolizing the tremendous resources of their own countries. Thus a great part of the world's resources are being used up for this purpose of perfecting instruments of death. Even if there's not a nuclear war, and even if the nuclear test explosions are not dangerous to human health, the very course one is forced to take is one that is detrimental to the interests of mankind, of the rest of the world and even to the people in their own countries.

As Ivan Illich has written, modern weapons can only defend civilization and so-called freedom by annihilating man.[2] Do you agree that, for instance, SALT[3] does not prevent a further increase in atomic warheads in rockets? There is a SALT agreement, but SIPRI[4] has used the term "cosmetic agreement" for it. Is man not faced with a very serious situation?

Yes, he is. The SALT agreements are good from the point of view that they show that two parties can agree upon something. But even for the defensive strategic weapons it means that they increase their ABM's in order to get there. Then for the offensive strategic weapons there is no limit even on a quantitative basis as they can put more bombs in each missile. They can make *qualitative* development; there is no end to their so-called improvement.

Secondly, there is no limit at all to the quantitative increase. The field remains open for competition. The additions are so high in the Soviet Union and in the United States that it certainly cannot but encourage China to try to go ahead also. At least these three world powers are not showing any signs of stopping this competitive course towards destruction.

In other words, they are now moving from quantity into quality, and actually the mad race goes right on.

Yes. They have been improving quality all the time. The only aspect on which they are trying to put some limitation is the quantitative one. That is not the worst. The qualitative one is much worse, because if you produce new quantities of nuclear weapons, you dispose or you use resources, plants, iron, electronics and so on. But if you are racing towards qualitative improvements, you take and utilize the human brain to a much higher degree, because it involves research and development. I believe that brainpower is much more scarce in this world than, let's say, electricity. What the poor countries need more than anything else is, of course, to get all these hundreds of thousands of scientists and engineers to work on their problems, on constructive problems and not on destructive problems.

What did the Khrushchev-Kennedy agreement to stop atmospheric testing actually mean? Underground testing went right on, endangering the planet and human life. Now there is a so-called SALT agreement?

The Kennedy-Khrushchev agreement on the nuclear test ban has not meant anything, least of all, to reduce the armaments race. Not a single thing. They are going on just as they did before. I see really no end to it if the military people don't change their attitude, I do think the scientists are in the course of changing theirs. There is much more discomfort on the part of scientists to work, for instance, with chemical weapons. They really are criticizing what is being done. We always have had the great heroes among even the atomic scientists, who have been wondering whether they did right or not, like Oppenheimer.[5]

Yes, Andrei D. Sakharov in the Soviet Union—

Yes, Sakharov and several others in the Soviet Union. They came to a congress in Sweden. They have said recently that all scientists should agree at least to stop work on biological weapons. I have greater hopes about the scientists revolting against the present situation. Scientists will lead public opinion to revolt against this, and that will influence the politicians. Then I hope the politicians and statesmen will in turn exercise power over the military.

In other words, the scientists should move the people to stir the politicians to do what is needed.

Yes, exactly. The people themselves have not got that source of energy. Because they are also dumbfounded by the mass media or by television. They believe much more in slogans like "superiority," "national honor" and "we must be the greatest," et cetera—which is just nonsense. Every nation cannot be the greatest, anyway. It is better that we band together and try to make the best of the planet.

The Forrester team at MIT has now tried for the first time to create a global model in order to study what should be done for survival and what interactions of damaging factors to all life in reality are.

Yes, if you stress the word "beginning," I think it's very good. It opens up a field of interest to many people, but it certainly could not be considered as a model on which one should start to work for an implementation, but rather to start with critical studies of alternative futures of different kinds. We have been very much interested in Sweden in this field. As a small country we are of course afraid of the huge nations, the superpowers, especially of their planning from a military point of view. The multinational firms—big business and so on—will plan the future of the world according to their interests. They are actually also planning for *our* future. We want to have an influence on it. We are very eager to set up some units in Sweden to follow the thinking in the planning field which is going on and to contribute in certain sectors, where we have resources enough for doing it.

I have just been chairman of an official committee. We have deliberated in our report on how the future should be studied in Sweden. We must remember the interests of the common man, of the municipality, of the provinces, of the various groups and we must see to it that the thinking of the future, which should be combining their interests, will be balanced, but that it should take into consideration also the interests of future generations. We should not decide too much. We should not tie the future too much for them. We should leave a number of decisions open to them. That is a very difficult proposition in everything that has to do with planning.

The New York Times *warned in a speech by Professor Mason Willridge of the University of Virginia that gangsters or evil people some day will be able to threaten humanity by making an amateurish nuclear bomb.*

That is possible. Assassins and bandits have much greater potentialities than we realize—even with regard to chemical weapons, for instance, lethal gases and so on. You see examples of that kind of explosives, which they send in little letters to various persons in different countries. That might not bring real havoc to great numbers of people, but I think the possibilities for implementing plans of brutality by individuals or by gangs is something we must take into consideration much much more than before. SIPRI is just now producing a massive and harassing study on all kinds of chemical weapons, for instance. You are no doubt familiar with the 900-page study the institute recently published on "The Arms Trade with the Third World"?

Yes, I went to see Dr. Frank Barnaby [director] and have written about this most important study in the press. But are you hopeful that scientists will be able to arouse ·sufficiently mankind and in time before we are really into disaster?

No, I could not say I am hopeful. But we do not need to be hopeful in order to try to forestall evil until it happens. I do believe that everybody who understands at least something of these problems has the duty to speak up. I would say that particularly we in the smaller and neutral countries—who are not bound by considerations towards one block or another—we have an extra responsibility to tell the truth as we see it, hoping that that in the long run will influence the world. There is nothing to believe in anymore if you don't continue to believe in reason.

NOTES

[1]July, 1972.
[2]*Deschooling Society*, Harper & Row (New York, 1970), p. 158.
[3]Strategic Arms Limitation Talks.
[4]Stockholm International Peace Research Institute.
[5]J. Rober Oppenheimer, US nuclear physicist.

37.   Ralph E. Lapp

Ralph E. Lapp was born in Buffalo, New York, in 1917. He received his Ph.D. in physics from the University of Chicago. He is one of America's best-known critics in the field of atomic-energy uses and development.

From 1945 to 1946 he was connected with the so-called Bikini Island bomb tests. He has been an adviser to the Pentagon on atomic matters.

Among numerous articles and books, we mention *We Must Hide* (1949), *Nuclear Radiation Physics* (1954), *Atoms and People* (1956), *Kill and Overkill* (1962) and *The Weapons Culture* (1968).

Dr. Lapp, what are your views on the steady increase in use of nuclear power as to the endangering of the environment or human society?

My view on nuclear power is that we have to have this new source of energy in order to supply the power for the future, as our fossil fuels —especially the premium fossil fuels, oil and natural gas—are being rapidly depleted. It is not so much a question that we cannot find more oil and natural gas or exploit coal resources, we certainly can. But the nature of our modern society in the twentieth century is that we are all trying to shinny up the industrial ladder as fast as we can. In fact, some of the less-developed countries are even proceeding at their stage of the game faster than we are. This means that there is an enormous demand upon resources, especially the fossil fuels which are a one-time inheritance and which cannot be replaced.

The United States has exploited fossil fuels like no other country in the world, to a point where today it is forced to import twenty-five percent of all its oil and is now importing natural gas from Algeria. Indeed, it's beginning to import natural gas in liquid form. So great is the need in the United States for these premium fossil fuels that we are going to get gas from the desert in Africa. Liquified after being pumped to a coastal port and then put upon a special tanker.

In frozen condition?

In liquid form and then transported in supercooled state across the ocean to a port facility where it will be pumped ashore as a fluid again and then held until it is needed to be gasified. This gas comes out of the Algerian desert at probably a few cents a thousand cubic feet, but by the time the Boston housewife gets it, she will be paying two dollars and a half for it. That's an enormous markup in the price of a commodity. We've gotten so hooked on this fossil fuel and on the things which are produced from it, namely, electricity, that we have to go where the fuel source is. Now I happen to believe that nuclear power comes along as a necessary extension of our reserves of fuel. It is of course a completely different kind of fuel from the fossil fuels which are burned in the presence of oxygen in a combustion technique. This of course forms the major source of pollution which comes from the smokestack of a power-plant. There is also the pollution from the more than one hundred million tailpipes of the mobile vehicles in the United States when the products of gasoline and diesel oil combustion are exhausted. So the Americans have in their ingenious way combined an enormous gas machine in the form of hundreds, indeed thousands, of stationary sources, burning coal, oil and natural gas and in the form of something like one hundred and thirteen million four-wheeled vehicles which gulp down gasoline. Now, the problem is that we are in the United States converting ourselves into an increasingly electrified country. Mid-century only ten percent of our fuel went into producing electricity, today it is gone to about twenty-seven percent; by the end of the century fifty percent of all the fuel will be burned just to produce electricity. We are becoming an electrified society, and the rest of the world is following in our footsteps.

Some scientists seem to feel that energy someday could be tapped from the sun, which would give man unlimited energy.

Yes, when I talk of nuclear power, I talk not only of power from uranium, but also of power from the fusion of light elements, such as hydrogen, that is of course an unlimited source of energy for us. It is not without its problems. Nobody knows how to predict the time scale for it. We have a general idea of how such a machine burning hydrogen in a nuclear sense would look. But we don't know how to make one, nor do we know how to cost it out and tell at what price such a machine would produce electricity. But the fuel for such a machine is virtually the fuel of the oceans itself—the heavy hydrogen that is contained in water itself. So we will really be ocean-burning and of course with the magnitude of the oceans we literally have solved the energy problem of this planet for a billion years.

The public will ask, Where will nuclear waste go?

The basic problem in the heavy-metal power—which is uranium and thorium—the basic problem is to ensure that the energy release that is accomplished in machines known as nuclear reactors, that the hazard is confined at each point, from the time you take the uranium ore from the ground, mill it, refine it, convert it, fabricate fuel elements, burn them inside these nuclear plants and then reprocess the radioactive fuel to get new fuel and finally ending up with the residual waste, the very long-lived, radioactive elements, which form a unique problem for man. We must find—and most countries must find it within their own territory—a unique cemetery. A place that will be undisturbed for centuries to come, because that is the time it takes for these radioactive elements to lose their potency. One cannot look at countries in Africa and think of any political regimes that will be stable for centuries to come. We in the United States are a relatively young democracy. We think we have political stability. How long it will persist I don't know. But very few countries have political stability, or a history of it. The necessary repository will in my opinion be some sort of salt mine, in which to store the radioactive waste in perpetuity. This, however, is not an unsolvable problem. I believe that sufficient research is going on now so that we will be able to put these wastes in underground containment and that these will be safe.

For centuries to come, without endangering mankind? But didn't you write that the nuclear plants that are being built, mainly in the United States, tend to be constructed closer and closer to cities? What are the dangers?

My basic philosophy about a nuclear power plant is that until you prove them safe—and safe essentially to a very high degree—until you can prove these plants safe enough to locate close to a metropolitan population, you put them relatively far from a dense population. My reason is not because I have no confidence in nuclear-power design, but because we are dealing with a unique problem in the history of man. Never before in the history of this planet have we placed such a unique hazard so close to a large population.

About the only parallel that I can draw is that if you construct a high dam and then build a city at its base. That isn't generally done; and if you did it, the people at least would know that the dam was there and that they were in line of sight of the risk. And they would have some experience with how often dams break and if you got in trouble, the dams started to weaken, the engineers could release the water from the dam gradually, as was done in the case of Los Angeles after the 1972 earthquake. That's about the only parallel I know. But, for instance, eleven miles from Philadelphia, a nuclear-power plant is being moved in toward a very large population. In my opinion we have not demonstrated to the public that there is that degree of reliability in the safety systems for that plant, that it does not pose a rather severe hazard to the population, in case of an accident.

Yes, but demonstrating to the public is still something else than whether it is truly safe. In your opinion it is safe?

In my opinion the issue is in doubt. The issue is in doubt because we are dealing with very complex systems. We have not operated power plants or the new ones at this power level. We have very little experience with plants of this kind. Therefore, to say a nuclear-power plant is safe in advance is to say that you are depending on models which have been constructed to predict the behavior of the system. I know we have to rely on models, but the question is when you rely on models, how do you get the public to accept the model? This is very clearly the case in nuclear safety, because nobody wants to take a full-scale nuclear power plant and treat it to an experiment. It is too expensive, much too costly, to have an experiment of that kind. So what you do is you construct a model for this plant and then you subject it to an analysis to see how it will behave. But what you like to do is to carry out a series of small-scale experiments to prove the model out. Some of these experiments have been conducted in the United States by the Atomic Energy Commission.

Since we cannot prove even to the scientific community that these machines are that safe, I believe that we must (1) intensify the safety research program; (2) hold the line of the deployment of these plants, so that they are not too close to cities. Some plants—such as one not far from where we are today, namely, the Calvert Cliffs plant (forty miles east of Alexandria, Virginia)—if there were to be a severe accident, there would not be serious consequences in terms of thousands of people who may be exposed to radiation from the plant, because the plant is favorably sited with respect to population at risk.

In your June 22, 1972, article in the New York Times Magazine *you mentioned the possibility of building atomic islands in the sea—like eleven miles outside Atlantic City, New Jersey. Has that been proposed on official levels? Is it being considered at all?*

Since I wrote this article on power islands for the New York *Times Magazine*, the public-service company in New Jersey has announced definite plans to build a $1.1 billion installation three miles off the coast of New Jersey, northeast of Atlantic City.

You mentioned eleven miles in your article. Is three miles not dangerous?

It's three miles from the shore, but over eleven miles from Atlantic City. I believe that in this particular case we have the problem of the calculated risk for a state which has no more rivers on which to locate plants. It's essentially run out of cooling water and these plants all require a very large amount of cooling water. When you are up against it, you find out that there is no really good place left for New Jersey—or for New York City. Therefore, going out into the ocean essentially solves the thermal-pollution problem, the so-called hot-water problem, so you don't destroy unnecessarily aquatic life. The other problem of nuclear safety still remains. But I believe that in this case, if we examine the wind patterns from the site, you will find out that the risk to Atlantic City is not nearly the risk, for example, that you would have from the plant they would plan to locate at Newbold Island, eleven miles from Philadelphia. All of these projects would involve risks.

Dr. Lapp, in managing the future of the planet, MIT (the Forrester people)[1] have tried to make a model of the planet in order to start a catalogue on how to manage it. Do you feel a model of that type has any value when no variables are included concerning atomic energy and the kind of power or energy that might save us in the future?

Over about the past seven years I have been doing a great deal of work myself on trying to look at the future, looking specifically at the year 2000. But I soon realized that you cannot look at such a short time ahead. You have to look actually to the year 2100 and beyond in order to see it through a perspective of some of the problems we face.

With respect to the question of the computer model of the planet, I believe that the MIT approach was a first attempt, and it was a brash one in my opinion. The danger of such a model is that people are prone to computer worship. They don't realize that all of these computers depend upon the wisdom that was put into them. They have no self-wisdom. There is no judgment or value system generated inside a piece of electronics at this stage of the game. When I look at people predicting the quality of life in the twenty-first century on the computer model, it makes me very unhappy, because I do not believe we can define the quality of life in computer terms. So, I don't expect the computer to print out predictions of the quality of life. That's utter nonsense, and I think people have a right to get mad and irritated when scientists make such outlandish predictions.

But, to put the best complexion on this, where a model will provoke people to think about the future realistically and see that there are finite resources on this planet, then I say hallelujah, I am for it. To that extent I go along. However, I do not believe you have to entrust the destiny of man to computers. I believe that the human brain, the three-pound piece of software inside my cranium, that still has great excess capacity and that it can itself analyze the problem and take into account many variables and make predictions which will, I think, have certain values.

For example, I believe that it is quite possible to construct a model of fossil-fuel resources of the planet and to sketch in for the twenty-first century how we will deplete these fossil fuels and how we will come to depend primarily in the next century upon nuclear power for our energy. The fact is that our fossil fuels are in very short supply. Demand for them is so great, with a growing population and with a growing per capita consumption, that we are virtually "blowing" our fossil-fuel resources in a short space of time. The whole fossil-fuel period in the United States or in the world will be a transitory era, which is in between the wood-burning phase and the nuclear-burning era. Our problem is how to get from here to there.

Gasoline, for example, is probably the most critical fuel for the United States since its economic viability depends on mobility. I happen to regard the internal-combustion engine as the most infernal invention ever made, because to me the internal-combustion engine is more revolutionary for the twentieth century and its economy than atomic energy. As a nuclear physicist this may sound a little bit off beat for me to make a prediction of that kind, but I have been looking at the twentieth century.

I have just completed a book called *The Logarithmic Century*. I call the century logarithmic because when I plot anything—whether it is consumption of cigarettes, whether it's production of kilowatt hours of electricity, whether it's burning of gallons of gasoline per year—everything goes up in a logarithmic ascendancy. So when I look at the actual course of events in the twentieth century, I find that the United States has been leading the pack of nations. It is leading them at such a rate that it is really incredible that we in this country, with our high degree of technological finesse, have not anticipated the shortages that are certain to come. We are blind, and the reason we are blind is because of our democratic system. Our democratic system is politically quantized to think in two-, four- and six-year time periods. These are the respective terms of office for congressional representatives, the president and senators—these men in office think of their time period when they will be reelected. It is very hard to get them to think in twenty-five-, fifty- and a hundred-year time units because they think that's not of importance to their constituents. This is a basic fault in the democratic system, and we must overcome it.

Therefore, I welcome studies such as the MIT studies, because they shake us up a bit. We may not like them but they make us look to the future and we have to be future-oriented. For example, I said that gasoline is the most critical commodity which is required to keep the United States in business. Two-thirds of the population of the United States is located in one hundred metropolitan areas, sprawling complexes of central cities, of villages, towns, which are interconnected with congested highways on which every day we have an inward and an outward flow of tons of millions of vehicles. This inward and outward flow is largely based upon occupancy of the automobile with 1.2 people on an average. I calculate what I call the energy cost of such transportation, and it is fabulous. By the way, in reckoning my energy costs I reckon far more than just the cost of the gasoline. I reckon in energy times the cost of the automobile, the cost of servicing the automobile, the cost of repair—

—The "ground," as Marshall McLuhan[2] would call it.

Yes. And when I do that, I find out that we have on our hands an extremely energy-consumptive machine. Yet we have gotten ourselves into a fix. Our people are so sprawled out in ameban geometric patterns that it is almost impossible to devise an efficient and reasonably priced mass transportation system, which can service people who live ten miles from the center of the city.

Dr. Lapp, Japan is having the same problem. In China, Chou En-lai[3] told a recent visitor that there are one and a half million bicycles in Peking. Apparently he would not like to see them replaced by automobiles. Holland is overrun by cars. The entire world is suffering by now from this disease. How to tackle these problems on a global scale?

Well, precisely. In fact, I have a little chart, which of course we cannot inject in conversation very easily, but a chart in which I plotted the population of automobiles on the planet in the year 2000. It just gives me the willies because of the fact that while we are building this number of automobiles, we are also trying to make these automobiles less polluting, and in the process we are going backwards. These new automobiles have low-compression engines, and they have all kinds of antipollution devices which take energy. The result is that the car today in America, going in and out of the city, gets only about eight miles to the gallon, in a modern car. I am much more concerned about the conservation of our resources, than I am about the pollution because it seems to me that if we cannot keep our people mobile—if we cannot get them from here to there, from home to work, to the shopping centers—if we cannot do that, our economy will go stale.

The situation is terribly bad, you know. It is easy to say, "there are solutions to this." Fine. If you don't drive a Cadillac, but were to drive a Volkswagen, you could get twice as many miles per gallon. But imagine what it would mean if you could conceive of anyone in the White House telling General Motors that they should make Volkswagens. I assume they would like to make Volkswagens if they could sell them for the price of a Cadillac. But if they would sell Volkswagens at Volkswagen's price, what would happen to General Motors' stock? This is at the heart of our economy. About one out of every six and a half people in the United States has his job keyed to the automobile. When you tinker with the automobile economy, when Detroit's production is changed, the whole economy of this country is changed.

So if we want to talk about curtailing growth, we must realize that there are severe consequences. Therefore, I believe the economists are correct when they say you must include the measure of cost of the system as you project to the future. In fact, in analyzing many things, I found a whole variety of constraints imposed upon various energy systems or various commodity systems. In the case of cigarette smoking, it's virtual saturation of the market. I mean, there are some more people who might smoke, but you cannot increase the market very much more, it's near saturation. The biological insult is a limiting factor here. In the case of power plants, it is our sure ability to build power plants and to finance them. I think this is a more limited factor than anything else. We will have to have by the end of this century one thousand nuclear-power plants, each one a million kilowatts in power. These plants will by the end of the century be costing a very large amount of money. This is a problem even for the United States with all of its wealth. But think what it means to a small country to try and get up on the industrial ladder if it has to go the nuclear route. They will have to pay almost the same price we are paying. I am almost inclined to believe that one of the impacts of nuclear power is that the rich countries will continue to grow richer and the poor countries will get poorer.

Let's put some of these energy things in perspective. We in the United States are of course energy affluent. We consume energy like there is no end to it. Really the Americans cannot believe—even though they have been told it by some high authorities—that it will ever stop. They say energy crises are an invention of the petroleum industry. They just want to sell, get a higher price and sell more oil. In point of fact, it took even time for the petroleum industry to realize it, because they normally think only in terms of about fifteen years in the future. But now we have problems here. When we look at other countries—India, for example—India has fifteen percent of world's population, but currently uses about one and a half percent of the world's energy and much of that energy is provided by burning animal dung. This is truly a backward country, and what happens when India attempts to climb up to an industrial state of development which is higher than it presently has? It has to get capital to finance it. Now, where do less-developed countries manage to get the money to finance these new developments? It's fine to say to a country, "Oh, we could build a nuclear-power complex which will produce electricity for chemicals and electricity to run pumps to provide agricultural water, but you have to have the capital to make it go."

*   *   *

NOTES

[1] See conversation no. 34.
[2] See conversation no. 12.
[3] Prime Minister of the People's Republic of China.

38. *José M. R. Delgado*

Professor José Manuel Rodriguez Delgado was born in Ronda, Spain, in 1915. He studied medicine at the University of Madrid, where he still teaches. In 1965 he was nominated professor of physiology at the School of Psychiatry at Yale University, in New Haven, Connecticut.

Professor Delgado developed electrodes for permanent implantation in the brain. He further studied problems of radio stimulation on the brain, and the social behavior of colonies of monkeys. Physical control of the mind by direct manipulation of the brain is an entirely novel event in man's history. His book *Physical Control of the Mind: Towards a Psychocivilized Society* was published in 1971. A cover story for *Time* magazine, "The Mind: From memory pills to electronic pleasures beyond sex," devoted considerable attention to Professor Delgado's work (April 19, 1971, pp. 29-34).

Albert Szent-Györgyi,[1] the microbiologist, feels that man is apt to follow the dinosaur.[2] You said somewhere that man is about as stupid as a dinosaur.

There is a very fortunate difference between the dinosaurus and man: The difference is that we have awareness about our own existence.

Furthermore, we are developing the technology to investigate the mechanisms of awareness, of personality, and therefore of our own future behavior. The dinosaurs did not have the technology or the intelligence to establish the feedback that we are initiating now, which is the feedback of intelligence on the destiny of man. Until very recently, this was not possible because we did not have the methodology to explore the intracerebral mechanisms of behavior.

Man has always considered himself from a political, economic, and philosophical basis. But in fact, he was really an outsider. In the past the only thing that we could do was look at each other from the outside. The most essential link between all men, the processes within their thinking brains, were totally out of reach. This is the new door that technology has opened for us. In addition to general information about mankind, we now have access to knowledge of how the intracerebral mechanisms act. Until now, we could only give information to man and expect to evoke some responses. That is what education is all about. Because we did not have any idea about brain functions, which constitute the connecting link between sensory inputs and behavioral outputs, we could not comprehend the possibilities or limitations of the intracerebral processing of information which was resulting in the expression of behavior.

Is it true that the ten billion or so nerve cells in the brain are preprogrammed and therefore that it will be extremely difficult to influence them?

The answer is no. Like other animals, we have preprogrammed instincts and very elemental motor activity. What is most essential in man, however, is not his elemental preprogrammation but depends on stimuli which come from the outside. This is one of the findings of recent investigations on how the brain is structured.

What do you mean by outside environment?

Waddington[3] said long ago that we have a dual inheritance: genetic plus cultural. One of the important differences between man and animals is that animals' behavioral repertoire is largely preset. When a cat is born, it knows how to walk. When a rat is born, it knows how to eat. These creatures have many programs already established that they do not need to learn. Man is born with a far more immature brain. Today we know that the chemical structure of this brain, which will be developed and formed through the years of childhood, is to a great extent dependent on the amount and quality of sensory inputs it may receive. In the absence of visual sensory inputs, the visual pathways of the brain will not develop properly. In the absence of auditory inputs, the auditory centers will be abnormal. Therefore, our experiences have a material representation, and messages from the outside world are stored, perhaps as symbolic codes of chemical formulas, inside of the brain. Information from the outside is transformed somehow into symbolic matter within the brain. These are facts that we know today.

We should ask what are the most important elements of being human. Naturally what is "human" is a question of definition. Let's take, for our discussion, something very simple like conversation, language. Man has preprogrammed mechanisms of speech, but without exposure to this type of communication, he will never learn to talk. The anatomical structure of a chimpanzee's larynx is different, and it would be impossible for him to modulate the sounds that we make. Probably the temporal lobe is also programmed differently in the chimpanzee, making the animal difficult to teach.

And is it nonsense that we are called descendants of apes?

No, that is not nonsense. It depends on your understanding of what we are discussing. The blood in our veins is similar in composition not only to that of chimpanzees but also to the blood of other mammals and even reptiles. Therefore, we should define the question more precisely. We are descendants of a long biological evolution, but we should not speak in generalities. We must proceed item by item. For instance, sodium chloride, the main component of sea water, is still present in our bloodstream, testimony to our evolution from remote ancestors which swam in the world's oceans millenniums ago.

When we speak of human nature, we are talking about something completely different. The chimpanzee does not have the preprogrammed mechanisms in its brain that would enable it to talk and associate words in the complex way that we do. Therefore, in relation to your question, some of man's behavior is preprogrammed, but it is only a possibility, not a reality. To develop these potentials, to talk, you need to be taught. If you are not exposed to English or Chinese, you will never speak these languages. You have in your brain, however, the capacity to learn languages. Thus, anatomical structure and preprogramming of instincts should be distinguished from the wide range of variability in possible human development. Would you like to be human? Would you like to talk? Then you need to learn. Would you like to be human? And to have ethical values? You may acquire ethics, but they are not inherited, and must be learned. The most basic qualities of man come from the outside.

In order to understand human potential, you must go inside man. The unique qualities of human behavior have their origin within the thinking brain, and the new technology allows us to explore its working neurons. The tremendous difference between animals and man is that we have the awareness and technology to investigate and influence our own behavior. We have already acquired tremendous mechanical and atomic power with which we can modify nature. We now live in the artificial climates of our cities. This is the present condition of mankind. Civilized man does not live in—and is never again going to live in—the jungle, where he would be old at twenty-five and would probably be dead at thirty. This is just not comfortable. It is not practical. It is not "human."

So we will continue to live in the modern environment of expanding metropolises. The only choice is whether we are going to use or misuse human intelligence in order to plan our cities. If we are not intelligent, our cities will not be functional. Then instead of helping man to enjoy a healthy and interesting life, his surroundings will turn out to be a handicap, imposing pollution, overcrowding, and their corollary problems. We cannot afford to make this mistake: We must organize our environment properly and learn to modify nature for our benefit. In a similar manner, the careful planning of man's social relations is absolutely vital.

Do you feel that the planning of our planet as a whole is essential? You are talking of planning the planet in a social way according to a frame of reference—

—of the nineteenth century. It is inadequate in today's society because new elements are evolving. The old political ideologies, including Marxism and capitalism, cannot work. They were the products of conditions which were realities in the nineteenth century, but today we need new frames of reference, and they must be found soon. This is my bias. This is my opinion: that we need the biological understanding of man with the new premise that our problem is not to discover "Who am I?" or "What is man?" That was the classical position. That was static. What we need now is to know the neurophysiological potential of human beings. What is the main organ responsible for "humanness"? The brain.

We need to know what it can do. Then, based on biological reality, we can plan the kind of human beings that we would like to structure for the future.

Naturally that requires unlimited imagination and involves grave risks, but we have no choice, because just as we are building cities today, for better or worse, we keep on producing children. Because they are not born all prewired (and that is why your first question was important), their behavioral frame of reference must be provided. The sole question is, Who is going to choose it? This we *can* decide. Shall we allow the intellects of future generations to be formed by chance? In this way we may have some safeguard that human beings will not be automats. But don't random stimuli influence thought processes as much as rigid sets? We could program people, increasing the automatism that we experience today. What we must recognize is that at present most of us are ninety-nine percent programmed by our culture, by our civilization, by the mechanization of our cities. We are programmed by television, by books, by information that we receive from the outside. Very few people are strong enough to think for themselves and qualify the avalanche of information coming from the outside. Therefore most of our behavior involves carrying out activities planned by the mass media. Conduct is determined not by our genes but by the medium in which we live.

Now the choice could be to augment this behavioral programming and establish some institutions and central agencies strong enough to effectively control human development.

In the form of universities—

In the form of universities, government, or anything you like. To me, these methods are repulsive. To me this is what I would not like to see done.

An Orwellian[4] nightmare is alive today?

Exactly. This is what people do not realize. They are concerned about being controlled in the future without realizing that they are being controlled today. Most of us are the products of specific cultural systems. Now, Big Brother, the directive power, could do something else, which is what I would like to see done: to emphasize in education the elements of human dignity and personal freedom. To me, the most precious aspect of being human is the opportunity to use one's own ideological and emotional framework in order to do something original. But even originality must be inculcated, developed, and encouraged from the outside. You see, we are not born original. While we are all unique individuals, we are not necessarily going to make unique contributions; all of us are different, but few are original. If you want to create original, independent human beings, you need to cultivate these qualities in childhood.

I would strongly favor teaching people the trick that has been played on all of us: that we were patterned in early life when we had no choice or defense. We did not choose the framework of our own minds. Each set of parents, as spokesmen for their particular cultural environment, arbitrarily and in a dictatorial way imposed their own ideas on us. Before a child's brain mechanisms of choice have developed, he must be guided. We need to give little babies a frame of reference.

During later childhood, when their brains are more mature and they are able to gather information and make decisions, we can favor the development of a new kind of human being by encouraging them to evaluate their frames of reference and to challenge the sensory inputs given them. We can then ask them to be cautious about the set value patterns they have been exposed to, and reward flexibility, not rigidity. Thus we could encourage children to express their own individuality, keeping in mind that they will always act with the cultural tools we have provided. With these building blocks at their disposal, we could ask children: Be original. Be not only yourself but a different kind of yourself. Try to live for some purpose and go toward some future in which you can make a special contribution. Parents could provide the conditions in which children could develop in this way; the initial choice is theirs, and the responsibility is society's.

This is what we might plan for: the creation of a new kind of man that I call psychocivilized. Psychocivilized man will have far greater awareness of the determinants of his own behavior, and an intimate knowledge of his potential, based on the possibilities and limits of his own mind. He will realize that we are not (as I was taught) individual, independent human beings, but creatures totally dependent on social and cultural exchange. A man who comprehends his inescapable involvement with his surroundings will appreciate that the quality of his environment is of primary importance in determining individual development. Thus, in order to be a freer "himself," he may need to improve his surroundings. There are profound social implications of this new concept of what man should be. We cannot live isolated from our medium, and therefore we need to improve it. Since we form part of the medium, let us also improve ourselves and try to help those around us.

Isn't that what Mao Tse-tung is practicing in China?

Not really, because in China, as in most other countries, education and indoctrination are practiced empirically with predetermined aims but without an intimate knowledge of man's working brain. Rather than accept doctrines blindly—it makes no difference their political or theological color—we should try to exert the precious human qualities of awareness and individuality. Leaders should be respected but not idolized. The words and desires of a great man are not always right: Leaders may provide inspiration without necessarily being arbiters of all scientific and spiritual values. Each person should use his own intelligence to accept—or reject—doctrines and frames of reference, trying to develop ideas as original as possible.

Toynbee[5] foresees a kind of benevolent form of dictatorship. Skinner[6] advocates positive reinforcement.

My view is quite the opposite, because what I would like to see is not a benevolent dictatorship, but the contrary. When you give a person the encouragement and possibility to develop himself as an individual, then he will have a rather critical view of any dictator, no matter how benevolent he is. I envisage a society which does not constrain the individual and does not impose the modes and morals of a dictator but, to the contrary, encourages the person *not* to accept blindly the frames of reference received from either the past or the present. Everyone should have the opportunity to compare information given him with other cultural sets. Thus, in the future I see a more self-reliant and self-controlled man, not a society of creatures ruled by a benevolent dictator. The psychocivilized man will be free and independent because he will know the tricks of dictators and propaganda directors who try to control his own behavior; with this knowledge, he will be equipped to resist indoctrination.

But isn't it impossible to change characteristics in the interaction between heredity systems and the environment?

No. We are not changing characteristics, if by that you mean genetic inheritance. What we can do and should be doing is to give man a different kind of environment, more favorable to his development.

* * *

You encourage the already present characteristics to develop more, to get additional branches on its tree.

Exactly.

Proust[7] made a famous effort to recapture the past. How important is memory in this exercise of using intelligence?

Memory is the bank where all of our frames of references are stored. Memory forms the bases of our personality.

Is it true that the brain collects a million billion bits of information in a lifetime?[8]

I would be doubtful about how many items can be collected, but as usual, the important thing is not how much money you have, but how you use it.

Could computers someday assist or replace human memory?

I think that the role of the computer is as an accessory of memory. We are using computers today to store information. That is fine, but there are many other applications to be explored. For example, in one of our latest published studies we established direct communication for the first time from the brain to the computer and back to the brain. We did this in a chimpanzee equipped with implanted electrodes and a tele-metric device that sent information from the amygdala, a deep brain structure, to the computer. The computer recognized a special spindle pattern in the recording of spontaneous electrical activity from the amygdala; and each time it appeared, the computer produced a square wave which activated radio stimulation of a negative reinforcing area in another part of the chimpanzee's brain. The animal soon "learned" not to produce amygdala spindles, because every time it did, it received an unpleasant stimulation. In this experiment we demonstrated that one part of the brain may influence another with the link of the computer.

Our experiment, in spite of its complexity, is still rather simple. Perhaps the technique could be applied to man. This is a speculation, and what I say may be incorrect: Perhaps a computer could detect something clear-cut, such as the beginning of an epileptic attack, and then trigger a brain stimulation which would inhibit the attack. This could have tremendous therapeutic possibilities. We are only just entering this exciting new era because this instrumentation was developed within the last three years.

Naturally, advances are related to technology. I can show you our new unit for transdermal stimulation of the brain in animals, which should be used soon in patient therapy. Now we can reach the depth of the brain, stimulating it through the intact skin, by totally implanting this tiny unit, which needs no exterior sockets. It is used routinely in our laboratory animals, eliminating the possibility of infection, and making the animals available for radio stimulation at any moment.

More recently we have developed the sister instrument for transdermal recording from the depth of the brain, and when it is miniaturized, we will have two-way communication with the behaving brain by means of totally implanted units. Now, let us speculate a little. In the future, we will be able to link this "in and out" information with computers. The "Cyborg," a combination of man and machine, will become a reality, but don't be too impressed by this technology—it has its limits. The only thing that we can do in this fancy experimentation is to activate what is already in the brain. Stimulation certainly cannot transmit ideas or teach a language; for this we need to use normal, sensory inputs. This is the limitation of electrical stimulation of the brain or ESB, which has often been misunderstood by the press and the general public. It has been incorrectly assumed that with electrodes we are now going to be able to control everybody, and that a dictator is going to push buttons to handle the masses.

Whereas the fact is that you can only evoke by ESB behavioral patterns already there.

Exactly. This is the fortunate qualification. We can stimulate a point in the brain to cause an arm movement that may be skillful, provided that this arm has previously been trained to perform the movement skillfully. Stimulation of the second temporal convolution may cause a patient to talk, but naturally he will use words that he has learned in the past. Brain stimulation cannot create a new individual—it cannot change personality.

One possible application of computers to brain research involves the—highly speculative—communication of an emotional state from one brain to another, by means of a computer: It could perhaps be programmed to recognize an intracerebral electrical pattern coincident with a state of excitement or "happiness" and transmit a message to a second person to induce a similar emotional state. This may be possible with ESB, while it is not possible to direct or induce robotlike behavior.

How can we promote the dialectical relationship between consciousness and concrete reality?

Probably by acquiring a conscious understanding of this reality and by analyzing the neurological mechanisms involved, without being misled by fantasies.

It's like telling children about Santa Claus and programming them from the cradle onward against realities.

That's right. That's why I propose the establishment of psychogenesis, which means the creation, the genesis, of the psyche. Instead of programming in an erratic and contradictory way, as we are doing today, let's try a more intelligent method. You may ask, "Through a big brother?" and I answer, "Perhaps." But with a different orientation: with awareness of what types of human beings we would like to produce, based on unavoidable biological realities.

As it was sung in the American musical, *South Pacific*, "You have to be taught . . . to hate." It is known that patterns of aggressive behavior can be effectively instilled in little children; in some countries they are taught bayonneting the enemy, superpatriotism, and hatred of other nations or races, as a part of formal state-school training. Forms of aggression and prejudice are learned all over the world, not through formal education, but in the streets, in the struggle for survival. On the other hand, a young child could just as easily learn judo, to play the piano, or to speak three languages, by the same age. Society determines the substance and quality of information given to each new generation. Children need to be taught even to walk and to talk. They will learn, for better or worse, a wide repertoire of other forms of behavior, and we might as well try to promote patterns that will increase individual happiness and world peace.

Who will decide—the Japanese, Chinese, Indians, or others?

We are all deciding these things now, the Chinese in a different way than the Americans. The lack of common goals for mankind, which is bound by a common destiny to share the planet earth, is in part the cause of present conflicts. Attempts to reach international agreements are often handicapped by man's ignorance of his own neurological decision-making mechanisms, by the intellectual distortion of uncontrolled emotionality. Human beings cannot be dealt with only in statistics and in terms of productivity: We must also take into consideration the existence of sensitive and reactive brains.

In preparing a global model, how could education be included?

We already have global norms in public health, travel, and in international law. Scientific research about atoms or cancer cells is carried out with similar instruments and comparable aims in different countries. The landing of astronauts on the moon was televised around the world, arousing enthusiasm for a great adventure shared by all mankind. These facts mean that we possess the technology and that we have started a global education. What is still missing is agreement on common goals for the human race, the realization that international cooperation is more useful than selfish economic exploitation, and the awareness that in the same way as we are changing the surface of the earth with our cities and roads, we are also changing the brains of human beings with knowledge and behavioral imprinting.

The future destiny of man no longer depends on natural chance: It is determined by our planning and intelligence—or lack of it. Our attention and efforts should be centered on the neurological mechanisms of the intellect, and the development of the brain's maximum potential, without forgetting that we are in the middle of a feedback, with ideas, emotions, feelings, and actions in a continuous exchange with electrical, chemical, and anatomical phenomena which are at the fingertips of our scientific curiosity. Man is not the final product of creation, but an evolving creature which is learning to direct its own evolution. Man is inventing the man of the future.

NOTES

[1] See conversation no. 6.
[2] See *The Crazy Ape*, Philosophical Library (New York, 1970).
[3] See conversation no. 2.
[4] George Orwell (1903-50), British novelist and essayist.
[5] See conversation no. 5.
[6] See conversation no. 7.
[7] Marcel Proust (1871-1922), the reference is to his most famous work *A la recherche du temps perdu* (Remembrance of Things Past).
[8] See *The Human Brain, Its Capacities and Functions*, Isaac Asimov, New American Library (New York, 1963), p. 338.

39. Elisabeth Mann-Borgese

Elisabeth Mann-Borgese is a senior fellow at the Center for the Study of Democratic Institutions at Santa Barbara, California.

Mrs. Mann-Borgese was born in Munich, the daughter of famous German writer Thomas Mann. She studied at Zurich and Chicago. She is a member of the American Society of International Law and the American Society of Arts and Sciences.

She is an author of several books, *Ascent of Women, To Whom It May Concern, The Language Barrier* and *The Ocean Regime*. She is the widow of Dr. Borgese, an Italian professor of literature.

You are mainly preoccupied with world organization, with international organizations. Limits to Growth—as a first step to design a planetary model—does this strike you as an important endeavor?

Well, the way you put the question, I would have to answer it negatively. I do not think that this book, such as it is, will be the beginning of a world order, let us say. I put myself on the side of the sixty people in the developing and socialist nations, whom you are going to interview subsequently, which is where I think I belong anyway. This does not diminish the importance of the book. I think the book is very important, even if I disagree with most of its premises. I think that the book points up the need for a global management of resources. I one hundred percent agree. I think that it demonstrates this need forcefully, and that is very valuable.

But what does the report lack, in your opinion?

The report in my opinion is defective in some respects. It is defective because it leaves out a number of absolutely crucial variables in its calculations. I mean an economic statement that leaves out the social dimension of the problem is to me as far remote from reality as anything. I think in this I would concur with the criticism advanced by my friend

Gunnar Myrdal.[1] Another thing which of course is almost inevitable, is almost intrinsic in this method, is that the projection is based on present trends, on present technologies. If there is one thing sure, it is that there will be very dramatic changes in these things. So, for instance, I mean if one speaks of the limits, not of growth right now, but of resources, I think there the projections are probably wrong because the technologies that we are developing, let's say in the field of energy production, are changing. This problem just may change aspect altogether within the next fifty years, I would say.

By borrowing energy from the sun and further nuclear fusion development—

I think in particular of fusion energy. We will have a source of energy which will be certainly cheaper than any that man has tapped so far. We will have unlimited sources of energy because the deuterium from the oceans is unlimited. We will be freed of geopolitical restraints as far as energy sources are concerned. This, I think, will amount to what you might call an energy revolution. Mind you, that if one has potentially unlimited energy, as I think we will have, that means—if I may quote my colleague, Professor Roger Revelle[2]—theoretically illimited energy means illimited resources.

How about food?

Even food. The amount of proteins that one can produce out of oil, theoretically would be sufficient to feed the world population twice over. I don't say that it is going to work out that way. I don't say that we are not going to head toward starvation and crisis and disaster, because I think we are. I say merely that one can make a projection which is as far from the reality as Mr. Meadows' is, or just as valid.

But organizing the planet—would that not require first inventory taking like the Club of Rome has tried to promote?

Absolutely. Inventory taking and monitoring is an inevitable premise. One has to base whatever one does on that. I think that the MIT as a methodology is very, very important and will continue to exercise quite some influence. But this is but one projection. It is an interesting one, but I need not accept it as the only valid one. I think that the emphasis on the *Limits to Growth* is very one-sided and is certainly not well received as you will find out when you go to the developing nations. It is not well received among people whose economy must expand and must grow. One then has to convince them that it's not meant that they should stop their development but that what we have in mind is a redistribution of resources, a redistribution of wealth. When they will be sure that we are earnest about that, they may change their mind. In other words, the *Limits to Growth* to me is another word for socialism. If one is ready to accept world socialism, then one can accept *Limits to Growth*, otherwise one cannot.

In other words, you concur much with the speech that Robert S. McNamara made in Stockholm.

Oh, yes, I think that he has made some very, very important statements, in Stockholm and even before, in Canada.

Have you seen a speech for the World Bank in September, 1972? He mentioned, for instance, that the World Bank is financing birth-control measures in Indonesia, which will cut the Indonesian population between '72 and the year 2000 by fifty million people.[3]

Well, I have a notion he may be kidding himself.

Why?

Just like the pollution problem or the environment problem, the population problem is so immensely interacting with so many other things that if you think that you can single it out and cope with it in isolation by emphasizing birth control techniques one is kidding oneself.

What to do about the unbelievable barriers between scientists of all different disciplines, who compete with each other instead of working together on solutions to save the planet?

One finds the same thing in peace research. All these thousands of organizations and they don't talk to each other, thereby making the whole enterprise futile. Of course, systems analysists and economists and whatnot must work together. I think one of the basic lessons of these last twenty, twenty-five years is that all these attacks on the world's problems have to be international and interdisciplinary, otherwise we just won't get anywhere. But the fact is that if one attacks problems that way, one runs into immense difficulties: nationalism, parochialism, departmentalism, but not only among people, but also among the funding agencies, because your projects usually fall between each and every chair and if one deals with environment, for instance, then one is told, our funds are only to finance national projects. If you deal with international aspects of it, well then one must go under international relations. These two things must be done together and can no longer be separated with the hope that Maurice Strong's[4] new agency will make a new departure in this direction. The philanthropic organizations, the funding organizations have not caught up with the changes of the last twenty-five years. The financial infrastructure is very far behind, and this makes work extremely difficult.

From my dozen years of work at United Nations headquarters, I know it was always said, "Wait until China joins, then we will really have an international organization." The first thing Peking did was veto Bangladesh. What is your view on the future of international organizations in general?

I think that international organization is evolving very rapidly. Pure diplomacy, old style, has no future, unless it, too, joins the trend toward the interdisciplinary essence of problems.

What exactly do you mean by interdisciplinary order?

I mean that international life today consists no longer merely of relations between governments. It is no longer merely political. There are a lot of other interests and a lot of other forces which are not governmental and not political and they overcut and undercut nation-states. They have to interact properly with politics if we want to get any practical result. The United Nations reflects the world of thirty-five years ago. It is not set up to cope with the problems of our day. The functional agencies in some respects are more fortunate—I mean WHO and so on. But even they are very, very limited. I think the time has definitely come to develop new forms. I have very high hopes. I have spent my last four years on working on the problem of ocean space, in close cooperation with the US Seabed Committee. I think that the new international organization that will emerge for the management of ocean resources will be a breakthrough toward a new form of international organization, which I would say should join together economics, industry on the one hand, science on the other, and politics—a new form of international organization which then may be applicable to other forms of resource management or of transnational activities in general.

How would Thomas Mann[5] have viewed Limits to Growth? *He was rather pessimistic about mankind's future anyway, wasn't he?*

My father was definitely not very much interested in economics, nor was he a materialist. He was not. He was a humanist throughout. The question of economic growth would not have been uppermost in his mind, I think. But many people today tend to throw out the baby with the bath. Of course I agree with the idea advanced by many developing nations like the Chinese on the one hand, and the humanists on the other hand (and the Chinese are humanist, very profoundly, in a deep sense), that economic growth is not everything, that there are other values in life besides economic growth. But that does not mean throw it out. It means put it into the right perspective. With this aspect of the thesis of MIT, I agree. But once one puts one's emphasis instead on stopping it and on slowing the progress of people who instead need faster and faster progress, then I disassociate myself from it.

But Aurelio Peccei[6] is working for human equilibrium, no?

I think that whatever I said today is in agreement with what Aurelio thinks. I have had long talks with him over the years. I found nothing to disagree with him at all. He is a humanist in the best sense of the word. I do not think that nowadays and especially in dealing with international relations, which means in dealing with the people of the Third World, one can say that economics is secondary. It is not secondary. It is as important as anything else. That does not mean to say that it is the only thing. Certainly considerations of distribution, of equilibrium, of social values, of social justice, are inseparable from purely economic considerations. I think as a matter of fact, to deal with economics in itself when you look at world organization, is old-fashioned, is as old-fashioned as to neglect it, to ignore it.

You know that I am aiming at the second volume of interviews prepared in mostly the Third World. Would you think it a positive development to schedule for '74 a Bandung-type[7] conference between the seventy minds of the first volume and the seventy minds of the second volume?

It is a splendid idea. I think as a time schedule we have time enough to organize that. I think it is a splendid idea, I look forward to it. I want to be there.

A last question: Are you working on a book?

Unfortunately I am working on about three books. One is coming out now, called *Pacem in Maribus*, and concerned with activities to design an international ocean regime.

You borrowed the name from Pope John.

Yes.

What importance can we attach to the ninety-one nation convention signed in London in November 13, 1972, not to dump any more poisonous waste into the ocean?[8]

It is a step in the right direction. There are a number of steps in this direction now. But, by itself, it is not enough. First of all, dumping accounts for only a minor part of pollution. The most important sources of pollution are land-based. Pollution of the oceans is just one of the symptoms of the breakdown of our entire industrial-urban system. And this leads me to the second point: One cannot deal with pollution by itself. One can cope with it only if one addresses oneself to the basics of resource management and development. The emphasis on pollution controls betrays a Western bias. Which does not necessarily mean that it is wrong. It certainly means that it is too narrow.

NOTES

[1]See conversation no. 35.
[2]See conversation no. 28.
[3]See Robert S. McNamara's speech for the World Bank, September, 1972, p. 4.
[4]See conversation no. 30.
[5]Thomas Mann (1875-1955), German novelist.
[6]See conversation no. 70.
[7]Indonesia's first president, Sukarno, called the first Afro-Asian conference of nonaligned nations in Bandung on the island of Java, Indonesia, in 1955.
[8]The National Marine Fisheries Service of the United States reported early in 1973 that no less than 665,000 square miles of the Atlantic Ocean from Cape Cod (Massachusetts) to the Caribbean were thoroughly befouled by floating oil, tar and plastics.

40. Hugh Montefiore

The Right Reverend Hugh Montefiore, Bishop of Kingston-on-Thames, near London, was born in 1920.

He attended Rugby School, St. John's College at Oxford University, Westcott House and Cambridge University.

In 1954 he became dean of Gonville and Caius College in Cambridge. In 1963 he was nominated vicar of the University Church of Great St. Mary's also at Cambridge.

Since 1970 he has been Suffragan Bishop of Kingston-on-Thames. He is also a trustee of the Ecological Foundation of Great Britain. Among other works he has written *The Question Mark: Can Man Survive?* and *Doom or Deliverance?*

You spoke in your 1971 Rutherford lecture of "man as knocking against the limits of the world." This is exactly what Limits to Growth *tries to get across.*

Yes, man is knocking against the limits of the world. He is only knocking. He hasn't actually reached the limits of the world yet. But obviously if he continues to increase the number of his species, if he continues to increase the rate at which he uses raw materials and consequently increases the rates of waste, pollution and environmental deterioration, then he will—quite soon—reach the limits of the world. I hope it won't happen. My interest is in stopping it.

Pope Paul condemned contraception in his Humanae Vitae. *You have called this document, ecologically speaking, the most disastrous Christian utterance of the century.*

Yes, it is ecologically disastrous because it prevented the largest church in Christianity, with millions and millions of adherents, from using contraceptives in good faith or in good conscience. The Pope put restraints upon that, whereas I think the church should be leading the way towards a stewardship of mankind just as much as a stewardship of resources. This document was disastrous in as much as it turned its back upon this.

Teilhard de Chardin felt that humanity no longer was imaginable without science, but neither was science possible without some religion to animate it.

We have got to ask ourselves what science is. Science is simply knowledge about the natural world, about its nature and about its functioning. Science in that sense is not a way of life at all, it simply tells us how the natural world works; or anyway it comprises certain hypotheses about the way it works based on empirical observation; and hypotheses, of course, can be amended or proved wrong later. Now, this gives you no "way of life" whatsoever. There may be a certain form of religion called "scientific humanism." But that is not science, it is only a series of value judgments based on what people think is valuable for them and consistent with their knowledge of science. I suppose it is a form of secular religion. Man cannot live without religion of some kind, because he needs ideals to inspire him and a worthy goal at which to aim. Some religions nowadays are even entirely secular. I myself believe that a transcendental religion of some kind is necessary, not only because it is true but also to meet the deepest needs of man's spirit.

You said in your writings, that no doubt one day the world would end, but you also spoke of a duty towards posterity.

It is a natural human instinct that parents should wish well for their children. Indeed it is implanted in us by the process of evolution that we should be concerned with our progeny, and so we all naturally are concerned for the welfare of our children. I think the extent of our duty to posterity is to keep open for them the options and to retain for them choice about the way in which to live and the way in which they wish to treat the world. We must not so abuse the planet that the environment will have permanently deteriorated.

But the degree of laissez-faire that is presently permitted to private capital will have to be considerably restricted. Who will restrict it? By a world management?

I must say that this question not only applies to private capital but also to public corporations and to government corporations, which can abuse the resources of the planet just as much as individuals. Restrictions will have to be placed upon them, first of all by national governments; and that can only be done by the consent of the people. Hence, the attitudes of the common person are of paramount importance. We should also reach international agreements, the more so because it is the multinational organizations which are so immensely powerful in this field. Multinational organizations can only be controlled by international agreements.

You have quoted Maurice Strong[1] several times, but he does not believe in a united world government.

I did not say "by united government." I said "by international agreement." That is another matter. I myself think that the world of tomorrow—if civilization as we know it is to remain—will have to be far more regionalized; people will have to identify themselves with townships, with neighborhoods, with communities, with regional areas, if they are to feel that they are participating and hence act with a sense of responsibility (because unless you participate, you do not act responsibly). But the fact that we shall require more regionalization also means that we shall require more international agreement. International agreement is not the same as world government. It means that countries are agreeing about certain tactics, not that they elect a world government which then tells them what to do.

But who polices the agreements?

I don't know. I haven't thought about this in sufficient detail. I take it that there will be a kind of sanction. I think that even though you decide to have a United Nations Army, no one would want to enforce this kind of thing by military means. You have to do it by international agreement and therefore by agreement to ostracize those countries which break the agreement.

But how to arrange the containment of world growth without some form of world body?

I can tell you that this afternoon, this very afternoon, at this moment,[2] an agreement with ninety-one countries is being signed here in London, concerning the dumping of toxic materials into the oceans. If this can be done, then these kinds of agreements can be extended.

Yes, just as the world agreed through the United Nations that we should aid the Third World. What happened in Unctad III in Santiago de Chile? You know that not a single affluent society has yet given one percent of its national growth in direct aid.

Yes, I know all this. But it is very important to emphasize that the cure should not be worse than the disease. It would be comparatively easy to solve the problems of the environment by a government which is authoritarian whether fascist or socialist, but this cure would be as bad as the disease. I see no other possible solution than the gaining of the consent of a majority of people on the globe—or anyway of their governments—for international cooperation. I do not regard this as impossible. When I first started writing about the environment, some six or seven years ago, people thought I was mad. Well, perhaps I am, but not in this respect. When I look at the way in which knowledge has spread, attitudes have changed, action is beginning to be taken, as seen at the Stockholm Conference, then I do not regard this as impossible. I am not a doomsday man in this matter.

Sir Julian Huxley told me that the fishes are returning to the river Thames. There now is a minister of the environment in the British Cabinet. Isn't that seal part of a general deception?

I am sick and tired of the river Thames. Whenever national pollution is brought up, we are always told how many fish have been caught in the Thames at London Bridge as never before. Even at County Hall they put them in a tank as though this had solved our environmental problems. Of course there are aspects in which life in London is far better than ever it was environmentally. Look out of the window now. You will see a lovely clear November day, whereas twenty-five years ago you might as well have had a peasouper fog. Again, the Thames is cleaner. Yes. There have been things done, but this does not alter the fact that far more needs to be done than smokeless fuel or the fact that we drink all our water in London four or six times over. As for the ministry of the environment, this is just a conglomeration of three big ministries; and I do not myself think that the ministry of the environment has as yet tackled seriously the major environmental problems, such as a national policy for transport, or the question of a selective increase of growth, rather than encouraging a five percent package growth all round. I think it is a help to have a ministry of environment, but I don't think that as yet they have grappled with the very radical questions which face us.

Speaking about the young, you mentioned the suicide rates going up.

In a way, the young are our only hope in this matter. Firstly, because they are, after all, going to be in charge of the world very shortly; and secondly, because they are, on the whole, fed up with the consumer society. It's so materialistic, so concerned with the rat race, and of course many of them opt out. Many of them cannot take it, the rate of those who attempt suicide has gone up, there has been an alarming increase in drug taking and in alcoholism among the young. This is all part, alas, of the disintegration of our culture, which is a very complex matter but it's partly caused by the increase in urbanization and the materialistic outlook of our culture. So there are the dropouts. But the great majority of the young do not drop out, and therein, I think, lies our hope, because there are many of them who are determined that we will not continue our kind of affluent society, with each person seeking only to be better off than the neighbor next door.

I've worked among young people for nineteen years, and I regard them now as far more honest and better at facing up to real problems than they were when I first started living and working among them. The tragedy to me is that the institutional church lacks credibility to so many of them. Whereas they are determined that the present situation shall not go on, they have no real world outlook, no shining ideal of that to which they should aim, no real inspiration and vision of the Kingdom of God which they might help to build. And hence, one tends to see a lot of negative attitudes towards authority and a tendency towards anarchy in the proper sense of that word. The young lack this vision, and they also lack a self-discipline which is going to be necessary to build a better world. The proper use of our resources is something which is going to require a great deal of self-discipline. The "permissive society" is usually thought of in terms of sex, but it is not going to help forward environmental improvement because permissive attitudes spread into the whole life.

* * *

Do you think Limits to Growth *has contributed to the raising of the consciousness of mankind to the realities of the planet?*

I think it did a lot of good, and I think it did a lot of harm. I think it did a lot of good because it raised these questions and received a great deal of publicity; I think it did a lot of harm because I think the model that was used on the computer was nothing like sufficiently sensitive and detailed to produce a correct answer. For example, with this great increase in population, you will have also eventually what's called "the demographic transition," so that population does not go on increasing exponentially. When it comes to resources, you get some negative feedback when things go short, you use alternative resources, there are, I think, a great deal more complexities and difficulties, than those represented in the model. I am no expert on computers, but I think the model must be much much more sophisticated to carry a great deal of credibility. I am only criticizing as a first shot. I think the method of using a computer is as valid in this sphere as it is in any other sphere. It is an aid to thinking, it is no better in its results than in what you put into it, but it can make the kind of complex calculations which the human brain unaided cannot make in accurate detail, so it's a step forward.

The "MIT boys," as they are called by those who disagree with them,[3] *are the first to recognize this, but it was a first decisive step.*

Yes, but this is really only the first step because, throughout this matter, the basic issues are questions of our attitudes, our motivations, our expectations. To tell mankind what will happen if we go on as we are is merely to prophesy about the unseen and the unknown, which they probably won't believe. What is required for humanity is a change of interior attitudes.

How to achieve that?

In my judgment such a fundamental change in deep-seated attitudes will only come about through—I measure my words—something like religious conversion and a sense of direct accountability, as well as by a clearer vision of where real happiness and joy lies, not in things but in people.

* * *

NOTES

[1]See conversation no. 30.
[2]November 13, 1972.
[3]Professor William D. Nordhaus; see also conversation no. 19.

41. Robert M. Fano

Professor Robert Fano was born in Torino, Italy, in 1917. In 1939 he came to the United States. He received his doctorate in electrical engineering at the Massachusetts Institute of Technology in 1947. In 1956 he was nominated professor of electrical communications, and in 1962 he was appointed to the Ford Chair in the school of engineering at MIT.

Professor Fano has worked and published works in the field of network theory, microwaves, electromagnetism, communications and computers. He has made special studies on the social role of computer-communication systems.

During my tour d'horizon, with various personalities around the world, I met with many opinions about the usefulness of computers. Dr. Edward Teller[1] felt them to be extremely dangerous and misleading. Herman Kahn[2] stressed that the first eight computers in the United States were under his direction and that he knew enough about computers to consider them untrustworthy. Do you feel computers are the most useful means to tackle problems of future global management, like the Forrester[3] team has done?

Computers have roles both in making studies about the operation of society, as well as in the operation of society itself. They are fairly distinct roles. Particularly in the first role computers are excellent instruments for answering questions that are formulated. The real difficulty does not lie in the solution but in the formulation of the question. That's where the arguments about the use of computers in studying growth really lie, in the formulation. The formulation remains entirely in the human domain. The computer will answer what is being asked and not what ought to be asked.

Edward Teller said, for instance, a computer cannot tell me who is a friend.

Here we arrive at an aspect of computers which is quite important. If we want to tackle problems that are too complex in structure for a human to be able to deal with alone and without help, we must be sure that we make possible a very intimate collaboration between computer and man. On the other hand, we know fully well, as I have stated in all my papers, that the process of problem-formulation and the process of problem-solution are essentially concurrent. One never knows whether one has formulated a problem correctly without exploring some of the consequences of the formulation, which really means exploring the solution of the problem. The process involves, first of all, formulation, observing what is the nature of the solution, then one checks whether something has been left out of the formulation, reviews human aspects that have not been taken into account, for instance, restrictions or limitations that have not been put in the formulation. Then one reformulates, solves again, sees what comes out and keeps formulating, solving, formulating, solving until one obtains a formulation that, as far as the person knows, appears to be correct. One no longer sees any consequences of the formulation that are in conflict with what instinctively one knows to be true. The ability of interacting very closely with computers, the ability to mix what I may call "human information processing" with "computer information processing" is extremely important.

Could the computer—what Marshall McLuhan calls "the ground of the brain" [4]*—be viewed as an extension of the brain?*

I'm always wary of this terminology, but I do believe that one can in a sense call the computer an intelligence amplifier, in the same sense that we can think of some of the power tools that we have today, an electric drill or a washing machine, which are muscle amplifiers, as devices that increase, augment power. Not only power, but also the precision and skill of our muscles. It's very true. One can do with a power tool precision work that just the unaided hand could not do. Well, in the same sense computers can be regarded as having the power to augment the power, the precision, the skill of our mind. That's, indeed, the way I look at it.

But I think there is another aspect of computers from a social point of view, which is even more important, namely, to facilitate a meaningful intellectual communication between people. That will be in the future the greatest importance of computers in society. If we use computers in the communication process—we think of communication as telephone, television—all that these devices do is to eliminate distance between people. One can talk on the telephone over thousands of miles as if it were next door, but they help in no way to relate the intellectual process of communication. How can I really convey better what's in my mind to your mind. They don't help in that respect, and that's where we need help.

You have written that a book contains knowledge which does not become available to a person until he reads the damned book. Could computers be brought in to speed the process of reading and learning? [5]

There are two aspects to that question. First of all, is there any way of storing knowledge in directly usable form, i.e., a person is able to utilize the knowledge without himself absorbing it, and practicing the intellectual skills involved. The answer seems to be a preliminary yes. There exist programs today that store knowledge in a way that people can utilize directly. For instance, the particular example of work done here at MIT by some colleagues of mine, particularly Professor Moses and Professor Martin. They have created a computer system that has the knowledge of an extremely competent mathematician. As a matter of fact, I heard one of them claim that he cannot think of one mathematician who has all the knowledge that is in that system.

I think that the answer is yes. It seems to be possible to store knowledge in computer programs in directly usable form, that's one aspect. But I was talking about the process of facilitating communication between people. Let me give you an example of what is involved. Two people are interested, generally speaking, in the same sort of thing; but, as often is the case, one point of view is different from the other. If I am a good teacher, I try to understand your point of view and explain it from your point of view. That's the skill of a teacher. But it is not very easy for me to know exactly your point of view. If you are going to really understand what I say, a translation process has to take place. That is, you have to translate this knowledge into your point of view, or in other words fit it into your frame of reference, fit it and tie it to the rest of the knowledge that is in your mind. This process of translation is extremely difficult and complex, and this is—in my view at least —one of the barriers to human communication. People talk with one another but don't communicate. I think that computers eventually will be able to help people in this respect.

Let me give you some trivial examples of this: Suppose that in describing the computer—let's say some object—I think of that object—let's say by looking at it from the front—that's my interest. (This is of course a trivial example.) Your interest is to look at it from the back. Now, a computer can very easily turn it around and change the display. I describe it from one point of view; the computer translates the point of view—literally speaking, the direction from which you look at it—and you see it from the other end. In more general terms you can think of a computer as having the knowledge stored, perhaps acquired from a person, but then be able to present it to another person in a different way, as the other person requests. In effect the computer may converse with me and absorb knowledge from me. The knowledge is stored. Another person converses with the computer and extracts the knowledge in a form and from a point of view that suits him. This is for the future, but if one looks at what is being done today, we will be able to do that in the future. One begins to see examples of that sort already appearing. Small examples, trivial, but we are on the way. That's one form of communication.

Another form of communication is what I call communication in the presence of data. When we sit down together to discuss something, we may need pages and pages of papers, of data. We are forced to look at it together. This is awkward. Computers can facilitate this a great deal. They can have the information stored, and we can interact with one another and with this information through a computer. Consider a meeting—this experiment in fact has been carried out—like a committee meeting in which each person sits in front of a computer console, computer display. The communication between them takes place through the computer with the result, for instance, that one hears or sees somebody talking about something. It involves information that perhaps we talked about before or which is background information. I want to see it. While the other person is talking, I ask my computer and there it appears, the details of what the other is saying appears for me selectively. The others are not bothered unless they want to. There is a wealth of information that is put into the conversation this way.

—On a kind of TV screen?

That is right. This screen is at the fingertip of each individual as an individual, and he does not need to bother other people. One just finds out what one wants. Someone else finds out something else.

Professor Delgado of Yale University speaks in his interview about the transmission of emotions by computers from one part of the brain to a certain part of another person's brain;[6] now, there is a very wide new range of computer utility.

I am reluctant to comment upon it without knowing what he means about emotions.

The computers that were sending the Apollo 17 up in the air gave some trouble, and scientists spoke of computer hypochondria. Technicians had to adjust these computers like psychiatrists, to prevent a further delay. Do we need now computer psychiatry?

Those words are mysterious and out of the world. Let me debunk them a bit. The story is this. We are characterizing human behavior with certain expressions, and really we are faced with an extremely complex organism. We are observing certain behavior characteristics. We have no idea how they come about. We ask ourselves what are the mechanisms internally that result into that external behavior? We characterize this with expressions such as the one that you've used. Computer systems are becoming so complex that it is often difficult to understand where certain unexpected behaviors result from. Computer behavior? Yes. There are tendencies to characterize general patterns of behavior in an anthropomorphic way. It's natural and not surprising that a certain behavior of the computer could be associated with certain words.

For instance, I remember years ago people were asking me whether a computer could show preference for certain people. In a trivial sort of way, yes, you could say that you can apple-polish a computer, just like the old story about apple-polishing a teacher. All it boils down to is this: If you know how the computer behaves, you can fit your behavior to suit the computer, in which case the computer will preferentially do what you want.

Let's assume the Chinese will be capable of designing computers within the next decade. Then of course we would need a new science, because Chinese computers would be reacting to Chinese behavior. Would Chinese computers be able to talk to American computers or European computers? Next we will see the consultation of behaviorists versed in Oriental behaviorism to adjust our computers.[7]

No, no, let's not go into science fiction. On the other hand, there may be a grain of truth in what you say. Since computers are designed to interact with people, they're fitted into a certain culture. It isn't that Chinese computers will be very different from, let's say, American computers, but rather that it will be fitted in a certain respect to the Chinese culture rather than another—in the same sense furniture does. The furniture you will find in a Japanese home is different from what you find in an American home, since Japanese have a different culture, different habits of life, and the furniture is designed accordingly.

Yes, but human emotions interact entirely differently even between Japanese or Indonesians—let alone between Japanese and French. If human emotions, human behavior, interact, come out in these computers, you are going to get a different kind of interaction between man and the computers in the Far East, for instance, as compared to in the West.

It could be. But let me talk about this question in a more general sense to characterize it. The fact is that there is a rather strong coupling between computer systems and the community of people that is affected by their use. By strong coupling I mean that the characteristics, the initial characteristics, of a computer system have effects on the community around it, possibly social effects. The characteristics of the community around them influence the evolution of a computer system. Let me make clear that a computer system is not a static thing. New programs are written. Things are reorganized. It evolves in time just like a community evolves in time. The two evolutions influence each other very strongly. There is evidence to that effect. In those terms you can see social phenomena being very closely related to the characteristics of computer systems and vice versa, i.e., you can see initial characteristics of a computer system that may have very strong influences on the evolution of the community around them, including relationships between people and even affecting the values of the community.

Would there not be a danger then that some evil power would get hold of the programming of the computers and therefore program the community according to possible vicious ideologies? We get into Skinnerian philosophy of programming the environment in order to program the individual.

I am not particularly worried about that. It's a kind of a detail, in a sense. What I am speaking about is something much broader and in a sense much more dangerous than that. Basically the way you would utilize computers in the operation of society depends also on the structure of the computers themselves, what is available. For instance, to draw things to the extreme, there are computer systems that do not interact with the users directly, and there are the computer systems that can fairly easily interact with individuals. Depending on which type of computer system you use in a particular operation of society, you force the community to operate in a different way. An example has to do with the seat of control. There are certain computers that force a mode of operation—or I would say not force, but induce—further and further centralization of control. Another way of utilizing computers is the easing of decentralization of control, a computer that maintains an overall coordinating activity. This can have a big influence on the entire behavior of the community. There are subtle things like computers that can protect individual privacy or that won't.

Do you feel that computers in the immediate future will assist man by accepting the fact that the planet is finite and that we have to come to a form of managing this planet?

There is no question in my mind that computers can be very helpful in that respect. I would say even more. I am seriously afraid that advanced societies such as the society in the United States, may fall under their own weight of complexity without the help of computers, which is going to be an essential tool for survival of a complex society. It is not just a question of planning. It is a question even of operation. Because what you can plan depends on what you can actually implement.

When one talks about managing the globe as a whole, one does not talk only about planning but implementing workable solutions. These workable solutions imply much more collaboration in close interaction between all parts of the globe, that I cannot expect to be feasible except through extreme utilization of computers. This is why I was talking about facilitating human communication. It is not enough to make a plan. One has to be able to execute it. The execution requires tight interaction between people about many different matters. People need better tools to cope with this greater complexity, otherwise it's going to fall apart.

To come down to earth for a moment. I noticed outside your office some signs and recommendations. Universities are asking for computer experts. The Rand Corporation[8] asks for them. Yale University is running a Ph.D. in computer technology. Tell me in a few words how are young Americans reacting to the science of computers? Are you hopeful that you can educate a generation that can tackle problems?

There is no question that the interest among students in what is called computer science and engineering is growing very fast.

Both boys and girls?

As a matter of fact I regard computer science as a branch of engineering. I would say that is the particular branch in which substantial interest from girls keeps growing.

NOTES

[1]See conversation no. 45.

[2]See conversation no. 46.

[3]See conversation no. 34.

[4]See conversation no. 12.

[5]See Robert Fano, "Computers in Human Society—For Good or Ill?" *Technology Review*, March 1970.

[6]See conversation no. 38.

[7]See *The Human Use of Human Beings: Cybernetics and Society*, Norbert Weiner, Discus Books, Avon (1950).

[8]In Santa Monica, California (Think Tank).

42. *Noam Chomsky*

Professor Noam Chomsky has become famous in recent years for revolutionizing the understanding of the meaning of language, while his radical critiques of American foreign policy have made him one of the most influential spokesmen of the left today.

He was born in Philadelphia, Pennsylvania, in 1928. He obtained a Ph.D. in linguistics at the University of Pennsylvania in 1955. His doctoral thesis, written while at Harvard University, was called "Transformational Analysis." In 1955 Chomsky joined the Massachusetts Institute of Technology with a joint appointment in the department of foreign literatures and linguistics, and the Research Laboratory of Electronics. In 1966 he was appointed to the Ferrari P. Ward Professorship of Modern Languages and Linguistics.

Among his best-known books are: *Aspects of the Theory of Syntax* (1965), *Cartesian Linguistics* (1966), *Language and Mind* (1968), *American Power and the New Mandarins* (1969), *At War with Asia, Problems of Knowledge and Freedom, Studies on Semantics in Generative Grammar* (1972), and *For Reasons of State* (1973).

MIT computers have produced Limits to Growth *as a first step to study the way to global equilibrium. How useful do you think that kind of approach is to the world's problems?*

Without commenting on the empirical adequacy of the Forrester study and related studies I don't think that there's any doubt whatsoever that their general point is qualitatively correct, i.e., there are limits to growth, set by natural, by physical and chemical law. It would be inanely optimistic to simply assume that technology will somehow develop and overcome any problem posed by the finite limits of resources and the finite capacity of the ecological system to tolerate pollution and destruction. Of course, that's not the case. There is no doubt, that irrational economic growth will press the limits of natural law at some stage, probably not a very distant stage. This is a prospect which has enormous social consequences.

The crucial point—which, as far as I see it, is not brought up by the Forrester study but is quite central, nevertheless—is that as the prospects for limitless growth fade, a major technique for social control will be lost. The idea that economic growth will continue without limit has been a very effective device for controlling and limiting demands for redistribution of wealth, for example. And this is quite explicitly understood. Walter Heller, chairman of the Council of Economic Advisers under President John F. Kennedy, made it very explicit that the notion of limitless growth could be employed to bring about consensus instead of conflict by overcoming the demands for redistribution of wealth, which would certainly be heard if one could not look forward to gaining more of life's benefits by some other method.

Of course, the privileged are willing to tolerate talk about redistribution only as long as it is rhetoric. They are never willing to see talk translated into action, which means that as soon as the limits of growth are seriously faced, a violent class war might erupt in which the tremendous resources of destruction that are available to the privileged will be used to destroy anyone who challenges privilege—whether it's a Third World country trying to separate itself from the Western-controlled global economy or whether it's disaffected groups in the industrial societies themselves.

Bertrand Russell[1] once said that there would never be real freedom in democracy until those who do the work control the management. That's the kind of class war you just referred to?

That is right. It's conceivable that owners of capital will tolerate workers taking control of their own insurance programs. They might call it "co-determination," as they do in Germany. But when it comes beyond that to an actual share of management and profit and determining the direction of an enterprise and the character of the work that is done, of course that will not be accepted. At that point serious struggle will arise, the kind of struggle which has been suppressed by the prospects of unending growth.

Would that explain the barrage of protests to Limits to Growth *by economists like Samuelson or Kaysen?[2]*

It is very striking that the liberal and progressive economists have on the whole been quite negative towards this thesis that growth will reach certain limits. I think the reason is exactly the one expressed by Walter Heller, which I quoted. He pointed out quite correctly that when, in his phrase, you don't have to rob Peter to pay Paul, when anyone can gain, then consensus replaces conflict. That is perfectly true. It's perfectly true that if you can promise to everyone that his lot will be better tomorrow, then even the underprivileged and the dispossessed have reason to accept a society which is strongly prejudiced against them. But those reasons disappear, as Heller and other liberal economists quite understand, as soon as these prospects no longer exist.

Do you feel H. G. Wells'[3] dream of elegant engineers ruling with perfect benevolence (instead of our new mandarins) will come through some day?

I tend more to accept, with some qualifications, a much earlier prophecy than H. G. Wells'—namely, that of Bakunin[4] and other left-wing social critics since. Bakunin saw the scientific intelligentsia as a new class. It would be the most despotic, the most authoritarian, the most ruthless class that would ever rule in human society, and would control the resources of wealth and knowledge, and force the uneducated masses to live and work and march to the beat of the drum, or words approximately to that effect.

However, I think there's one qualification necessary in Bakunin's original forecast of the rise of the new class, which as far as I know was the first such prophecy. Also in the many later variants on this theme, I mean recently by people like John Kenneth Galbraith[5] or Daniel Bell,[6] who claim to see a transfer of power into the hands of the technical intelligentsia. In my opinion they are wrong in seeing a real transfer of power into the hands of a scientific intelligentsia. Rather what we are seeing, in this stage of industrial society, is that the technical and scientific intelligentsia—Galbraith's educational and scientific estate—are able to perform very significant services for those who really do own and manage the central institutions of society. In fact, they are able to provide them with the results of science and technology and scientific management and so on. Far more significant is that they are able to legitimize authoritarian control of wealth and institutions by masking this control in the aura of science. Everyone knows that science is good and noble and worthy, and everyone is deeply in awe of technical expertise. If the intelligentsia can make it appear that authoritarian control by the privileged and allegedly the talented is a necessary condition of modern life, then they will have succeeded in legitimating precisely that kind of privilege. I believe that probably is the major contribution of the intelligentsia in the service of power and privilege.

How to influence the complex, biologically given system of the human mind, globally? Where to start to influence man's mind?

I think the best way to influence the human mind is by presenting evidence and argument, by persuasion and by explanation. These are by far the most effective techniques for influencing the human mind. It is perfectly true that one could invent the kind of behavioral technology that would make you stop smoking, if you smoke. But it's also equally true that with a rational explanation as to why you should stop doing it, you might very well come to the same conclusion. Now, the proper way to influence the human mind is by the art of explanation. There's nothing much deeper that can be said than that. Any other techniques of influencing the human mind are simply another form of service to those who want to wield coercive power. Ultimately I think one should look forward to a society in which choice and decision reside in the hands of freely associated individuals. One precisely does not want to employ the controls of the behavioral technologists or, for that matter, the techniques of the military interrogator or prison guard. It is important not to be caught up in the fraud and pretense of scientists who claim otherwise.

Wouldn't you agree with Skinner[7] that survival is the planet's foremost value right now?[8]

He actually says that survival of a culture is the highest value of that culture. With that view of course I do not agree. I think that there should be very significant changes and alterations of cultural and social institutions. Changes that one might call its replacement rather than its survival. But survival of the species of course remains a value.

Toynbee[9] has warned of the Germanization of America. The US is the second largest state management in the world right now. How do you see its future develop?

There is not going to be any simple reform or in fact any complicated reforms that will change the present situation. There's the matter of outright aggression, as in the case of Vietnam, which is in fact a traditional colonial war in which the United States is trying to destroy a radical nationalist movement struggling for independence and to extricate its society from the global economy dominated by the United States. In the traditional manner, the United States is unwilling to tolerate this, and it uses the vast resources at its command to destroy the indigenous nationalist movement. Nothing particularly new about that. It's the scale that is new. But the phenomenon is familiar from history.

But is there a visible trend towards a Germanization of America?

Not because they are Nazis. It's because there's nothing else available. There is no other technique for government intervention in the economy, other than the production of waste. This has to do with the fact that the government cannot act in such a way as to conflict with the needs of the real rulers of the society. The government, for example, is not going to pour money into a mass-transportation system when most of the top corporations get their profits from irrational use of the automobile. Nor is the government going to produce anything useful because if it does, it will compete with the private empires that control the economy. Furthermore, government intervention in the economy has to be tolerated by the taxpayer who pays the bill.

Incidentally, the same liberal economists introduced one of the most regressive tax proposals of modern times in the United States. The taxpayer can be whipped into line when he believes that his life is threatened, so he'll be willing to pay for military expenses. The state religion is powerful enough so that when national prestige is on the line, as in the space race, then the citizen can be beaten into submission and will tolerate spending for it, for a time. But these various conditions on governmental intervention in the economy—namely, that it not conflict with the interests of ruling groups but rather enhance those interests, that it be tolerable to the citizen who has to pay for it—if you look into those conditions, they virtually determine that government intervention in the economy will be the production of military waste, of military goods which will sometimes be used, as in Indochina.

Philip Handler, the president of the National Academy of Science, explained to me how the participating scientists in the National Academy often are not even aware of the gap in the use of language. "They would not be able," he said, "to put down on paper what divides them." In your field of cognitive psychology and linguistics, would it be possible to bridge these still-prevailing gaps between politicians, diplomats and scientists?

I would not like you to think—because it is not true—that linguistics and cognitive psychology have contributions to make in this domain. It is an interesting and important field. I happen to devote my intellectual energies to it. But we are not going to solve the problems you raise. It's misleading—and it's in fact part of that subversion of science that I mentioned earlier—to believe that this is a matter for scientific and technical expertise to solve.

The answer to this problem is in the hands of every single human being. It requires no profound insight into the mysteries of science to see it. People are under ideological controls which are determined very specifically by the structure of privilege and power in their societies. In the United States there is an official state ideology which is propagated daily and drilled into everyone from childhood onwards. Quite naturally people who are incapable of extricating themselves from that ideology will have a very distorted and perverted view of things that happen, of the affairs of everyday life and things that happen in the world or what they see in front of them. I think this is true of every other society as well.

The answer is to try to gain understanding of social and political processes, to see how power is being exercised. There is no contribution of science that is going to make any significant contribution. Data are available to people. People have to decide to use their intelligence, to free themselves from ideological constraints, to penetrate the duplicity and the distortion that is an intrinsic component of any system of power, ours or any others. People must try to investigate for themselves what no scientist could tell them, namely, what are the conditions for decent human existence and how to achieve them.

But with one-third of the world illiterate and another third of the world having no schools whatsoever and with the population increasing to seven billion by the year 2000, how to do it if we are to live?

The major problem of *Limits to Growth* is not posed by the under-developed world. It's posed by the advanced industrial societies, where people are literate, where people are committing their vast resources, material and intellectual, to destruction, to waste and so on. It is here that people have to extricate themselves from the ideological controls that distort the thinking about these matters. One cannot pass the responsibility over to scientists, and one cannot pass the responsibility over to the illiterate peasants of the Third World. The responsibility lies right in the hands of every citizen of an advanced industrial society.

How then do you view the period immediately ahead?

If in fact the limits of growth, which certainly exist, become apparent in this period, then I believe there will be a very significant social upheaval in the industrial societies, as the great mass of people who are underprivileged, dispossessed, oppressed in many ways, recognize that they no longer have any reason to accept a system of inequality and injustice which is prejudiced against them. Not having such a reason, they will begin soon to explore the ideological assumptions, to challenge them and to challenge institutional structures that are oppressive and unequal. As soon as they begin to do this, they will be met with force, because those who have power and privilege will never tolerate any serious challenge to that privilege.

I cannot predict the outcome of that kind of struggle. Clearly it will depend on the state of consciousness and organization achieved at the point when massive force is used to crush efforts to attain equality and justice.

Incidentally, I think that something of the same sort can perhaps be expected on an international scale. Just as the privileged and the affluent in a particular society will use force and terror and violence to protect their privilege if ideological controls no longer work, the same is true of the relationship between advanced industrial societies and the so-called developing and very often not-developing world. If some—say, some Third World society, so-called—decides to extricate itself from the global system which is prejudiced against it and decides to use its limited material and human resources for its own benefit, then one can predict with a high degree of probability that the privileged of the world will not tolerate that behavior and will attempt to crush it by force, as, for example, they have been attempting in Vietnam for the last twenty-five years.

I recall there was a study, in fact, one of the very few studies of the political economy of American Foreign Policy—by a conservative group incidentally. They pointed out, absolutely accurately, that the primary threat of communism is the unwillingness or the inability of the communist powers to complement the industrial societies of the West, i.e., their unwillingness to play their role in the game of comparative advantage, their backward and subservient role. That is the primary threat of communism, and it is in fact true. What we call communistic societies are societies trying to undertake a kind of do-it-yourself program of development with mobilization of the population and generally some kind of authoritarian control over it. What we really objected to was that they no longer complement the industrial societies of the West.

If that tendency develops elsewhere in the world, of course, the threat will be resisted by force if necessary, by the use of all the resources of technology and science which are available. I think these are plausible speculations for the next half-century.

NOTES

[1]Bertrand Russell (1872-1970), British philosopher, mathematician and writer.
[2]See conversations no. 8 and no. 11.
[3]Herbert G. Wells (1866-1946), British novelist and writer on social and political problems.
[4]Mikhail A. Bakunin (1814-1876), Russian anarchist and writer.
[5]Harvard economist.
[6]Harvard sociologist, see conversation no. 66.
[7]See conversation no. 7.
[8]See also Chomsky's sharp criticism of Skinner's *Beyond Freedom and Dignity*, "The Case Against B. F. Skinner," *The New York Review of Books*, December 30, 1971.
[9]See conversation no. 5.

43.　*Kenneth B. Clark*

Professor Kenneth B. Clark is president of the Metropolitan Applied Research Center in New York City and teaches psychology at the City College of the City University of New York

He was born in the Panama Canal Zone in 1914. He received a Ph.D. in psychology from Columbia University. He has taught at Queens College and joined the faculty at City College in 1942. He has been a visiting professor at Columbia University, at the University of California at Berkeley and at Harvard University.

In 1970-71 Professor Clark was president of the American Psychological Association. He has served as social science consultant to the NAACP (National Association for the Advancement of Colored People) and was awarded the Spingarn Medal by that organization.

In 1955 he published *Prejudice and Your Child* and in 1965 *Dark Ghetto: Dilemmas of Social Power.*

Psychologist Rollo May, in his latest book Power and Innocence,[1] *discusses in one of the first pages your controversial speech[2] before the American Psychological Association in Washington, D.C., in which you proposed that man might use a "peace pill" on the Brezhnevs, Nixons and Maos.*

The term "peace pill" was a press invention, a misinterpretation of what I said. I can understand the need of the press to compress complex ideas into a form that the general public can grasp immediately, and this is the kind of risk that anyone who deals with complex ideas has to take. What I discussed was the need at this juncture of human history for the psychological sciences to move toward what I call a systematic psychotechnology, that is, to develop a kind of research which gears itself to controlling man's primitive, barbaric, destructive characteristics and enhancing his positive qualities. This is needed, I believe, because the beginning of the nuclear age has projected man into a period of history which not only is unprecedented but for which we are unprepared. The past development of man—his past ideas and concepts—does not give us adequate ability to cope with the present dangers of nuclear destruction.

The Nixons and the Brezhnevs, after all, were programmed in the thirties.

Yes. What the physical scientists did to us in 1945 was to make the past no longer really relevant to the demands of the future. My thinking is based on the assumption that the engineering feat of the physical sciences, which resulted in exploding man into the nuclear age, almost obliterated past assumptions about the nature of man and what can be expected of him in terms of social and moral development. It projected man into a period in which he could no longer take his chances on trial-

and-error techniques in working out his relationships with his fellow man.

What has now become imperative is for the psychological sciences to accelerate research about the nature of man, towards the immediate goal of controlling man's negative, barbaric aspects which were undesirable but at least tolerable in a pre-nuclear age. But now, in the nuclear age, man's own destructiveness is probably the greatest danger that he faces. The only possible safeguard against this, that I see, is to accept the difficult and controversial, but nonetheless immediate challenge, which goes against almost all of man's previous conditioning, of controlling the primitive and the negative in human beings.

Professor B. F. Skinner[3] approaches the same problem but with a method different from mine—he suggests manipulation of the environment, the society, the conditioning. I suggest manipulation of the internal biochemical systems of man as an organic system, because I believe this is what in the final analysis determines man's psyche. Another controversial proposal of mine was that men with power should be dealt with most immediately—not criminals, not lower-status people, because these are not the people who pose the immediate danger to mankind. The people who pose immediate danger are the relatively few human beings who have tremendous power, greater than any other human beings have ever had in the history of mankind. I say these are the people who must be the concern. These are the people whom we must insist are controlled in terms of the maximum of personal and mental health, which I define as the dominance of the positive qualities of love, compassion, empathy, sensitivity. It is my thesis that these are controllable physiologically. This is not a "peace pill." It is a serious research for a very serious end.

Have you done experiments where positive results were gained from biochemical interference with negative inclinations?

No, I haven't personally done experiments.

It has to begin.

It has begun. The tremendous research of Delgado cannot be ignored. Delgado[4] has demonstrated, I think beyond question, that there are certain portions of the brain which control specific emotions; some portions which control negative emotions, some which control positive emotions. This is the biochemical basis of feelings, emotions, motivations in man.

* * *

Dr. Clark, you were talking about men in power. Anybody who becomes a professor in a university, or a managing director of a company—anybody who takes a position of importance in our modern society—would have to have a basic education, pass examinations, be screened. But in the political system as it runs now, the one with the loudest mouth and the one who cheats the public most gets into political office. We use sixteenth-century methods of "choosing" politicians.[5]

Yes. Twenty-five years ago I wrote a paper for the Association of Psychiatrists in America in which I raised this question of the need to address ourselves to the methods by which leaders are selected or non-selected. By that time I was concerned about the fact that success in the competition for political leadership in democracy seemed to be determined by the degree to which the individual had certain competitive qualities which I felt were not particularly adaptive at that date of human development, however were still being used.

After the atomic age burst upon us, I was even more convinced that the qualities generally considered necessary for leadership—aggressiveness, tough-mindedness, a certain kind of insensitivity which is called realism—had to be reexamined. I suppose at this stage I can be called unrealistic in my strong suggestion that we must now substitute others for those qualities. To be specific, we must replace them with qualities of sensitivity, empathy, kindness, and the ability to translate these into policy and action. These are the qualities of leadership which are now required, but we are still using the old qualities in selecting or in permitting competitors for leadership to be successful. I can understand how my critics would consider this unrealistic, because it really is in a way asking for a—

Utopia—

I have been accused of being a kind of sentimentalist, an idealistic utopian. But to me that is the only adaptive realism of the present and the future. It seems naive because it is asking man to redefine those qualities which are essential for survival. In a nuclear age the Darwinian concept of survival is antithetical to survival, and a reversal of the Darwinian concept is now hoped for.

But would you say that even concepts like capitalism or Marxism are

*based on realities of another era? Aren't new frames of reference neces-
sary to plan the future?*

Unquestionably. I suppose the only contribution that B. F. Skinner
and I are making in the face of all the attacks we have attracted is beginning the dialogue necessary for the new frame of reference. I hope we
have time.

That's what the computers of MIT and Limits of Growth, *the study of
the planet as a whole, aim at. But we seem always to be talking about
our part of the world. How about China, India, Africa, Asia, Latin
America?*

I want to reply to your question in two parts. First, I am not particularly impressed with computerizing ideas or plans or designs. I know
that this is in some areas of science the current fashion. My feeling is
that the computer puts out nothing other than what's put in and that man
has the ultimate responsibility of putting into the computer what he wants
to get out.

I'll remove myself from any further discussion of the computerization
of global models. What I am concerned with are individual human beings
and their relationships with other human beings and groups of human
beings. There is a complicated set of problems and variables that have
to be pieced together in order to fully understand how to control man's
negative behavior. I welcome the philosophers in the effort. I welcome
the empirical scientists. I welcome any group of human beings who recognize this as the critical problem which human intelligence must somehow find a way to solve.

Secondly, I agree with you that this cannot be an isolated effort. The
theorizing and the research that has to be done, the mistakes that will
inevitably be made, cannot be restricted to the artificial boundaries of
nations. I agree with some of my critics who say that it would be devastating to have any one major power with this kind of new perspective
when other major powers will be operating in terms of past perspectives.
I believe that research on this problem, which I have defined as the significant problem of contemporary human society, should be international.
It should not be nationalistic and secretive, like the atomic research. This
problem involves the survival of mankind and the best minds of all the
nations should be involved in working on it. This would be a built-in

safeguard. I hope this can be a genuine United Nations scientific research project. Probably the most important thing that the United Nations could contribute to the future of mankind is getting into the research and allowing no particular power to dominate it.

It is therefore essential that we "re-shape life," as Boris Pasternak[6] said. How then can we improve the direct corelationship between consciousness and concrete reality? Through chemical biology?

One of my graduate students recently made an observation that was the first time I had heard this thought vocalized. You are coming close to it. He said, "You know, as I read Skinner and you, the thing that is underlying your ideas of necessary psychotechnology is a concept of reality which is different and somewhat disturbing." I asked him what he meant and his reply was, "Most of your critics define the reality of being human in terms of everything that has happened in the past." Bombing Vietnam into obliteration is accepted as a definition of reality. And in the medieval times reality could equally be defined as having plagues.

American bombers are a plague—

I listened to the young man and I said, "Yes, you are right." The first part of my paper on psychotechnology really was dealing with the question of the fragility of reality. It was dealing with the inherent fragility of human consciousness; in fact, of human existence. When you get right down to it, the human being, in his conscious and intellectual being—in his thinking and behaving—is totally determined by and dependent upon the degree to which the membranes of the cells in his circulatory system or his brain maintain their integrity. So if we really look at it, the total reality of our existence is determined by fragile forms of biological matter, the basic cells. The nature of that reality is modifiable by intervention, by changing the internal biochemistry within which these cells are operating. Certainly we know that about drugs. We know it about alcohol.

In this regard I guess I am breaking with the logical positivists and with the absolutists. In my paper I referred to human pathos, which to me is man's desperate struggle to try to be an absolute entity. Man can do a lot of damage to himself in his inability to accept his own fragility, in his inability to accept his finite mass. His struggle to be something absolute can make him impose upon other human beings absurd, fantastically ridiculous cruelty. It is absurd and ridiculous because the individuals who have power can never be successful in using that power destructively because they too will be destroyed. That is my concept of reality. Reality is nothing more than what you are and what the brain can perform. These things are time-limited, they are relative, and they are also in a curious way unpredictable.

Professor Delgado is preoccupied with the question of how to safeguard the original man. He believes that man's ideological and emotional setup is original, and in order to safeguard dignity and freedom, to use Skinner's phrase, the original man should be preserved and promoted.

My reservation is that I really don't know what original man is. One could define that as primitive man. I agree with Professor Delgado that any form of psychotechnological intervention cannot create characteristics in the human organism. The potentials of the human organism are limited by a whole host of determinants from the evolution of the species. But basically what one would be dealing with—and certainly my ideas would be based upon this—are potentials that are inherent in this organism and particularly in the governing system of the organism, the nervous system. But the destructive, nonadaptive characteristics of man appear to be stronger than the potentially positive characteristics. I think Freud was right when he talked about the id, the unconscious qualities of man which in the past did seem to have positive adaptive functions, in that they made it possible for human beings to survive in a competitive structure. The primacy of those functions, which are no longer adaptive, make them clearly stronger. I think that it's a general principle in biology that the more primitive the structure and the function in the organism, the greater the strength, the greater the persistence. However, the positive potentials, the potentials for love and kindness, are more recent in the evolutionary process of this organism, clearly dependent upon higher ascendancies of the nervous system. But they are there in potential.

What I am suggesting is that we accelerate their development, that we don't wait, because we cannot wait for the normal evolutionary process to give them a dominance over the subcortical membrane functions. I am suggesting that we determine how we can make them stronger and more dominant, and once we have determined this, that we apply our knowledge. This is what we do in medicine. The great danger to man now is not medical ignorance, it is ignorance of the organism and of psychology, which we have to deal with in order to prevent psychological plagues which can result in the destruction of mankind.

C. G. Jung[7] once said that the destruction of Hiroshima was not a disaster in technology but a disaster in psychology.[8]

Yes, I am in complete agreement with that. What fascinates me is that so many of my colleagues in psychology refuse to face this understandably difficult reality. The Vietnam disaster is as psychologically backward in the latter part of the twentieth century as the medical sciences were in the sixteenth century. We cannot afford it any longer.

How hopeful are you that Faustian[9] man will not drag himself to doom by his own machines and his own supertechnology?

I don't know whether the shackles of the past—such as man's obsession with dominance, thus his obsession with technological progress— can be overcome by man. I know these are very powerful shackles. They are the shackles of the mind. If you saw some of the letters that I receive! Some of the most venomous letters come from members of the clergy, almost suggesting flagellation. I read these letters and I do not take them personally, I just take them as further evidence of the nature of the problem that we have to deal with, the fact that the reality of the present is determined by the reality of the past. People's perceptions of themselves and society, of cruelty and barbarity, are still determined by the special interests, the special pleadings, the rationalizations of the past. And if one were to concentrate on that, one would say it's hopeless.

Would you agree that in the past four or five years—actually parallel to the increased war activities since 1965 in Vietnam—a frightening development has taken place in the United States?

Yes, this is again another example of psychological disaster. As America has bombed the North Vietnamese with the greatest destruction imposed upon any people anywhere, a group of nonindustrialized people who are unable to retaliate against our cities, we have in return bombed our own minds. We have devastated our ability to understand fundamental moral and human problems. And this is the only explanation for the pervasive and to me quite dangerous apathy among the vast majority of the American people, in the face of continuing crimes of devastation which we have inflicted upon the North Vietnamese.

That's probably also why the 1972 presidential campaign was the most depressing of the past twenty-five years of my reporting in the United States. People seem to feel that whether you vote for one candidate or the other, there's nothing to be done, everyone is lying anyway. Where is the faith in America that I knew in the forties?

Faith in America seems to have been transformed into a curious kind of apathetic pragmatism, being sold as political realism, which I suppose is another symptom of what I call the bombing of our minds. This is what happened in Germany, with the rise of Nazism. I think what it reveals is the pathos, the absurdity, the tragedy of man, because this is the kind of power that in my thinking can only be defined as a sort of self-perpetuating tragedy. It is a use of power to justify the tragedy of past uses of power. You get into this kind of cycle that I don't see as just the extension of power, but as a sort of psychological devastation, a psychological bleakness, an acceptance of immorality as if there is no difference between immorality and morality.

You know, power is not only corrupting, it is what causes a whole species to disappear. That kind of power to me eliminates the possibility of any future vitality.

NOTES

[1]*Power and Innocence, a Search for the Sources of Violence*, W. W. Norton and Company (New York, 1972).

[2]September 4, 1971.

[3]See conversation no. 7.

[4]See conversation no. 38.

[5]See Dr. Arnold A. Hutschnecker, "The Lessons of Eagleton," New York *Times*, October 20, 1973.

[6]Boris Pasternak (1890-1960), Russian poet and novelist.

[7]Carl G. Jung (1875-1961), Swiss psychologist.

[8]See conversation no. 45. Compare nuclear physicist Edward Teller's response to the same question to psychologist Kenneth Clark's.

[9]The famous German character, Faust, sold his soul to the devil for power or knowledge.

44. *Michael Harrington*

Michael Harrington's *The Other America* (1963) stirred the American nation to act against widespread poverty in the richest nation on earth. He has been for many years an executive member of the Socialist Party national executive committee and became party chairman in 1966. In 1972 he resigned as cochairman of the Socialist Party-Democratic Socialist Federation in protest over criticism voiced in the party against Senator George McGovern, then a Democratic Party candidate for the presidency of the United States.

Michael Harrington was born in St. Louis, Missouri, in 1928. He studied at Holy Cross, Yale University and the University of Chicago. From 1951 to 1953 he was editor of the *Catholic Worker*. In 1953 he joined the Socialist Party.

In 1965 he published another best-selling book called *The Accidental Century*, followed by *Toward a Democratic Left* (1968) and *Socialism* (1972).

You have asked yourself the question, quoting Voltaire,[1] *how should society be retooled to prevent the masses from destroying themselves?*

Well, I think that the basic problem from my own point of view, which is a democratic-socialist point of view, is to democratize economic and social power. In the United States that means democratizing the power of the corporation, which under the present circumstances operates as our major planning agency for the future of the United States. That is to say, a private institution, partaking in governmental decisions, radically transforms the quality of American life.

In the communist countries it seems to me that the fundamental problem is the same although the context is completely different. There, too, I think the problem is one of democratization, much as the Czechoslovakians in 1968 argued, or as the Poles and Hungarians in 1956, or perhaps even as the Poles again argued during the strikes of 1970 and '71. There you have a totalitarian bureaucracy, which is a planning agency, but in some ways is as private, as antisocial in many ways as the corporation.

I think that the fundamental problem is the problem of democratization. One of the great limits on this, one of the great difficulties, is that if the projections of the Club of Rome study are true, then it seems to me socialism has become an impossibility. Socialism at least in its loftiest and highest aspirations thought that it would be possible for there to be a change in the psychology of mankind. Specifically, socialists argued—and I quite agree with the analysis of the past—that it was economic scarcity which was the chief material source of competitiveness, of aggressiveness, of various forms of domination and repression. They argued further that if you had a society of abundant technology and a democratic movement controlling that technology, that under those circumstances people would be much less competitive, could be much more cooperative, much less aggressive and instead have relationships of brotherhood, sisterhood et cetera. I think the problem of the *Limits to Growth* hypothesis is that if it is true, then one has removed permanently the possibility of abolishing that fundamental scarcity which is at the root of so many of the basic human emotions.

Therefore, I think those people have tried to argue that a spaceship earth forced to ration all of its resources would be a socialist earth. It would obviously have to be a pliant earth, a managed earth. But I think it would be psychologically, culturally and, in the broadest sense of the word, humanly, profoundly at variance with socialist ideas of emancipation. Of course people wouldn't have enough, and therefore they would still be looking over their shoulder at their neighbor wondering if their neighbor has gotten a little more than they. The hope is democratization. I think a profound limit is if we don't have enough resources for everybody to have a decent life, I don't think we would even have a good society.

Because the gap between the rich and the poor seems to grow wider instead of being bridged?

Right. Even if you stabilize the gap, even if you narrow the gap somewhat, still, the mere existence of widespread scarcity would, for example, put black-market emotions at work. People would spend a lot of time trying to figure out how to evade the rationing system and how to get more for themselves. That has certainly happened in historical experience every time there has been a rationing system in the twentieth century.

It has been accompanied by a black market and a considerable amount of corruption. What I am saying is I think that the *Limits to Growth* thesis is profoundly antiutopian, is profoundly pessimistic.

Is it realistic?

Well, I have a number of areas where I don't think it's realistic. I share the criticism made by so many, many people, that *Limits to Growth* postulates a kind of neo-Malthusianism in which the demands of resources grow exponentially, while the technological ability to satisfy those demands only grows arithmetically.

But it is a first step. This was the first step to make a catalogue of the planet as a whole. When I go to Yale and talk to Professor Nordhaus,[2] who made a model (as an economist) of the planet, and ask him to see Forrester[3] to combine their wisdom, he says, "We don't deal with system-dynamics engineers." They evade each other, like Chomsky[4] and Skinner.[5]

That's obviously enormously problematic. I find Skinner's writing strange. I think he tries to portray himself as an enemy of freedom and dignity. In fact, in his latest book, *Beyond Freedom and Dignity*, he is basically arguing that it is possible for man by conscious intervention to change the circumstances which affect his behavior and, as Marx said, "to educate the educator," and takes an activist position. To tie Skinner into the *Limits to Growth*, the problem I find is that if we have this permanent condition and scarcity in the world economy, then I think a Skinnerian or any other kind of proposal for intervention to make men really decent toward one another won't work.

A second aspect of the *Limits to Growth* study, which is unrealistic, is it comes out with the model of economic stability, of basically no economic growth. It does not ask the political questions as to whether that is possible. That is to say, it does not ask, Will the Third World peoples accept a permanent condition of inferiority to the peoples of the advanced capitalist and communist economies? I don't think they will. Secondly, the report does not ask, Will the peoples of the advanced capitalist and communist economies accept a stopping of their growth rate and a stabilization of their advantage at only a certain level? I don't think they will accept that.

Professor Tinbergen[6] *in Rotterdam is now working on a new model. The Japanese are working on several models.*

I have felt for a long time, though, that what we need is world economic planning. What we need are world economic models. In that sense I think that the Club of Rome is a step in the good direction by recognizing the problem of quantifying economic data and trying to analyze economic trends for the globe as a system. I think the *Limits to Growth* has gone beyond the national limitations of so much of our thinking. I felt for a long time that some of the world economic models that people of the United Nations have been developing should be given much more emphasis. Because, for example, if we had some really good models of world economic development, then our trade and aid policies—which, thus far, particularly in the United States, adversely affect the peoples of Asia, Africa, and Latin America—then those policies might actually be made to help them.

You also touch on the question, "If man cannot control products of his own brain, there will be no place to hide for mystics or for anyone else."[7] *How will developments in biological feedback, studies of the brain, studies of behavioral control, how will these present efforts massively studied everywhere enhance chances for survival?*

I think that the breakthroughs in biology, the behavior control, test-tube babies which they are working on in England, which Watson of DNA fame argues will soon be an experiment that can be easily done, the fact that scientists in the United States are talking about the parents being able to determine the sex of their children, the possibility of cloning, that is to say, producing identical copies—I interpret all these events in a broader context.

It seems to me that a fundamental problem certainly of Western capitalist societies for over a century has been that technological revolutions have taken place without a corresponding political and social revolution. We introduce into society, into the economy and into the environment an internal-combustion machine without asking what are its consequences. We have a profoundly social technology but there is still very much a laissez-faire attitude toward its uses. We allow private centers of power to determine the public choices really of this technology.

We have, I think, the most extreme case where it is possible for mankind scientifically to reverse the Darwinian process of natural selection, where you had a cool, remorseless process whereby the individual and the genetic stream adapted itself to an environment and where nature was a very bloody and vicious arbitor of human destiny. Now we are on the verge—or perhaps we have even entered the age—of human selection, of where people can make these choices, of where you can have genetic engineering, of where you can perhaps cure some genetic diseases by actually trying to change the chromosomal makeup of a human being. If we blunder into that world in the same way that we blundered into the world of the automobile, God help mankind. This is an area where if you make a mistake, the mistake can have a multiplier effect through the next thousand years. Therefore, I find it, on the one hand, exhilarating that many diseases perhaps can be controlled; on the other hand, I find it frightening that we will not politically and socially utilize this genius. That's why a statement I made is "There is really no place to hide for a mystic."

One response to this, which some people have made, is to try to hold back that investigation, to outlaw experiments in this area. There have been proposals, for example, to outlaw experimentation with test-tube babies. But I think that simply postpones the problem. You cannot outlaw this technology. It's coming. The very fact that it is possible means that it will come into being. I am very disturbed about that component of the future.

*You wrote that the Soviets discovered that totalitarianism could not keep out jazz or cool music. In other words, you are not necessarily speaking only of our part of the world, the capitalist world, as you include the socialist countries as well in your observations. How hopeful are you for the future—*Limits to Growth *models or not?*

I tend to be optimistic for a reason. My feeling is that it is really impossible to know whether the future is going to be good or bad. It is quite possible that it will be quite bad. But as long as the question is open, as long as there is a very serious possibility that these technological advances can be utilized for the good, as long as there is any possibility that we can end scarcity and thereby inaugurate a new era of human moderation, then I think one is morally obliged to be optimistic. That is to say: to fight, to struggle and to see to it that the good possibility comes out. Because one of the determinants of whether the good or the bad prevails—and all of these very ambiguous situations we face today—is going to be the decisions of individuals as to whether it is worth struggling to make the good prevail over the bad. So in that sense I really refuse to try to project the future. Because I insist that part of that projection is our willingness to try to create it, and my emphasis is on the need to create it, which will then change what it will be.

NOTES

[1] Voltaire (1694-1778), French philosopher and essayist.
[2] See conversation no. 19.
[3] See conversation no. 34.
[4] See conversation no. 42.
[5] See conversation no. 7.
[6] See conversation no. 3.
[7] Michael Harrington, *The Accidental Century*, Pelican (New York, 1965), p. 276.

45. *Edward Teller*

Professor Teller was born in Budapest, Hungary, in 1908. He studied physics at Leipzig where he received his Ph.D. in 1930. He taught at many institutions, including Yale University, London University, George Washington University and Columbia University.

From 1943 to 1946 he worked at Los Alamos Science Laboratory on the A-bomb. He later worked on planning and predicting the functioning of atomic weapons and the hydrogen bomb. Since 1952 he has been connected with the Livermore Radiation Laboratory in Berkeley, California.

He has written, among other works, *Our Nuclear Future* (1958), *The Legacy of Hiroshima* (1962) and *The Constructive Uses of Nuclear Explosives* (1968).

There reigns deep concern in the scientific and humanitarian world about the future of mankind. Skinner[1] calls it a matter of survival. The Club of Rome has made a start by looking into the question of how to manage the globe.

I happen to believe that the matter of survival is very important. People have always been concerned about it. They always had reason to be concerned about it. Preceding the year 1000, it was generally believed in the Christian world (perhaps not by everybody, but by many) that the world would come to an end in the year 1000.

This particular view many people share today. There seems to be a predisposition in many people to prophesy the end of the world: in the year 1000 because 1000 is such a nice round number, in the year 2000 for reasons of pollution, for reasons of nuclear explosions and for reasons of the population bomb. I believe that the arguments that are advanced today are by no means more reasonable than the arguments that were popular one millennium ago.

In the Middle Ages, when there was crowding in the cities, when they possessed much dirtier methods of transportation than we have today, the result was widespread epidemics. The black death indeed looked for a while as though it might wipe out mankind. In fact it was a menace comparable to any that we are facing today, although there are fully justified worries today.

I claim that with respect to reasons to be worried in our present situation, there is nothing new. There is something new in the type of answers that one gets. There are lots of people who think that they can in some scientific fashion predict the future, calculate the future. We are getting news from all over the world and since all this information is available now, people begin getting ideas that there is a chance to manage the world. I tend to believe that these people are greatly overestimating their powers of influencing the world and even are overestimating their ability to foresee what the essential questions will be.

It is my opinion that the way to deal with problems is to deal with them one by one. To deal with the small problems, to deal with the big problems and to be a little more modest than most operational analysts seem to be. Even perhaps more modest than most of the scientists seem to be.

I would like to repeat to you a very old story, a religious one. It is not part of the Christian religion, but a legend of a conversation with

Buddha. When one of his disciples asked Buddha how one should behave in respect to women, Buddha replied, "Do not look at them." The disciple answered, "But Master, I have already looked." Then Buddha said, "Then do not talk to them." "But Master," came the reply, "I have already talked." Then Buddha said, "In that case, my son, try to preserve a small amount of common sense." This is my advice to the operational system analysts. It's the same as Buddha's advice was to the young man: "Please retain a minimum of common sense."

How do you view the future of computers in relation to assisting the management of the future of mankind?

I believe that of all remarkable inventions of the last decades, the fast electronic computers are in fact the most remarkable. They are so important because they can perform any intellectual function, with only one provision: that this intellectual function be really precisely described. Once the computer can perform, it can perform more rapidly and more reliably than any human. This, of course, may mean that our intellectual activities will become obsolete because the machine can perform them better. However, there is a small restriction, which I slipped in and which is very significant indeed.

This small restriction is that I must be able to describe an intellectual function with complete precision. I, for instance, have the ability to recognize a friend. But I am completely unable to describe in any detail how I am doing it. A computer therefore cannot be taught to recognize a friend (even if he had one) because the simple process of recognition is in fact not so simple and has in fact not been described as yet.

Generally it is the boring portion of our work which we are able to describe accurately. Computers can be used to carry out these boring tasks for us. On this basis a symbiosis can be worked out because a man and a machine together can be very much more effective than a man alone.

The danger arises when the man forgets to make his essential contributions and leaves too much to the machine. He makes a few assumptions which he did not think through sufficiently, and then lets the machine spew out the results. These results will never be any better than the original assumptions.

I do not believe that we are going to become obsolete. It will take a long time before you, as a journalist, will prefer to interview a machine, rather than to interview a fellow human being.

Freeman Dyson[2] *mentioned to me von Neumann's*[3] *initial notes on the manufacture of a self-producing machine, "machines that are sophisticated enough to reproduce themselves." Like computers, these apparatuses would be unable to blush, but in what way would this development influence the possibilities for the survival of the human race?*

There will be no influence. The human race will survive. Whether we shall be better or worse depends on the question whether we use or misuse our new tools.

But let me mention a task for the machine that is simpler than the task to blush. The rules for limericks can be spelled out in a reasonably explicit manner. We can make machines that could write limericks. If we could then publish a volume of mixed limericks, partly man-made, partly machine-produced, and if the reader could not pick out which is which, then we might have made progress in understanding what that peculiar word "humor" means.

José Delgado[4] *does believe that a man-machine will be possible in the future, at least on the basis of activating what is already present in the human brain.*[5] *In the study of cybernetics and the modern mind, apparently scientists did succeed to transmit emotions by computer from one human to another and back.*

For that you hardly need a machine. You can have it in any marriage.

The greatest danger of the computer is that when used by fools, these often claim that they are scientists. What is worse, they are believed.

The great promise of the computer is that it can give a wider scope and a more rigorous control to human imagination. Of course, our imagination is limited. But in the long run imagination is apt to win.

Some psychologists believe that the more we know about the function of the brain, the less we run the risk that technology will be used as in the case of Hiroshima.

I do believe that it would have been much better to demonstrate nuclear explosives before using them in anger. I am not one of those happy people who are convinced that they are right. I feel strongly that the war should have been ended with the help of science and without bloodshed. Science would be incomparably better off in that case, and mankind would be happier.

But while I feel this strongly, I am not convinced that I am right. Arguments can be made on either side. The clarity and the simplicity which could decide such complex questions is lacking, and the more I talk with the people who are most imaginative and have the most critical minds, the more my doubts multiply, though my feelings (against the bombing of Hiroshima) remain unchanged. The functioning of machines requires a very special kind of clarity and simplicity. In decisions of this kind a contribution by machines, whether such contributions are direct or indirect, are in the distant future—if indeed they ever should become possible.

It is only simpleminded people who are, in their opinion, always right and who believe that science or machines can save us from mistakes. It may be justified to call these people fanatics.

The fanatics among the scientists are no less dangerous than the fanatics in religion. In fact science is the religion of the modern age, and in that sense we must beware of scientific fanatics more than of any other kind.[6]

Recently you made a trip to Asia. What were your impressions? To what extent could technology ease poverty and misery there?

I did visit the peaceful parts of the Far East. In almost all countries I did see misery, but I also did see a definite will to develop, and I saw that this will is being translated into action. The Indonesians know very clearly that technology is an absolute requirement if they are to attain a way of life that is fit for a human being.

I also noticed practically the same government in every one of these countries. They are relatively mild forms of dictatorships, with some limited free speech, and with two great saving features: none of them are proud of being dictatorships and all of them use the not-so-democratic powers in order to accelerate progress. This holds for Taiwan under the old Chinese regime and it holds for Singapore under a younger Chinese, the most ingenious and cultured Lee Kuan Yew (who was a socialist and whose strong measures are therefore not criticized by the liberal press), as it also holds for General Suharto, who saved Indonesia from a slide into a worse dictatorship and who initiated practical progress for which a most desperate need still exists.[7]

In all of these places technology stands in as high a respect as was the case in the United States during those decades (which now seem to lie in the distant past) during which the foundations of the power and prosperity of the United States was established.

It was a remarkable contrast at the end of my trip to visit Japan. Their technology and democracy are highly developed. The Japanese seem to be able to do everything faster than anybody else. They perfected technology more rapidly than any other country and switched from dictatorships to democracy at a breathtaking rate. Now their society seems to be well under way toward disillusionment in technology and maybe also in democracy.

My strongest impression from this trip is the simple statement that people are people, whether in the East or in the West. They need technology, and they have not really solved the problem yet how to live with technology.

I strongly suspect that the answer to the question is a thousand times more complex than the answer proposed by the Club of Rome.

Please permit me to ask a question related to your own field. Expectation that fusion power could be obtained as a significant energy source until recently was deferred to the twenty-first century. According to the Atomic Energy Commission, scientists at a fusion reactor at Princeton University achieved the highest densities and temperatures ever reported. As we understand it, the problem was how to take a thin gas of hydrogen plasma and raise it to the enormous temperatures required to permit fusion and the generation of more energy than is employed to start the reaction. Do you expect an early breakthrough in the use of H-bomb power in the world's energy crisis?

I hope for early results. But that will amount to no more than a demonstration—a toy of the scientists. Even if that toy is big and expensive it will not solve the energy crisis.

For that we need engineering. In this century fusion will not contribute a decisive chunk of economically useful energy. It is always easier to get an uncontrolled reaction than a controlled one, particularly if you must produce at low cost. Fusion power will not contribute to the solution of the present crisis. Perhaps it will help in the next one.

The energy crisis is a particularly good example of a self-induced catastrophe produced by the prophets of doom. They have exaggerated dangers from pollution. In part they are right, but they now oppose the building of nuclear reactors, which are among the cleanest of all sources of energy. They talk of thermal pollution and seem to worry about the fish which have to swim in water, whose temperature is raised by three degrees, rather than about people who are deprived of needed energy. They complain of added amounts of radiation which are much less than the levels of natural background radiation to which we have been exposed from our very inception. Indeed, our quadruped ancestors have been irradiated by what is now called the "maximum permissible dose" starting at the time when living beings emerged from the ocean. At that time the environmentalists among the fish should have warned about the unnatural conditions living beings will encounter on dry land. But the fish were mute. This, one may consider fortunate, or else a disaster—depending on one's point of view.

If nuclear reactors could be built at a rate which is reasonable according to the state of technology, and if this development were not impeded by the exaggerated fears of those who see the end of the world approaching, then a considerable contribution could be made to the demands for more energy by reactors.

There are other ways to approach the same problem. One of them, which lies in my field of specialty, is the use of Plowshare, the constructive employment of nuclear explosives. By using nuclear explosives we could stimulate gas reserves which are contained in rock of small pore size and which cannot be pumped out by conventional methods. We could utilize oil shale at a modest price. We could get the residues of oil of depleted oil fields as the Russians are doing now.

Free speech is a wonderful thing and we must insist on it. One also should listen to that free speech with some criticism, otherwise countries in which free speech is suppressed, as in Russia, will win the race of technology. Indeed, in Russia the Club of Rome has little influence. This is an advantage for the Russians. But I would rather have a thousand Clubs of Rome than one Politburo.

There is one point on which one must lay great emphasis. The energy crisis is not the result of wasteful use of energy in the United States (even though this is asserted by many Americans). It is primarily the result of the rest of the world catching up with American standards. In Western Europe and in Japan this process is in full swing. In the developing world it is just getting under way, and indeed is getting under way much too slowly. People are entitled to a better way of living and new pathways in research could produce the needed technology to combat pollution and at the same time to provide everyone with plenty of energy.

I have mentioned only a few ways to alleviate the energy shortage. There are many more. All of them utilize research and technology. Many of them are bound to succeed.

You have expressed disagreement with those who see great difficulties in the future. What would be your own prediction?

I believe that in the year 2000 the world will be very different from its present state, which is unstable and is not likely to endure. Life will be either much better or much worse.

Which will be the case depends on all of us. Discussions about the future undoubtedly are full of wrong statements (I would be quite willing to apply this to my own answers). But irrespective of these mistakes, discussions of this kind are needed. They constitute a powerful influence which will form the future.

NOTES

[1]See conversation no. 7.

[2]See conversation no. 60.

[3]John von Neumann (1903-57), mathematician connected with the Princeton Institute for Advanced Study.

[4]See conversation no. 38.

[5]See also *Cybernetics for the Modern Mind*, Walter R. Fuchs, Macmillan (New York, 1971).

[6]See also *The Technological Society*, Jacques Ellul, Vintage (New York, 1964). A penetrating analysis of our technical civilization and of the effect of an increasingly standardized culture on the future of man.

[7]The author, who spent a number of years in Indonesia and personally knew Sukarno and knows his successor, Suharto, feels obliged to note that Dr. Teller ignores the fact that Suharto's illegal coup of 1965 caused 500,000 Indonesian deaths (an estimate of the *London Economist*) and that while Dr. Teller dined in Jakarta in 1972, Amnesty International issued a communiqué that (at least) 55,000 Indonesians are still locked up in concentration camps without having legal rights or lawyers since 1965.

46.   Herman Kahn

Dr. Herman Kahn is director of the Hudson Institute at Croton-on-Hudson in New York.

He was born in Bayonne, New Jersey, in 1922. He studied at the University of California at Los Angeles, where he followed classes by Nobel Prize winning Linus Pauling.[1]

In 1945 Kahn joined the Douglas Aircraft Corporation. In 1947 he went to the Rand Corporation in Santa Monica, California, where from 1948 to 1961 he was on the staff of military intelligence. In 1961 he founded his own think tank, the Hudson Institute.

His most important books are *On Thermonuclear War* (1960), *Thinking about the Unthinkable* (1962), *The Year 2000* (1967), *Can We Win in Vietnam?* (1968) and *Why Antiballistic Missiles?* (1969). In 1972 he published with historian B. Bruce-Briggs *Things to Come: Thinking about the Seventies and Eighties*.

Victor Hugo once said that nothing is more powerful than an idea whose time has come. Do you feel Limits to Growth *is one such idea?*

It's an idea whose time has come in perhaps three different ways. First, man's impact on the environment is now very significant and very widespread, and therefore, we must increasingly incorporate the costs of environmental damage and of preserving the environment in our calculations.

Second, it may be important to start asking the question "What are we doing today that will be helpful to our grandchildren or our great-grandchildren, or even further along?" These generations are unrepresented in most calculations and decisions in the political and economic process. There is almost nothing in the price system which discounts more than ten or twenty years ahead. Most governments do not look ahead much more than five years, in spite of what they may say or claim. Individuals often do plan ahead for their family twenty, thirty, or more years, but in terms of our society as a whole, nobody's worrying specifically about the grandchildren or great-grandchildren. Actually, we do not know if, in practice as opposed to theory, it is necessary to discount much more than ten to twenty years ahead. But the possibility of this necessity is becoming increasingly clear.

Finally, limits to growth is an idea which fits into the ideology of upper middle class intellectuals more or less worldwide, but particularly in what we call the Atlantic Protestant culture area, and therefore it has become a very influential idea. Actually limits to growth type of thinking in some ways derives from a more fundamental problem. One can quote Nietzsche: "Inescapably, unhesitatingly, terrible like fate, the great task and question approaches: How should the earth as a whole be administered? To what end should man—no longer a people or a race—be raised and bred?" My own belief is that the answer will include a concept which is common to almost all Asian religions, the concept of "Many mountains up to heaven, many roads up each mountain." In particular this concept would include what we at Hudson call a mosaic culture, in which many different individual and group answers to Nietzsche's question exist fairly comfortably side by side. When I say many mountains up to heaven, I mean by "heaven" a post-industrial culture. This post-industrial culture probably will largely have emerged in the next 50 to 100 years in most of the OECD countries.

What culture?

Post-industrial culture. The major characteristic of the post-industrial society can be seen by analogy with the U.S. today, which is a post-agricultural society. The U.S. produces a great many agricultural goods, and in that sense, is what we would call a super-agricultural society, but less than four percent of the work force produces more than ninety-five percent of the food and products we need. In the same way, we think of this post-industrial economy as a super-industrial economy in the sense that it produces a fantastic amount and variety of goods, but only a small percentage of the people are needed to carry through this production. There will be plenty of raw materials, pollution will be managed, and a very high standard of material consumption for everybody will become possible. This concept of a post-industrial economy and eventually a post-industrial culture for society is the exact opposite of that of the Club of Rome, which argues extreme and absolute limits to consumption.

Before I attempt to support my position, let me first stress some areas of agreement with the Club of Rome.

First it is important to ask about the impact of current policies on the lives of our children, grandchildren and great-grandchildren. It is also important to realize that there are uncertainties in such calculations. If there is no obviously safe policy, one will not pay a great cost today for very uncertain gains in the future, particularly when policies entailing such costs may turn out to be counterproductive for the grandchildren and great-grandchildren. The burden of proof for anybody who is arguing for the acceptance of great costs today in the name of the long-term future is on the advocate of such costs. But none of this detracts from the fact that concern for the grandchildren and great-grandchildren has been found increasingly legitimate.

The second thing so strongly expressed by the Club of Rome studies is the observation that there is no such thing in nature as an exponential growth curve that continues indefinitely. Almost all curves in nature start out slowly, increase rapidly, build to an inflection point, then turn over or taper off. The issue is when do they turn over and why. According to the Club of Rome, this turning over would be due to starvation, pollution, and resource limitations. I believe the turnover will occur because of prosperity and changes of values. When people have just about as much as they want, they will not be willing to sacrifice leisure or other things for more production. We are currently doing a study at Hudson Institute on what we call the Prospects for Mankind. We argue that the world population is likely to taper off around 15 billion plus or minus a factor of two, and gross world product at about 300 billion plus or minus a factor of three. Current gross world product in 1973 will be about four trillion dollars, and I believe that the Club of Rome has argued that even this level cannot be maintained indefinitely, or at least not much above this level. We hope to put about 20 to 50 man years into this study, at the Hudson Institute, and to date, we have put in between one and two, thus we have completed less than five percent of what we hope and expect to do. Within that five pecent or less, we have already changed our mind a great deal about the nature of the problem and what one can say with confidence. In fact, I don't believe we will make as many changes in the rest of the study as we have already done in these first months. Not because we have become rigid, but because I think we have a fairly good outline of what the study will produce in some areas and in other areas we don't have any outline at all, so we cannot change our mind.

Where did we change our minds? We had thought we would have to assume very great improvements in technology, or at least a natural

growth of technology as well as a rather high level of competent management both worldwide and locally in order to deal with all the problems.
We now believe that we can deal with most or all of the problems that
are coming up with current or near current technology. This means that
since future technology should be better, it should be even easier to deal
with our problems. While we don't know how high a level of management it will take to deal with all of the problems, we now believe that
most of the problems can be dealt with by only a medium level of compe-
tency and skill and that while there must be many international rules
and regulations, these probably do not require competent, powerful world
government. We are not saying this is true of all the problems, but we
are saying this is true of many of the problems which we are beginning
to study.

There is another way in which I would agree with the Club of Rome,
but this agreement is also a disagreement. The Club of Rome talks about
the present predicament of mankind. I would say they are completely
correct because the problem exists; but then the Club of Rome argues
that the problem will go on for 100 to 150 years.

Back in June 1955 John von Neumann wrote an article in *Fortune*
magazine on the prospects for mankind. I believe it to be an extraordinarily intelligent article, and for years we handed out copies of it at almost
every meeting in which these kinds of issues came up. This article points
out that by the year 2000 there will be great necessity for what we call
zoning ordinances. These are regulations to control or correct pollution,
over-crowding, land use, ocean use and so on. Generally, we believe
that if one looks at gross world product in historical terms, and that if
we could hit the highest rate that has ever been reached or will be reached
in the next decade or two, a rate of about six percent, this takes us to
an inflection point on the curve of gross world product. We believe,
and not completely coincidentally, that what we call the 1985 technological crisis will occur at about the same time, and this is exactly the crisis
that von Neumann was talking about. It is fairly impressive that he picked
the 80's as the date back in 1955, and nothing has happened since then,
as far as I am concerned, to cause the date to change. In other words,
we are arguing that in the next decade or two a big hunk of man's problems will occur and if we get through this period, we will still have
many problems to solve, but they ought to be relatively easy to deal
with on the whole, at least as compared to the big hunk of the 70's,
and 80's, and perhaps the 90's. These problems go all the way from
the current highly advertised "energy crisis" to the problems of arms

control, new weapons, how to deal with genetic control and all kinds of new drugs, and the like. How to deal, say, with cloning when it becomes feasible would be one example of the critical decisions technological advancement is going to present in the next couple of decades.

Cloning?

Yes, cloning. All these things are coming up together. We don't believe that they will be such big problems fifty to a hundred years from now. We rather suspect that the backbone of these problems will be broken by the year 2000. We will always have problems with us. There's never a situation without problems. But hopefully, the problems will not be getting exponentially worse. From the year 2000 onwards, many of the current problems should be pretty much settled, though, of course, brand new problems will arise.

A form of equilibrium?

Yes. The Club of Rome, which thinks the real crunch will come fifty or a hundred years from now, is in a way being very optimistic. Problems of the next ten to twenty years are of vital importance. On the other hand, the Club is very pessimistic because it says we'll have a brick wall there, and there's no way to get around it. That seems to be dead wrong! And what do I mean by dead wrong? Here I have to be very careful. What is the position of the Club of Rome? Resources are running out. Pollution and other devastating byproducts are almost certain to get out of control. There are disastrously increasing gaps, both domestic and external, between the rich and the poor. Policy-making is becoming increasingly difficult, perhaps disastrously so. Industrialization and technology and affluence are all traps. We're taking a different position on the basis of our current study. Almost everybody is getting rich, some faster than others.

May I interrupt here? The adviser of President Nixon, on food, has said, seven hundred million poor Chinese is a problem, but seven hundred million rich Chinese will wreck China in no time. Aren't we talking only of our part of the world?

No, no, almost everybody is getting rich, some faster than others.

Among those getting rich faster than others will be the Chinese. I think the last people to get rich will probably be the Indians and maybe parts of Black Africa and some of the Moslem countries. I am willing to bet five to one that the Chinese will get rich quite rapidly.

Could you imagine two cars in Chinese garages per family?

I could, but I don't think that will be the answer they choose. If they do, there'll be big traffic jams—at least for a time.

Does this planet carry enough natural resources to make those automobiles that would be needed in China?

I can find the necessary resources for you today and I don't need any improvement in technology to do so. It would be necessary to do some redesigning and to make some substitutions. You might use a lot more aluminum, a lot more iron and a lot less of some alloys. In the future, we shall probably find more alloys or superior substitutes, but if we depend only on currently known substances, one has to make a large number of substitutions. If properly managed, there will be plenty of resources for a wealthy China, including resources for pollution suppression and pollution absorption. There are two ways to demonstrate this proposition. One is to use what we call the use-expanding model. Basically, the proper model of a resource is not of a fixed bowl or a fixed pie. We should think of resources as a process, like a muscle or a skill. Within rather large limits, the more you use the more there is. In the fixed bowl or fixed pie model what I use, I take away from you, what you use you take away from me. In the skill or process model we don't have to fight over a fixed pie. If the fixed pie model were correct the world would be in very bad shape: World peace would not be possible. The rich and powerful would seize the resources and hold them and keep down the poor. Almost no other result would be practically conceivable.

Would that also be true within nations, for example, Cuba?

Yes, but Cuba is an authoritarian society. Incidentally, Castro's redistribution was also at the expense of the workers. Cuba is very interesting in this respect. I don't know whether Castro is good or bad for Cuba. History will judge. But he is bad for the short and medium term growth of Cuba. Their GNP now is about the same as when Batista was there.

But you did write that the poorest people have a better life and more government services under Castro than they had under Batista?

This seems to be correct. Every little village has a sewing machine, has a school, feels itself to be part of the system. Few now feel left out of the system completely. But the plantation workers and many others in Cuba are working harder and for less money. They are angry.

But on the global scale, wouldn't the rich nations have to come down like the rich classes in Cuba, and wouldn't the poor countries like Latin America, Africa and Asia have to be pulled up at the expense of the rich nations? It would get us angry, and we would indeed have less, in order to get a more equal distribution of wealth?

I would be perfectly willing myself to be part of such a solution, if it were the only way to make the poor rich. I would be willing to see my own salary drop quite a bit, but perhaps not to the extent it would have to drop. I could imagine an egalitarian system today, and I find that I myself am much more willing to do this than almost anybody I know. My own belief is that it is inconceivable as a practical matter to imagine the rich countries depriving themselves of most of their income to help the poor. The rich are strong and the poor are not. This condition is not likely to change significantly over the next three or four decades.

The status quo will be maintained?

No, I think that many of the poor will get very rich and get powerful too. The status quo will not be maintained. It will not be maintained because the poor will get rich. Not because the rich voluntarily get poor. You see, that's a very different statement.

Everybody will get rich?

Eventually, except for the hard-core poor. Some will do it in two or three decades and some will take five or six, and some will take ten or fifteen. This is not a prediction. This is an extrapolation, a projection. This is a scenario. But a scenario which I feel has a high degree of validity. Let me go back to the big shock of our study: We said to ourselves, if we really have serious problems in getting rich, we should be able to find solutions. We tried to find such problems. We failed to find any unsolvable problems. I'm overstating right now. Now I want to make the correction. What we expected to happen was that we were going to find different kinds of problems. We have learned in the past that if we are dealing with a big system model, it is very important to focus the attention on the important interactions. That is, it is almost useless to use a model which treats each interaction with equal intensity. It would just be too big to handle and you would fail to get any information out of it. What we said was, let us first try to find those problems which by themselves or with interactions look very important, and then see if we can imagine the kind of technology which it would take to fix it, or the kind of change in the system which ameliorates or eliminates the problem. Let me go over the list of problems which the neo-Malthusians have said we have. First: that we will run out of resources. But it is not that we have no more coal to burn because coal is running out, but that we will have only high sulphur coal left to burn. That's not a simple running out, that's a pollution problem. We don't want to burn it because of the high degree of sulphur. We looked at the major raw material type resources and came upon none that looked disastrous; we even looked at more subtle resources like chromium, and we can find none there either that looks disastrous. (Throughout, we should remember, this holds only if we expect middle class, not upper class, standards of living.) Therefore I have given many members of the Club of Rome and others, a standard challenge. If there are critical resource limitations, what are they? In almost all cases I have studied they can be dealt with by current and near-current technology.

But what about the second problem—if the resources are not really usable because of side effects such as those that occur when burning high sulphur coal? Here the situation is more complicated. We don't even know what all these side effect type problems will be. But as far as current problems are concerned, and the ones which people worry most about in the long run, they seem perfectly amenable to simple technological solutions—if there are enough resources to use these technological solutions, that is if we have enough wealth. In fact one of the most important justifications for economic growth is that it provides the resources we need to deal with these problems.

The third issue that the neo-Malthusians focused on is what they call disastrously increasing income gaps. It is true that there are some fixed resources. The distribution of these resources is decided both by the rich and the poor, depending basically on what the rich will be able to get away from the poor. The richer they are, the more they will be able to get away. Such situations occur very rarely and we usually find that the richer the rich get the richer the poor get, because it is the very riches of the rich that create technologies and open up opportunities for the poor.

But what about the political problem? The resentment of the poor will become disastrous.

In most cases we feel that this concept of resentment about poverty is a concept that develops within a particular social or economic group, and rarely has much applicability across groups, even if they are intimately in contact with each other. If you polled almost any peasant or worker, or most businessmen in Latin America, in Africa, and in Asia, you would find they don't care whether the gaps are bigger or smaller. They want to get richer, that's all. And if the fastest way to get richer is by bigger gaps, fine. If the fastest way to get richer is by smaller gaps, fine. In practice the easiest and fastest way for the poor to get richer is by exploiting bigger gaps. So that's what they want. The emphasis on gaps as a problem is widespread in certain circles, but in most cases it is perceived as a problem by the rich, not by the poor.

Let us move on to the fourth point—that policy-making is increasingly difficult, perhaps disastrously so. There is no question, in my judgment, that policy-making is going down in quality, so that we do not deal with problems as well today as we did twenty years ago. Policy-making is worse today. If it gets much worse, I think it would be disastrous. What makes it worse is as much a decrease in the quality of the discussion as an increase in the difficulty of the problems. If you can get rid of some of the low-quality discussion, I think that the policy-making might be adequate.

Why do you think economists are so critical of the Club of Rome?

Partly because they are professionals in this kind of issue and really understand it—and also understand from experience the weakness of the input-output model used by the Club of Rome—partly because they have their own educated incapacities and think the price-system and market will always work and do not understand that there are some new elements to this situation.

* * *

Their capacities could be parochial, could be a little outdated.

I would put it this way. I will agree with eighty to ninety percent of the typical position of the economists who reject the Club of Rome. I do think that many don't fully understand the possible impact of even quasi-exponential growth or of some of the new problems and issues which are coming up.

Do you feel that a beginning has been made to pool experience, talent and wisdom in this field to aim at the future with the aid of computers in order to think of these children and grandchildren, to make the world livable fifty years from now?

I think you've put one phrase there which annoys me very much: "with the aid of computers." In the late forties and early fifties the United States had at one time about eight high speed computers; all of them were working for me. I have done lots of computer problems in my life. I enjoy computers. I have yet to find a problem of this sort in which computerized studies are very useful. I find that usually those who most use computerized studies understand this the least. It is very interesting to me that we have never used computers at Hudson for any other than tactical exercises and engineering studies. You don't need computers for most serious policy problems or even systems analysis.

We have been aware for many years of the ga-ga problem: garbage-in, garbage-out. We now call it the ga-go problem: garbage-in, gospel-out. The most interesting aspect about this whole matter is that many people worldwide have been distrustful of the use of computers for complicated problems. And all of a sudden there comes an answer to problems which they like, and now they say the computer is good. Why? Because they like the answer. If they didn't like the answer, they would have said, "Who believes it, it comes from a computer."

But who likes the answer that the world is in danger of being wrecked in twenty years?

Many in the upper-middle classes everywhere—or almost everywhere. That's why this is a class-interest issue. At the age of fifty I have become a Marxist. I now ask myself, "Look at the class interest. Look at the class attitudes. Who profits?" All right. Who is it who gets hurt the most by growth? What class is concerned?

The working class.

No. The working class does well by growth. It does well!

Not if growth runs amok.

The working class is the last to be hurt. The things that happen first in growth that people don't like are overcrowding, too many cars, urbanization. The working class likes that.

But how about increasing unemployment, labor unrest?

But growth has, by and large, not caused an increase in unemployment. Show me one country where an increase in growth has caused massive unemployment. The big unemployment in the world is in the undeveloped world, not the developed world.

In Europe at the moment we have them.

You have recessions, yes. You always have recessions. Okay. If you tell me that a modern dynamic economy has recessions, absolutely. You will have cycles. Many workers understand that, and will accept it. As long as he does well on the average. The big unemployment of the world is in the underdeveloped world. Let's remember that.

In your view McNamara was right in Stockholm when he said we need economic growth in order to help fight poverty in the Third World.

Absolutely. You need economic growth because the mass of people are poor.

Let me talk a little bit about what we call the Paneqole program. Paneqole is an acronym for peace, affluence, national and ethnic identity and freedom, quality of life, and equity and ethics. We don't believe you can have absolute peace, but more or less the kind of coexistence Khruschev described in his 1961 speech, at least for the near future. By affluence we mean over $1,000 per/capita, and European standards of living soon afterwards. By national and ethnic identity and freedom, we refer to national or ethnic identity, not necessarily to individual freedom. Many cultures do not really like individualism; they think it a selfish and unworthy concept. On quality of life, we mean middle class and lower middle class standards worldwide, while adopting as much as possible from the way the upper middle classes and the rich live. And as for equity and ethics, we originally included the concept of justice, but justice is too expensive, so let's say that men should at least be fair, and let's remind people of their obligations and responsibilities as well as their rights and privileges. Justice is a worthwhile ideal, but a very expensive ideal.

What do you mean by that?

Justice for the Arabs is death for the Israelis. Justice for the Israelis is death, or at least expatriation, for some Arabs. Justice is the most expensive commodity in the world: it means blood. As much justice as you can get is the most noble ideal of mankind.

I believe in justice. Justice plays a very big role in my life, but I am not a fanatic. I'm not a maniac about it, even though I feel very uncomfortable whenever I see an unjust situation. Justice to the American Indian means two hundred million white Americans get wiped out. I think in some ways justice is more important than love. I am not a Christian. In a way I am very Jewish, and in the Jewish religion justice is important, even more important than love, but not more important than human beings.

Earlier you said that this situation of rich and poor was a fact of life which is unavoidable.

If you wish to make the poor rich rapidly, the most rapid way to make them rich is to increase the gaps. The most efficient method we have ever found of making poor people rich rapidly is having a lot of very rich people around. Now, it happens that the ideology goes the other way. The ideology says it does not happen. Look at South Africa. In South Africa you have got about two million whites and ten million blacks. Those two million whites are trying to keep the ten million blacks poor. They cannot do it. As the whites get rich, something percolates down to the blacks. Wages are going up for the blacks. Also their training, their education, everything. The whites will continue to try to keep the blacks down, but get rich themselves at the same time, and will find it impossible.

The most obvious thing in the world is that riches percolate down. What do the rich nations or classes do to the poor? They supply capital.

They supply technology. They supply services. They are great big markets. There is nothing about the Chinese culture that made it especially efficient for industrialization until the twentieth century. Every Chinese culture outside mainland China now grows ten percent a year or more. Why? First because modern technology is now available to them to do what they did not do by themselves, that is, invent it; and modern markets are also available to them. So the Japanese grow, the South Koreans grow, the Taiwanese grow, Hong Kong grows, Singapore grows, and so on. Brazil grows like mad today. Why? Because of modern technology and modern customers. The fact that people don't understand this is their problem, not the world's problem.

But do you still believe that in this finite planet we will find infinite resources to answer the demands of rising standards of living?

I assume there must be limits. I don't know how the limits change over time with improved technology. I wouldn't make the final decision right now. With current and near current technology, we can support fifteen billion people in the world at twenty thousand dollars per capita for a millennium—and that seems to be a very conservative statement. We can do it with an adequate standard of life, adequate quality of life—at least by middle-class standards, but not necessarily by upper-middle class standards. The upper-middle class does have to give up many of its most cherished standards, if the middle class is to live well. For example, it's a suburbanized world. There will be suburbia, everywhere.

Let's think of it this way: In the twentieth century the world urbanized. Up until the eighteenth century for every person in the city there were ten to twenty people outside the city. The world is now suburbanizing in the same way as it previously urbanized. In the twenty-first century, if things go smoothly, the world will probably become suburbanized. That's not that bad. There're a hundred and fifty million square kilometers of land in the world. There are only sixty million square kilometers of more or less level available land. You put ninety million aside for recreation and other useful purposes. That's a lot. Of the sixty million kilometers of usable land, you use twenty million for human settlements and ten million for factories, for commercial, industrial, and service activities—half the land. The other half is for agriculture, entertainment, leisure. But basically it's all being used. The amount of park space may go way up. But wherever you go in the world, you will see suburbia.

You are hopeful?

For those who like suburbia, I am hopeful. For those who don't like suburbia, I am talking about a tragedy. The upper-middle class does not like suburbia for the poor. They hate it. Let me be very blunt about this. Say you're upper-middle class in a poor country. You have status. You have prestige. You can buy immunity from the annoyances of life. You can buy a good maid. Joseph Schumpeter made the remark that one good maid is worth a household full of appliances. You have one of thousands of cars, not one of millions. The rich cannot do anything wrong. In other words, many things that the upper-middle class prizes so much disappear when everybody gets rich. The reason why *Limits to Growth* was eagerly accepted was partly because of the quasi-legitimacy of its concern, but even more because it was presented to a very receptive political and emotional milieu.

NOTES

[1] See conversation no. 56.
[2] Victor Hugo (1802-85), French poet, novelist and dramatist.
[3] Organization for Economic Cooperation and Development, headquartered in Paris.
[4] Jean Mayer, quoted in Richard Falk, *The Endangered Planet*, p. 29.
[5] *Things to Come*, Macmillan (New York, 1972), p. 21.
[6] At the Hudson Institute.

47. *Jean-François Revel*

French author, journalist and philosopher Jean-François Revel was born in Marseilles in 1924.

He studied at the Sorbonne in Paris where he obtained a Ph.D. in philosophy. He taught philosophy at the French Institute in Mexico City (1950-52), at the French Institute at Florence, Italy (1952-56) and has taught philosophy at Lille and in Paris.

In 1963 he withdrew from academic life and became a full-time writer and journalist. As Paul A. Samuelson does for *Newsweek*, Revel writes columns for the French weekly *l'Express*.

His book *Without Marx or Jesus: The New American Revolution Has Begun* (1971) has drawn sharp attention in the United States. He is preparing a history of Western philosophy, of which two volumes have been completed and which is to be published in the US by Doubleday in 1974.

The first line of your book[1] forecasts that the revolution of our time, of our century, will take place in the United States. What do you mean by revolution?

By revolution I mean change. What you have to take into consideration when we talk about revolution is not the kind of ordinary revolutionary phenomenology, as it is often used, but about the very substance of change. I'll give an example: We speak in France about the revolution of 1848. In my opinion it was not a revolution because it lasted about three months. Afterwards we had the Second Republic, which lasted about two years and then came a dictatorship for twenty years under Napoleon III. When we speak of revolution, we should observe the outcome, what went into the very depth of society. America today seems to me more or less the melting pot of a world revolution.

You mention on page 183 of your book why you think that the United States is a prototype nation for this kind of revolution. You sum up the reasons, like continued economic prosperity, rate of growth, affirmation of individual freedom, etc. This tremendous Americanization of the world, on the basis of what is happening in the United States today, versus Japan—do you think it's possible that Japan with its enormous rising influence and economic growth will achieve in the East what the United States did in the West?

Yes, I think it may have a great impact on Asia, namely, on China. Japan up until now has had growth without development.

* * *

What do you mean?

We will come to that later when we talk about the *Limits to Growth* because I think that's the key point of the issue. Japan had an economic takeoff but no cultural revolution. In my book I mention that a true revolution has five components. One of them, only one, is economic growth. The great revolution towards the end of the eighteenth century in England (I don't speak of the first industrial revolution of the seventeenth century, which was purely political and a classical type, it could have taken place among the Greeks and has nothing to do with—but I am speaking of the world revolution—the Atlantic revolution of the end of the eighteenth century: America, England, France, Switzerland, Holland) was made possible by the first economic takeoff which took place in the United Kingdom.

Japan has had its economic takeoff, but Japan does not create for the world new models of culture, of behavior, like we see in the United States—as the Women's Lib, pop art and pop music, counterculture, the communes, everything like that—exciting a transformation in sensibility, in the way we perceive the world. The complete turning upside down of the perception of the world accomplished by Jean Jacques Rousseau[2] was as important for the French revolution as, for instance, the political thinking of Montesquieu.[3] Rousseau reversed the classical vision and Rousseau created a kind of emotional drive, a new attitude about nature, toward education. If you notice, each time you have a many-sided revolution, you have an upheaval in education: Jean Jacques Rousseau during the eighteenth century, Ivan Illich[4] today. All ideas of a new kind of pedagogy that came to Europe some years ago were shaped in the United States in the beginning of the sixties. I am talking about a new kind of laboratory for a new culture, a new civilization.

I find your thinking the same approach as Limits to Growth, *which is attacking the planet with global thinking, the concept of a global revolution.*

The Club of Rome has raised an important issue. This was useful. It is pleasant to see an idea, a thesis which was devised in 1965 or 1966 by some pot smokers in Californian communes—individuals considered half-demented parasites of the affluent society—become a theme thought about by the great technocrats of our world. That's a typical example of the American revolution too.

I lunched recently with Herman Kahn.[5] According to him, the Gantal culture is dead. I told him, that the Gantal culture was not dead at all, since all that he was saying to me were ideas that were devised by the Gantal culture five years ago. The most effective revolutions are the revolutions that are taken up by their enemies and then go unnoticed.

Some experts say *Limits to Growth* was a little garbage-in, garbage-out. Nevertheless, perhaps the greatest benefit of the publication of this report will be that we will become more and more aware of problems of environment, of possible exhaustion of energetical resources and of course of problems of the Third World.

However, we must draw a distinction between growth and development. Growth is a purely quantitative concept, and you always have growth. You even have growth in Haiti or Tanzania. You have tremendous growth rates in Russia, but a bad quality of life, even a daily life, which for the average Russian citizen is a kind of underdeveloped situation, sometimes coming close to starvation, as we have seen last year.

Development is something else, development involves changes in the political structure and in the culture. What we saw at the end of the eighteenth century during the industrial takeoff in England and France was not only an economic growth. It was at the same time a change of civilization, political change, moral change, artistic change, philosophical change, change in the structure of the family, everything. The reason why so many countries in the Third World don't develop themselves and don't transcend poverty is, as Gunnar Myrdal has seen correctly, that we experts of the developed world have taken into consideration only the economic aspect. We thought that just sending money would do it, would create an economic takeoff without changing human attitudes, social infrastructure, a new administration and a new management.

In Latin America, for instance, to fight birth increase is impossible for cultural and moral factors. The Latin man wants children. When we give the pill to an Indian woman in Mexico, her husband beats her, because he does not want her to take the pill. He wants her to have many boys.

Growth is a pure economical concept. Development is something which lays at the point of convergence between economic accumulation and innovation at all levels. That will be my answer. I would say that the problem *Limits to Growth,* in the pure economic sense, is a technical problem, it's a problem of management. The fact that I decided I will spend less coal or oil for this or that is a purely technical problem. In that sense I am for *Limits to Growth,* but I could not support limits to development.

Proust[6] once observed that disease is the only doctor who can exact obedience from the patient. Would you say that the problématique *of the planet at the moment would warrant the declaration of an emergency?*[7]

Yes, I would say that. I would add, however, that I also think that there is no solution now, except on a world scale. I am only afraid we are too late. We are too late politically. I think that we have too much technology in certain areas of the world and not enough technology in other areas of the world. But in order to use technology as we use wealth or money in the developing areas of the world would mean that there would be a kind of world government to manage these areas. I don't see how the rich West could first ask General Amin[8] to limit growth because, first of all, he has no growth at all in Oeganda, or not enough at least; and second, even if he had an economic takeoff, the kind of civilization he's creating is something so abominable that what would be the point? The great problems are exponential growth of the developed world and the nondevelopment of the so-called developing world, which is not developing at all. They are world problems, and we have to cancel completely the fiction of the nation-state, the De Gaulle philosophy.

De Gaulle[9] never spoke of nations, but of states.

Yes. Therefore, I think that it's wrong that the Portugese government feels it has a right to do what it has done in Mozambique or Angola. Nations are historical accidents. Don't get me wrong, I do believe in cultural diversity.

You also mentioned in your book that you are against bilateral accords. They must be avoided like the plague, you wrote.[10] We see the United States and Russia achieving the SALT agreement, which makes us recall the Von Ribbentrop-Molotov[11] pact of 1939. How to globalize nuclear power treaties, how to make the world safe?

Here you are touching upon something very special: security problems. It's a fact that there are two big nuclear powers and a few little ones. The SALT talks are necessarily bilateral because there are but two big military powers in that field—

But their pacts won't make the world any safer—

They do to some extent, because it's not either completely and exclusively bilateral. There are some consultations of the Europeans by the Americans, for instance. Of course it is not enough, but it's better than nothing. Towards multilateral entente—I was thinking, for instance, of phenomenons like the slowly growing European unity, or the Stockholm Conference on pollution and environment.

All politicians, dictators as well as democratically chosen politicians, seem to run behind the consciousness of the people.

Yes. And what makes a revolution is when the vital difference is no more than five or ten years; when the difference is fifty years, everything is lost. But when the politicians understand that earlier, under pressure, since more and more people are becoming internationally minded, the wall between domestic affairs and foreign affairs is collapsing at last.

You went further. You said in your book, foreign affairs are dead.

They should be dead. I think as far as affairs are foreign, they are damaging to mankind. Why should they be foreign? Because they are all our affairs. We are of course aiming towards not a global village, as McLuhan says.[12] Perhaps we should speak of a metropolis—and not in the sense of an expressionist movie of Fritz Lang, but in the Greek city sense.

Maybe McLuhan used the term village with his characteristic sense of humor. But you agree, I assume, with the Limits to Growth *concept of starting to manage the planet like a big company, like Shell or Phillips.*

Yes, but we have first to regulate democracy. In the Third World you cannot. The people there have not reached the cultural level for that kind of massive operation. Theirs is a very slow change and this is a tragedy.

This is a political problem?

Yes, a political and cultural problem.

Noam Chomsky[13] spoke to me about the proletarianization of intellectu-

als. Do you believe that the minds, the thinking people, would be able to revolutionize—to gang up and put sufficient pressure on the politicans to really do the job that's needed?

The present political systems are completely archaic. The way individuals reach positions of power and I do not only refer to the fact that most of the world is governed by dictatorship, the so-called democratic one-third is very archaic too. Through publicity people win votes.

McGuiness, The Selling of the President.[14]

McGuiness is one. Did you see the movie *The Candidate*, with Robert Redford? I compare the modern political leader to the man who was riding the stagecoach, the coachman. Our modern society is a Boeing 747, and instead of a pilot, you would see arrive a coachman—from the American Wild West in the 1880s, with his whip and his spurs, his Texan hat—and he thinks he can fly that 747 the same way as he used to drive the stagecoach at the end of the nineteenth century.

The issue is more democracy. After all, it has always been the solution. There is not a single problem in the history of mankind which has been solved otherwise, by other ways than simply more democracy, more participation, cultural participation. The more people are able to understand issues, the more democracy we get. In the United States—and to a less extent in Western Europe—we can say that two-thirds of the population can really understand what's going on, compared to five percent a century ago. The world is closer to a working democracy.

The modern revolution—the new kind of revolution, let's not forget—is something new. It is not something that has already happened. A true revolution cannot be compared with any previous form of revolution, because otherwise it would not be revolution.

More and more people are getting an education. In 1990, ninety percent of young Americans will get a college education. Yet, we cannot solve the great problems of mankind, summed up by *Limits to Growth,* without world planning. At the same time people demand more and more personal freedom. Here lies the complete contradiction. We have to do planning as the result of a convergence of individual choices. That is what democracy really is.

I think that we reach the point where the big reconciliation will have to take place, between collective planning and individual creativity. One cannot say "I am against pollution" and at the same time say "I am going to do what I damned please. I am going to throw one thousand liters of oil in the sea because I am a free man.'' That's absolutely insane. One cannot speak in favor of both ideas, as we hear every day. We cannot say, ''il est interdit d'interdire,'' like we read on the walls of the Sorbonne. ''It's forbidden to forbid.'' We have to have growth; we have to stop growth. How to stop growth if you do not limit personal freedom? That's the world's political issue, the moral and cultural issue of our time. That is the heart of the question. There will be needed only one new type of social contract, of world social contract, which can lead to the solution of the problem.

NOTES

[1]*Without Marx or Jesus.*
[2]Jean Jacques Rousseau (1712-78), French philosopher and social reformer.
[3]Montesquieu (1689-1775), French philosopher.
[4]See conversation no. 32.
[5]See conversation no. 46.
[6]See Jean-François Revel, *On Proust*, The Library Press (New York, 1972).
[7]See also conversation no. 9.
[8]President Id. Amin of Uganda.
[9]Charles De Gaulle (1890-1970), former president of France.
[10]*Without Marx or Jesus*, p. 88.
[11]Joachim von Ribbentrop, then Hitler's foreign minister. Viacheslav M. Molotov, then Stalin's foreign minister.
[12]See conversation no. 12.
[13]See conversation no. 42.
[14]*The Selling of the President*, Trident Press (New York, 1969). A devastating, insider's account of the 1968 presidential campaign and election of Richard Nixon, also described as the ''electronic election,'' during which maximum use was made of television and influencing the public by electronic media.

48. *Herbert Marcuse*

Marxist philosopher Herbert Marcuse was born in Berlin in 1898. He studied at Freiburg and Berlin, where he obtained his Ph.D. in philosophy.

In 1934 Marcuse came to the United States. He was professor of philosophy at Brandeis University from 1954 to 1965. He was then appointed to the University of California in San Diego. His most worldwide-known pupil was black activist Angela Davis.

Among his best-known works are *Reason and Revolution* (1941), *Eros and Civilization* (1954), *Soviet Marxism* (1958), *One-Dimensional Man* (1965) and *Negations* (1969).

We are discussing the usefulness of the efforts by MIT and the computers of Forrester[1] *and the Club of Rome to make a close study of how to manage the planet in the interest of all of mankind and not the rich nations alone.*

I think this study is of the utmost importance, because it shows from a new angle the destructiveness and aggressiveness which is inherent in the capitalist system. At the same time it shows its historical limits. They speak of redistribution and organization of all the resources of the planet. I believe that such a reorganization is only possible through and after the abolition of capitalism. From the beginning the whole question of survival is for me a radical political question and presupposes the effort to change not only certain things within society but society itself.

Yes, but the capitalist system tends to become stronger and stronger.

Stronger? And Vietnam? Chile? Cuba? And even where we can speak of economic growth, as in the Latin American states which depend on American power, this sort of economic growth goes hand in hand with the increasing impoverishment of the vast majority of the population.

* * *

But if the rich tend to become richer and the poor probably continue to become poorer, a clash seems inevitable.

The clash is inevitable and will be the content of a whole period of history. I certainly believe that there are already forces within the capitalist system at work which indicate the limits of the system.

But now the poor countries owe seventy billion dollars at this point to the rich nations. They have to pay seven billion dollars service charges on that amount of money borrowed from the rich nations. How will they ever be able to get out of this trap? [2]

Well, that's just it. They will never be able to get out of this trap unless there is a change in the advanced industrial countries themselves. I do not believe that the fundamental change can be the work of the Third World alone. It presupposes a change in the metropolis, which in turn would then trigger off the radicalization of the Third World.

You were optimistic, especially in 1968-69, when you drew attention to the fact that not the working class, but the universities and the ghettos presented the first real threat to the system from within. [3] *How would you view the situation in 1972?*

In the first place, let me correct this. I never said or wrote that the universities and the ghettos would or could replace the working class as a revolutionary force. I only made the point (which I think has been corroborated since again and again) that in the United States today the working class is not a revolutionary force and that in the prevailing nonrevolutionary situation, the students, the ghettos and the women's liberation movement represent preliminary, perhaps even premature, forces of rebellion. But they are the only ones we have today. I have stressed that unless and until the working class does become politicized, these forces will continue to operate in the forefront of the anticapitalist movement. I do not believe, for example, that the student movement is dead. I believe that it is in a period of regrouping and reexamination, the main question being, Which form of organization to give to the movement? Up to now it was mainly the lack of any kind of effective nationwide organization which caused the temporary weakening of the student movement.

* * *

Professor Marcuse, how do you explain, especially for foreign European opinion, the fact that so many young people in this country voted for Nixon?

I would say for two reasons, which have to be actually discussed separately. First because the repression and, consequently, the conformism have been intensified since the advent of the first Nixon administration. They continue to be intensified, so that these kids know perfectly well that if they had any radical activity on their record, that they will have a very very hard time to find a job later on. Therefore, they comply, their votes reflect this compliance. Secondly, it is the disillusionment and the disappointment that all the great efforts of '68-'69 came to naught and that the repressive government today seems stronger than ever before.

The killings at Kent and Jackson State,[4] would you include that in efforts to scare the student movement?

Certainly I would. However, this is only the most brutal and the most obvious form of suppression and destruction. There're others, such as economic and social discrimination, which do not work with open terroristic means but are very effective.

Are there any signs of an emerging revolutionary movement?

It has to be emphasized again: in this country, there is no revolutionary situation. This is not surprising at all, given the fact that the system still works, and that the power structure has been immensely strengthened. However, there are strong indications of deterioration (I discussed them in my book *Counterrevolution and Revolt*): malfunctioning in vital areas (the fuel crisis, transportation); rapid decay of the cities; race war; widespread protest in the factories (wildcat strikes, sabotage, slow-down, absenteeism); collapse of the capitalist "work ethic"; inflation, unemployment, blatant poverty; destruction—

But foreigners do not understand how the United States has managed to incorporate the labor movement into its power structure.

It is not difficult to explain at all. The integration of organized labor into the capitalist societies is a rational and very material process and certainly not only pertaining to the ideological level. First of all, the relative height of the standard of living: No matter how dehumanizing the work on the assembly line is, no matter how exploitation is intensified today (and I think it is more intensified than at any previous stage of capitalistic development), the fact remains that the organized worker today lives much better than his parents and grandparents ever lived. He has more relative security. He has more comfort, and after all, this counts. I find it ridiculous that people who call themselves dialectical materialists simply disregard all these facts as merely belonging to the "sphere of consumption," as if the sphere of consumption would be something that Marxists could neglect or relegate to a secondary level. This is a first reason, the material foundation for the integration.

The second is the apparent lack of an alternative. If you talk about socialism, the worker thinks of socialism as it exists in the Soviet Union and in the Soviet satellites. That he does not want, and he prefers his present state and society.

You agree with Shirer[5] that the United States might be the first country to go fascist by democratic vote. Do you see an indication that this country is moving further towards a form of authoritarian rule?

When I talked about going fascist through the democratic process, I thought of very concrete examples. Take the very large vote for Wallace[6] in the 1968 election or the strong labor vote for Nixon in the 1972 election. I also referred to the manipulation and to the computerized, electronic control of the population, wire tapping, undercover agents, etc. And perhaps most important, the rise of the executive branch of the government above all effective popular control, the decline, or rather self-emasculation, of the legislature, the silence and submission of the majority of the people in the face of the war crimes in Vietnam. Moreover, the training of "counterinsurgency" forces, the police, national guard and so on. If the capitalist system should further transform itself without being abolished, it would be a transformation into fascism.

Do you have any indication that we are moving towards the transformation of capitalism in this country and in the rich nations in general?

I think they are more than indications. The transformation of the capitalist system itself within its own framework is going on before our own eyes. If you compare capitalism today with the laissez-faire capitalism of the past, there is already a tremendous change. What we have today, what is usually called monopolist-state-capitalism, is such a transformation within the framework of the capitalist system—complete regulation of competition, the ever more active and widespread intervention of the government in the economy, the new imperialism, the paralysis of the democratic process.

IBM[7] stock is worth forty-five billion dollars on the market right now, but the government is taking action to break it up—

I think that would be the first antitrust suit that really did something to the capitalist system, so if I had IBM stock I would not worry.

I would like to ask you one more question on Limits to Growth *and what the Club of Rome is trying to do.*

May I answer your question before you ask it? It is in my view not so much the question of limiting economic growth as of fundamentally redirecting economic growth and economic activity, above all the mobilization and exploitation of all available technical and natural resources towards the abolition of poverty and inequality the world over. This may well necessitate even further economic growth, but economic growth used in a radically different direction.

NOTES

[1] See conversation no. 34.

[2] See also conversation no. 53.

[3] See Herbert Marcuse, *Counterrevolution and Revolt,* Beacon Press (Boston, 1972), p. 36: "Not the working class but the universities and ghettos presented the first real threat to the system from within."

See also Herbert Marcuse, *An Essay on Liberation,* Beacon Press (Boston, 1969), p. 16: "By virtue of its basic position in the production process, by virtue of its numerical weight and the weight of exploitation, the working class is still the historical agent of revolution."

[4] On May 4, 1970, Ohio National Guards killed four students at Kent State University during an antiwar demonstration protesting Nixon's invasion of Cambodia. Eleven days later, on May 15, Mississippi police killed two more students at Jackson State College after antiwar protests had erupted there.

[5] US author William L. Shirer.

[6] Former governor of Alabama, George Wallace, who ran for the presidency of the United States on a "third party" ticket, the American Independent Party.

[7] International Business Machines.

49. *Mary McCarthy*

American writer Mary McCarthy was born in Seattle, Washington, in 1912. She attended Vassar College and worked in her early years as a drama critic. In 1948 she taught English at Sarah Lawrence College.

She now lives in Paris and is married to an American diplomat working at the OECD headquarters.

While best known for her novel *The Group,* Mary McCarthy has in recent years become known for her criticism of American policy. Her books *Vietnam* (1967) and *Hanoi* (1968) were widely acclaimed. Also written recently, *The Writing on the Wall* (1970) and *Birds of America* (1971).

To paraphrase Charles de Gaulle on Sartre, "Mary McCarthy c'est aussi l'Amerique." [1] *How does it feel to live in Europe as an American with the critical world situation as it develops?* [2]

I've lived here in Paris for more than ten years. However, I don't think I have a European point of view at all. It has had advantages to be a little detached from the United States during this frightful period of the war in Vietnam, which isn't over obviously. The disadvantage is that if you want to try to take some action, it's difficult from here. If you want to organize opposition, it's very very hard by long-distance telephone. If you want to write a letter, as I have just done, to the *Herald Tribune,* [3] on subjects connected with the war, you know it will only be read by Americans abroad.

You could send it to Harrison Salisbury or John B. Oakes of the Times *in New York. You'll get your views printed there. You should.*

Yes, but somehow one is moved to write a letter in the place one lives. Incidentally, living in France seems to create a great deal of envy. Americans are very, very envious of people who live abroad and will try to put you down because of it. But I'm not an expatriate. I live here because my husband works at the OECD.

How did you experience this era, in which on the one hand Mr. Nixon opens bridges to China and the USSR and at the same time organizes Christmas carpet bombardment on a scale the world has never seen before?

It's a mystery really. I never believed in Nixon's good faith in these negotiations. I never believed in that October 26, 1972, accord.[4] I didn't think he would stick with it.

An election gimmick?

I don't think that could have played such a big role. He was sure of getting reelected anyway. Still, many people remain hostile to Nixon's policy and believe he was serious about ending the war. They thought it was to his interest to make peace in Vietnam. Once he had opened these lines to China and Russia he absolutely needed, they thought, peace in Southeast Asia. But it doesn't look as if he felt he needed it so badly.

Why the US stays in Vietnam and Indochina in general is a mystery. The only explanation I can come to is a kind of Marxist explanation, and perhaps fundamentally as much economic as political. The crude Marxist reading does not make sense. We don't need their raw materials. We don't need their rice; in fact, we're now exporting rice to South Vietnam. We don't need their rubber. Anyway, we've destroyed the plantations, and much of the trees. We don't need their bananas. Some offshore oil has been found there—but that's fairly recent, 1969, I think —and might help explain our hanging on there now, but not our earlier determination. We can't be sticking with Thieu[5] for pure colonialist or even neocolonialist motives.

But I do think that a choice was made by the VC[6] and their followers in South Vietnam for a noncapitalist way of life. This was a preference and something quite different from what happened in Poland, Czechoslovakia and so on, where the people really never had a choice. If Poland is communist, it is not a black mark for US-style capitalism, not at all, whereas the free choice exercised by the supporters of the Vietcong . . .

Like in Chile?

Exactly. It's very much like Chile. If they're allowed to win in Vietnam . . .

Carl P. Rogers[7] *stressed that what made him sad was the spread of what he called "a colossal hypocrisy in politics."*

Yes, I agree. It's absolutely horrifying, and almost more horrifying than the Christmas carpet bombing were the official lies that were told about it. Lies about that Hanoi hospital[8] and so on. And then this awful business of how we're going to help them reconstruct their country afterwards. It is completely mad and allows Americans to feel innocent, to feel good.

But to go back to Nixon's peace brinkmanship. My estimation—I may be wrong—is that Nixon first thought he wanted to buy the October accord. But as soon as Kissinger[9] came back with the provisions agreed on, if not actually signed, he suddenly realized, "I could have done better. Hanoi agreed to this, and that shows I could have done better." This is my analysis. I think he will back away again from another accord. . . .

—That's the level of Nixon's mind.

Yes. But it has been true of every American President, one way or another.

But you have to grant Eisenhower[10] *that he did get the war stopped in Korea, and fairly soon after his election. When Nixon ran for President in New Hampshire in '68, I was with him. He was saying over and over again, "I learned from Eisenhower and I'm going to stop the war in Vietnam." But he's still bombing, five years since!*

I remember that, yes. I remember that was one of his campaign lines. Eisenhower stopped Korea, but it isn't really over. There are still seventy-five thousand American troops in Korea—a thing everybody forgets. On the one hand, Eisenhower pursued a relatively prudent and moderate policy in Vietnam, compared with his successors. On the other hand, he was the President who decided not to have those Vietnamese elections, after the Geneva Conference of 1954. The fact that Washington, which permitted the assassination of Ngo Dinh Diem, will not politely dump Thieu indicates enough. If we withdrew support from him,

Thieu would no longer exist. As long as Thieu is there, it proves to me that Americans are not willing to get out of the country.

But what puzzles me, the Americans should have learned by now that by supporting Chiang Kai-shek,[11] *who is another Thieu, they harvested Mao Tse-tung. It's like supporting Batista*[12] *and getting Fidel Castro. When will Washington learn?*

Yes, but maybe there really are not any middle people nowadays. That's the liberal line: One should have supported some nice social-democrat, rather than Batista, then one wouldn't have any of these middle people who are viable, so far as the US is concerned. To them "middle" is already too far to the left. I come to think this more and more by looking at the disastrous developments happening in Chile. Allende was a perfect marvel of this nice social-democratic type.

But to return to our subject. How do you feel about what Jean-François Revel has called the Americanization of cultures?[13]

I think my answer is that I don't know. I think that some of the current forms of it are simply fashions, modes, and may well not last very long. Even I would hope that the drug culture may not last very long. I don't know. Americans are terribly, terribly susceptible to swings in fashion, and when they may set styles the styles spread. I also think the consumer-society mentality plays a curious role in all this. With the music, the clothes, jewelry, love bands, macrobiotic food, there are new commercial opportunities there. There are counterculture shops. Hippies work in shops that sell dropout clothes. This means a new youth market which has turned into a world market.

It's amazing how Japan on one hand is totally Japanese still and on the other hand has imitated the Americans on a scale as probably no other Asian country has done.

My feeling, I must say, about all this is very, very pessimistic. One only has to look around to see that really Notre Dame de Paris cannot cohabit with the Tour Montparnasse. It cannot. And of course I infinitely prefer Notre Dame de Paris. But you can't have both, and if you try, you get dead, preserved cities, museum cities surrounded by those ghastly housing developments, these cynical . . . habitations for workers and on the whole for poor people. Inside that ring is a petrified museum city that can be visited by tourists. It's impossible.

Paolo Soleri[14] *tries to design new cities through miniaturization. Are you familiar with that?*

Yes.

Jean-François Revel has written that either world government must come into being or nothing else will remain in being.

I am against world government myself. Especially with these dangerous and totalitarian tendencies of modern society. I think world government could be infinitely worse than what we've got now. Revel imagines a nice democratic world government. It might not be like that at all. Supposing there had been a world government headed by Hitler![15] The advantage of the present plural system is that there are still places that people can escape to. During World War II, it was Switzerland or Sweden, or eventually the United States. I am opposed to any tendency towards world consolidation which would mean that there would be no place to escape to in the event of a new totalitarian world tyranny.[16]

Yes, but on the other hand, Limits to Growth *very much warns that we are reaching the ceiling in resources, in pollution and in population. I don't even want to talk about a more just distribution of wealth between rich and poor nations. How then to come to a better management of this planet, without having a more effective political apparatus to work with than the United Nations?*

I don't believe that any of that is going to happen.

Don't you feel it should happen? After all, there are United Nations and institutions like the OECD.

Yes, but they have no power. I simply do not believe that any of that is going to happen. If we do get a world government, it will probably be a world government imposed by a tyranny.

Toynbee[17] *reminded me that the Romans reverted to temporary dictatorship in times of crisis and then returned to democracy afterwards.*

That's possible, but if a world government comes, it will *not* come about, I think, through agreements and round-table discussions. It would come about through force. If it does come about through force, then at some distant time in the future this force may be somewhat softened, modified, that is possible. But it's the only way that I can see this ever to happen. I also feel that it's quite possible that we're on the verge of some global peace, semipeace, at least between the three big powers, between China, US and the Soviet Union, and that a kind of semiauthoritarian, semitotalitarian society, with lots of consumer goods, will prevail in all these countries, with different accents.

Including Russia and China?

Yes. My sense is that these countries are moving closer together, especially the US and the Soviet Union. The US is becoming more reactionary, more totalitarian, and there is some slight *adoucissement,* [18] at least for the consumer in the Soviet Union. Some people put more hope in China, partly because it's newer and partly because, I think, we know less about it. We know the Soviet Union all too well. Too well to hope much from it, in the way of change or development. I've never believed that the US was fascist, but I think it might slide towards some new form of general oppression.

Repression also of the press and television?

Authoritarianism is very likely to develop in the United States, and in some ways it will be a kind of nonidentical twin with the Soviet Union, with different history, different life-styles, and so on.

Actually that would then bring them closer together.

Yes, I believe it.

Do you feel with the Club of Rome that there's reason for deep concern in these areas?

Oh, yes, indeed I do. So far as I know the thesis of the Club of Rome, I agree with it. But again I don't see that much of this will be done. Perhaps it is worthwhile if even some of it is done.

* * *

Through public opinion, pressure could be exerted on politicians and decision-makers.

Well, look at the pollution issue in the United States. The US is much the most polluted country in the world, even allowing for the Rhine—

—The sewer of Europe.

Yes, I think the US—if you combine noise, air pollution, river and lake pollution—the US is by far the worst. There has been enormous publicity about it. People have worked for it. There has been a whole ecological fashion. And it accomplished zero.

Nixon has just recently withdrawn money even to achieve some limited goals in this area.

Which shows, it seems to me, that public opinion cannot influence anything, not on a big scale. You have to keep on trying to stir up public opinion, but I am more and more coming to the belief that what is known as public opinion does not exist anymore.

You think of the fact that sixty-eight percent of the American people voted for Nixon while most of them are against the war actually.

As a writer—not when I write novels, but in those three books about Vietnam—I try to address myself to public opinion. But I have slowly come to realize that I'm addressing a vacuum. There's nothing there. Public opinion was probably based on the newspaper, rather than on television and radio. Perhaps newspaper readers, and masses of newspaper readers, constituted a thinking public that reacted to events. TV spectators do not.

Marshall McLuhan[19] tries very hard to find what on earth television does do to our minds.

Yes, but he is for it, and I am against it. I am completely against television, I think it could be abolished.

*   *   *

You think it pollutes and corrupts the mind?

Yes, I do mean it. I haven't had my television set out of the closet since General de Gaulle withdrew from politics, not since he died.[20] Yes, I did have it out once for a friend, a writer friend who was on French television. No, I really am against television. It's no sacrifice for me to keep that set in the closet. I forget it is there.

You slipped in the word French television, but French television is rather controlled; are you also against the CBS, NBC and ABC news?[21]

Those people are such fudge really. The idea that they represent any kind of radicalism is to me absurd. To me the best argument for television would be the BBC, British television in general. Also your Dutch television. I've seen it, I was in Holland over Christmas. We watched a certain amount of it—and it seems good. They have wonderful color, the best color in the world, I think, the Philips TV color. Anyway, I am against television.

I noticed—speaking of this question of public opinion—an effect on myself. When I happened to be in New York, coming back from Japan to Paris at the time of the Kent State murders, just after the Cambodian invasion. I saw it all on TV in New York, like everyone else in America. We were kept glued to TV for at least a day, maybe two days, every hour when there was news. We kept seeing the same thing over and over. The same sequences every hour just like with the Kennedy assassination,[22] when you kept watching Kennedy get shot, the funeral, Oswald[23] get shot, the same scenes over and over and over. I realized that by the end of the first day, I had no more feeling about Kent State.

Immunization—

This image had completely destroyed itself like some strange chemical reaction, it no longer had any power.

TV watchers don't know the difference any longer between John Wayne[24] and My Lai.[25]

No, I wouldn't take such a moralistic line. The deadening happened to me, and I am not in danger of confusing John Wayne with My Lai. I think it's an effect of the medium itself. The effect is just anesthetizing.

People first used to say it was wonderful, a very positive thing that everyone, in every American home, saw the horrors of Khe Sanh[26] and Hamburger Hill.[27] No doubt, this Christmas they must have been watching the carpet bombing of Hanoi, around the Christmas tree. I don't know. But I'm sure all feeling had died. I don't think that reading the newspaper has that numbing effect. In fact, it stirs one to want to do something, if it is only to write to the editor of the paper. The press creates around it an informed body known as public opinion, which after all didn't exist in the Middle Ages when the image predominated and rumor spread by word of mouth. There were waves, paroxysms, of emotion in the Middle Ages. It spread through whole countries. Just before the year 1000, people were terrified that the millennium was coming and the world was going to end. If only the Club of Rome could whip up waves of panic like that! But there was no such thing then as public opinion. It is a modern bourgeois phenomenon, and I think it's disappearing together with newspapers.

When I met with Professor Lévi-Strauss[28] at the Collège de France, he seemed sad about the state of the world and said that he would have preferred to live a hundred or two hundred years ago.

I agree with him. Yes, absolutely. A hundred years ago certainly. That was a very interesting time. Or even two hundred years. I might have lived in the sixteenth century. I also feel sad about the world. I particularly feel sad, not for young people, but for people who are babies now, and the future that is in store for them. After all, we won't see the worst, we won't live that long. Even our children, I don't think, will see the worst. But our grandchildren, my grandchildren, the grandchildren of people my age.

That's what the Club of Rome is so concerned about, Aurelio Peccei[29] has seven grandchildren. He feels after building Fiat factories in Latin America that he should spend the rest of his life in trying to work very hard for the improvement of conditions on the planet for all babies.

Of course one should keep trying, but I am not very hopeful that anything will be done in a large way. I think that is chimerical. Perhaps small initiatives may be taken, yes.

*   *   *

But globally?

I don't see it. Realistically I don't see it. If we can't even outlaw atomic weapons! If that happens, I will have some faith in the possibility of global agreements on population control, environment control, food resources. Arms should be easier, in principle, since agreements can be negotiated by governments and don't require citizens' cooperation. But so far as I can tell, nobody in power is offering even a distant hope of bilateral atomic disarmament (not reduction—disarmament), let alone a global accord. At the same time everybody knows about the danger of the spread of nuclear weapons. It will soon reach the point when any nation can manufacture its own bomb, like kids making LSD in the family kitchen or growing marijuana in mother's herb garden. The next step will be bootleg nuclear stuff.

My advice to anybody who cares about the future is to stop thinking big, thinking "global," and try to create free socialism in individual countries. Here in Europe small countries have the best chance of that. Not that that is easy either.

NOTES

[1]"Mary McCarthy is also America."

[2]The conversation took place in Paris at the time of Nixon's carpet bombing during Christmas, 1972.

[3]Paris edition of the New York *Times*.

[4]The date of the reported initial agreement to an armistice reached by Henry Kissinger and Le Duc Tho during their Paris negotiations at that time.

[5]Nguyen Van Thieu, president of the US puppet regime in South Vietnam since the assassination of Diem.

[6]Abbreviation for Vietcong, originally a pejorative nickname for the Vietnamese Communists and used interchangeably—if inaccurately—with the NLF, the National Liberation Front.

[7]See conversation no. 31.

[8]Bach Mai hospital in Hanoi was heavily bombed by US B-52s, although Pentagon spokesmen initially denied the raid.

[9]Henry Kissinger, Nixon's assistant for national security affairs.

[10]Dwight D. Eisenhower (1890-1969), thirty-fourth President of the United States.

[11]Chinese Kuomintang leader, fled to Taiwan after the 1949 Chinese Revolution led by Mao Tse-tung.

[12]Fulgencio Batista, former Cuban dictator, forced to flee Cuba after 1959 Cuban Revolution led by Fidel Castro.

[13]*Without Marx or Jesus*, pp. 73-76. See also conversation no. 47.

[14]See conversation no. 10.

[15]Adolf Hitler (1889-1945), German fascist dictator.

[16]See also Hannah Arendt, *Totalitarianism*, Harcourt Brace & World (New York, 1951).

[17]See conversation no. 5.
[18]Softening.
[19]See conversation no. 12.
[20]In 1970.
[21]Columbia Broadcasting System, National Broadcasting Company, American Broadcasting Company—the three main television and radio networks in the US.
[22]November 22, 1963.
[23]Lee Harvey Oswald, accused assassin of President John F. Kennedy.
[24]US actor and movie hero, specializing in cowboy roles.
[25]Vietnamese village destroyed by US troops, the majority of whose population—including the women, children and infants—were murdered in cold blood by US soldiers.
[26]Another reminder of war atrocities in Vietnam. However, the author would like to stress that while Vietcong atrocities are not discussed during this particular conversation, the reader is reminded of cruel behavior on the side of US opponents in Asia.
[27]A famous battle in Vietnam, where young American soldiers were ordered by superiors to defend to the last man a particular hell—which was later abandoned. Among those who intervened on behalf of the opponents to such insane military orders was Massachusetts Senator Edward M. Kennedy.
[28]See conversation no. 24.
[29]See conversation no. 70.

50. *Eugene Wigner*

Professor Eugene Wigner was Thomas D. Jones Professor of Mathematical Physics at Princeton University in Princeton, New Jersey, from 1938 till he retired in 1971. In 1963 he received the Nobel Prize for physics.

Professor Wigner was born in Budapest, Hungary, in 1902. He obtained a doctorate at the Technische Hochschule in Berlin in 1925. In 1930 he came to Princeton as lecturer. In 1937 he became an American citizen.

He is still teaching at Louisiana State University in Baton Rouge, Louisiana. For many years he has been adviser to the US Atomic Energy Commission in Washington, D.C.

Alva Myrdal[1] said in Geneva recently in July, 1972, that during the past eighteen months there had been sixty-six atomic explosions. Are we in danger because of these continued experiments with hydrogen fusion?

Those experiments do not hurt many people. I think the danger from the radiation produced by weapons tests has been exaggerated—in many cases grossly exaggerated. Most of it comes, of course, from USSR tests. The real danger is that it won't stay with tests and it won't stay with experiments, but that either threats will be made of nuclear attack or that a nuclear attack will take place. Contrary to much of what we read, even that would not exterminate mankind, but it would be a trauma for the future to come which might be terrible.

But could we envision the use of limited nuclear weapons in Vietnam or in any area of conflict?

In Vietnam I don't think there is a danger because the United States will not use nuclear weapons there. I don't believe that the North Vietnamese will have nuclear weapons at their disposal. There is no real danger there of nuclear weapons. Actually I am more afraid of blackmail than of nuclear warfare. In other words, I am afraid that one day one country will go to another country and say: Unless you permit us to station regiments in St. Louis, Chicago, Boston and so on, we will kill tomorrow this many and that many of your citizens.

Like Hitler did with Rotterdam.

Like Hitler did with Rotterdam. That is what I am principally afraid of.

How safe is mankind from defaults in atomic planning, like atomic power generators?

Mankind is safe because such disasters can only strike a limited region. But a limited region could be struck, since we are all stupid. We cannot foresee with certainty how things will function. Some problems with reactors exist, but I cannot believe that the total calamity which will be caused will be significant on a global scale.

Would you go along with the approach of the Club of Rome, that in order to manage the planet we would need a model to study the interactions of pollution, population, resources, etc.?

I think these things can be exaggerated. I think we have to watch pollution, but if I look now above your head, I see the blue sky. And certainly we have enough welfare, enough affluence in America so that we don't need more pollution due to added production than we now have. Now, the population may increase, and that may increase the production and hence the pollution. Do you know how much the average temperature increases in the United States as a result of all the power which we produce? You see, if you look up, that we waste power a great deal; but the temperature increase is one-hundredth of a degree. That is not significant. We do put into the air, though, a number of things which it would be better not to have there. We do many, many things which are bad, including misinformation in the media, which is also pollution.

Misinformation on science in the media?

On everything. On the police, on how people vote, on almost everything. Misinformation on Vietnam. Also on pollution, and we should fight it. But the effect of physical pollution to mankind in its present form is, in my opinion, being exaggerated. I don't want to support the physical pollution of our environment, I want to reduce it; but there is a difference between wanting to reduce something and considering it to be a menace to mankind.

But look at Japan, there are very serious problems.

The density of population in Japan and the Netherlands is very much larger than the density of population in the United States or than the density of population in other areas of the earth. And you are right: If the density of population increases to such an extent, much more attention should be paid to danger of pollution. But even then I don't consider it as a menace to mankind. There are many things that need to be changed, but don't menace us. If you look around, you see books. They don't menace my life. Just the same, I would like to put them into order. But I fight against many things which are not a menace to my life and similarly we should strive to improve the atmosphere and surroundings.

* * *

When Rachel Carson wrote the Silent Spring *the fight against insecticides began. You spoke about misinformation, well, Hannah Arendt would say, "The liar is defeated by reality." Did that book by Carson not help to raise the issue as* Limits to Growth *might help likewise?*

Yes, it did help to raise the issue, and I admire that book. I admire her courage, her imagination. But I don't have to say that somebody fights for the survival of mankind in order to admire her. I think it may be worth doing even if it isn't the saving of mankind.

But do you foresee the world moving towards a form of world management?

I have an ideal for the future of the world, which is no longer "one world." I think that if we have a single government in the world, it will be autocratic, suppressing. My ideal is that there should be many nations —perhaps not many but several nations, perhaps even several cultures. And the different governments should vie with each other for the loyalty of their subjects. They should permit emigration from their country, as the United States permits emigration from our country, and settlement in other countries, so that people, if they are unhappy with their government and with their rulers, could move elsewhere. And that would induce the governments to cater for the welfare and happiness of their people rather than strive for power.

In La Condition Humaine *Malraux[2] changed the revolutionary into a painter. How can we make the world livable for all these people from all these developed and undeveloped, rich and poor? By changing them from what into what?*

If I tell you how much the general welfare in the world increased in the world in my own lifetime, you would be amazed. I read a short time ago four signs of poverty: The first one was no running hot water; the second was no automobile; the third one was no radio. My grandfather was a physician. He lived in what was considered then reasonable affluence. He had no automobile, he had of course no radio and as for running hot water, he did not have running cold water either. And just the same he lived in happiness: Our welfare increased tremendously, and I do not believe that lack of welfare is a principal cause of unhappiness. I consider this as one point where the young people are right, the affluence is high enough.

*In other words there is a limit to this affluence, and there should be
a bending back or a zero growth of affluence in the rich world in order
to let the rest of the world catch up.*

In that sense zero growth of affluence for this country is enough, and
indeed it will soon have very small increase of affluence. Most people
have everything they need. There are many things, spiritual matters,
where much improvement is possible. I admire many things which other
countries do concerning welfare, but in America we have enough food,
we have almost enough lodging, we have enough means of transportation, we have enough books; these are not our problems.

*Twenty percent of the American population lives under the poverty line,
so that would give the others a chance to catch up too.*

This twenty percent under the poverty line reminds me always of the
teacher who complained that in spite of all his work, in spite of all his
effort and all his industry, half of his class was still below its average.
The people who now live under poverty level, I would like to improve
their lot, but it is much better than the average life was fifty years ago,
it has a much higher standard than the average life had fifty years ago.
Nobody has to go hungry. Once I decided I want to find out how much
I *have* to spend for food. I went to the grocery store and looked for
cheap food. I bought chicken backs and wings for eighteen cents, enough
for three dinners.

*Robert McNamara in his September 1972 speech before the World Bank
said that none of the rich nations in the world really reached the
minimum goal of aiding the underdeveloped nations. Would you feel that
we have an obligation here to the rest, the largest half of mankind, while
we go on spending billions on nuclear rockets?*

Well, I think, as I told you, we help mankind because we discredited
aggression. Aggression is one of the worst enemies of mankind, like the
desire of some autocratic rulers and dictators to extend their power—as
North Vietnam is trying to do. I will say this, even if I make myself
unpopular.

*All right. We in Europe always feel that our freedom is guaranteed unfor-
tunately by your nuclear rockets. We recognize this fact. But on the other
hand, would you tell us how many times can the United States destroy*

the Soviet Union at this juncture or how many times the Soviets could destroy us and the money this costs?

This is one aspect of the misinformation which is rampant. I can present a calculation which I carried out myself. The Soviet Union has a possibility to evacuate its cities. If it evacuates its cities, and if we were to shoot all our rockets at the people and if the Russian antiballistic defenses were totally ineffective, we could kill a tremendous number of people—tremendous—about six million. More than half of what they lost in the second world war and almost a third of what they lost as result of all sorts of semiexecutions.

But, Dr. Wigner, that still leaves the common man with the question, Is it necessary? Albert Szent-Györgyi[3] calls Brezhnev and Nixon "pigs," who continue to take the immoral responsibility to go on making more and more and more rockets, and they announce that the United States can destroy the Soviet Union a thousand times, et cetera.

That's just a foolish, incorrect, arbitrary statement, which is not true at all. Russia has a population of two hundred forty million. The United States can kill, if the Russians evacuate their cities, six million of them. That is not being able to kill everybody a thousand times. This is the possibility to kill every sixteenth person—no, every fortieth. The United States has not increased its missile power for two and a half years. In fact, the United States has decreased its missile power in the last two and a half years because the Russian missile defenses made this necessary. Not the civil defenses, the missile defenses. As a result of that, the United States was forced on MIRV, that is, to increase the number of its missiles, but decrease their size much more, in order to maintain a certain deterrent in spite of the growing ballistic-missile defenses of the Soviet Union. The last two and a half years the missile power of the United States decreased and did not increase. We did not increase it because we hoped Russia would follow soon. Russia did not follow and increased its missile power by a large factor. If somebody says the United States increased its missile strength in the last two and a half years, he is giving out false information.

Recently the New York Times *mentioned that one US atomic submarine costs a billion dollars. For the same amount of money one could build a transit system for a US city. Why the hell do we have to spend such fantastic sums of money on nuclear submarines if so much social work needs to be done?*

I don't know. The New York *Times* is not infrequently spreading misinformation. I don't have it in my head how much a nuclear submarine costs. I don't know it.

Nietzsche foresaw the devaluing of all values. I sense that you are an optimist.

I am an optimist concerning the physical future of mankind. I am worried about what we should strive for. There is a beautiful Hungarian poem saying that man needs a goal, that he always strives for something, good or evil. Man needs a goal in order to lead a life that he enjoys, and I don't know what the future goal of man will be. In the past, in my generation still, it was to earn a decent living. This comes now free, at least in our countries, for the majority. I don't know what people will strive for, I am worried about the spiritual welfare of mankind, not about his physical welfare.

Baudelaire[4] felt that we needed beauty in our lives to survive.

That is the problem. Where does the beauty come from? The fight for survival I think will be over, unless we can control the growth of population. If we can control the growth of population, the fight for survival will be won, and I am then worried about the fight for spiritual values, for purpose, a goal to man, a meaning. This is the problem that worries me, not the physical problems.

NOTES

[1] See conversation no. 36.
[2] André Malraux (1895-   ), French author.
[3] See conversation no. 6.
[4] Baudelaire (1821-67), French poet and critic.

51. Harrison Brown

Dr. Harrison Brown is professor of geochemistry and professor of science and government at the California Institute of Technology. He is also foreign secretary of the National Academy of Sciences in Washington, D.C.

He was born in Sheridan, Wyoming, in 1917. He studied chemistry at the University of California and obtained a Ph.D. at John Hopkins University in 1941.

From 1942 to 1943 he worked as research associate at the plutonium project of the University of Chicago; from 1943 to 1946, assistant director of chemistry at Oak Ridge, Tennessee; from 1948 to 1951 he was associate professor at the Institute for Nuclear Studies at the University of Chicago.

He has published numerous books, among them *Must Destruction Be Our Destiny?* (1946), *The Challenge of Man's Future* (1954), *The Next Hundred Years* (1957) and *A World Without War* (1961).

You are the foreign secretary of what is considered the largest consulting operation in the world, the National Academy of Sciences in Washington, D.C. How do you view the international community of scientists in the seventies?

The primary task of my office in the National Academy of Sciences is to maintain and develop close working relationships with our colleagues in other countries, no matter where these countries might be and no matter what the political differences between our governments might be. We have very good relationships with the socialist countries. We have very good relationships with the countries in the Third World. We have very good relationships with our sister academies in Europe, Australia and elsewhere.

* * *

And China?

We are just beginning to develop relationships with China. We have hosted now two groups of Chinese: The first group was a medical group, which spent three weeks in the United States; the second group is a group of natural scientists. Including physicists, biologists and chemists, and that group is just now touring the United States as our guests. I must say that here again, although there are very real political differences between our governments, as scientists we get along extremely well together.

There are apparently about seven hundred and fifty thousand working scientists worldwide. We are able to communicate with each other. We are able to talk with each other. There are gaps of course, stemming from the fact that we are in different fields. A biologist might have some kind of trouble communicating with a physicist, but we scientists are able to communicate with each other far more effectively, I think, than nonscientists are, coming from different cultures. It is startling to me how the members of the scientific community worldwide tend to look at the problems of the world in the same way. We have the same general view of just what the major problems really are that require solution.

A United Nations university has been now decided upon.

The "United Nations" of the scientific world is called the International Council of Scientific Unions. It is made up not of nations but of organizations of scientists. We believe that every group of scientists should have access to the workings of the International Council of Scientific Unions. As a result we have as members a major scientific society in West Germany and the Academy of Sciences in East Berlin, the Academies of Sciences of both North Vietnam and South Vietnam, the Academies of Sciences of both North Korea and South Korea.

In The Challenge of Man's Future,[1] *you discussed among others the exponential growth of amebas—which brings me to the Forrester Law and the Club of Rome—how do you feel this initiative is being looked upon in the United States or in the community of world's scientists?*

It is quite clear that the study *Limits of Growth* has aroused man's passions both pro and con. My own view is the following: It is absolutely essential that we attempt to look into the future. Unless we do so, it's almost certain that mankind is going to paint itself into a corner from which it will not be able to extricate itself. Our ability to look into the future is not very good. We are learning a great deal about how to forecast. Nevertheless, in spite of the fact that our current competence is not very extensive, it is important that we try and continue to improve our techniques. It is very important, for example, that we look at the interrelationships between population growth and technological change, between technological change and our natural resources, between technological change and the human environment. It is very important that we look at technological change in terms of social change. How are new techniques changing the ways in which people live? When we look at the full scope of human history, we see major changes in society which have resulted from the adoption of relatively simple technologies. Basically, for example, the change from a food-gathering technology to an agricultural technology produced perhaps the greatest single social and cultural change in mankind's entire existence.

How to describe your concept of four futures? [2]

If I were a cosmic gambler looking at the world from a great distance, examining what goes on, I would outline the planet's future in the following order of probability. I think the most probable, basically, is that the instabilities will be so great and that nationalism will influence our existence to such an extent that it is only a matter of time before somebody drops "the bomb." Then, of course, there would be a major catastrophe. I don't believe that such a catastrophe would destroy all humanity. But I do believe that it would be extremely difficult for a new civilization to emerge from the ruins of the old. We saw that happen in the Middle Ages, when the fantastic civilization of Rome disappeared and the generations which followed cannibalized the old civilization. It took centuries before something new could be created. We must keep in mind that we are now living in an age when there are no longer resources of the high grade which were available to us when we built our civilization. As each year passes our resource base will diminish still further. This does not mean we cannot keep going, we certainly can. It is solely a matter of developing adequate technology and a matter of energy. If need be, we could maintain a very high level of civilization using ordinary rock, which is the lowest common denominator of resources. But suppose such a civilization were to stop? A primitive group without the tools cannot live off ordinary rock.

The next most likely future is one in which we in some way manage to avoid the catastrophe of "the bomb." If things continue the way they're going now, it is quite clear that humanity will remain divided into two quite separate cultures—the culture of the rich and the culture of the poor. No matter what indicator we use, whether it be gross national product per capita, energy consumption per capita or steel consumption per capita, these are increasing in both the rich countries and in the poor, and they are increasing at the same rate. What this means is that the rich countries will continue to remain, per person, twenty times as rich as the poor countries. They will continue to consume twenty times as much energy per person as will the poor countries. Yet the poor countries are increasing their energy consumption and at the same time they are becoming more crowded. As a result one can foresee the perpetuation of a minority of rich and an expanding population of poor. One can visualize the emergence of conflict between the two groups and a continuing complete separation between the two from the point of view of ways of life.

A third possibility is that in light of the sensitivity of highly industrialized civilization to disruption and also in the light of the very slow rates at which countries are developing under democratic systems and the more rapid rates at which they appear to develop under strong totalitarian systems, it seems to me that in both cultures—both the culture of the rich and the culture of the poor—we are gravitating more and more towards strong totalitarian control. We see this in Latin America. We see this today in China, where many of my Chinese friends say quite freely that China cannot possibly develop under a democracy. My Latin American friends say, Argentina cannot develop under a democracy. Brazil cannot develop under a democracy.

Or Indonesia?

Indonesia is another example. When we couple this with the situation which is emerging in the West, where we see more and more conflict —conflict resulting from the fact that it is so easy to disrupt society—we see the effects of highjacking, of blackouts, of strikes. A single well-placed bomb in a power system in an eastern city could disrupt the entire eastern coast. It is only natural that governments react and exhort stronger and stronger control. It is not difficult to imagine the emergence of a totalitarian world.

I am not saying that I am advocating any of these three futures. These are indeed three terrible prospects. The last, the fourth future, I believe is attainable. It also is the least probable. I am convinced that man has it within his power to create a world in which all people worldwide can lead free, abundant and even creative lives. We have that power. It remains to be seen whether we're really going to be able to mobilize that power and use it. We have fantastic power, when it comes right down to it, power given to us by the fact that we have such unlimited quantities of energy, a fantastic technology. Hunger in the world today is absolutely inexcusable. Poverty, disease, the traditional scourge of mankind, are inexcusable.

If I had to point to one enemy that is preventing us from using this power, I would point to nationalism. We live in a world of a hundred and thirty sovereign countries. There was a time in history when this made some sense, since the world then was large. Today the world is very, very small. The thought of perpetuating this fiction of a hundred and thirty sovereign countries is the most dangerous notion one can have today. It is terribly important that in some way these countries come together under a common rule of law, under a common government for all of mankind.

When we look back over the history of my own country, in our very early stages of development, we were in grave danger of ending up as thirteen separate, sovereign states. Fortunately this did not happen simply because we had a remarkable array of extraordinarily intelligent, competent individuals, such as Thomas Jefferson,[3] Benjamin Franklin,[4] Alexander Hamilton.[5] Hamilton once formulated a question which he asked himself: Why was government instituted at all? His answer was: Because the passions of men will not conform to the dictates of reason and justice without constraint. He was arguing for a federal rule of law as applied to the individual. That is what we ended up with in the United States. Thus far it's worked fairly well. I suspect very strongly that if the world really is going to get itself out of the present mess, we must look forward to a rule of law in the world as applied to the individual. We must recognize that nationalism is an anachronism. We must recognize in the long run there must be one world, otherwise there will be none.

NOTES

[1]*The Challenge of Man's Future*, Viking Press (New York, 1954), p. 8.
[2]Ibid., pp. 220-67.
[3]Thomas Jefferson (1743-1826), US statesman and third President.
[4]Benjamin Franklin (1706-90), US statesman.
[5]Alexander Hamilton (1757-1804), US statesman..

52. *Edwin M. Martin*

Ambassador Edwin M. Martin is chairman of the Development Assistance Committee at the Organization for Economic Cooperation and Development in Paris.

He was born in Dayton, Ohio, in 1908. He studied at Northwestern University in Illinois.

In 1945 he was adviser on Far Eastern economic affairs in the office of the Assistant Secretary of State at the State Department in Washington, D.C.

In 1946 he became acting director of the Office of Economic Security Policy; in 1948, deputy director in the office of international trade policy; in 1949, director of the office of European regional affairs. In 1952 Mr. Martin was appointed special assistant to the Secretary of State. In 1964 President Lyndon B. Johnson appointed him US ambassador to Argentina.

To consider the question raised by *Limits of Growth* and choose a course of action, it is necessary to make certain assumptions. I describe my positions thus because they can be no more than that; they are not susceptible—except one or two quite marginally—to logical debate or factual proof. You may allege that that too is an "assumption" in the same sense. I accept the point, but it is mine.

I believe the following:

1. The uncertainties are too great to make forecasts based on the use of resources other than those of this earth and its atmospheric envelopes.

2. Man has an absolute priority in the use of the resources of this earth for his well-being.

3. His well-being can have as many meanings as there are people, but I include only his well-being while "alive" on this earth.

4. Each generation has a responsibility for the ability of the earth to serve the well-being of future generations, but how high a priority to

give this claim and for how far into the future is an individual political choice incapable of objective definition.

5. All human beings are born with an equal "right" to have a satisfactory life on earth—inequalities being the result of the actions of man, past and present, and hence changeable by man.

6. Those now living who have unsatisfactory lives, do so largely because of chance factors which have determined in what countries they were born, into which communities and families, and with what genes.

7. There is therefore a heavy obligation on those who have been lucky, to improve the levels of well-being of others, an attitude sometimes referred to as Christian charity or humanitarianism.

8. What constitutes a better level of living will differ widely between cultures and often between individuals and for each over time, the latter changes seeming to accelerate in recent decades.

On the basis of these eight points, I would draw the following points with respect to *Limits to Growth:*

1. For a repetition of current life-styles, there can be foreseen serious problems of pollution, resource exhaustion and population excess, but the date depends on an unpredictable rate of technological progress *and* on our skill at managing our societies' politics.

2. There is no reason to suppose that the current life-style, with its high average component of consumption of energy and things, will persist, rather the contrary seems likely, with important consequences with respect to the time pressure under which science must produce better answers.

3. Nevertheless, the majority of mankind lacks enough material goods, private and public, to permit a very minimum decent level of well-being, or life fulfillment. Hence, substantial further increases in output of things, consumption of energy and production of pollution will be required, regardless of whether zero population growth is achieved. The major adjustment needed in the foreseeable future is not in output but in the distribution of consumption. For the better-off people, the slogan should be not "zero growth" but "zero consumption growth." Apart from redistribution within rich countries, major new channels must be found to shift both production and consumer goods from rich countries to poor ones.

4. This necessity to expand global output for a good many decades, considering the difficulties to be overcome in slowing population growth

and the political obstacles to redistributing output globally, demands a major continuing effort to find new sources of energy and raw materials, to use and reuse them efficiently and to reduce their polluting effect. These will be major challenges for our scientists and technologists. It is vital that a decline in many societies in respect for material things not be accompanied, as it sometimes already seems to be, by a decline of interest on the part of the ablest minds in pursuing careers in scientific and technical research and innovation.

5. This continued pressure on resources provides added reason to reduce as rapidly as possible the waste of scarce resources, which is represented by production of military weapons to defend one part of mankind against another. These fears, if continued, can greatly complicate the lives of future generations. This is just one example, though an important one, of our great dependence for material and nonmaterial well-being, now and for the foreseeable future, on our political skills. These too still need careful nurturing in future generations.

6. While recognizing the importance of preserving resources, which we believe—we cannot know—will contribute to the richness of the life experience of future generations, we should not allow this concern to impede too greatly efforts to improve the lives of those now alive for whom existence is barely possible. This includes concern for our flora and fauna. The variety of species does enrich the lives of a small percentage of us, but one shouldn't forget the thousands, at least, of species which nature herself has eliminated.

From your remarks on Limits to Growth *in the 1972 report on Development Corporation,*[1] *you gave the impression that you thought* Limits to Growth *was a little too pessimistic. You felt rates of growth and future disasters could be substantially modified by man. What makes you believe in the rationality of man?*

I think, as you quoted me, I said *can* be substantially modified. This does not imply that I am sure they *will* be. I am convinced that if man can find the political will and the political organization to deal with this problem—which includes reduction of waste, of which arms expenditures are one, which includes a proper financing and advanced planning of science and technological research addressed to the problem, which includes a willingness of the best brains to work on these problems—then I think that the possibilities of finding additional resources, of finding new sources of energy, of reducing the pollution impact of production can be achieved. I would emphasize that with concern for the position of the developing countries, I feel that we must find ways to continue producing more. The problem is not limitation of production for the foreseeable future, but a redistribution of consumption, so that many people—the majority of the world's population—who are now living at a subsistence level, can live halfway decent lives. Even though this may mean, in order to keep total off-cut within reasonable bounds, that people now living with two cars and a motor yacht, will get along with considerably less. I do think that man can effect this also by changing beliefs in what is important in the world and that we are seeing a generation in the richer countries which is less interested in material things and believes less that personal wealth is the answer to man's happiness. This could change consumption patterns and hence production requirements in a way which will postpone the date of crisis.

Carl G. Jung once said that "the imposing arguments of science represent the highest degree of intellectual certainty yet achieved by the mind of man." [2] *Do you believe that scientists could get the necessary ball rolling, to get the decisions taken that are necessary?*

Perhaps it's my generation but I am on the whole a pessimist of what men of science acting in the social field, in the political field, can do in having an important influence on how the life of society should be conducted. By and large these are people who are looking for certainties, who are used to dealing with absolutes and who find difficulty in dealing with the compromises that are necessary between the multitude of individuals with different capacities, wants and ambitions, which is the very heart of all political life. Discoveries that scientists make may have a very important impact on social, political and economic life; but as individuals I feel their interventions have on the whole been naïve, unsophisticated and not always helpful.

But the shock effect of Limits to Growth, *put together by scientists, had a healthy influence on public opinion.*

This is right. The book, with all its defects, did focus attention on a problem in a way which was useful. I am not quite clear that it was done by scientists. It was a system-analysis approach, which tends to derive from social sciences, which must be distinguished rather clearly from physical sciences, natural sciences.

NOTES

[1]See 1972 Review, Efforts and Policies of the members of the Development Assistance Committee, OECD, Paris, p. 28.

[2]Carl G. Jung, *The Undiscovered Self*, Little Brown Company (Boston, 1957), p. 3.

53. *Alexander Trowbridge*

During the years 1967-68 Alexander Trowbridge was President Lyndon B. Johnson's Secretary of Commerce.

Born in Englewood, New Jersey, in 1929, Mr. Trowbridge was educated at Phillips Academy at Andover, Massachusetts, and Princeton University.

He began his career with the California Texas Oil Company in 1954. He was connected with Esso Standard Oil Company from 1959 to 1963. In 1970 he was nominated president of the Conference Board in New York City.

Limits to Growth, *sponsored by the Club of Rome, is saying that if uncontrolled growth were to continue, without urgently needed checks and balances, it would be like arguing that the earth is flat. Do you deem it necessary that the technological-industrial world take careful note of a study like* Limits to Growth *and the studies that are planned following it up?*

There is no doubt that this kind of challenge, as seen in *Limits to Growth,* is important and necessary as a warning signal and as a stimulant to discussion in ever-widening circles. Debate is a better word, since the findings of the study are being seriously argued. The processes by which the analysis was carried out, the underplay of technological impact, the silence on pricing mechanisms as determining factors—these aspects of the Club of Rome study have created extensive debate. But no one can deny that we need long-range forecasting and planning, and we need to act now on the critical findings of such forecasts if they are valid.

I happen to be more optimistic over man's ability to solve these problems than we see in the gloomy exponential curves of the *Limits to Growth*. Man's ability as a rational human being has enabled us to survive similar predictions in the past. While the problems facing us are tougher to solve, we are increasingly better equipped technically to solve them—if we have the will.

I am also impressed by the widening concepts of corporate social responsibility that I see in the business world, and the recognition of the social impact of economic activity. We see it both in the United States and in other countries as we work with major firms associated with the Conference Board. Managerial leadership is increasingly geared to the total social, political and economic context in which they work, recognizing the inextricable ties between political and social stability with economic viability. While the "bottom line" measurements of corporate results will always be read in economic terms, we will also see greater and new sets of criteria which attempt to measure the social value of the organization's activities. I see real hope in the engagement of private sector leadership in seeking ways to stimulate social and political health, as well as economic prosperity.

Sir, why do you think mostly the economists in the United States have so strongly criticized the report of the Club of Rome on price mechanisms and details of the model, while it obviously was a first beginning? Why the sometimes irrational negativism?

Frankly, we shouldn't be surprised that the *Limits to Growth* has stimulated strong resistance. Our outlook is still heavily economic, geared to the development of new material wealth. When a study portends the ultimate end of that quest and indeed challenges the very rationale that supports it, I think it is understandable that the reaction is strong and the debate lively.

Another factor is that a number of critics, most notably Carl Kaysen[1] in the July, 1972, *Foreign Affairs,* say that we cannot afford to cry over future wolves when we have numerous tigers on the current scene. He fears diversion of attention from such problems as the international monetary system or the gap between developed and developing countries. If we become convinced that the end of the world à la *Limits to Growth* is in sight and therefore readjust and redirect our efforts and priorities to potential problems more than existing and immediate ones, then we are being misled. This may not be a very long-range perspective, but is certainly an understandable one.

Now, Mr. McNamara made an important speech to the World Bank September 25, 1972. From the point of view of foreign aid, the developing world owes at the moment already seventy-five billion dollars to the rich nations. They have to pay approximately seven billion a year in service charges. How will the Third World ever get out of this trap?

It may well be that these kinds of massive debts will have to be either stretched out or declared dead in some form of moratorium. There are clearly some countries so heavily indebted to international institutions or national governments that they will never get out from under. And yet examples of successful turnarounds do exist, in Brazil or Indonesia, for example. Indonesia still carries huge debt burdens, but it has become a center of interest for new private foreign investment as a result of improved political stability.[2] Secondly, if the developed countries can ever come to agreement on a system of generalized preferential trade arrangements for developing countries—an admittedly elusive target —their chance to earn more and hence repay more could be improved.

I see another area where hope may be justified. The shift in the developed world is moving towards a greater portion of gross national product and of labor-force utilization in the service sectors of the economy. In the United States over sixty percent of our GNP is generated by service and distribution industries, by government and by education. Over fifty percent of the work force is in the nonmanufacturing, nonindustrial sectors. In Japan and numerous other developed economies, the growth of the service sector is also strong. At the same time, inflationary trends in the developed world have become almost endemic. I would guess that these two factors will lead to ever larger flows of private foreign investment into developing countries, and a consequent increase in their ability to earn through exports of lower-cost finished products to those developed countries where, by choice or by inflation, economical production has decreased.

* * *

The SIPRI (Stockholm International Peace Research Institute) has reported that since 1961 the United States used 338,000 tons of napalm alone. The armaments race in the Third World is galloping onwards. And here McNamara reports that none of the rich nations—next to Italy, the United States gives least—reaches even one percent of the GNP in aid to the poor peoples on the planet. [3]

It is quite true that developed countries do not reach the one percent of GNP target unless you include, as the Japanese do, the total amount of private-sector development going to developing countries. While not part of the national effort, in that it is not a reflection of official commitment or budget, it is still part of the development process.

As to your comment on massive expenditures for war, I again may be excessively optimistic, but I am struck by the rapid and substantial developments in the last two years in big-power relations. The extent of the changes in US-USSR and US-China relations, plus modus vivendi operations in Germany, have indeed been impressive. We would be foolish to assume the millennium has arrived, or that the antagonisms and deep philosophical and political differences have disappeared suddenly. But surely there has been a remarkable reduction in tension—and more will follow once the Vietnamese question is settled. Viewed in terms of 1945-70, developments in 1971 and 1972 have been astounding, and if handled wisely our future relations do offer serious opportunities to reduce arms expenditures. The SALT talks plus the balanced reduction of conventional weapons—all hold promise for ultimate release of official resources for positive application to the developing countries and for closing the gap between have and have-not nations.

The prime question revolves around our will. Do the developed nations, and does the United States, still believe as we did during the Marshall Plan and the '50s and '60s that our long-term interests will be served by closing that gap? We cannot overlook the strength of economic nationalism in the US, or the EEC, or Japan or Canada. It could overflow its boundaries and send us all back to the days of isolationism and economic stagnation. We are weary, in many ways, of the burdens of leadership. It will take the best kind of political and business leadership, in all countries, to avoid succumbing to this weariness. But this gap really must be closed on a steady, consistent basis, in the interest of survival of us all.

* * *

NOTES

[1]See conversation no. 11.

[2]The author protested this statement strongly on the basis of facts and figures, maintaining that the present, highly corrupt Suharto regime has achieved no political stability at all except in carrying out an effective military dictatorship, the classical breeding ground for popular insurrections, as seen earlier, for instance, in China against the Kuomintang clique. At the special request of Mr. Trowbridge, the entire conversation on this subject was later scrapped.

[3]James Reston summed up in the February 4, 1973, New York *Times*: "World military spending has increased by 82 percent in the last ten years, from 119 billion dollars (in current prices) to 216 billion (US) dollars in 1971."

54. *Lester R. Brown*

Lester R. Brown is a senior fellow with the Overseas Development Council, a private, nonprofit organization in Washington, D.C.

He was born at Bridgeton, New Jersey, in 1934. He studied at Rutgers University and at Harvard University.

Formerly he was administrator of the International Agricultural Development Service and served as policy adviser to the Secretary of Agriculture on world food needs and agricultural development abroad.

Mr. Brown has written the following books: *Man, Land and Food* (1963), *Seeds of Change: The Green Revolution and Development in the Seventies* (1970), and his latest book, *World Without Borders* (1972), has drawn wide attention in the US and abroad.

What exactly is the Overseas Development Council?

The Overseas Development Council is a nonprofit research and educational institution established in 1969 to improve the relationship between the United States and the poor countries. We are a small bureaucracy by Washington standards, numbering some twenty individuals, half professionals and half supporting staff. We are supported financially by three large foundations—Ford, Rockefeller and Clark—and about forty multinational corporations. We do not contract work and are financed entirely through grants.

Do you advise the World Bank?

We work with the World Bank in the same way that we work with any other organization whose primary business is international development. We work with the Agency for International Development, the OAS, the Inter-American Development Bank, other development agencies, the UN agencies and so forth.

Limits to Growth *was a very controversial report right from the start of its introduction in the United States. Where does this controversy originate?*

The *Limits to Growth* is a threat to many people. It's a threat to economists, for example, whose tool kits contain tools designed primarily to stimulate and encourage growth. Those tool kits will become somewhat obsolete if growth is no longer the objective. It's also a threat to people more generally because it brings into question the entire matter of life-style.

You referred in your recent book to the need to evolve a new social ethic for all mankind. What is the nature of this new ethic?

The circumstances in which we find ourselves in the late twentieth century call for the formulation and eventual adoption of a common social ethic. This new ethic must be responsive to the need to accommodate ourselves to the finite ecosystem in which we exist. Among the components of this social ethic would be such things as the basic changes in attitudes toward childbearing needed to stabilize global population, the need to abandon the concept of planned obsolescence which underlies a modern, materialistic industrial society such as the United States, the need to recognize that we share the resources of the globe in a way that we haven't before, that is we depend on common sources of petroleum reserves, of marine protein and of waste-absorptive capacity. As we press against the limits of these resources, we must begin thinking of how we share them. Interestingly as we begin to press against the limits of various resources we find that the interdependence among countries rises very rapidly.

Let me cite an example: The state of Florida two years ago was experiencing a severe drought. It was threatening agriculture and it was threatening wildlife in the Everglades. The state of Florida signed a contract with a rainmaking firm to make it rain over the Florida peninsula. It did eventually rain, but at the expense of the surrounding oceans. If Texas had signed that contract, it could have been at the expense of Mexico. If Pakistan had signed such a contract, it might have been at the expense of India. This is just one example of the way the interdependence among countries increases as we attempt to expand the supply of scarce resources. There are corporations, some of them quartered here in Washington, D.C., which will sign a rainmaking contract with anyone in the world who will pay them. It can be farmers' associations, state governments, national governments, or ministries of defense. There interventions cannot go unregulated. We have reached the point where we need a supranational institution to regulate the intervention of national governments and international Monetary Fund attempts to regulate actions of national governments which affect the international monetary system.

That is exactly what Sicco Mansholt of the Economic Market in Europe is advocating; supranational institutions. But then comes the next question: How to police them?

The question of enforcement is a difficult one. My own feeling is that if we are to get a shift in global priorities in an increasingly interdependent world, it requires supranational institutions that have not only purpose but muscle. For example, we must think of giving the UN much more peace-keeping authority.

To cite another example: Last year global military expenditure totaled two hundred and four billion dollars. That sum exceeds the income of the poorest one-half of mankind. I submit that in an increasingly interdependent world that's not an acceptable ordering of global priorities. The sum of national priorities does not add up to a rational set of global priorities. The time has come to begin thinking in terms of global priorities based on the needs of all mankind.

Discussing this new organization of global relations and building bridges, do you think in order to construct a global infrastructure, the Forrester Law approach might be a useful tool?

The *Limits to Growth* emphasizes the limits of at least a number of important resources, ranging from arable land and fresh water to waste absorptive capacity. As one begins to recognize that there are limits to how far one can go, at least in some areas, without irreversible changes occurring, we see an interesting psychological shift in thinking at the international level. As long as the global economic pie, if you will, or the supply of any given resource on which economic growth depends, can be expanded indefinitely, the rich can say to the poor, "Be patient and wait, your turn will come, things are expanding." But once the reality of the finiteness of some resources at least, begins to dawn on people, then the issue shifts in a very dramatic way. The issue is no longer how do you expand the pie, but how do you divide it. This is a very important question.

You mentioned in your book World Without Borders *that leaders of poor countries could very well claim in the near future the marine protein supplies of the oceans for their own protein-deficient diets. Then, of course, there will be a clash, and they have just as much right to claim as anyone else.*[1]

As long as there were more fish in the ocean than anyone could hope to catch, how the catch was distributed was no problem. But once we reach the point where we're pressing against the limits of oceanic protein yields as we are now doing for several important commercial species of fish, things begin to change. Recent years have witnessed heavy investment by the industrial societies of the north, the Soviet Union, Japan, the United States in large fishing fleets, in floating fish factories, in advanced technologies, such as sonar, for locating and catching fish wherever they can be found throughout the world. The poor countries, who very much need marine protein, cannot compete in these terms. They don't have the capital. They don't have the technology. The only way they can compete is by extending their offshore limits, which they are now doing. Some fourteen countries have extended their offshore territorial limits from the traditional twelve miles to two hundred miles in order to protect such coastal fishing areas.

In 1972 mainland China joined the ranks of the poor countries, supporting their two hundred mile offshore territorial claims. This is significant because mainland China is the first nuclear power to align itself with this effort by the poor countries to increase or protect their share of world protein resources.

Marine biologists now feel that the world catch of many species of fish is very close to the maximum sustainable limit. We are confronted with the need of establishing global limits on the annual catch of various species and then dividing that catch country by country into national quotas. The question is how to do that. The rich countries, of course, would like to freeze the pattern where it is, because that would enable them to retain the predominant share of the world's marine protein supplies. If one were to distribute the catch on a per capita basis, then the poor countries would get two-thirds and the rich countries one-third. That would not be an unreasonable position. There's also the possibility, which you mentioned, that the poor countries, which are suffering severe protein malnutrition among their people, may propose a formula whereby they will get first claim on this common global resource. After all, many of us in North America or in Europe are overfed anyhow, consuming far more protein than we need.

Or we feed it to animals.

Exactly. For our indirect consumption in the form of poultry, for example. One of the important questions that needs to be addressed is how to distribute the earth's resources and wealth. As Americans, representing six percent of mankind, we consume a third of the world's resources. It has been part of the conventional wisdom in the international development community that the two billion people living in the poor countries could not aspire to the North American life-style, because there simply was not enough petroleum, iron ore, protein and so forth.

It might be bad to have in China seven hundred million people, but seven hundred million rich Chinese would wreck China in no time.

Perhaps not only wreck China but seven hundred million Chinese with two cars in every garage would put an enormous stress on the world's petroleum reserves, needless to say. As long as Americans could depend primarily on indigenous resources, whether it be petroleum, minerals or what have you, the question of how much was consumed was largely an internal matter. But as we come to increasingly depend on others for resources that we consume, we must confront the question, Why should six percent of mankind be permitted to consume a third of the world's nonrenewable resources? As Americans we must begin asking ourselves that question because, increasingly, others are beginning to ask it and we must be prepared to respond. I have suggested to audiences I have talked to in recent weeks that if they wanted an interesting and challenging exercise, when they're at their desks, to sit with a pad and try to explain in five hundred words why we as Americans should be permitted to consume a third of the world's resources. It is not an easy question to deal with, but it is one that we must increasingly confront in various situations where the terms under which the United States gains access to reserves of oil and mineral in other countries are being negotiated or where formulas for allocating common resources are being considered.

NOTES

[1]See pp. 37-38.

55. *John R. Meyer*

Professor John R. Meyer is president of the National Bureau of Economic Research in New York and professor of economics at Yale University in New Haven, Connecticut.

He was born in Pasco, Washington, in 1927. He attended Pacific University, the University of Washington and received a Ph.D. at Harvard University in 1955.

In 1962 Professor Meyer participated in the Presidential conference on problems of the US economy. The same year he took part in a White House panel on civilian technology. In 1964 he was a member of a Presidential task force on transportation. From 1970 to 1972 he was a member of the Presidential Commission on Population Growth and the American Future. He also is a member of the Computer Science and Engineering Board of the National Academy of Sciences in Washington, D.C.

Samuel Butler [1] already stated that all progress is based upon the universal desire on the part of every organism to live beyond its income. Limits to Growth *is an effort to catalogue to what extent the planet is living beyond its means and its limits.*

It was certainly a very useful effort at drawing attention to certain problems that would exist if we did not modify our behavior. On the other hand, it is reasonably clear that the underlying assumptions are much too rigid. *Limits to Growth* assumes that human beings cannot and will not adapt to changed circumstances. By contrast the natural instinct of an economist, whenever viewing these problems, is to always assume that there are self-correcting tendencies in human behavior. But economists may be much too optimistic on this score. Many points, assumptions and warnings delivered by the physical scientists and others collaborating on *Limits to Growth* are well taken.

John Kenneth Galbraith once said that conventional wisdom becomes increasingly irrelevant, since economic growth renders many things obsolete, and one of these things is economic theory. Why have economists been extremely critical of the model at MIT?

Partly because the rigid assumptions that were built into the model just go contrary to basic economic training, empirical findings and theory. Economics as a science is offended by many of the underlying assumptions in the model. Nevertheless, economists may have been too quick to dismiss *Limits to Growth* on these grounds. Economists perhaps underestimate the importance of some of the problems to which the analyses of *Limits to Growth* are pointing. Economists perhaps are too prone to be optimistic about the self-equilibrating corrective character of much of human behavior. The truth perhaps lies somewhere in between. If you ask me where the balance resides, I would say it's rather more on the side of the economists' thinking—in terms of flexible parameters and adaptive behavior—than on the side of the rigid parameters and noncorrective behavior that underlies the *Limits to Growth* analysis.

Nevertheless, you have created here at the National Bureau of Economic Research a computer study in economic research and management. In other words, you do not discount the method of the use of computers for this kind of project.

I am quite enthusiastic about the potentialities of the computer as both an aid in modeling and general economic research. That is an additional reason why I feel in some ways *Limits to Growth* may be most unfortunate. For example, I worry that *Limits* may prematurely and improperly discredit the design, building, construction and use of large-scale behavioral models using the computer. The *Limits to Growth* model is based upon, in technical jargon, a closed-loop fixed-parameter system. That approach worries me. With those characteristics (fixed assumptions about technology, consumption behavior and so on), if you extrapolate out far enough, you can always derive some limiting solution which will probably be quite disturbing. The basic point is, though, that those assumptions—about fixed parameters, fixed feedbacks, nonadaptive behavior—are probably incorrect.

Would it be useful to promote close cooperation between systems engineers and economists and bring assumptions into such a model both disciplines are in agreement with?

The MIT team did not utilize enough economics. MIT has one of the most distinguished departments of economics in this country or in the world. What the communication problems are at MIT I don't know. My guess would be that some of the engineers and scientists involved in this—not all by any means—may not have been as outgoing as they might have been in seeking out the inputs of economists. I really do not think that MIT economists are much different from economists elsewhere; they're more than willing to talk about these matters, even willing to volunteer. Economic expertise certainly exists in the Cambridge, Massachusetts, area and in one way or another was available to the Club of Rome team. One therefore has to ask the question: Did they really want those other inputs? Of course, Forrester's work[2] is basic to the *Limits*, and his earlier industrial and urban dynamics are really characterized by the same weakness. Forrester appears to revel in not having read the basic works in the field in which he's modeling and not having consulted with those who have spent time studying the relevant phenomena. Maybe there's some case for simplification, but ignorance can be carried much too far, and when a simplification goes to the point of embodying empirical generalizations that just run contrary to all previous investigations and study, then one has to be skeptical.

Are we moving to what you would call a multipower world management, a global management of the globe?

I find it difficult to think in terms of either/ors. I do think, though, that perhaps a message that's really well taken in *Limits to Growth* is that compared to the past, we have to pay more attention to higher levels of planning. Whether this happens at a global level, at a national level, a state, a regional or a local level, is a matter of pragmatic adaptation and depends on the problem. For example, I hope that we will have more regional-planning districts in the US so that we look beyond, say, a central city, so as to place some of our land-use transportation and general urban planning problems in a much larger geographical context. I am certain, on the other hand, that some problems quite clearly do have important international complications. The environmental impact of the supersonic transport, for example, is a matter of concern not just to the British or the French, who've developed the plane.

Do you expect maybe a clash coming up between labor and the Limits to Growth *ecologists?*

I wouldn't want to characterize it as labor as such. You can have various kinds of clashes between have-not and have groups, certainly internationally. I've heard rumors that, for instance, the Brazilian government welcomes "dirty polluting industries" if they would create more employment in some of their backward regions, where chronic underemployment and low incomes now exist. In the long run, of course, that might lead to a new set of problems. After incomes rise in more backward parts of the world, they might ask: Why should we have all of those contaminating industries? Then a new cycle, in a slightly different form, might ensue from these ecological and environmental problems. I think in the US, with our very heterogeneous and diverse society, with special minority-group and poverty problems, you can already see some real confrontations occurring on these environmental issues. Maybe some of these are false and can be modified by high-level political action and diplomacy; but some may be very difficult to reconcile because they come down to basically fundamental choices or priorities we must set about how to spend public budgets.

Herman Kahn[3] has calculated that this world could carry twenty billion people at a per capita income of twenty thousand dollars per person. What would be your reaction as an economist to futurologists thinking like that?

First, I would want to check the arithmetic very carefully. Secondly, even if it were true, I would rather not live in such a world. I would rather live in a world with far fewer people, because of the many adverse externalities which could derive from such numbers. I am not sure, by the way, that Herman Kahn wouldn't also agree with that, and perhaps was motivated to do his calculations by just such considerations.

NOTES

[1]Samuel Butler (1835-1902), British writer.
[2]See conversation no. 34.
[3]See conversation no. 46.

56. *Linus Pauling*

Linus Pauling is professor of chemistry at Stanford University, in Stanford, California.

He was born in Portland, Oregon, in 1901. He received his Ph.D. in 1925 at the California Institute of Technology, where he became a member of the teaching staff from 1922 to 1964. He has also been visiting professor at Cornell University, the University of Illinois, MIT, Harvard University, Princeton University and the University of Madras, India.

Much of his scientific work has dealt one way or another with the nature of the chemical bond. He studied the structure of proteins, the molecular basis of general anesthesia, the rule of abnormal molecules in causing disease, and abnormal enzymes in relation to mental disease. He also studied the theory of the structure of atomic nuclei and the nature of the process of nuclear fission. During recent years much of his work has been centered on the application of chemistry to biological and medical problems.

In 1954 Professor Pauling was awarded the Nobel Prize for chemistry. In 1962 he was also given the Nobel Peace Prize. He received the International Lenin Peace Prize, the Gandhi Peace Prize and other awards and honors. Among some of his best-known works are *No More War!*, *The Architecture of Molecules (1970)*, *Science and World Peace,* and *Vitamin C and the Common Cold* (1970), which was dedicated to Albert Szent-Györgyi.

Are you familiar with the study of Limits to Growth?

Yes.

Do you think it is a useful effort to organize the planet, to catalogue the planet, in order to better manage it in the future?

I think it is not only useful, but it is necessary and essential that we do this. I think that the course that we have been following is one that does an injustice to future generations of human beings. We must begin to catalogue our resources and to analyze our uses of these resources with this ethical principle in mind, that it is not proper for us to steal from future human beings all of the wealth of the earth.

In 1976 several dozens of countries, a quarter of all the nations in the world, will possess large nuclear reactors for the production of electric power. In the United States alone, by 1990, there will be some three hundred power reactors. How safe is this?

* * *

These reactors are not safe in the sense that there is no probability of a catastrophe. There have been enough reactor accidents to show that accidents with reactors will happen. I myself believe that nuclear reactors based upon nuclear fission should not be built, because once they are built—with hundreds of millions of dollars invested in each one—it is almost certain that they will be used. They will do damage by released radioactivity and they constitute a real hazard to the public, to the people as a whole or to the earth. There will be a chance that some serious accident spreading a large amount of radioactive substance over the surface of the earth will occur.

It has been forecast that it is even possible that gangsters would make homemade nuclear devices, and that atomic scientists do not take sufficiently into account the irrational behavior of people, like the threatening by highjackers to blow up the nuclear facilities at Oak Ridge, Tennessee.

Yes, of course, this is a real danger I have not mentioned, namely, that fissionable material cannot be completely controlled. It is possible to steal from a plant that produces fissionable isotopes a certain amount of fissionable material without this loss being discovered. This fissionable material might get into the hands of unscrupulous people, even the leader of some small nation. Or just some private person or organization which could then use it to the detriment of the world.[1]

That really could be possible? The catchphrase—a teaspoon of strontium 90 would be enough to kill the human race—is then true?

I would say that if you could get each person to take his share of this teaspoonful, it probably would do the job; but to distribute one teaspoonful of strontium 90 into the atmosphere would not kill the human race. There have been much larger quantities spread already in the atmosphere. This is enough, however, to do damage, to cause some people to die of cancer and to cause children, infants, with gross physical or mental defects to be born. In my book *No more War* and also in my Nobel Peace Prize lecture I gave my estimates of the amount of damage from nuclear tests that had been carried out up to that time, 1958 and 1963 respectively. In 1963 I estimated sixteen million: The bomb test carried out would in the course of time cause sixteen million infants who were born to have gross physical or mental defects, and who would have been perfectly normal if bomb tests would not have been carried out.

This gives an idea when there was only six hundred megatons of nuclear explosives exploded up to that time, part fission and part fusion, in 1963.

Who makes certain that it is not dangerous to the planet to have underground tests?

Yes, who is it? I remember fifteen years ago when it was said that Secretary of States John Foster Dulles volunteered for all of us to be guinea pigs in this study. Dulles was one of the criminals, I would say, who had moved us ahead in this direction without proper consideration of the amount of damage being done to people. Of course, the Atomic Energy Commission suppressed the information that was available. It was very hard to get any information on these points out of the AEC. The corresponding authorities in the Soviet Union of course followed a similar course with suppression of the information about the amount of damage done to people by nuclear radioactivity, radioactivity from the nuclear bomb tests.

At Cal Tech[2] it was established that underground nuclear power plants would be feasible.

Yes, it's just a matter of spending somewhat more money to put power plants underground. I don't think that this means that there still would not be a hazard. There would still be some danger, because there is the possibility of the blowout from an underground plant too, and the contamination of ground water, say, by radioactive substances. It is my belief that we should control the amounts of energy that are used. Following my own basic ethical principle, the principle of the minimization of human suffering. I believe that it is not important to the well-being of mankind, the happiness of individual human beings, to have larger and larger amounts of energy available and to allow day-to-day simple economic considerations to determine the nature of the life that we shall live. We could get along with means of transportation much simpler and much better than the ones that we have now. We do not need to have seventy miles per hour as the standard speed of operating on highways, or to have the ability to accelerate so rapidly that you can pass other high-powered cars on the freeway. We would be just as happy, perhaps even happier, if we restricted the amounts of energy that now are being used. The propaganda by the power companies—to build more and more power plants, that we shall have to have four times as much energy per person twenty years from now as we have now—is really harmful and dangerous.

You mentioned we need a little more money to build underground atomic plants. But the Baltimore Gas and Electric company is giving up its two planned atomic units, costing seven hundred million dollars, because of environmental opposition. Other companies, like Con Edison, are cutting down on expansion, because they don't have the money needed. Where could the money be found to make nuclear plants safe and underground?

I don't advocate it. I was just commenting. I advocate not building nuclear power plants. I think that we can get along without them. We should lead simpler lives. Our economy, I believe, should be controlled in such a way as to preserve the wealth of the world.

Here you join Limits to Growth *again.*

That's right. I advocate that. I believe that we should have a decreased population. The quality of life is decreasing. We have inflation of the amounts of goods that one can buy. The quality of the food that the American people eat is lower than that fifty years ago or even twenty years ago. It is deteriorating rapidly. When I lectured in New Delhi in January, 1967, I said that I believed that in the United States should live only one hundred and fifty million people. We have at present some two hundred and ten million. I tried to analyze the mode of life, the needs for labor, the amounts of consumer goods that were made available, the food, the drinking water, the opportunities for recreation, the need to preserve primitive areas, forests and so on. I reached the conclusion that there are already too many people in the United States. For India I estimated—they had just reached five hundred million in January of 1967—that there should be only one hundred million people in India instead. In other countries of the world the optimum population which would permit every person to lead a good life should be perhaps one billion rather than three and a half billion. I do not believe that the goal of the United States should be to have a ten percent increase each year in the Gross National Product. I think we should level off the GNP, even decrease it, and decrease likewise the population.

It might interest you that Dr. Herman Kahn[3] told me that for millennia we would have enough resources and we could easily feed twenty billion people. My question would be scientists seem to show such enormous gaps in beliefs and theories of what's possible and what's not possible, that the public must be at a loss whom to believe.

When I was debating with Edward Teller,[4] of the University of California, fourteen years ago, someone said to my wife, "Now, your husband says one thing and Dr. Teller says another thing. How do I know whom to believe?" And my wife replied, "You just look at them and listen to them and decide who is the one to believe." In this case too. Herman Kahn was a student in my class. He came to only three lectures and then gave up the course. I don't think Herman Kahn has attacked these problems from the standpoint of ethics and morality. It has been said that everything that becomes scientifically and technically possible will be done. This is nonsense. There is no reason for us to try to do everything just because it is possible. There is no reason to have fifteen billion people on earth even if it is technologically possible or to keep them alive by using all possible resources, sacrificing everything to the job of just keeping people alive. The thing to do is to decide how many people can lead reasonable lives on earth and then work toward the goal of permitting this number of people to lead these lives.

What role do you ascribe to scientists in the future management of the globe?

Of course I think that everyone should have some knowledge and understanding of science, but I don't believe that scientists should run the world. They should contribute. I believe that a scientist has two duties: First, as a citizen, to help get his fellow citizens the benefit of what special knowledge and insight he has, this is educational; the other is to make up his own mind about questions and to tell his fellow citizens what his opinions are. It is important that these opinions be expressed, but we should not have any oligarchy of scientists.

If we are going to manage the planet like the Club of Rome is advocating, how to get away from mostly mediocre politicians to say the least, or corrupt dictatorships?

The planet is not run only by mediocre politicians and other powerful people, but by immoral politicians, immoral powerful generals, and immoral business people. The principle of business is to sacrifice everything to profit, even morality and ethics. This the government is supposed to control, but of course governments are immoral too. They have not taken the broad view. They do not look into the future. Governments do not make decisions because of their ethical soundness, instead they are expedient and selfish. This is what we have to change. There is a basis, a fundamental basis to science, namely, honesty and willingness to accept the truth. This is the most fundamental principle in science. This very principle of honesty and willingness to search for and accept the truth is one that needs to be introduced into government, the government of the world. This is going to be difficult to do, but I think that we should strive to achieve this goal. Analysis of the problems as done by the Club of Rome is extremely important. There should be a basic principle involved, and I believe that the principle that I've formulated and have described in many places, the principle of the minimization of human suffering, taking into account the suffering of future generations of human beings, as well as of people now in existence, is one that could be used as the basic principle for all decision making.

NOTES

[1]See Alva Myrdal, conversation no. 36, and Ralph A. Lapp, conversation no. 37. See also New York *Times Magazine,* February 4, 1973, Ralph A. Lapp, "The Ultimate Blackmail," in which Mr. Lapp discusses the chances nuclear thieves would have if they stole Uranium 235 or plutonium. The Lapp article also quotes Soviet UN delegate Omitri N. Kolesnik declaring during a recent United Nations debate on terrorism: "Robin Hood was armed with bows and arrows, but modern terrorists prefer to have rifles and bombs, and tomorrow it is quite possible they will have death-carrying germs or maybe stolen atomic bombs. And with the help of these bombs they can blackmail the government, p. 29.

[2]California Institute of Technology in Los Angeles, California.

[3]See conversation no. 46.

[4]See conversation no. 45.

57. *John Rawls*

Professor John Rawls teaches philosophy at Harvard University. He published in 1971 *A Theory of Justice*, which according to the New York *Times Book Review* of December 3, 1972, is one of the five most significant books reviewed during 1972.

John Rawls was born in Baltimore, Maryland, in 1921. He obtained a Ph.D. in philosophy at Princeton University, and taught both at Cornell and the Massachusetts Institute of Technology. In 1962 he was nominated to the faculty at Harvard University.

Justice seems an expensive commodity. How would you formulate the two main principles of a required social justice, which would be needed for an equilibrium in a society, which seems a priority of the greatest importance. How could this be achieved in the immediate future without losing the kinds of freedom we have now—we are talking now about the Western World, of course.

What I described in the book[1] is a kind of justice that would be characterized by two different principles: One that would apply to political institutions and to the right of civil law and economic institutions; that principle says that liberties ought to be equal, that all citizens ought to have in a certain class equal liberties. If these cannot always be equal, at any rate there should be a sense in which the total system of liberties is equal for all menbers of society. The other principle deals with the distribution of economic and social advantages and it concerns the organizations, say, of firms, universities, and other forms of association; the other principle holds that social advantages and economic goods ought to be always, so far as possible, distributed, that those who have more make a contribution to those who have less.

But is this somewhat utopian theory not contrary to the grain of human nature, to accept less growth, less wealth, for the benefit of all?

* * *

This raises a very different kind of question, namely, to what extent is the view that I discuss a kind of view that might hold within an advanced industrial and technological society? What you mean is, How far can different nations be expected to make sacrifices or, to use your phrase, to share the wealth with others in the world? There's a complicating factor about the imperfections, to use an euphemism of governments elsewhere. Political problems arise. In my book I discussed more or less what form justice would take or should take under reasonably favorable conditions within one society.

Is it not against the nature of man to be willing to share the wealth of one small minority with the overwhelming majority? Also in affluent nations? You know what Michael Harrington[2] in the Accidental Century *pointed out, that forty million people in American were still poor.*

Whether it's against their nature I don't know. It has been argued that what the nature of people is depends upon the society in which they grow up. I'm inclined to think—although I cannot give a real argument for this—that if you had the kind of society that I try to describe and if people grew up and developed under those kinds of institutions answering to these principles, then I think that they would be prepared to share. At least within the same social unit. I do agree that it's a lot harder to make this argument if you're talking about people in other cultures and other nations, where you don't have some kind of common political institutions in regard to regulating each others demands. It is a lot harder, I agree, to extend any such notions on a global scale. There's no doubt about that.

You argue in your book with Hobbes[3] that man should enter into a social contract. But how do you envisage this?

Well, it is not any sort of actual historical contract. What I imagine is a certain way in which people view their relations. They can be asked, or at any rate they might entertain this thought and try to see how this view would work, so that they asked themselves what sort of contract or agreement they would make, if they were under a certain sort of condition. The ideal would be to ask oneself, What would I be prepared to agree to if I did not have certain kinds of information, if I did not know my special position, if I did not know some things about my particular taste? And questions of that kind.

Those are reasonable sorts of constraints for people to accept. The ideal would be to try to develop in some detail, the kind of principles that people would agree to if they lack certain kinds of information. For example, take international law: If a representative state did not know who had the larger armies, who was best situated and all the other military information, then it might agree to certain principles of international law; but it is the possession of so much information about particular contingencies and imbalances of power that makes it hard to reach an agreement. The same thing applies between members of the same society. If we don't know our social class and if we don't know a lot of other things about ourselves, then it's possible for us to recognize that we would assent to certain sorts of general principles. I try to argue in my book that those turn out to be things that we would recognize as principles of justice.

But the science of computers, the "computer spaghetti," as Kenneth Boulding[4] says, is flourishing at such a fantastic speed that in the near future people will not have less information about each other at their fingertips, that it would make it even harder to enter into a social contract.

I don't mean that people actually lack this information. In order to construct a moral theory, the kind of contract that one ought to make is that one, so to speak, agrees not to rely on certain sorts of information. One reasons as if one did not have that information. Although, of course, actually we do have that information. The moral argument has to be that there are moral grounds for excluding that information and not using it. The theory is not designed as a political theory in a sense that it is to account for the things that actually happen. It's not meant to account for actual international behavior, or actual political behavior. It's supposed to account—insofar as it accounts for anything—for the sorts of moral judgments that we might make when we are ourselves impartial and uninvolved. It would account for the sort of moral ideals that we have—insofar as we have any—and could be persuaded to act on them. It's supposed to be a moral theory, not a social theory.

It would require moral geometry to work this theory out?

I make the assumption that one does not have certain kinds of information, that we have certain general sorts of ends and all these other things, and then from those assumptions I try to show the way. The argument is intuitive and has lots of gaps, as it has now. But the idea is to show that certain sorts of moral principles would be adopted and agreed to under these conditions. Conditions being those of an idealized sort that need certain kinds of constraints.

But, as you call it, we must develop a sterner, more fastidious kind of justice. Increasing people's awareness for this kind of social justice you speak of. Would you tend to agree with Skinner[5] that there could be ways to achieve these results by rearchitecting, by redesigning, by programming the environment in order to make this kind of approach generally available?

Well, I think it's true. Most would agree that the kind of institutions that we live under, in fact the kind of desires that we come to have and the kind of ideals, moral or otherwise, that we acquire, there's no doubt that most would agree that a certain amount of programming would have to be done. The important issue is by what principles is the environment to be programmed. The view which I am suggesting in my book is that in choosing a principle of justice or in arguing a certain conception of justice, one wants to adopt a conception that if it is institutionalized, that if the institutions satisfy their conceptions, people do come to have the kinds of desires and ideals that will affirm their conception—in other words, that they will come to adopt it. One argument that I argue, indeed, is that the principles of justice I propose are of the kind that they do encourage people, as if they were actually followed, to adopt these very same principles. They have to be kind of self-reinforcing. Where I would differ with Skinner is the principles on which I think it should be programmed and how it should be done, as well as the end result which we are aiming at.

Where does politics and dire reality come into this? Because society is definitely still run by politicians, who have no notion what you are talking about.

Well, I wouldn't say they had no notion. But undoubtedly they have a different one, or they don't pay all that much attention perhaps to any moral notions. This is a problem. How one gets from a situation where any social ideals or justice that one thinks to be correct are not followed—how one moves from that to a situation where they are followed, that's a part of the moral theory that I haven't really talked about very much. Indeed, hardly at all, because that involves all kinds of, particularly political, matters about the sort of strategy that one should follow in trying to bring those things about.

Limits to Growth is based on a global how-to-manage-this-planet. It seems rather hard to make even a beginning of entering social justice into the present global structures. How do you view this overall dilemma we face at this late hour?

I haven't attempted at all to discuss any of these matters, global matters. One ought to recognize—and I would be the first to recognize—that it's obvious; that—as all philosophers do, discussing various kinds of morals, ideals and the like—they have to recognize that these are, viewed in a certain way, very impracticable, while any political action to bring them about is very, very remote. How to create a more just international order? I have not actually discussed any of these matters. Frankly, I am very pessimistic that the kind of ideas that I discuss would have any real substantial influence on that process.

You know Camus⁶ believed that the absurd was born out of the confrontation between the human need and the unreasonable silence of the world, in other words you have set forth in great detail a highly valuable theory on how to improve social justice in your country, in this part of the world.⁷ How hopeful are you that mankind, increasing to seven billion people in the next twenty-five years, will live then, by what kind of justice?

I don't really know. Of course nobody knows. I guess I am a bit pessimistic. I see the direction even in my own country less bright than it was twenty years ago. It is a matter of political fact that the military have a lot more influence in our country than they used to. This is a result of more and more of our taking over certain gaps in the structure of world power. All this is having bad effects. We haven't been able to solve the problems of racial minorities in our country. I think that the presidential leadership the last few years has been very bad in these respects. I am not really very optimistic, even in my own country, that one would see in the near future the definite trend towards a more just society in a sense in which I would conceive it. It's practically possible in America, there is a material base for it. But I don't think that socially it's bound to come into existence.

Have you had any reactions from politicians on your best-selling book?

No, I haven't.

NOTES

[1]*A Theory of Justice*. See review by Marshall Cohen, "The Social Contract Explained and Defended," the New York *Times Book Review*, July 16, 1972. See also "Five Significant Books of 1972," New York *Times Book Review*, December 3, 1972. See also Tom Alexander, "The Social Engineers Retreat Under Fire," *Fortune*, October, 1972. See also Stuart Hampshire's special supplement in *The New York Review of Books*, February 24, 1971, pp. 34-39.
[2]See conversation no. 44.
[3]Thomas Hobbes (1588-1679), English philosopher.
[4]See conversation no. 65.
[5]See conversation no. 7.
[6]Albert Camus (1913-60), French author, Nobel Prize for literature.
[7]*The Myth of Sisyphus*, Vintage Books (New York, 1955), p. 21.

58. *Edgar Morin*

French sociologist Edgar Morin was born in Paris in 1921. He studied geography, law, economics and sociology. From 1950 to 1962 he was director of research at the CNRS. He is also director of programs at the Centre Royaumont pour une Science de l'Homme. While at the Salk Institute for Biological Studies at San Diego, California, he examined the possible relationship between biological and sociological theory. From 1957 to 1963 he was editor of the magazine *Arguments*.

Among his best-known books are *L'homme et la mort* (1951), *Commune en France* (1967), and *La brèche* (1968), and *Rumeur d'Orleans,* (1969). A new work, *Le paradyme perdu: la nature humaine,* is scheduled to appear in 1973.

You seem to feel that man is already on his way to a final collapse—don't you feel the rising awareness of the present dangers begun after Stockholm and the recent publication of Limits to Growth *might reverse the tide?*

Yes, I think the breakthrough in our ecological consciousness dates back to the years 1968 to 1970. It grew from an encounter of a spontaneous, romantic back-to-nature movement and a serious attempt to create a science that regards the environment not strictly in mechanical terms but in terms of ecosystem and organization. This breakthrough is an event of fundamental importance, and this is the reason why I used the expression "the year one of the ecological era."

This ecological consciousness is closely related to the fact that pollution is not the heart of the matter. Pollution is a local manifestation of certain disturbances which are so clearly perceptible to man that they inevitably lead to a local awakening of consciousness and a number of more or less delayed responses. In short, I think many pollution problems are in themselves to be solved by purely technological means. For instance, the problem of the exhaust fumes could be solved within a few years by the construction of a "clean" engine or a set of traffic regulations. This also goes for many problems concerning the so-called urban pollution. I think it is indeed a real consciousness, because people are aware that the actual problem is not pollution—pollution is only a translation of a much more fundamental problem: the fact that our economic development is absolutely uncontrolled and unregulated; and what's more, the exponential growth rate has even been taken as a regulating standard. In other words, nature has been assumed to take care of all our financial, budgetary, economic, and moral problems.

This is an extremely paradoxical situation—we have tried to regulate our problems by a device that eventually ended in an absolute disregulation. This is very important, and I think this uncontrolled growth is the real problem. It's not so much a matter of exhaustion of raw materials and energy sources—we have still plenty of energy sources, like solar energy and the energy sources of the oceans. The biosphere is an extremely complex planetary ecosystem in which a fundamental cycle is taking place, from the plankton in the seas to the primates, from the photosynthesis of the plants to ourselves. And it is very important to know whether we have not poisoned the very essence of this system and, by doing so, brought about a general deterioration of life, that is, our life.

In fact, the real problem covers a field that always has been regarded as the exclusive property of war industry. It is clear that war industry leads to death. It is clear that production of guns and tanks endanger human life. But we never suspected that peace industry, life industry, could have the same effect. But it has, in two different ways: First, through the absence of any civilization; and besides, through the absence of any control of the natural ecosystem.

It is impossible to establish the exact moment on which the deterioration of mankind will take place, it may arrive suddenly, it may even take years. But nevertheless, the problems are of fundamental importance, not only for the essence of human civilization, but also for the essence of man himself. Because from Descartes[1] onwards the notion of men has always been separated from the notion of nature, as if they were two absolute different entities. Besides the fact that we are unable to predict when the general deterioration of human life will take place, the most dramatic element is perhaps that the problems may simply prove too big for us.

I think we have to distinguish two different kinds of ecological consciousness, concerning respectively what I call the "big" and the "little" ecology. The little ecology occupies itself primarily with the problem of pollution. It shows us a concrete example of pollution on a local scale, and indicates at the same time by which technological means the problem can be solved. The big ecology is concerned with a much more fundamental problem, which is only to be grasped if we manage to think theoretically—

From a global point of view—

Exactly. We need a global point of view. We have to oppose the technocratic way of thinking that divides all problems. This permits a high degree of exactitude, but at the same time it omits a very essential element, the link between the different constituents that make up the whole. We need a global point of view. We need a theoretical frame. We need a base for our reflections. And as soon as we find this, we become aware of the real nature of the problem. This could be the starting point of a new course of development, which is indispensable. To quote a very beautiful phrase of Michel Serres, "the problem is no longer how to control nature, but how to control the control." This is a fundamental problem of a political nature. Today the whole human race is entangled in an imbroglio, and the outcome of this is of decisive importance.

Do you think Limits to Growth, *the attempt of the MIT team to catalogue the planet, is a step toward a control of this imbroglio?*

The study of MIT has two sides, and it all depends which side you look at. The first side, that attracted me very much, is that for the first time in the history of mankind an attempt has been made to feed a computer with data concerning humanity as a whole. No doubt the study of the MIT team was in itself clearly insufficient, but it was a first step that could bring about a new way of thought—the global point of view —and this is absolutely essential. The second positive point is the fact that we are so thoroughly technocraticized that it is very important that this concern about the ecology was instigated in one of the sanctuaries of modern science, MIT. It is a very positive development that the prestige of modern scientists is serving a cause which is fundamentally correct, even if all the empirical data in the study are not.

But there are also negative points. The first negative point is directly related to the positive point I mentioned earlier. It is the fact that the study in itself is clearly insufficient and absolutely worthless except as an alarm signal and a contribution to the awakening of the ecological consciousness. In addition to this, there is the notion of "Limits to Growth," and as a direct consequence of this, the notion of "nongrowth." This is a very bad myth. The people of MIT tried to combat the myth of growth, but in doing so, they created an antimyth, which is as irrational as the original one. My objections to this are twofold. In the first place a matter of principle: There is a growing awareness today that we identified the notion of economic development with a notion of a purely quantitative growth. In other words, we flatten a multidimensional, qualitative notion to a strictly quantitative notion. In addition to this, we identified the notion of the social, human development with the notion of economic development. This means we carried through a double reduction. First, we reduced a very rich and very mysterious term—because, what's "human development"? That's what we want to know—to an economic criterion. And besides, we reduced economic development to growth statistics in terms of income and production. Actually the real problem of today is that we must try to leave the one-dimensional universe of the word "growth" and reformulate the problem of economic development in its own terms and submit it to the problem of the human development in its totality. By formulating the problem in this way, we may reach a solution; whereas, phrases like "non-growth" keep us entangled in quantitative and economistic ways of thought.

The second error is that the expression "nongrowth" suggests a stationary situation, which is in fact out of the question. The very problem is that we must try and keep things moving. We live in an age of perpetual change, and we must control and direct change. In fact, a state of equilibrium is a mere illusion. These are the two fundamental errors in the report, of an ecological consciousness to attack the ideas of the MIT team, as well as those of Mansholt,[2] with great violence and a reasonable degree of success. And what's more, the matter of nongrowth was brought forward rather lightly and in a purely Western perspective. It created the impression that in the advanced industrial societies an idea had arisen to slow things down a little. And although this did not have to suggest a direct expression of Western neocolonialism to the developing countries, it must have seemed at least an unconscious manifestation of the secret desire to maintain the present hierarchical structure of power and privilege. In fact, these views are absolutely unacceptable to the Third World.

But there is another aspect of the ecological awakening that involves very serious problems. Until recently economists always held a "closed" view of the profit and loss account of industrial development. During the hypertrophied expansion of transport, communication and certain kinds of industry, they never took into account the whole set of neurasthenic and psychosomatic disturbances which affected the factory workers and the populations of the cities. They made idyllic calculations in which the effects of the industrial production were only beneficial, whereas public health, hygiene, etc., used to be considered on a totally different level. The budget was gradually burdened by an accumulation of new diseases, but its relation to the industrial development was usually ignored.

Today a new consciousness breaks through, and especially in the field of pollution—legal dispositions are being prepared to force industries to counteract the effects of their own pollution. This is a difficult but by no means impossible matter in the industrial societies, where powerful concerns may contemplate recycling processes. It is of utmost importance to the developing countries as well; but again, it won't be easy to convince them to go and deal with this matter.

These problems must be tackled on an international and global level. But unfortunately this is quite impossible today, because we are still entangled in the *Realpolitik* of the superpowers, as we could observe in Stockholm. We are passing through a very serious crisis, because we are involved in a system—in a system of thought, in a social system, and in a system of international relations—in which the contradictions and paradoxes are such that one involuntarily starts to think of a metasystem, which is to solve and integrate the most fundamental contradictions and paradoxes. In short, we need a radically new international and global society—

How are we to achieve this?

—But once this understanding has been gained, we become immediately aware that this solution, the only realistic and concrete one, is at the same time, the least realistic and concrete one, because it is impossible to realize. We cannot confide in our political leaders, nor in our political parties; and nothing would be left to us but despair, were it not that there are certain examples in the past, which are, to say the least, encouraging. We can ask ourselves how man managed to invent language. It is beyond our understanding that man could create such a complex system as the double phonetic articulation. How could life invent the genetic code? How came the first nation into being? It is almost impossible to find adequate answers to such questions. How are we to construct a new society? That's also a very difficult question.

You think of Skinner?[3]

No, no, absolutely not. I think such a transformation is to be organized by the exact opposite of the stimulus-response theory. Usually it is generated by an unconscious and very profound maturing process, by an encounter of unconscious and conscious creative powers. Thus comes into being what we call a movement. I think we need such a movement right now, a movement of a radically new nature, not moulded on the classical political party. We need an international movement, which can take concrete form and initiate a process—

A psychological movement?

Psychological and sociological and, I would say, praxistic as well. But this is by no means a simple enterprise—

The different cultures, the Japanese, the Americans, the Africans—

Yes, but it is very striking that the new consciousness takes the same shape almost everywhere. In a way the ecological question is a unifying problem. We can find examples of international movements in history. There have been four Internationals. All of these were subjected to rather depressing vicissitudes, but nevertheless they existed; and this proves it is not impossible to create an international movement. But we must not model it on the existing political parties; and at the same time this movement should be prevented from becoming a mere gathering of academics and intellectuals.

In that case the masses would be excluded.

In generating an awakening of consciousness a deep-felt conviction can be as effective as an intellectual judgment. Actually, the masses are already ecologized. What other reason could there be for the overall impulse in our societies to flee the cities? Why the general dream of owning a house in the country? Why do we behave like would-be farmers as soon as we have left town? Why do we change during the weekend? Why do we fish? Why do we hunt? There is a very urgent need of physical activities.

It's only a mania, buying a second home in the country, but how are we to change the desires?

It's not a matter of having a second home or not, it's not a matter of owning something or not, it's a matter of returning to a pure environment. There is a growing demand for this, now that our civilization is becoming more and more urbane and abstract; and we are getting more and more dominated by an artificial rhythm with traumatic effects to our personality.

I think anyone living in a city possesses a certain degree of ecological consciousness, even if this is sometimes unconscious. There is a need to ignore this consciousness. This kind of unconscious consciousness—if I may put it this way—has in a sense contemplated the enormous problems posed to humanity. That is to say, this ecological consciousness that incites people to flee the cities, gradually assumes the character of an escape. This escape has to be transformed into its counterpart, a recovery of one's self. There are germs of something new in our society, and these must be transformed so they can pave the way for a new movement. This means that new ideas must crystallize, they must be carried by tens, hundreds, thousands, millions of people, and they must be put in practice. This is our problem.

But do you think the scientists, the sociologists, the psychologists can lead the way? For we cannot expect anything from politicians. Nixon does not read Skinner; neither does Pompidou.[4] Who must launch this new movement? The young?

Yes, the young in the first place. But in the earliest stages it's always the people living on the fringes of society, the people trying to break away from something, from their class, from their caste—and this could be the scientific caste as well. Contemporary science is extremely bureaucratic.

Unfortunately we can't expect anything of today's scientists. Science owes its practical successes to the fact that it dissociated itself completely from goals and values. The results of this process have been very remarkable, but an unexpected side-effect has been that science and scientists tend to ignore any problem concerning goals and values. In this process science itself has become object of goals and values outside its own particular field. In other words, science has become part of the social dialectic.

Once it was generally believed that science could solve anything. This was at the end of the nineteenth century, when Renan[5] wrote about the future of science. This naive belief in the omnipotence of science has maintained itself quite a long time, especially in the United States. Even Einstein[6] still lived up to the image of the sage prophet addressing warnings to mankind. But actually Einstein was the only scientist of his generation who could play this role. In fact, it took only a few years for Moses-Einstein to change himself into Jeremiah-Oppenheimer. For Oppenheimer—Einstein's successor in a way—was not anymore a

Moses, he was a Jeremiah, who lamented that the men in power had produced an atomic bomb which threatened to wipe out humanity. And I think we have already passed the era of Jeremiah, the era of Oppenheimer. We have reached the era of Job.

The scientists are sitting on the dunghill, because all the marvelous inventions they produced turned out to be shit for the human race. And they are beginning to realize this. Nobody is more vulnerable, more helpless, facing scientific inventions than the very scientists who created them. And this is the reason why they entrench themselves in their small bureaucratic world of standing, status, and prestige. But it is a traditional mistake to think that scientists can enlighten the human race—what's more, it's sheer madness.

If you look about you in this world, you realize that we lack the support that used to be found in a privileged class. In the eighteenth century the intellectuals were considered a privileged class; but today we know that the intellectual world is on the other hand completely neurasthenic. It is madness to think it can provide the answers. In fact, we don't believe anymore that the intellectuals carry the light. The working class has also been considered a privileged class, the guardian of truth. But although the working class plays a very important part in the dialectics of progress, they do not carry the light either. And what's more, the champions of the myth of the proletariat attach so little value to their own theories that they leave no stone unturned to force their own ideas upon the workers. There simply is no privileged class, nor a privileged race, nor a privileged people, and that's the reason why I feel we must start from the point from which humanity always has started, that is the prophets, Buddha, Mohammed—

A new Marx?

Or Marx. Prophets always just started to think, then they propagated and defended their ideas, and found people who were prepared to share their insights. Nietzsche has said: "I write for nobody and I write for everybody." Right now, we must appeal to everybody.

NOTES

[1]René Descartes (1596-1650), French philosopher and mathematician.
[2]See conversation no. 20.
[3]See conversation no. 7.
[4]Georges Pompidou, president of France, successor to Charles De Gaulle.
[5]Ernest Renan (1832-92), French philologist, historian and critic.
[6]Albert Einstein (1879-1955), German physicist who formulated the theory of relativity.

59. *Alan Coddington*

Professor Coddington teaches economics at Queen Mary College of the University of London.

He was born in Yorkshire, England, in 1941. He obtained a degree in physics in 1963 and a Ph.D. in economics in 1966.

Professor Coddington regularly publishes articles in the *Manchester Guardian*. Among his published works are: *Theories of the Bargaining Process* (1968) and, with Dr. P. A. Victor, *Ecology-Economy: Your Environment* (1972).

What do you mean "the cheermongers"?[1]

By the "cheermongers" I mean those who have taken it upon themselves to assure us that there is no serious threat posed by the combined effects of pollution, natural resource depletion and population growth. In particular, it would include those who have sought to deride or discredit the views of people like Paul Ehrlich[2] and Barry Commoner[3] as well as the kind of concerns displayed in a study like *Limits of Growth*.

The cheermongers have attempted to do this in a variety of ways: partly by the use of protracted sneers (in which the analogy with hellfire-

preaching about the end of the world appears with wearisome regularity);
partly by appeals to their own alleged superior sophistication regarding
the many technical issues involved; and partly by advancing actual arguments. I would contend, however, that these arguments, under closer
scrutiny, turn out to be simply affirmations of spontaneous optimism:
a kind of global micawberism. Of course, it is the underlying mood of
spontaneous optimism which gives the cheermongers' views their unity.

What are these views?

Naturally, not all cheermongers share the same views, but there is a
cluster of ideas which have emerged quite clearly from the general cheermongering literature. At the most fundamental level, cheermongering
involves reaffirming one's faith in the adaptive capabilities of industrial
society. I am deliberately using a vague term like "adaption" to include
adjustments which are brought about in the political, economic or the
technological sphere. Actually, most cheermongers pin their faith on the
adaptive capabilities of the global economic system, but their ideas are
by no means confined to economic processes. When I say that the cheermongers have faith in the adaptive capabilities of industrial society, I
mean that they believe that the processes which they envisage being set
in motion will be both sufficiently sensitive and sufficiently powerful
to avert any social dislocation that could have arisen from natural-
resource depletion, pollution problems or population pressures.

You think that the cheermongers' faith is misplaced?

I do not know whether their faith is misplaced or not, although I do
not happen to share it. My point is that we should recognize their position
for what it is—the product of a rather large act of faith—and not accept
it in the form it is presented, as the product of dispassionate analysis,
superior sophistication, or, most notably, the inescapable conclusions
from incontrovertible economic principles. It is certainly true that many
economists have taken a cheerful view of these matters, but I think we
have to see this as an occupational hazard rather than as a necessary
product of economic reasoning. The main claim they make is that natural-
resource depletion is not a problem since the spontaneous working of
the market system will provide the incentives for the substitution of new
materials, the development of new techniques and the introduction of
recycling processes as the prices of increasingly scarce materials rise.

But the speed and sensitivity of such adaptive processes in real economics is a matter of such uncertainty that it becomes, inevitably, the object of conjecture, which is an unbridgeable gulf away from the abstract models of economic theory. Just how powerful such adaption will be in a world of cartels, government intervention, high technology, ill-defined property rights and so on, no one knows.

These remarks are relevant to a common reaction to the *Limits to Growth* study. This reaction is that the world is a great deal more complicated than the model used in the study, especially in that the model abstracts from certain types of adaptive processes; it is then concluded that the model must be hopelessly misleading or even worthless. Now, the interesting thing about the *Limits to Growth* model is, indeed, the great emphasis it places on self-reinforcing processes, in direct contrast to the adaptive processes which are the focal point of neoclassical economics. Which of the two kinds of process is the more powerful in the long run is an interesting and important question, and one that should not be simply begged. In particular, one cannot establish that the self-reinforcing processes of *Limits to Growth* are not worthy of study simply by pointing to the existence of adaptive processes. Of course the world is complicated; of course the *Limits to Growth* model is a drastic abstraction; of course there are adaptive processes complicating the picture. But what follows from all this?

Only skepticism. And skepticism is not an attitude which, in an unprejudiced observer, is supposed to apply only to the conclusions of the *Limits to Growth* study. As it happens, I am skeptical about the conclusions of the study, as I should imagine Denis Meadows is, too. But I am also skeptical about the conclusions from alternative formalizations addressed to the same issues; and I am particularly skeptical about formalizations which are insinuated rather than stated. On pollution, the cheermongers' faith switches from the economic to the political sphere. In this case they recognize that government intervention is necessary to establish a charging system whereby polluting activities will be brought within the workings of the economic system. It is asserted, however, that all problems of pollution may be solved in this way. Indeed, a well-known British cheermonger, Professor Wilfred Beckerman, recently claimed that ". . . the pollution problem is a simple matter of correcting a minor resource misallocation by means of pollution charges" and went on to argue that the objections to such a scheme may be disposed of with the aid of second-year economics. What remains unclear is whether this reflects more on the incontrovertible viability of such a scheme, or on the inadequacy of second-year economics for analyzing the problem.

Even if one regarded the imposition of pollution charges as an acceptable approach, a number of problems immediately arise. First, one needs a method of recording and measuring the pollution of each type caused by each individual and each firm. Second, one needs a system for deciding the charge appropriate to the location and for collecting the resulting revenues. And third, one needs a method of detecting those who are cheating the system, together with legal sanctions to impose on them, this being a matter which may involve international as well as national law. All that economic theory tells us is how, under idealized conditions, to relate the charges to the costs imposed by the polluter. In fact, making such regulative systems workable and responsive to the problem rather than to goals of bureaucratic origin, are problems requiring political will, legislative skill and administrative competence of an order that makes one hesitate to categorize it as a "simple matter."

So we see that in this case the underlying faith of the cheermongers concerns the adaptive capabilities of the political system: a faith in the wisdom and skill of governments in devising a regulative scheme based on pollution charges. Again, I do not share this faith, but I leave it to others to decide whether it is misplaced or not.

How does all this relate to economic growth?

Our cheermongers are wholeheartedly in favor of economic growth. But since they see resource depletion as unproblematic and pollution as something that can be dealt with in a straightforward way, it is quite natural for them to view increased production with a delight unmixed with concern for the effects other than on the supply of goods and services.

They do, however, in the context of economic growth, introduce some further arguments. For example, they stress that economic growth does not involve the *physical* growth of some fixed bundle of goods, but the growth of the *value* of some ever-changing bundle. This may increase in value not just because it contains more materials, but because the materials are transformed in ways which make them more effective in satisfying human needs and wants. This stress on the value aspect rather than the physical aspect of materials and resources generally obviously helps to undermine the idea that there is some definite relation between producing, on one hand, and resource depletion and pollution, on the other. It supports the contention that there is no necessary relation between the growth of flows of value and the growth of the underlying flows of materials in physical terms.

But again, this line of thought merely complicates the picture and, properly, leads to skepticism rather than to optimism. As the technology of production and consumption changes, so the relations between physical and value flows change. So the question becomes that of whether future technology will be less prodigal of natural resources and less polluting than current technology. Or, assuming that such a technology could be developed, the question becomes: Would it be workable within the framework of our institutions? And, if so, Could it be pushed into operation by suitable government policies? And it is on these questions that the cheermongers have nothing to offer except reassurance.

So it becomes apparent that this issue, like all the others, resolves itself finally into a matter of spontaneous optimism. In this case it is technological optimism: a faith in the prowess of future gadgets to solve the problems associated with the widespread use of present gadgets.

Another argument that the cheermongers have put forward is that environmental concern reinforces rather than undermines the need for economic growth, on the grounds that restoring, protecting and improving the environment absorb resources, which need to be made available. But this view is question-begging, for the environment may be preserved not only by the restoration of damage which has been done, but by the prevention of activities which have caused damage.

It is not only question-begging to suppose that reversing damage is always better than preventing it; this view also presupposes that the undesirable effects of economic growth are indeed reversible. And this is just not so. No amount of extra resources will enable radioactive waste to be transformed back into fissionable isotopes. And one is at a loss to think of reverse processes that could be implemented in the case of fertilizer run-off, soil erosion, and the concentration of pesticide residues in food chains.

Since pollution is essentially a process of things becoming intermingled and scrambled together, its reversal is either hopelessly expensive or quite impossible. That is what entropy is all about. The arguments that economic growth makes available the resources to undo its own undesirable effects and still leave resources to spare is a swindle. For the effects cannot be undone. What is being offered here is, at best, certain cosmetic exercises to mask the effects or push them into the future.

* * *

Some critics of the Club of Rome have seen in Aurelio Peccei and his friends a latest version of the Robin Hood Symptom.

Yes, they have a very peculiar argument to the effect that environmentalism and antigrowth sentiments have Sinister Class Overtones. This is founded on the fact that the propagators of antigrowth sentiments are all members of the middle class, and, according to the cheermongers, this should make us very suspicious of their capacity to pronounce disinterestedly on this issue. But the force of this objection is puzzling, since the cheermongers themselves all have impeccable middle-class credentials. The cheermongers, however, insist that antigrowth sentiments are the disenchantment of the relatively privileged and well-off (other than themselves) with the result of further spread in wealth, results which undermine the quality of the amenities they enjoy: a quality which generally falls as the amenities are more widely used. But to expound this "middle-class conspiracy" theory, one has to be highly selective in one's examples, confining them, in fact, to congestionlike cases; for it remains totally obscure why the middle class should be uniquely vulnerable to, for example, pesticide residues or radioactive emanations.

What then is your own position?

In the terms I have been adopting, I am very doubtful about the adaptive capabilities of industrial society in the face of the problems it is generating. I am particularly dubious about the role of technology in these processes: it has not shown itself to be markedly responsive to social needs or even, in notable cases, to economic pressures. The Concorde springs to mind as an important example of technology unfolding according to its own goals and logic.

And I am particularly concerned about the load that will be thrown onto the political system with the need to regulate more and more activities with potentially disruptive environmental effects, bearing in mind that the regulative machinery at the global level is decidedly flimsy. Even at the national level, the success with which governments have pursued orthodox economic objectives does not inspire me with great confidence in their capacity to achieve both these *and* targets involving natural-resource conservation and pollution abatement. It seems quite likely to me that the relatively autonomous unfolding of high technology together with the unwieldy and uncertain workings of the political system could provide sufficient perverse adaption to more than offset the degree of benign adaption that the economic system may be capable of. In which case, one is thrown back onto global responsibilities of the individual citizen—an already overworked and markedly ineffectual instrument. None of this makes me particularly cheerful.

NOTES

[1] See Alan Coddington, "The Cheermongers: or How to Stop Worrying and Love Economic Growth," *Your Environment,* Autumn 1972. See also Coddington, "The Economics of Ecology," *New Society,* April 9, 1970.

[2] See conversation no. 13.

[3] See conversation no. 26.

60. *Freeman Dyson*

Professor Dyson teaches physics at the Institute of Advanced Study at Princeton, New Jersey.

He was born in Crowthorne, England, in 1923. During the war years he served at operations research headquarters of the Royal Air Force (1943-45). He studied mathematics at Cambridge. In 1947 he came to Cornell University on a Commonwealth fellowship. In 1957 he became an American citizen.

He has worked on the TRIGA reactor and the Orion spaceship at General Atomic in San Diego, California (1956-59). He has also been a consultant for various weapon laboratories in the United States, for the Space Agency and the Disarmament Agency.

Do you feel like Arthur C. Clarke[1] *has written—"we are not the*

*only castaways upon the tiny raft of the Solar System as it drifts forever
along the Gulf streams of the Galaxy.''* [2]

I don't know. I am very much interested to find out.

How does Clarke know?

It's a question of faith. Many of my colleagues have this religious
belief that we are not alone in the universe. I hope they are right. The
universe will be a much more interesting place if they are right.

Toynbee[3] *felt that this odyssey into space was a waste.*

In the long run it is certainly no waste. The way we have gone so
far is not the right way to go. We have come to a dead end in the Apollo
program. That is no surprise to anybody who has been involved with
it. It has been done in a very extravagant and in many ways unintelligent
way. Still it has been done. That is the main thing. I would rather have
gone to the moon this way than not have gone at all. What we shall
need if we are to do anything sensible in space is to travel cheaply in
space. Ships like the Apollo remind me strongly of the great airships
of my youth, the R 101 in England and the *Hindenburg* in Germany,
these marvelous, beautiful, fragile ships with their absurdly small
payloads. They are just like the Apollo ships. What we need is the
equivalent of the Boeing 747. I think we shall have it, but it will take
a while.

Do you feel the Soviets approach space exploration more intelligently?[4]

I wouldn't say so. It's very difficult to judge because they don't publish their costs. I would say theirs has been done slightly more stupidly
than ours, but this is a matter of judgment. They also have had wrong
objectives.

In what way the wrong objectives?

They have been more interested in the rocket than in the payload. As
far as we know, the people who run the Soviet space program are even
less in touch with scientific objectives than the people who run ours;

but I speak from great ignorance, since very few of us have ever had the chance to talk to these people.

With the lessening of dangers, the improvement of relations, do you believe there is a fair chance for closer and more open communication with your Soviet counterparts in space?

We already have quite good communication with my counterparts, that is, the people who snipe at the program from the outside. I think there is also reasonably good communication between the people on the inside, but we have not succeeded in establishing very good communication between the people on the inside and the people on the outside in either country. However, these are small issues as compared with the future of mankind.

The US just succeeded to put into completion the first map of Mars, through seven thousand television pictures, thirty-five million miles away. What's the importance of this achievement?

This is impossible to say. One did not know what was the importance of discovering America when it was first discovered.

Is it a step ahead?

It's an enormous step. It's the first time we've had a clear view of any planet other than our own. What it will lead to I am not capable of saying, nor is anybody else. The next step is to send two orbiting ships in 1975 or '76 to have a much closer look. It will take a very long time to see what are the sensible things to try to do. At the moment we are just at the very beginning of exploring the planet Mars.

You have expressed in the New York Times *the view that it is important to gather more intelligence on the galaxies, on the universe.*[5] *Is that possible? Is it being done with the use of computers?*

The way to approach this is to have a look and to see what is there. Most of the apparatus is not very sophisticated. We have to look with ordinary optical telescopes of the kind we already have. We do need more telescopes of all kinds. At the moment there is an acute shortage of ordinary old-fashioned telescopes. There are many more astronomers with good ideas than there are telescopes. We are beginning to have a look from space which shows us a lot of new things. The most important thing that's come out of this space program, as far as science is concerned, is the discovery of x-ray sources in the sky. This is a completely new kind of astronomy. The beauty of this is that it is comparatively cheap. The most important science that has been done in this space program has been done for less than one percent of the cost of the program. All the space astronomy has been done with unmanned satellites. X-ray astronomy in particular has mostly been done with quite small rockets. Such observations don't need billions of dollars. In fact, they're done much better without billions of dollars.

You are talking now about what you call infrared astronomy?

No. Infrared is done from the ground, mostly.

And that flourishes?

Yes, it flourishes. But there's still an acute shortage of telescopes.

Don't the Soviets now have the largest telescope in the world?

It's not quite running yet. It is true it will be running in a short time.

It will be an important step forward.

It's not clear. The Russians are skeptical about it. It seems it has not been put in the right place. It's not being very well handled as far as we can tell. However, we shall see. It will be a good instrument, I am sure.

You spoke recently of a possible entirely new development, which you called "the greening of the galaxy." Are new discoveries in the universe probable which will place the limits of the planet in a different perspective?

One thing you can say for sure about the future, it will not be the way anybody expects. Of course that includes me. I don't pretend to predict what's going to happen. The kind of predictions made by the Club of Rome—or rather by Forrester and Meadows—look to me even less convincing than most of the others. What I have learned in looking at the world over the last thirty or forty years is the fact that qualitative changes always outweigh quantitative ones. Whenever the world seems to be going in a particular direction as a result of quantitative changes, then some new qualitative factor comes up which changes the whole nature of the problem. This has happened time and time again.

Hydrogen fusion—

Hydrogen fusion may or may not have this effect. I think it is not a sufficiently great qualitative change. It's only a small variation. Many of the big changes are rather intangible. It was only a few years ago that people started seriously talking about zero population growth. We already are closing down an elementary school in Princeton because there are not enough kids. That took only five years or so. It goes ridiculously fast. I think this will happen time and time again within the next hundred years. Whatever people will be worrying about in a hundred years' time, I am willing to predict will not be the problems that Forrester and Meadows are so excited about. Of course, I could be wrong. We all can be wrong. But the main thing to me is to be always prepared for the unexpected twist.

But coming to the possibility of growing trees on comets and feeding on biological byproducts—

We don't expect any great surprise from physics, which is my own part of science. We could be wrong there too, but I think it is likely that physics will not be the main frontier of scientific advance in the next hundred years. Biology will be the main frontier. There will be enormous changes in what we think about ourselves, what we think about our environment, as a result of learning how biological processes work in such a way that we have a real mastery of them. This hasn't yet happened. I think it's very likely to happen within the next fifty years. We will then have the same kind of mastery over the basic processes of biology that we have achieved in physics and chemistry. That will be a very great change in the whole place of man in the universe and in the scheme of things. I don't say the next thing as a prediction but I raise this as a question. It could happen that in a hundred years from now the main question which concerns us will be, shall we be one species or shall we be a thousand species?

What do you mean by that?

Shall mankind remain one species or shall we diversify to such an extent that we become a thousand separate species.

Spread over the galaxies—

Not necessarily. Maybe here on earth. It is not necessary to go into space to face this problem. We have it already here.

In order to have these thousand different species live on one earth, we need a form of rule of behavior acceptable to all. You talk about biology being the future, but where does behaviorism and psychology come in?

Of course, that's probably ninety percent of the problem. I absolutely agree with you. Only I don't think that we shall make people behave the way we want them to. I think the question will be, How do people wish to behave?

In absolute freedom?

I hope there will never be a world in which we decide how people shall behave. That is not what I would want to do. I think the question is, Are our social institutions flexible enough to cope with the kind of diversity which is coming? This is to me the big problem. I think we have some hope. There's every sign that social institutions in many ways are getting more flexible than they used to be. This I find a very healthy development. All kinds of behavior are now allowable which thirty or forty years ago were not. This I welcome. I think that we're going to see much more of it.

And doomsday?

I am thoroughly against prophets of doom. They've never done us any good.

*   *   *

But would you consider it feasible that civilization instead of being bound to the limits of the planet, would propagate from comet to comet, from star to star, into new living space, new space to feed us, new space to live?

Spacing mankind out into a larger living space, I don't say from star to star, that's in the remote future, but within the solar system; the question is, Do we wish to do it?—rather than, Can we do it? If we wish to do it, we certainly can. It remains to be seen whether we shall wish to. It would seem to me likely that we will need a larger living space to solve the problem of diversity, which is, as I see it, the main social problem of mankind. It may help us to solve a great number of these problems if we can open up new frontiers in the solar system away from the earth. I hope that this will be done in an informal way, in the same sort of way that the expansion of Europeans over the planet took place. Not that some supergovernment decides to launch a tremendous project to colonize the solar system. I hope that it will rather be small groups of people who make up their minds that they would like to be on their own and who will organize the necessary resources and go ahead and do it. That is why it's so important that it should be cheap, so that a couple of hundred people can acquire the necessary resources. I think that this will happen, but I have to admit that a lot of inventions still have to be made before it will become feasible.

One of the very important developments which I look forward to is the self-reproducing machine. This idea was first studied from a theoretical point of view by the mathematician von Neumann.[6] The self-reproducing machine is our own copy of the processes of life. When we have understood in sufficient depth the way in which living things reproduce themselves, the way in which the processes of heredity, of differentiation of an organism, occur in nature, then it will be open to us to use these processes for our own purposes in building machines, i.e., to make machines which are sophisticated enough to reproduce themselves. Already we see in principle how to do it. Von Neumann designed such a machine on paper. It had only half a million distinct parts. A real one, of course, will have a lot more than that. It has to be a complicated beast. But when such machines are practical, it will make the process of colonizing new worlds tremendously easier. You send one rocket to the moon with a rather sophisticated machine on board. This machine will be programmed to reproduce itself using nothing but rock and sunlight. It can manufacture its own parts. It can be programmed to construct whatever one would want to construct to make the moon ready for human habitation. This is the sort of way in which it seems to me the economics of space could be transformed, not by slight improvements in propulsion systems, but by radical change in the qualitative nature of the problem.

When you have self-reproducing machines, the problems of economics have a very different flavor. The accumulation of capital would become much more rapid. The costs of doing things would become different in such a radical sense that it no longer is possible to predict at all what you can do and what you cannot do. There's no reason as far as I can see why self-reproducing machines shouldn't also be important here on earth. There is lots that one can think of doing here. There are greater limitations on the earth. We have human beings around who're likely to get in the way when self-reproducing machines are let loose. Self-reproducing machines on the earth will obviously cause all kinds of ecological problems which we will have to handle with great care. These machines will also make the transition from poor to rich a great deal easier. Perhaps, looking at it in capitalistic terms, you can imagine an industrial development kit which is marketed by one of your big companies like IBM, which a poor country can buy for a modest down payment. One machine is shipped from the IBM factory to the country in question, and this machine then reproduces itself, differentiates, organizes an industrial plant, a complete modern communications network, and all the rest of what it takes to modernize a country.

But what would these developments do to the ever-increasing populations? More machines, less work, more unemployment. Self-reproducing machines will cause, in India or Brazil, disaster.

I didn't say that I had a solution for the social problems of mankind. I merely say that such technological developments are quite likely to happen. They're going to change radically the nature of our problems, but problems will still be there. They may be worse, but they will certainly be different. I think it's very likely that one of the consequences of this will be a greater alienation of the mass of mankind from economic problems, a greater alienation of people who run the machines from the people outside, who are only bystanders. We will be moving more and more in the direction of what is called by the pundits a postindustrial society, a society in which the majority of people are no longer concerned with earning a living in old-fashioned style. After economic problems are solved other problems always arise to take their place.

They might leave for the moon—

I don't say that they should leave for the moon. I say those who wish may leave for the moon. Those who wish to stay here will have to find ways to occupy their time, ways of living which they consider satisfactory. I think this may not be such a big problem for Indians as it will be for us, because in some ways the Indians are closer to the postindustrial society than we are. It may be we shall have to learn to live like the Indians rather than the Indians learning to live like us. It may be. It is hard to predict. What is perfectly clear is that the problems which will arise for mankind will have large aspects which will be common to the rich and the poor countries. In certain respects the self-reproducing machine will be a great leveler. It will mean that anything a rich country can do, a poor country can also do. It will mean that the problems which the rich countries have will also be problems for the poor countries.

NOTES

[1]Wrote with Stanley Kubrick the Metro Goldwyn Mayer film *2001: A Space Odyssey*; has written many books in the field of space.

[2]Arthur C. Clarke, *Report on Planet Three and Other Speculations,* Harper and Row (New York, 1972), p. 84.

[3]See conversation no. 5.

[4]"Now that we have sent out man to surround his machines, we have affirmed that technology is still only a part of culture, we have also affirmed that the culture of America is still significantly different from the Soviet Union. The Russian decision in favor of mechanized space flight illustrates the iron lock dialectical materialism has on their archaic industrial culture," William I. Thompson, "The Deeper Meaning of Apollo," New York *Times*, January 1, 1973. See also conversation no. 68.

[5]New York *Times*, November 27, 1972.

[6]See also Boyce Rensberger, "Man and Computer, Uneasy Allies of Twenty-five Years," New York *Times*, June 27, 1972.

61. Frank W. Notestein

Frank W. Notestein was born at Alma, Michigan, in 1902. He studied at Wooster College and received his Ph.D. from Cornell University in 1927.

For more than two decades Professor Notestein taught demography at Princeton University in Princeton, New Jersey. He has also been director of the Office of Population Research. From 1946 to 1948 Professor Notestein organized and was the first director of the Population Division of the United Nations in New York. In 1959 he became president of the Population Council, also in New York.

Limits to Growth has expressed great alarm about the growing population of the globe. It predicts some seven billion people by the year 2000. Herman Kahn told me that the planet could easily carry twenty billion people at the per capita income of twenty thousand dollars per person. Edward Teller said in Berkeley that according to his information the planet could hold one hundred billion people. For the common man it is very difficult to make up his mind what the situation really is.

I think it is probable that the world will get to seven billion. It might get to six and a half by the end of this century. It is irrelevant to ask how much the globe can carry. This is not a meaningful question. If there were no intervening political, social, and economic frictions, so that man could do the best that man knows, then the carrying capacity becomes indefinite. But if there were no friction, there would be perpetual motion. What the carrying capacity of the world would be in some never-never land of a distant future is irrelevant. The problem is, Here we are, where are we going? What are going to be the constraints? What advances of civilization, of rationality, of compassion and of lowering of pain can be made, and how? What is the course, among the conceivable courses, that we want to take? People who see the problem only in terms of fifty billions or two hundred billions are talking arrant nonsense, even if you are citing great names. I think they have not given much attention to the problems of social process.

Do you feel that the computer study by the Club of Rome—did they take social interaction into account sufficiently?

No, I did not take that study seriously, except as a first slight academic exercise. Their variables were too limited. They did not have adequate data even for the variables under consideration. Any statistician knows that an unlimited projection of past trends without change runs into an impossible situation. I think this is an interesting beginning, but to suppose that it has practical reality is foolish. I do not think one approaches the problem in the present state of our ignorance by putting doubtful figures into a machine. You will get out precisely what you put in. I think that is exactly what the Club of Rome did.

Dangerous you would say?

Dangerous to take it seriously as a real forecast in a real world. But interesting and important as a first step in studying what is obviously a serious problem. Do not misunderstand me. I do think that the world has very serious problems of population growth, problems that involve the welfare of all our children for a very considerable time. But they do not come to a focus either on some ultimate limit in a never-never land or on putting into a machine a certain number of variables and getting out the horror that is put into that machine in the first place. This is not the way to attack the problems.

Do you expect positive results from the first Population Conference that is planned for '74?

Yes, the situation is much more favorable than it used to be. Many years ago I organized the Population Division of the United Nations as its first director. Then the constraints on what one could do were extraordinarily strong. One could publish scientific information and one could blandly summarize the literature. But the minute one talked about population policy, about action, there was trouble. With the neo-Malthusians on one side and the Soviets, Roman Catholics and Moslems on the other, we could get very little agreement on anything save that people should be healthy, wealthy and wise—as well as more numerous. Since then, the disagreements among students of population who represent the world's main ideological and religious positions have been very much reduced. Now we can discuss real issues constructively, as I hope we shall in the UN conference planned for 1974. It, by the way, is not the first but the third world conference on population sponsored by the United Nations.

Mr. McNamara made an interesting speech[1] in September, 1972. But Professor Revel of Harvard thought he was kidding himself when McNamara said that the money the World Bank was giving to Indonesia for population control would cut the population of Indonesia between now and the year 2000 by fifty million people.

Mr. McNamara did not mean that the population would be fifty millions smaller than it is today. What he meant was that it might reduce by fifty millions the population that would otherwise be there by the end of the century.

Of course, but would that be possible?

I do not know, but just possibly. It would require cutting the growth by less than fifty percent. Remember, if twenty-five years ago you had told most students of population that in the next twenty-five years the Taiwan Chinese population would reduce its birth rate by almost fifty percent, they would have told you it was impossible. There would have been much talk about the way in which ancestor worship and the familistic society supports high birth rates. Much the same would have been said about Korea. But they would have been wrong. Birth rates may fall even faster in the future as educational advances and family planning programs improve. Who knows? The year 2000 is still a generation away. If you will excuse me, Indonesia is a particularly difficult case. Its demographic troubles come in part from the fact that the Dutch colonial system was almost a laboratory case of economic development in the absence of social change. The Dutch did a magnificent job of running the terraces up the hills, of standardizing the specialized agricultural products of the tropics for the world market, and of protecting the health of the people—all with a minimum of change in the social structure. The Dutch did the modern part, the Indonesians did not have to.

We didn't take care of the basic education on any wide scale. The result was lower death rates and more people, but a minimum impact of modernization on the social structures that supported high birth rates.

Professor McTurnan Kahin estimated that the Dutch East Indies in 1940, a nation of some 70 million, had 637 lads in college.[2]

Yes, and how many ladies? I visited there in 1948. One can only have admiration for the engineering accomplishments of the Dutch in their former colonies. They lifted the carrying capacity of the land, dropped mortality, and left intact the social structures that supported high birth rates. They, if you will, attained the maximum of imposed progress. They fostered the absorption of many modern techniques without resolving the kind of social contradictions that self-management requires, and today we have low mortality, high density, and high birth rates.

I found in your Population Council reports that the United States, if it has an average two-child family, will reach in the next hundred years three hundred fifty million people. If it has a three-child family on an average, it will reach in the next hundred years one billion people. As a demographer, would you say it is extremely important whether American families on an average will have a two- or a three-child family? The New York Times *recently reported, by the way, that the US reached below zero population growth already.*

Of course it is important whether we have two or three children on the average. That is a difference of one-half, and one-half is a substantial fraction! It matters by hundreds of millions! When they say that our fertility has dropped below the level that gives zero population growth, they are making a conventional, and not very real, statement. If we imagine that the rates of bearing and dying that took place in each age group this year were those of a birth class passing from birth to extinction through death, then such a cohort would not have replaced itself at the age-schedules of bearing and dying observed in 1972. It is a little like the speedometer of a car. When it reads 100 kilometers an hour, that does not tell you that you have gone 100 kilometers in the past hour, nor does it forecast that you will have gone that far at the end of the next hour. It tells you something interesting but highly conditional—how far you will go *if* you continue at the present speed for an hour.

If fertility and mortality were to continue at the levels of the year 1972 and there was no net migration, our population would begin to decline gradually in about seventy years, after the proportions of people in the childbearing years and the older ages had adjusted to these schedules of bearing and dying. In short, we have a situation in which the population is actually growing by about .7 percent per year, on a balance of fertility and mortality that, if continued for three-quarters of a century, would yield a gradual decline. I will have to leave it to you whether we are *below* zero growth or not. Nevertheless, something very important has happened. The birth rate has dropped very rapidly in spite of a large increase in the proportion of the population in the young childbearing ages. Interestingly enough, it has happened at the same time that governmental support for extensive programs of family planning have been reaching all parts of the population for the first time. For the first time family planning is beginning to become a real possibility for the poor as well as for the well-to-do.

If the gap between the rich and the poor were not to grow wider, if we were to continue our limitless freedom, what to expect?

Indeed, to solve the world's ultimate problems, we need at least another half-hour. Of course, the world differences in income levels need to be reduced, not, I think, by taking from the rich, but by lifting the productivity of the poor, partly by permitting them to limit the number of their children if they choose, thereby enhancing the opportunities for healthy development and education. This talk about ending economic growth seems to me to be great nonsense. The world has not begun to exploit its productive potential, even in its more developed parts. And the rich countries have not begun to assist the less-developed regions and peoples to catch up with them. Let's not worry about constraining freedom of choice until we have given freedom a chance, as neither my country nor any other has thus far done. We hear a great deal about resources these days, but let's never forget that the only ultimate resources, apart from space and perhaps the plant and animal gene pools, are people, their health, their education, their skills and their organization. I think that until we, the prosperous of the world, are willing to make very substantial investments in fostering the development of these resources throughout the world, the problems of poverty will not be solved. The great wasters of resources are not the rich governments, the rich corporations or the rich people, unfortunate as some of their activities are. The great waster of resources in the world is poverty.

NOTES

[1]Address to the Board of Governors, September 25, 1972, p. 4.
[2]*Nationalism and Revolution in Indonesia,* Cornell University Press (Ithaca, 1952), p. 32.

62. *Richard N. Gardner*

Professor Richard N. Gardner holds the Henry L. Moses Chair of Law and International Organization at Columbia University in New York.

Mr. Gardner was born in New York City in 1927. He graduated from Harvard College after majoring in economics. In 1951 he attended Yale University Law School. From 1953 to 1954 he taught at Harvard University and later practiced law in New York till 1957. That year he joined the faculty of Columbia University and became in 1960 a full professor. In April, 1961, he left Columbia temporarily to join the John F. Kennedy administration in Washington, D.C. From 1961 till mid-1965 he served as deputy assistant secretary of state for international organization affairs. Currently he is also a member of the board of trustees of the United Nations Institute for Training and Research (UNITAR). In 1970-71 he served as a member of President Nixon's Commission on International Trade and Investment Policy.

Professor Gardner published *Sterling-Dollar Diplomacy* (1956), *In Pursuit of World Order* (1964), *Blueprint for Peace* (1966) and *The Global Partnership: International Agencies and Economic Development* (1968).

That *Limits to Growth* is an important first step goes without any question. It is the first time that anyone has been daring enough to confront the future as a whole with the most modern instruments for forecasting and analysis. It is now clear, particularly in the light of some of the criticisms that have appeared in the World Bank study, that some of the methodology and some of the assumptions, particularly in the field of resources, may be legitimately criticized. But even the authors of the Club of Rome study admitted that it was only a crude first step. I think we ought to compare Aurelio Peccei[1] and Dennis Meadows to those early mapmakers in the fifteenth and sixteenth centuries, who tried to draw maps of the New World. We see now that the maps were not very good, but they were a useful beginning. We may regard the Club of Rome as the pioneers in the geography of the future.

Former UN Secretary-General U Thant[2] expressed in my interview extreme concern about the way things are going.

I think any sensitive, thoughtful, informed human being can only face the future with the deepest anxiety. There is no doubt that if things go on *as* they are now, we face disasters of unimaginable severity if not in this century, then certainly within the lives of our children and grandchildren.

I myself have launched an initiative in the United Nations, as the US member of the board of trustees of UNITAR, the UN Institute for Training and Research. This initiative is to establish a commission on the future.

The weakness and limitations of the Club of Rome are partly due to the fact that the club was mainly composed of Europeans, Americans and Japanese. It has not been sufficiently broadly based. Therefore, its legitimacy has been called into question, particularly in Latin America and Africa and Asia. My effort in the United Nations is designed first of all to meet this objection by having a commission on the future which would be representative of all the great cultures, religions, ideologies and intellectual traditions of the world. Then no one can say it is biased.

Moreover, our study will not be limited to growth and its limits, but will encompass three other areas in addition: developments in communications and education, technology (direct broadcasting from satellites, computers, information retrieval); developments in the biomedical sciences (birth control, death control, sex selection, genetic engineering) and trends in alienation and participation (the generational gap, attitudes of youth, the worker on the assembly line, the drug culture, boredom, the problem minorities). The "wise men" in this UNITAR commission would maintain a continual review of these four problem clusters. Perhaps one or two others will be added. Hopefully, the commission will bring in a report on the first of January of each year. This report one might call "the state of the future."

What have been reactions to this think tank within the United Nations so far from—especially—the socialist countries and the Third World?

The only honest answer is that we don't know yet. I should explain that this initiative was only possible because it was taken in UNITAR, which is a very unusual United Nations body. The UNITAR board of trustees consists of persons like myself, who serve in their individual capacities, as individual scholars appointed by the secretary-general. Unfortunately our Soviet board member has not attended the last several meetings, so his views are not known. We have not had a Chinese board member, simply because they have not chosen to appoint one as yet. China has left unfilled many of the places reserved for her on UN councils. As far as the developing countries are concerned, members of the board from those areas have shown considerable enthusiasm for this idea.

Of course the test will come when the first report is issued and we see what the reactions will be. Some governments may initially express reservations about this. There were also people who opposed Columbus' first voyage. There are persons who don't want to know about future problems because they are so hypnotized or fascinated by present issues.

I do not see concern with the future in any sense as an attempt to avoid the problems of the present. Quite the contrary. An analysis of where spaceship earth is going will result in a much more intense concern with the problems of poverty, with the problems of war, with the problems of the arms race, with the problems of environment and with all the other pressing problems now besetting the human race.

Would you expect that when this new project starts rolling, which will take probably one or two years before it really gets under way, political influence can be exerted and in follow-up, recommendations will be really pursued?

This, of course, is a very important question. Let me explain briefly the modus operandi. There will be a small expert staff in UNITAR serving this commission of eighteen to thirty-six "wise men."

Will they be based in Geneva or at United Nations headquarters?

Probably at UNITAR headquarters in New York. This small staff will be in contact with the great centers of research around the world, some of which have already organized themselves into a consortium, called IFIAS, the International Federation of Institutes of Advanced Study. Joseph Slater,[3] president of the Aspen Institute for Humanistic Studies, took that splendid initiative. Approximately twenty institutions have agreed to make regularly available an inventory of what they're doing, and what their conclusions are on all their work. With this material the UNITAR staff will prepare digests and summaries. The commission will meet once or twice a year and perhaps will divide itself into subgroups and committees. In any case, once it gets started, it will issue on the first of January every year a "state of man's future" report.

When do you expect the first report?

I wish I could say January 1, 1974, but you know well how difficult these things are to organize. I would hope by January 1, '75. My hope is that the leading newspapers of the world, since there is not much else to print on January 1, will devote two or three pages to printing the conclusions of this report.

The New York Times *will.*

Yes, I have some indications that they will. One would hope that the Washington *Post, Le Monde, Corriera de la Sera,* the *Times* of London—

And the Nieuwe Rotterdamsche Courant—Handelsblad.

—and I hope *Izvestia,* or even *Pravda,* will print summaries of this report. I see this as something that could capture the imaginations not only of insiders, intellectuals and scholars, but also of political leaders and forceful men around the world. It will be printed as a UN document. That is the beauty of this proposal, because the commission members will be serving in their individual capacities and will not be subject to any form of bureaucratic constraint in the UN. Then it will be translated into the UN languages. It will be placed on the desk of every single government in the world. My hope is that we will use the mass media in a very imaginative way to have transcontinental seminars on satellite television in which some of the splendid people that you are including in your book can regularly debate the conclusions of the ''wise men'' in a global, intellectual exchange.

One of the tragedies of our present time is that so many experts are often not talking to one another. We are afflicted by a terrible intellectual intolerance. Half of the people in your book probably aren't talking to the other half. If the world is to survive, we must break down these barriers. My hope is that this effort, launched in good faith and done, I hope, in a professional and intellectually acceptable way, will launch a process of global discussion of the global future.

How to break these barriers between intellectuals, even within the borders of our affluent, rich world?

I think the problem with many intellectuals—I don't say this applies to all or even most of the eminent people you have in your book, but it might apply to some—is that they have spent all of their professional lives wholly involved in the world of ideas without very much life experience and without the necessity to try to come to terms with other people in real human situations.

My own training is as a lawyer and economist, but primarily as a lawyer. We lawyers are engaged in what we like to call ''eunomics,'' the science of good arrangements. This science of good arrangements requires that one constantly structure institutions and procedures in such a way that human beings with rather different purposes, attitudes and values can somehow reach accommodations and communicate effectively. This is what's lacking in the world today. We have men of extraordinary brilliance as measured by their intelligence quotient, but with very little life experience, often with very little respect for facts. If the facts don't fit the theory, reject the facts. This one finds among the most intelligent people who are supposed to be the leaders of scholarship. If that is their attitude, how can we expect the man in the street to react, if the men in the ivory tower are destroying one another verbally and refusing even to speak to one another because of disagreements. That is hardly an example to set before the world.

What surprised me during the research for my book was that I had always felt politicians were unable to communicate, being glued to their political ideologies, but I found to my utter dismay that the same situation prevails among scientists—or worse.

In a way that's undoubtedly true.

And the masses are the victims. I mean the real groundswell of humanity is the victim of this immature and uncivilized behavior.

I think mankind is afflicted. I am by nature an optimist, but this is what makes me occasionally pessimistic. We are afflicted not only by national but by personal egoism. That is what eventually could destroy us. Many of these eminent people have such big egos that their principal preoccupation in life is to establish a piece of intellectual turf and preserve it against all comers, whatever the consequences. They're prepared to sacrifice truth—perhaps not consciously, but subconsciously—to the pursuit of ideology and to the pursuit of ego. This is wrong. The truly great men in history, the great scientists like Einstein, were modest men, constantly revising their ideas, listening with respect to people with other opinions. What has happened to the tradition of Einstein? What kind of men do we have today?

NOTES

[1]See conversation no. 70.
[2]See conversation no. 1.
[3]See conversation no. 69.

63. *Thor Heyerdahl*

Norwegian explorer Thor Heyerdahl was born in Larvik, Norway, in 1914. He studied zoology and geography at the University of Oslo. In 1937-38 he led his first expedition to Polynesia.

In 1947, on a raft named *Kon-Tiki,* in honor of a legendary pre-Inca sun king, he left Callao in Peru; and in 101 days Heyerdahl and his team crossed 4,300 miles of ocean, landing on the Raroia atoll in the Tuamotu Archipelago. Thus, he proved that scientists had greatly underestimated the seaworthiness of the balsa raft.

After numerous other expeditions, Heyerdahl undertook his *Ra* expeditions (1969-70). He finally crossed the Atlantic in his *Ra II*—3,270 miles in 57 days in a papyrus boat.

Thor Heyerdahl also takes an active part in meetings of the Club of Rome.

What was your foremost conclusion from your two Ra voyages?[1]

I expect you would want me to say that I proved my point that ancient people could cross the Atlantic in a primitive type of boat. But for me personally I found it more important to realize suddenly how small the ocean is, how very limited the distance is from one continent to the other and how polluted its water has become. On the trip that took only fifty-seven days, forty-three out of those fifty-seven days we observed oil clots floating about. Every day we actually saw plastic containers, nylon bags, empty cans or bottles or some other refuse from man, all the way from Africa to America.

One hundred years ago Her Majesty's Challenger *set sail from Portsmouth, England, on the world's first scientific voyage devoted to the exploration of the seas. That was a hundred years ago. Do we have enough facts, do we have knowledge about the sea, to explain the decline of the plankton, or to calculate how much time we have left to save the ocean?*

I think the situation is very serious, for the very fact that the visible pollution that has started must obviously be following some sort of potential curve. Only twenty years ago the world oceans were perfectly clear. We could still drag our plankton net behind our vessels and inside one would find only marine life. If we do it today, we cannot avoid collecting human pollution. I think that although science has advanced tremendously those hundred years, we have not been able to rid ourselves of the medieval concept of the ocean as being something endless. We think that if we pipe our sewers far enough off the beaches, the refuse will sort of fall off the edge of the world. We think that the blue ocean runs into the blue space and whatever we dump into the ocean will disappear. We think that the ocean is endless because it has no beginning and no end. But neither has a tennis ball. Today oceanographers are striving very hard to let the public as well as our decision makers realize that if we manage to pollute the ocean, to destroy life in the ocean, it means suicide. It would be the worst that could happen to man. The ocean was the source of all life on earth and is still its indispensable foundation, serving in addition as the global filtering system. Yet even with present-day knowledge we do not value it as such. We merely use it as our common sink, forgetting that it is landlocked in all directions with no outlet whatsoever, except for clean water evaporation.

The Americans already put atomic waste in huge containers on the bottom of the ocean. Ralph Lapp,[2] the atomic scientist, has already suggested building atomic reactors in the sea. What on earth could this do eventually to the sea?

I think this is the policy of the ostrich. If we find something to be so dangerous and so terrible that we cannot dispose of it ashore, we dump it into the sea, because then we don't see it and we feel it is not there. Of course if some material is that dangerous, we should keep it in some place where we can control it. Once it's at the bottom of the ocean, containers can crack open, something may happen and we have no more control over where it spreads.

—Pollute the entire bottom of the ocean and kill all marine life. You live on the Mediterranean. From where you live you can see the water and the Alps.

The situation in the Mediterranean is extremely dangerous. For the first time last year there were days when I had to tell my children not to go to the beach because the water was so terribly polluted. We could not swim. Only four years ago the water was always crystal clear. Of course the Mediterranean is a closed or almost closed ocean. We know that every year an estimated two hundred to three hundred thousand tons of oil are dumped intentionally into this great "lake." This floating oil slick is working against the cliffs of the Mediterranean, killing in some areas all littoral life, which happens to be of the greatest importance for the ocean as a whole, because most marine life will pass some stage of its life cycle either as eggs or larvae on the cliffs. If we manage to destroy life among the coastal rocks through toxic matter, this will have a deadening effect on life far away from the land.

On November 13, 1972, ninety-one nations concluded a global convention in London to control dumping in the oceans. How effective do you think that convention will be?

I think that the main thing is that we start to police these matters. This will be a great problem, because a great many people still think that all this is not so dangerous and they keep on dumping. I think it is also a matter of education. It's a matter of making people understand that the ocean is much smaller than we thought it to be.

In the North Sea, where so much of this dumping is going on, if people would only realize that if one builds a metropolis like New York City on the bottom of that sea, most of the houses would stick well above the surface of the water. That is how shallow it really is. It must be quite obvious that when we dump toxic matter into this shallow sea, it is going to have a disastrous effect on marine life, which again means that it is going to have an aftereffect on all humanity in the long run.

What are your expectations, for instance, of the New Institute for Marine Environment as part of the Natural Environment Research Council for Britain, which in 1975 is supposed to be in full operation with about a hundred and thirty scientists working in it?

Yes, that is an encouraging development. I am quite sure that the main thing is really to open up the eyes not only of the scientists, but also of the public at large. I think that there is still time, but time is very short. I should like to stress that while people are very much concerned about the pollution of the atmosphere above the big cities and the pollution of lakes and rivers, these are problems of minor importance. This pollution will be cleared by the wind and the current, but it will all end up in the ocean. The ocean is the only place where all this is accumulating and the only place where we must make sure to stop it from entering as fast as we can because it is much harder to get it out than to prevent it from coming in.

With your obvious love for the sea, do you feel the Club of Rome can be helpful in fighting for the survival of that sea?

Yes, I definitely think so. One of the main functions of the Club of Rome is to call attention to problems and to stimulate research bearing upon the future living conditions of civilized man upon this planet. This, for instance, was its sole intention in sponsoring the research behind *Limits to Growth*. Let me say that I feel the Club of Rome's work could be compared to an icebreaker. It is really not a question of how beautifully it moves through the ice but the fact that it is breaking the ice and making it possible for other more streamlined passenger steamers to follow. Scientifically, a lot of improvements could probably be made to a pioneering work like *Limits to Growth*, but the basic discovery that we are on a wrong track, on a collision course, and that it's a matter of time, no matter what adjustments we make to these curves—that is the most important result of the study. I don't think that the Club of Rome as such will solve these problems, but I do think that the members of the club, with their contacts with different scientific institutions, with different governmental bodies and so on, will certainly be able to stimulate deeper interest in the problem.

I should mention that at the 1972 annual meeting at Jouy-en-Josas near Paris, some of the scientists present took up some of these problems after the speech I delivered on the vulnerability of the ocean. They are now going to interest certain oceanographic institutions in research programs. We need to learn what is really happening, because today we don't know. We don't know what will happen if we kill the botanical plankton. There are some scientists who say it means that fifty percent of our oxygen will disappear. Some estimate seventy percent. Some even say it will take a million years for the oxygen we still have to evaporate. It means that opinion among the so-called experts is completely colliding. It is high time that we really know what will happen before we can start saying, "Don't worry, the ocean is endless and we can just keep on dumping."

Will these problems be studied with the use of computers?

I think that computers will be very useful in research of this kind.

Actually, isn't it shocking how little we know of the effects of what we are doing to the earth, how opinions differ? And do you think we will be able to correct some of our errors in time?

I think that long before we reach population numbers like seven billion or ten or twenty billion, we will run into problems that will stop a population increase. It is very likely that the pollution of the ocean is going to be one of them, because when we make calculations today on the food supply of the world—let us say for ten years from now—we figure out that while today you can catch eighty million tons of fish with the evolution of technical equipment, ten years hence, we could catch twice as much. This is on the assumption that there is an endless number of fish to be caught. Those who are involved in studies of the ocean realize that instead of increasing or keeping at a steady level, marine life is decreasing very quickly. Not only because of the strong evolution in fishing gear and techniques, but also, as I mentioned, due to the problem of pollution, particularly in the shallow coastal areas where ninety percent of all marine life is concentrated. If we are able to destroy the ocean, I don't think it's of any interest whether this or that person would be correct in assuming that some day there will be twenty or a hundred billion people, because we would never get to that point.

NOTES

[1]See Thor Heyerdahl, *The Ra Expeditions,* New American Library (New York, 1971).
[2]See conversation no. 37.

64. Lincoln Gordon

Ambassador Lincoln Gordon is presently a fellow at the Woodrow Wilson International Center for Scholars in Washington, D.C.

Lincoln Gordon was born in New York City in 1913. He studied at Harvard University and received a Ph.D. at Oxford University in England, where he attended as a Rhodes scholar (1933-36).

He was a member of the Harvard faculty from 1936 to 1961. He was William Ziegler Professor of International Economic Relations at Harvard from 1955 to 1961.

Ambassador Gordon was involved on behalf of the State Department with the creation of the Marshall Plan for Europe (1947-52). In 1961 President John F. Kennedy appointed him ambassador to Brazil. He left this post in 1966 to become Assistant Secretary of State for inter-American affairs. From 1967 to 1971 Ambassador Gordon was president of Johns Hopkins University in Baltimore, Maryland.

Among the books he has published are *Government and the American Economy* (1941, rev. ed. 1948), *United States Manufacturing Investment in Brazil* (1962) and *A New Deal for Latin America* (1963).

A number of us here[1] are engaged in a long-range project on what we call aspects of sustainable growth. We chose the title *Sustainable Growth* rather than *Limits to Growth* precisely because we had doubts as to the central thesis of the first Forrester and Meadows project for the Club of Rome. My own special concern is with international implications of problems of sustainable growth.

But let me say a few words as to what we mean by sustainable growth. We are concerned—as the Club of Rome has been concerned—with interrelations among population, resources, protection of the environment and rates and directions of economic growth. Unlike Forrester[2] and Meadows, however, I do not share the conviction that economic as well as population growth must be stabilized within the next generation in order to avoid global catastrophe at some point in the twenty-first century.

So far as the Meadows study itself is concerned, the critical analyses that I have reviewed and some work that I have done on my own convince me that their thesis is certainly not proven and probably not provable in global terms. The Meadows study is unduly pessimistic concerning depletable resources, unduly pessimistic concerning the possibilities of pollution control, and unduly pessimistic concerning the possibility that family-planning policy will in fact bring about lower rates of population growth even in countries that are quite poor.

Dr. Herman Kahn[3] estimates that this planet could easily sustain twenty billion people at a per capita income of twenty thousand dollars each.

I am a long way from subscribing to that view. I think that a global population of twenty billion would in fact imply conditions of life and life-styles that would be very unpleasant for most of that twenty billion. And indeed, while making these very sharp criticisms of the Meadows conclusions, I would say on the other side that there can be and will be and to some extent already are serious physical constraints on economic growth in some countries already, while in other countries there is the prospect of temporary constraints over certain periods of time.

Serious present constraints show clearly in resource-poor and already badly overpopulated countries. I would cite as examples Bangladesh and Haiti, on two different continents. Temporary physical constraints in other countries or perhaps even globally are conceivable if technological developments in the energy field are delayed, either because science does not work sufficiently rapidly or because of environmental limitations on what is done or because of the wrong policy decisions. Then you could have periods of time in which there is a lack of fit between the ultimate physical possibilities and what is actually done by society. In short, there is a mixture of physical constraints and institutional and social constraints, which I think make it not only unlikely but impossible that Herman Kahn's dream could be realized.

But let me come to what seem to me more interesting questions than the mere problem of physical limitations. They have to do with the interaction between physical constraints and what individuals or societies want. If one takes just the United States, the environmental concern has caught hold not merely as a passing fashion or fad, but as a deep-seated, widely shared concern. This is clearly true in particular localities or regions and may become true of American society as a whole. The general question arises whether people will want the mere expansion of conventional economic growth as measured by gross national product or GNP per capita. At present rates of growth in the United States, family incomes which presently average about ten thousand dollars would rise in seventy years to eighty thousand dollars per family at present prices. It is extraordinarily unlikely that anything like the present patterns of expenditure would still be desired, and major changes should be expected long before that figure is reached. Those changes would include the balance of leisure versus work, through shortening the working week very much more from the present average of about forty hours. Other changes concern the conditions of work, the satisfactions from work, the desire to spend one's working time in a more satisfactory way, and the use of additional available leisure. All of these kinds of changes are likely to slow down the rates of economic growth as we measure them conventionally. That is one major area which we are trying to explore in relation to the rich countries.

And what about the poor countries? You slipped in a phrase that was surprising to me. You said, if we look in the future and judge what individuals and societies will want. Would you believe that we approach the day, in view of the world's limits, that what individuals would want should be second to the interest of what societies need?

Let me speak first of the rich countries. Societies are composed of individuals. Clearly the consumption of the individuals is partly individual and partly social. There are many things that are collectively consumed. Environmental things generally are collectively consumed. Indeed there are—as others have pointed out—collective bads as well as collective goods. One of the changes in attitudes toward economic growth and consumption will be an increasing interest in collective consumption as opposed to individual consumption. That can be done partly through individual choice but largely requires social policy decisions, which means some kind of political process. We have some paradoxes at the moment in the United States. I interpret the results of our election in November, 1972, to indicate that on the one hand there is a great interest in improving collective consumption but at the same time a great skepticism that our instruments—our governmental institutions for providing collective consumption—really provide satisfactory results. Some solution will have to be found. I do not see the need for a sharp choice between individualism and socialism. There are all kinds of mixtures in the present situation. The social component, which is the fraction of total decisions that is made collectively through political decisions, will continue to rise. I would hope that a very large area could also be left for individual choices. When speaking of both individual and social preferences, I mean individual preferences expressed through markets and social preferences expressed through politics.

I was thinking in Skinnerian terms of losing some of that cherished "freedom." We can now move to the developing countries.

Yes, I wanted to refer to what seemed to me at least preliminary indications of some significant changes of attitude to economic growth in some of the poor countries, particularly some of the poorest as in South Asia. I wish we knew more about China because that is clearly one of the most fascinating countries in the present world. If one is concerned with poverty, some kind of economic growth is essential in order to reduce the tragedy which flows from bad health, malnutrition and all of the other social ills of poverty one knows.

But are Chinese citizens not programmed in a way that all of the population has to be taken into account? We are all in the same boat trying to get to a higher level. We must stop wanting things that we totally don't need, that overtax our economies and financial resources, and—I didn't want to interrupt you—

No, this is a good interruption. Let's take the case of cars for a moment, because I think they're a marvelous illustration. Now we are back to the rich countries. Automobiles are an excellent illustration of some of the critical problems involved in the relationship between individual choice and social choice. If anything like recent trends continue in the United States, Europe, Japan, even in the Soviet Union, it's fairly clear that individual preferences would favor one car for each adult. Yet the effects of that happening are strangulation of the cities. At some point there develops—and there are signs of this happening—a collective preference for a smaller number of total cars.

Here you have a curious conflict which the market cannot take care of. Many of my economist friends believe that environmental issues generally can be dealt with through market devices by doing what they call internalizing external costs. They say that if pollution arises from motorcars, the production of paper or electric power plants, all you have to do is to make sure that the polluter pays. The cost of curing the pollution or continuing the pollution should be added to the price of the product and then economic mechanisms will stop the pollution or bring it down at least to tolerable levels. I think that is true for many cases, but there are certain kinds of external social costs that cannot be internalized. Traffic congestion is a classic case of this type. The only way that kind of issue can be taken care of is by collective political decisions, specifically decisions that there will be built good mass-transit systems within cities, that there will be areas of cities which are forbidden to private cars entirely, that there will be better intercity transportation. All of these require very large investments of capital. There is no simple self-adjusting market mechanism that will do them. As technology gets more complex and as interdependencies, both within nations and across national frontiers, get more complex, I am convinced that the proportion of important decisions which must be made as deliberate social decisions will get larger.

To come back to China and the materially poor countries of South Asia: In a sense the Chinese model is what thoughtful people in South Asia are also thinking about in one respect, that is to say, instead of trying to promote economic development through what I might call the conventional path of industrialization, of intensive capital investment and the like, they would like to give emphasis to income distribution from the very start and to focus on the increased production of things needed by the mass of the people. That is to say, food for all, adequate nutrition for all, primary education for all, some kind of even rudimentary health care for all. As far as one can tell, China is in fact doing this. The great question is whether that kind of emphasis, in contrast to the more conventional type of development, can be translated into reality without a completely authoritarian brainwashing organization of an entire society. I don't know the answer to that question. I wish I did. I believe that in the next decade or so, perhaps sooner, we will see some interesting and important experiments under less authoritarian social systems to do that. I suppose that Professor Skinner[4] would be very happy with the Chinese way of doing things. I am not happy with it myself. I would think that as China develops, more and more thoughtful Chinese would become unhappy with it too.

Has it not been demonstrated in most of the developing nations that blindly copying the platitudes of Jeffersonian democracy did not keep them out of the hands of authoritarian rulers?

I was American Ambassador in Brazil for almost five years, between 1961 and 1966; I know the rest of Latin America quite well. I do not believe that Jeffersonian or post-Jeffersonian-style democratic institutions can work in a full-fledged manner in very poor countries. As a matter of fact they really only work in a handful of countries in the whole world in North America, Northwestern Europe, Australia and New Zealand. What does seem to me possible is to combine a great deal more authority which implies less democratic participation in the selection and removal of governments, with more open societies and more protection of individual freedom and choice than China seems to be permitting at the present time.

Or in the Soviet Union?

Yes, of course. In Russia the tensions of a closed society are clearly visible. During my long stay in Latin America, I could see a clear distinction between the question of effective democratic control on one hand and the question of a reasonable degree of civil liberties, protection of individual rights, intellectual freedom and reasonable freedom of the press. Take the case of France under De Gaulle after 1958. He had to cope with a disaster in Algeria. Looking at it internally, results were achieved by almost an authoritarian regime. But that regime still did protect the rights and the interests of individuals and the essentially open character of French society. It was not complete as the system of radio and television was turned into a propaganda machine on behalf of the government. But the free press was maintained. Certainly French intellectuals were not persecuted.

I am almost inclined to say that in the present United States government under the leadership of Mr. Nixon and his chief assistant Kissinger, Congress seems to be completely bypassed. The US of 1972-73 seems to approach the way De Gaulle ran France.

On the side of foreign policy, I would not disagree with you.

Nobody knows anymore what is going on, the White House alone decides foreign policy.

This is true. The Congress is out of it, and I don't think that this is a healthy situation. Nor is it a very durable situation. It will change very rapidly. The Vietnamese war was an enormous national preoccupation and a source of national disillusionment. It will be settled long before your book is published. My own guess is that a settlement will be reached before January 20, because I am convinced that Mr. Nixon wants to have that behind him when he is inaugurated for a second term.

But to come back to some of the rich and poor nations' relationships: I am particularly concerned about romantic overexpectation. What often is implied in the planetary approach is the expectation of a planetary government in the foreseeable future. We are a very very long way short of planetary government. Even within the European Community when one considers the problems that have yet to be resolved in developing a common currency, with all of the implications for federation which a common currency implies, one must be cautious about assuming that the world will move rapidly to global government. Moreover, large-scale migration from country to country or region to region seems to me no longer a major solution to the imbalances. I don't foresee in the next century or two anything like a total equalization of world standards of living. But in the richest countries there is now a growing tendency to question the advantages of growth as such. Growth is now considered more instrumental than an objective. Growth for what? Growth for more satisfactory living? Growth for quality of life? This may mean more leisure rather than work. If at the same time effective interdependence can be maintained between rich and poor, I would expect some narrowing of the famous gap between the two. That goal, it seems to me, is what serious efforts should be focused on. I don't expect the United Nations to be converted into a global government within my grandchildren's lifetime, to say nothing of my own. But I do think we should cultivate functional international institutions which will take area by area, try to identify specific problems and possibilities of convergence of interests, and then work seriously to make those convergences a reality.

NOTES

[1]The Woodrow Wilson Center of the Smithsonian Institution, Washington, D.C.
[2]See conversation no. 34.
[3]See conversation no. 46.
[4]See conversation no. 7.

65. Kenneth E. Boulding

Since 1967 Professor Kenneth E. Boulding has been professor of economics and director of the program of research on general social and economic dynamics at the Institute of Behavioral Science of the University of Colorado at Boulder, Colorado.

Kenneth E. Boulding was born in Liverpool, England, in 1910. He received his B.A. from Oxford University. In 1937 he migrated to the United States.

In 1968 he was president of the American Economic Association. Since 1970 he has been president of the Association for the Study of Grants Economy.

He has written some fourteen books, of which we mention *Economic Analysis* (1941), *The Economy of Love and Fear: A Preface to Grants Economics* (1973), *Economics of Peace* (1945), *The Skills of the Economist* (1958), *Principles of Economic Policy* (1959), *Conflict and Defense* (1962), *Disarmament and the Economy* (1963), *The Meaning of the Twentieth Century* (1964), *The Impact of Social Sciences* (1966), *Peace and the War Industry* (1970), and *Economic Imperialism* (1972).

Granted that wolf-crying is dangerous business, would you say, however, that the Club of Rome represents a real wolf? [1]

As I have said in my reviews of *The Limits of Growth* and *World Dynamics*, [2] the Club of Rome has identified a real wolf and his name is "Finitude." If I may be permitted an outrageous pun, however, not even the Forrester knows how far off in the forest he is, or whether he is advancing into the Meadows. The problem here is our inability to predict the future of knowledge, which is the most crucial element in the dynamics of society. This is not an inability which can be overcome by better methods, for it is inherent in the very concept of knowledge. If we could predict what we are going to know in the future, we would know it now—we would not have to wait! This does not prevent us from making useful guesses about the future of knowledge which have some degree of probability of being right, but it does mean that we should always be prepared to be surprised. The record of past predictions is very poor, and there is no reason to suppose that present predictions are any better than past ones.

You have called the world economy an "econosphere." [3]

We have to study the earth as a total system, and our knowledge about this system is still very primitive. In this regard, the natural sciences may be even more backward than the social sciences. We know more about very small things and about very large things than we do about medium-sized things like the earth. We do not know what produced the ice ages, we do not understand the dynamics of the atmosphere, we know very little about the oceans, we really know very little about the long-run dynamics of the biosphere, ecology as a science is not much better than cultural anthropology (interesting stories about strange species!), and we do not even know whether human activity is warming the earth up or cooling it down. There is real danger of a credibility gap developing, especially in the natural sciences, where all sorts of wild statements are being made about things we do not know very much about. The various systems of the earth—the lithosphere, the hydrosphere, the atmosphere, the biosphere, and the sociosphere—each have a certain degree of independence, but we must study their interactions.

We must avoid getting too much trapped in concepts of equilibrium, which is a construct of the human mind unknown in the real world, although a very useful construct, if used properly. The earth has been dominated by evolutionary processes for several billion years. These are fundamentally disequilibrium systems and it would be very surprising if evolution stops. There are indeed limits to growth, especially of any one species, but it is hard to visualize any limits to evolution, short of what Tennyson calls "the one far off divine event towards which the whole creation moves," about which we know very little.

What is wrong, really, with economics as a discipline in the latter part of this century?

What is wrong with economics is its inability to break through a framework of essentially Newtonian type models of equilibrium or very simple dynamics, into an evolutionary model which will throw light on the real dynamic processes of society. Perhaps this is too much to ask economics, for what is needed is a general theory of social dynamics. The Marxian dialectic is an attempt at such a theory, but I believe it to be profoundly wrong. In the long run, society is dominated by evolutionary not dialectical processes, which are, as I have said, just the storms on the evolutionary tide. Dialectical theory, therefore, produces a great deal of illusion, that is, false consciousness, and I think has caused a great deal of human misery. I have no great objections to a profit-seeking economy, if this is interpreted broadly that people are likely to make decisions which they perceive to be to their advantage, and I am profoundly unimpressed with most of the current substitutes for the market, most of which involve the use of threat as a social organizer rather than exchange. I do not think there is moral superiority in threats. On the other hand, we do face a very profound problem in the world of creating a viable world social contract which will produce a dynamic that will move the great obscenities of war, destitution and alienation towards extinction. Neither capitalism nor socialism can do this. Both are obsolete in the light of the real problems of mankind. We now need a period of very hard social thinking and social invention.

Freeman Dyson speaks of the greening of the galaxy; and self-reproducing machines of half a million parts, machines that produce machines; von Neumann had the thing down on paper; Dyson feels it belongs to the probabilities in the future. What would "this cornucopia of science,"[4] as Alexander King[5] has called these developments, do to an ever-increasing world population? Make everyone idle? Will no one work anymore?

I am extremely skeptical about all technological predictions, simply because the record of all past predictions is so bad.

What about the future of computers to assist man finding solutions to his social problems?[6]

Computers being part of technology, my remarks about the inaccuracy of all technological prediction apply here also. So far, I have argued that their impact has not been very great. They are a useful substitute for mathematics, one of the weakest of the sciences, at least in its pencil-and-paper form. I am still waiting for a significant idea to come out of a computer model. Thus, the Forrester[7] models are useful as Delphic oracle, but there are practically no ideas in them that were not in Malthus. In terms of ordinary day-to-day life, so far computers have given us continuous compound interest in banks, easy airline reservations, and have destroyed no doubt a large number of square miles of forest in order to produce unreadable printout. The computer produces information, but information is not the same thing as knowledge. In fact, as I have emphasized, knowledge is usually gained by the orderly loss of information, not by accumulating it; by the filtering out of noise, not by the piling up of data. The computer may well produce more noise than it is worth, but I am prepared to be surprised about this. If the computer can throw real light on the human learning process, it will be worth all the external diseconomics that it seems to produce.

Carl R. Rogers[8] *feels the world is moving into a Skinnerian direction, which he seems to regret.*

The Skinner[9] models are fine for pigeons but not, I think, very good for people, for the very fundamental reason that the value system of a pigeon is largely imprinted in its nervous system by processes of genetic growth, whereas the value systems of man are very largely learned by processes that neither I nor Professor Skinner understand. The Skinner model seems to me to be about as simpleminded as economics, and I have a great deal of faith that the enormous complexity of real people will always outwit the simplicities of the theorist. Still, I think simple models should never be despised. They can always teach us something. They will be more effective teachers, however, if we do not believe them too literally.

From my tour d'horizon *around some seventy men of letters and science I often found incomprehension and at times even utter disdain for each others' theories and work. Dr. Philip Handler (president, National Academy of Sciences) told me that a wide communication gap existed between most scientists: "They would not be able to write down on paper what divides them." How can peace ever be achieved on this shrinking planet if these problems of communication cannot be solved?*

The parceling up of the great republic of learning among the noncommunicating and hostile nationalisms of the disciplines is just as deplorable as the divisions of mankind into noncommunicating and hostile nations and sects. Not that I would abolish either disciplines, nations, or sects, for it is necessary for man to have small communities as well as large, and it is tremendously important to preserve variety of culture, if social evolution is to continue. The growth of knowledge is closely related to the practice of virtue, for instance, the practice of veracity, detachment and humility. Perhaps the greatest enemy of the growth of knowledge is pride, the deadliest of the seven deadly sins, and one to which, alas, the republic of learning is not immune. There is need indeed for middlemen in the knowledge industry. They will be despised, as middlemen usually are, but they will perform an essential function of building up communication among specialists.

Peace, whether in personal relations or in international relations, is something which has to be learned. It requires an evolutionary process in the direction of building up more complex forms of institutions, information, communication, and knowledge. It is now part of the fairly easily accessible evolutionary potential of mankind. This, indeed, is what gives one hope, for evolutionary potential does seem to have a mysterious tendency to be realized; how, we really do not know.

NOTES

[1]Reference to Carl Kaysen, "The Computer that Printed Out WOLF, a Critique on *Limits to Growth*," *Foreign Affairs*, July, 1972. See also conversation no. 11.

[2]Review of Donella H. Meadows et al., *The Limits to Growth*, see *The New Republic*, April 29, 1972, pp. 27-28. See also review of Jay W. Forrester, *World Dynamics*, in *Business and Society Review*, summer, 1972, pp. 106-9.

[3]Kenneth E. Boulding, "The Economics of the Coming Spaceship Earth," reprinted from *Environmental Quality in a Growing Economy, Essays from the Sixth RFF Forum*, Henry Jarrett, ed., published for Resources for the Future, Inc. by Johns Hopkins Press (Baltimore, 1966).

[4]See report by Alexander King to the 1972 annual meeting of the Club of Rome at Jouy-en-Josas, "The Club of Rome—the New Threshold," p. 4.

[5]See conversation no. 16.

[6]See also Robert W. Glasgow's interview, "Aristocrats Have Always Been Sons of Bitches," *Psychology Today*, July, 1973, in which Boulding states, "The crucial element in social systems is not information but knowledge. All a computer does is process information," p. 63.

[7]See conversation no. 34.

[8]See conversation no. 31.

[9]See conversation no. 7.

66. *Daniel Bell*

Professor Daniel Bell is a professor at Harvard University.

He was born in New York City in 1919. He received a Ph.D. from Columbia University in 1960.

Professor Bell was a writer editor of *The New Leader*. He was also labor editor for *Fortune* magazine. In 1969 he joined the faculty at Harvard. He is considered an expert in the history of radical movements in the United States.

Among his books, we mention *Marxian Socialism in the United States* (1952), *The New American Right* (1955), *The End of Ideology* (1960), *The Radical Right* (1963), *Towards the Year 2,000* (1968) and *Capitalism Today* (1971). His latest work is *The Coming of Post-Industrial Society* (1973).

Do you believe that the problems of growth are entering the political consciousness of Western people? Is there a beginning in managing the future with a global point of view?

You terrify me by ending up with the phrase global point of view. You mentioned earlier that somebody had said that I don't think wild enough—

That was William Irwin Thompson of York University, Toronto. [1]

—and now you're asking me to think globally. I am not sure I can think globally in this respect. I think that by training and temperament my inclination is always never to answer a question in its own terms. I won't respond to record your question, but will try to reformulate it. I am not sure the question is growth or not growth or growth used in an abstract way, but the question is always what kinds of growth, and for whose benefit. When people say there should be "limits to growth," I don't know what they mean. When people talk about the pace of change or the acceleration of the pace of change, I really don't know what they mean. They use these terms what we call synthetically, as intransitives, when they should be relational terms. Change of what? Growth for what?

Sometimes it is said one cannot predict the future. I tend to agree because there is no such thing as the future. These futures are different things. There are futures in technology. There are futures of particular countries. But there is no thing so abstract as growth or the future or pace of change or any of these phrases which slip so easily into discourse. My temperamental inclination, as I said, is always to say, let me try to make a distinction and then address myself to any particular dimension of the distinction that you are interested in.

You have written that a society that does not have its best men at the head of its institutions is a sociological and moral absurdity.[2] *The advance world is usually led by the mediocre and not by the top minds. How do you think we can ever get rid of this absurdity? Do we need a political redirection of our institutions?* Limits to Growth *talks about economics and of science and technology, but without substantially changing the direction of politics we don't get anywhere. How to improve the quality of our leadership? Can scientists influence?*

You're asking such difficult questions. If I knew the answers, I suppose I would have written them a long time ago. What I mean is very simply this: I don't know the answer in any realistic sense. What I am trying to do is try to think about how one would begin to go about finding an answer.

I think that it is a truism and quite banal to say that any society reflects the range of distribution of its people. It's very rare that in any society the best come very easily to the top. As you know there is something called a bell-shaped curve, which is a large growth of a sort of hump and then declining. You best use it as the small end of the curve and the people who are at the top of the hump usually are the ones who're most visible and they usually are, technically, the average or the mean. It is very rare to have a society that respects excellence or greatness in this way.

To some extent this is true for the fact that we all live in a bourgeois world, and the very nature of the bourgeois world is to be antiheroic. People who in a sense posture and become heroes are looked at askance. The only place where this has traditionally at all been possible has been the military, where you've had military heroes. They admire a certain degree of admiration. It's quite striking in this country, the only times you've had leadership outside the ordinary, except for one at the crisis situations, have been essentially when you had military heroes. You've had some of the generals who've been the presidents of this country. If you go back to Washington,[3] Jackson,[4] Grant,[5] Harrison[6] or Eisenhower,[7] of course they were all generals. There has been one field in a kind of growing bourgeois society which allows people of this sort to come to the top. It's very rare that you get a man who is a humble man like Lincoln,[8] or a shrewd man or an aristocratic man like Franklin D. Roosevelt,[9] who are able in crucial points to exercise leadership when it's required.

The problem always is what kind of rewards are created for a society. The difficulty has been that given the last two hundred and fifty years, we have created a very unique society in human history, which has been responsible for both the extreme good and the extreme bad. We created a society where the rewards were essentially material rewards. The extreme good of this is that it tends to raise the level of a large group of people who lived terribly miserable lives. I have never believed in romanticizing the past. I think people who talk about the fact that we've left nature and flipped nature are fools. The past has always been for most people in the world very terrible. One only has to read things like the statistics of mortality. Sean O'Casey—I remember his own autobiography—says that the fact is, going back only seventy, eighty years, in the Dublin slums half the children of the women died before the age of five. This was typical and is still typical in so many parts of the Third World. Clearly the whole nature of material advance has been one of the extraordinary benefits of the last two hundred years.

It also meant that we discovered a secret for increasing wealth without war. Before the 1700s and before the 1800s, most societies increased wealth essentially by plundering one another, by tax funding, by war, extortion, and this sort. Back in the early part of the middle of the eighteenth century we began to discover a new secret, called productivity, which is a technique for getting more out of less. This is the whole basis, of course, of the growth of wide-scale modern economies. This became part of bourgeois society too. It's a society which is oriented not to heroism. It's a society which is oriented not to high culture. It's a society which is oriented not to excellence, but essentially to material reward —and the motivations of the people who are at its heads.

Bourgeois society after 1815 managed to grow at the expense of the Third

*World. Without the resources from the Third World we in Western
Europe would never have grown the way we have been growing.*

No, that's not really true. I am not an economic historian. Perhaps
I am out of my depth here, but to a considerable extent the Third World
never entered into any of the economies of the advanced industrial
societies until the end of the nineteenth century, and even then didn't
begin to do so in any substantial way. Certainly there is very little substantial trade with the Asian societies. There is some amount of gold
taken from Latin America. Our majorities of economic growth between
1750 and 1890 were not at all in relation to the Third World. I am not
clear that all trade with the Third World—which itself seems a very loose
term—is essentially negative, or simply exploitative in this particular
way. It depends upon the particular place and time and country.

The Third World is a very loose term and unfortunately a very poor
one. I think any generalization made which tries to encompass all of
Africa, all of Asia and all of Latin America as the Third World is completely misleading and probably does them more harm than any good.
Latin America after all became politically independent in the middle of
the nineteenth century. It entered into the world economy in the middle
of the nineteenth century. My major point is to hold that economic
growth as it began in the Western world, particularly Western Europe
and the United States, was quite independent of the other segments of
the world and to that extent it didn't depend upon developing nations.
The major finding it seems to me was the whole import, of course, of
the technological revolution, like steam, then electricity and the whole
way in which the world transformed from that.

But let me go back to what's involved here, which is the cultural setting. Because what you did was to ask a very unique question in a way,
which people very rarely ask. You took a question like limits to growth
and then you asked a second question about the quality of leadership.
Very few people ever join up what is seemingly a technical-
economic-ecological-resource question with a sociological-psycho-
logical-cultural question. What I am trying to do is to join your two
questions in a kind of a thread. What does join them is that they're both
part of an economic civilization whose values are primarily economic
and whose mould is created by bourgeois society.

The positive side of it is essentially the fact that we have had an extraordinary rise in standard of living, with the Third World in a sense

envying us and they now want to emulate us. But at the same time we in the West saw a rise of a class whose motivations were primarily material rewards, whose motivations were not primarily scholarly, or for intellectual or aesthetic achievements. Historically speaking, I suppose this is—I hate to use the word—the price one pays. I don't think anyone ever sat down and said, Would I belong and pay that kind of price. But this was in fact, as they say in the jargon of sociology, the functional component of the economic sphere. To that extent, I still think of myself sufficiently of a Marxist to say that economics and culture become joint. They join or lock together in a common quality which is essentially here the creation of a new kind of economic civilization. These economic civilizations had both their positive and negative sides. Their positive sides have been the extraordinary explosions of economics and technology. Their negative side has been that they had a class of persons and leadership who normally reflected the highest of human achievements.

Are we moving towards more diversity? Are we moving towards a Skinner[10] method of programming the environment in order to get better people? Are we being pushed toward what John F. Kennedy once coined "voluntary totalitarianism"? Are we moving away from "individual excellence," as you would call it?

Let me not comment on Skinner, because I think that complicates the problems. Skinner deals more on a—what you might call it—a micro-level of society. I think the prevailing tendency—which has been accelerating, if you will, in the last hundred and fifty years—is that we move towards an increasing diversity. What is striking about any modern society is—if you look at this, let's say in Toynbeean terms—is what makes the management of any large-scale society so difficult, to manage the large number of multiple interests which have generated in a society as huge and as complex as it is. You have cultural intelligentsia, scientific intelligentsia, collective farm managers, army people, factory people, planters, what you have got is a multiplication of interests. At the same time you have a multiplication of cultural styles, which cannot be completely resisted. We now have not just obviously a global world, both economically and technologically. You have also an intellectual and cultural globality, which hardly means that you have homogeneity. What we do have here in many ways is the classical illustration of Rome during the time of Constantine, which is what used to be called syncretism.

You have a mingling and jostling of strange gods. People can choose. One thing which upsets people constantly is the fact that their children choose very differently from themselves.

I think to this extent there is an extraordinary situation, an extraordinary explosion, if you will, of diversity in the world and the openness to different styles of life, to different ways of choosing the way in which one wants to live. At the same time there is a different kind of pressure which creates the tension in the world, namely, the increasing need for regulation. If we talk of limits to growth, already you begin to mean that one wants to limit the population of a society. Which means one bars people from having more than three children. Or one can do so effectively by either taxing them, or making it more difficult to simply have more children. One can tax certain kinds of luxury—things like air conditioning—to cut down on use of electric energy. Inevitably we will have a world in which you have, as the economists would call it, more and more externalities. More and more spillover will be generated, which affects everybody else and the result is that one needs more regulation. A hundred years ago perhaps one could drive with horse and buggy down the road and not worry about anybody else. Today you have regulated traffic lights which break the flow of traffic.

One sees here an extraordinary historical problem. People want to be more and more different and encourage multiplicity and diversity. But the very fact of multiplicity and diversity means that you need more and more degrees of regulation, controls, orderliness, in order to allow for that kind of diversity. People don't always want to realize that it becomes a necessary condition for their survival in this particular way. I have always remembered a very shrewd remark of Bertrand de Jouvenel, many years ago, in which he said, "people double their income, they don't feel they're twice as well off as they were before." I think this is one of the important considerations at stake. People double their income and they demand more things. What happens of course is that in France, during the month of August, everybody goes down to the Riviera. Everyone goes down to Lake Annecy, which once was an unspoilt and very pleasant place. It then becomes a hearth of congestion simply by the multiplication of numbers. If you were to say to a Frenchman, "You must not take your vacation in August," he says, "You are interfering with individuality." That may well be, but if you don't interfere with individuality, everybody will then be standing in a crowd, hip and thigh next to each other on the coast of the blue azure.

* * *

Kant wrote that from such crooked wood as human beings are made, nothing exactly straight can be constructed. What is your view of our years ahead?

Since I believe in ending in paradox, I'll tell you a story: Once a man was asked, Are you an optimist or a pessimist? He replied, "I'm an optimist."

"If you're an optimist, why are you scowling?" The man retorted, "Because I don't think my optimism is justified."

NOTES

[1]William I. Thompson, *The Edge of History* (1971), pp. 122-29.
[2]See Anthony Lewis, "The Future of Equality," New York *Times*, November 26, 1972.
[3]George Washington (1732-99), first President of the United States.
[4]Andrew Jackson (1767-1845), seventh President of the United States.
[5]Ulysses S. Grant (1822-85), eighteenth President of the United States.
[6]W. H. Harrison
[7]Dwight D. Eisenhower (1890-1969), thirty-fourth President of the United States.
[8]Abraham Lincoln (1809-65), sixteenth President of the United States.
[9]Franklin D. Roosevelt (1882-1945), thirty-second President of the United States.
[10]See conversation no. 7.

67. Richard A. Falk

Professor Richard A. Falk has been Albert G. Milbank Professor of International Law and Practice at Princeton University, at Princeton, New Jersey, since 1965.

He was born in New York City in 1930. He studied at the University of Pennsylvania, the Yale Law School and the Harvard Law School.

He is also director of the North American section of the World

Order Models Project, World Law Fund. This project represents a global effort of scholars to develop feasible strategies for improving the quality of world order by the end of this century. He is also vice-president of the American Society of International Law and a member of the advisory board of the Fund for Peace and the board of directors of the Foreign Policy Association.

His latest book, *This Endangered Planet* (1971), drew considerable attention among a wide public in the US and abroad. Other works are *Law, Morality, and War in the Contemporary World* (1963), *The Stretgy of World Order,* four volumes, (1961), *Legal Order in a Violent World, The Vietnam War and International Law,* two volumes, (1970, 1971), *The Status of Law in International Society* (1970).

The seventh line of your book This Endangered Planet *mentions already the need for limits. Do you look upon* The Limits to Growth *as a step in the direction of organizing the earth?*

Yes. I think it was an important effort to crystallize people's awareness about two basic facts: that the world is finite, and that the way in which we're managing the planet at the present time is endangering those finite constraints under which the earth has existed for so many centuries. I believe that part of the success of *The Limits to Growth* was a consequence of its reliance on computer technology to convey an authoritative status to its conclusions. Of course, this success also constituted the study's principal vulnerability, because it relied somewhat prematurely on this form of quantitative presentation for what remains still essentially a qualitative argument. Quantitatively, we still lack the data necessary to build a computer-reliable argument about the "limits to growth" that could be used as a basis for reorienting the economy and political order of the planet.

Hugo Grotius, the seventeenth-century Dutch legal philosopher, was the first individual to suggest some sort of international body to organize and enforce international controls. In the meantime, four centuries have elapsed and where are we now? It is one thing for ninety-one nations to sign an agreement in London[1] promising no more oil will be dumped into the oceans, it is quite another to abide by the rule.

My own position is not a law and order position so far as the organization of international society is concerned. It's a strange irony that those who urge law and order for domestic society tend to be the most reactionary forces on international questions. The opposite contradiction often holds too. Those who are the most progressive domestically seem to yearn for a strong structure of order and enforcement on the international level. My own view is that in considering the type of world system that would be most desirable, one has to search for forms of order that have a very strong component of decentralization. A governmental solution is not what we need on a planetary level. What we need is a way of organizing the main functions of human existence around specialized but limited institutions. We need ways to secure a much more just distribution of the world's income and resources. We need ways to make human beings relate independently of the artificial interposition of national boundaries. These things require a new political consciousness, it seems to me, a new human awareness, which has the essential characteristic of moving toward a wider personal identity, eventually built upon the idea of world citizenship and human solidarity.

It has always been said that the United Nations as a tool of international diplomacy would be truly representative of mankind when China would come in. The first thing Peking did was vote against the entry of Bangladesh. Again, power politics played by all major powers. How do you establish rules to the game?

The basic reality of the United Nations is that it represents an extension of statecraft, not an alternative to it, and that it's very problematic as to whether many governments genuinely represent the peoples they claim to speak for. In many cases governments are primarily concerned with keeping themselves in power domestically, and in achieving as good a position in terms of international, political and economic influence as they can internationally. The game of nations is a competitive game with each society trying to maximize its own power, wealth and prestige. Given the finiteness of the world's space and resources, this inevitably means that the only way that one nation can normally gain is at the expense of the others, unless they can all grow simultaneously. The ideology of growth is intimately tied to stability of the state system, because without growth there would be no means to accommodate the separate imperatives of states to maximize their position in the world. Without growth each state could increase its power/wealth base only at the expense of the others. Such a neo-Darwinian image of the world system would deprive governments of any illusion that their separate aspirations were, if moderate, at least potentially compatible. The function of indefinite growth is to sustain the view that the state system need not entail a war of each against each, but that all can develop simultaneously. *The Limits to Growth* undermines the ideology of the state system in this central respect, and this is a notable and progressive contribution.

I don't see any prospect of dealing with the ecological challenge unless at the same time one thinks on a political level about how to reorganize international society in such a way as to displace and moderate the state system. One would not have to eliminate states, but it would be necessary to end their basic organizing relationship to power and wealth, and to dilute or transcend their control over human loyalties and allegiances.

But controlling population growth, pollution or any of these problems remains a matter of legislation and government control. We will always be stuck with laws, either on a national or international plane.

It is correct that we need norms and we need laws to crystallize those community norms and to assure their effective implementation. At the same time I think it's dangerous to assume that the only way to meet the problems of securing equity and equilibrium for the planet is by instituting some kind of a supergovernment that administers the whole of mankind. It is not at all clear to me that governments have the capacity to control human life and resources in a humane way, and therefore one may be creating a kind of Frankenstein in the process of trying to solve the immediate problems we're faced with.

A society like South Africa has worked out a very stable peace system. It has generally effective laws. Its police prevent a great deal of violence from occurring, and yet it is probably one of the worst societies in the world at the present time in terms of most values we hold important.

President Eisenhower held that law was the sole alternative to force in world affairs. Richard Nixon, the brain baby of Eisenhower, walked right into Cambodia which in effect was an illegitimate action in relation to the US Constitution. It looks as if proponents of law and order, whether in Czechoslovakia or in Cambodia, will trample any laws when its fits their purpose.

Richard Nixon is an ideal example of a leader who wants law and order for his own society, in the sense that law and order becomes a code word for police control and for a capacity to resist those groups dissatisfied with the status quo. Internationally, where there is no possibility of law and order of this variant, what Nixon wants is maximum freedom of action to secure the objectives of the United States as he sees them. This has involved a disregard of restraining norms, as for instance, in the case of Cambodia or in the persistent bombing of North Vietnam. Norms that are very well established in the history of international law have no meaning to either the governing group in Washington or, evidently, to governing groups in most parts of the world.

I had an interesting conversation in Hanoi a few weeks ago with the Swedish ambassador, an outstanding man, Jean Christoph Oberg. He was talking about the effects of the bombardments and the effect of European silence in the face of what America was doing in Indochina. He emphasized, properly I thought, the incapacity and indifference of these centers of civilization to the massacre of an innocent people, the willingness to stand aside and let the United States viciously carry on the war and yet conduct business as usual.

From the point of view of international law, American aggression in Southeast Asia entails straight war crimes, as Telford Taylor seems to feel. US warfare in Asia encompasses the worst atrocities ever committed by free society in the history of mankind.

Telford Taylor's views[2] have been changed somewhat by the disclosure of the Pentagon Papers,[3] because part of his hesitancy to attribute responsibility to the policy makers for war crimes in Indochina was based on the fact that he did not have documentary evidence comparable to the captured German war-planning documents used at Nuremberg. With the publication of the Pentagon Papers, one now has an adequate knowledge base, even from Taylor's point of view, to say that the leaders who planned this policy were guilty of, as you say, the most serious war crimes ever committed by a free society, and committed in a context where no serious justification in terms of national survival or even fundamental national interest was involved. It represents gratuitous criminality. Those who were planning the crimes in their air-conditioned offices were not aware and did not want to be aware of the lethal human consequences of what they were doing.

Professor Lifton[4] is publishing articles, for instance in the Saturday Review, *on how the war is being replaced by a kind of push-button war.*

One of the things that our kind of technology is doing is to permit the most frightful kind of behavior to be undertaken in the most cool, detached, and intellectualized way. At the same time the proliferation of high technology creates a kind of awesome vulnerability, as is illustrated a bit by a recent hijacking in which the hijackers threatened to blow up the Oak Ridge nuclear facility and release the radioactivity stored there, supposedly potentially equivalent to a thousand times the radioactive fallout caused by the Hiroshima bomb. With nine hundred of these facilities expected around the United States by the end of the 1980s, one is confronted with, on the one side, an enormously disassociated, technological kind of government where the distance from human values becomes increasingly great and where the computer becomes in a way the substitute for the mind, the spirit of man. On the other side, one is confronted with desperate men, who feel excluded from any kind of participation in this process, who have no hope of gaining their ends by normal means, and who are likely to possess an extraordinary capacity to disrupt the whole system.

Are we moving into the direction of authoritarian rule in order to combat some of the problems you just mentioned?

Yes, I think that's why people who are concerned today have such a sense of urgency. The longer we defer a fundamental reorientation of human consciousness, the more likely we become to seek the implementation of these essentially mad schemes to program the future by creating some kind of macro-learning process that conditions man to behave in accordance with the intentions of those that are doing the programming. It is a form of a kind of ultimate intellectual pride, that the human brain can somehow discover the basis for organizing a tolerable relationship between man and history and man and nature. One of the things that is so essentially needed at the present time is a recognition both of the potentialities and limits of technology, and our desperate need for worldwide ethical revolution. So long as we seek to evolve scientifically, technically, and materially, this new ethical revolution has to be based on a link between our social and political forms, and a reinterpretation of the conditions of human survival, and, hence, it needs to be sustained by a real world-order movement.

And reality?

Such a revolution has to have a kind of biological basis. It has to grasp the fact (and I think it's a fact that underlies the whole effort of the Club of Rome and *Limits to Growth,* as well as the effort of many groups around the world that are outside the established structures of power and wealth) that we need a new synthesis of knowledge and action, as well as a new synthesis of knowledge and feeling. We have both kinds of movements occurring at the present time. I think the MIT *Limits to Growth* effort is one creative response that emphasizes the relationship between knowledge and action, seen in a synthetic frame of mind. The authors have tried to grasp the interrelationship of the whole, because seeing any part is insufficient to understand the whole.

But the other half, which I think someone like William Irwin Thompson[5] is concerned with, is the whole relationship between thought and feeling, and the notion that consciousness, to be grounded in reality, has to take account of much more than the rational capacities of man. In certain ways this effort to probe the limits of consciousness, the rediscovery of the relevance of mystical traditions of thought, of the revival of interest in the way in which more primitive societies related to their environment, all this is part of the discovery of a bio-ethical basis for making the human condition not only survivable but tolerable and benevolent.

There are more conceptions of the future than the Skinner vision[6] of people programmed not to engage in bad deeds. This is a kindergarten vision of the future. Who could want the whole of mankind socialized into a Skinnerian kindergarten? It's not a world I would want to be part of. It's a world that so entraps the imagination and creative spirit of man that, though it's all in the name of utopia, by so seeking one contributes to the worst kind of annihilation of human destiny. There is nothing left to the individual creativity of man, and in that condition, the spirit dies, with no air to breathe. It's clearly a world in which the distinction between suicide and survival is only marginally discernible.

In contrast to the Skinner vision of the future is the World Order Models Project, an exciting collaboration in the work of bio-ethical revolutions. Groups of scholars in Africa, Latin America, India, Japan, Europe, Soviet Union, and the United States are each developing separate models of how to reform the system of world order by the end of the century. For the first time in human history there exists a self-conscious global enterprise, in which all sectors are projecting distinctive proposals for world order that are both visionary and concerned with the politics of change. We believe that the World Order Models Project will begin to provide men in all parts of the world with a basis for hope in the future and with a direction in which to direct their thoughts, feelings, and action, a focus, indeed, for the mobilization of all the vital energies of the human spirit. In this regard, we see the first stage in building a new world order to be one of consciousness-raising, the second to involve mobilization for action, and the third to involve the transformation of the secular institutions that now control power and wealth.

Efforts of the Club of Rome are aimed at increasing human awareness of the condition of the planet in this late hour. Communication satellites would tremendously add to the increase of human knowledge around the planet if used properly. The Soviets have threatened to shoot satellites down that would bring unacceptable information through its borders. Here we have a further legal problem of "visas for ideas."

I think that the underlying objective of trying to make ideas as mobile as possible in the decade or so ahead is one of the progressive forces in the world. Anything that cuts down on mobility is a reactionary impulse. But one has to recognize that a government like the Soviet government which is in a hostile relationship to its own population, cannot tolerate that kind of planetary mobility. It operates a closed society as part of the effort by Soviet rulers to keep control. How else does one maintain the degree of conformity in thought, feeling and action that the leaders in the Soviet Union feel necessary?

For this reason my own sense is that progress toward realizing a vision of the future in which notions like the *Limits to Growth* and a new world order become meaningful depends on prior changes within the principal domestic societies in the world; these are the critical arenas for world-order change. Progressive social change domestically, whether in the United States or in Europe or the Soviet Union, is the best hope that we have for a positive future. Progressive forces will have to gain access to power in order to reorient the centers of decision that run our planet. It is naive optimism of the most dangerous kind to think that the regressive elites that are in control of the predominant power structures in the world today are going to provide the moral and political leadership to generate a world that we would want our children and grandchildren to live in. Essentially these leaders of today are concerned with sustaining their own positions of power and privilege in relation to people that are poorer and weaker and victimized in different ways. It is these sorts of regressive relationships that tend toward social and political rigidity. It is terribly important that in the next decade or so we try to animate the change-oriented forces within principal societies in the world and hope that these forces gain enough access to power to reshape the way in which national governments envision their own well-being.

Until that happens I just don't think we can do more than prepare individuals to face unpleasant realities unflinchingly about the prospects of the future. I can see no hope in the present world power structure of securing real changes of the fundamental sort that are predicated on the basis of an analysis like that offered by the Club of Rome, which I agree with. I hope that the Club of Rome will begin to think seriously about tactics and strategies of change and about the politics and ethics of a new equilibrium between man and the capacities of the planet.

NOTES

[1]November 13, 1972.

[2]See Telford Taylor, US chief counsel at the Nuremberg war-crimes trial, *Nuremberg and Vietnam: An American Tragedy*, Quadrangle Books (Chicago, 1970).

[3]*The Pentagon Papers: The Secret History of the Vietnam War*, first published in the New York *Times*, Quadrangle Books (Chicago, 1971). A massive top-secret history of the United States' role in Indochina, ordered by Robert S. McNamara, then secretary of defense, on June 17, 1967.

[4]See conversation no. 23.

[5]See conversation no. 68.

[6]See conversation no. 7.

68.   *William I. Thompson*

Professor William I. Thompson teaches humanities at York University in Toronto, Canada.

He was born in Chicago, Illinois, in 1938. He attended Pomona College in California and received his Ph.D. at Cornell University in Ithaca, New York, in 1966. He has taught at Cornell, MIT and is now at York University. His sharp criticism of the Massachusetts

Institute of Technology is summed up in Chapter 3, "Getting Back to Things at MIT" in his latest book *At the Edge of History, Speculations on the Transformation of Culture* (1971).

He has written in recent years numerous articles, on the Op Ed page of the New York *Times,* and for various magazines, among them *Harpers,* "The Individual as Institution," September, 1972.

Would you agree with Erik H. Erikson[1] that man can no longer afford to cultivate illusions about his own [nature] or about that of his species or for that matter about those [pseudospecies] he calls his enemies?[2]

I think the threat of planetary annihilation is generating a response in terms of what Toynbee[3] called "challenge and response." Some of the illusions about the nature of reality we have are part of the old kind of industrial-managerial period, namely, that nature is dead, that you can work your will upon it, that nature is a void to be developed and turned into parking lots and Tokyos and things of that sort. As we move in a different direction of culture we are coming up with a radically new concept of a nature, mind, self and society. It's a question of a quantum leap in human evolution.

For example, one of the old illusions maintained by industrial society was that the world was split between nature (which was dead, inert matter) and consciousness (which was subjective and unreal and full of mere feeling). Feeling was never to be trusted because feeling was not real. Feeling would tell us that a forest was pretty and should be preserved, but reality with its economics showed that there was a profit to be made. Therefore, man was trained in industrial society to ignore his feelings, his body, the lower classes, the problems of poverty and things of this sort, and to move in a brave, masculine way, developing reality everywhere he could. Now, the illusion that reality is the split between matter and consciousness is absolutely false. It's more like a continuum in which there is mass, there is energy and then there is consciousness. You can slide back and forth in this continuum. Consciousness can now have a direct effect upon mass.

The way we've discovered this is the way human beings generally do, negatively. For example, take the planet: There is clearly negative feedback, coming in the way of pollution, telling us we are destroying the planet. We can see we're having an effect on nature because we are poisoning and destroying it to the point of destroying ourselves. Yet we cannot imagine that this is a situation in which there are linked opposites. We can see the feedback of consciousness on nature; we call it culture. In more positive ways, we can now detect the emergence of a new planetary culture which is totally redirecting the relationship of the mind and nature.

The Hopi[4] in their ancient culture could grow corn in the deserts through the focusing of psychic energy. Uri Geller is a psychic from Israel. He is here in the United States at the present moment working at various think tanks and scientific research facilities, proving to the satisfaction of physicists—of, say, Feinberg in New York—that through psychic energy he can twist and bend and break metal bars. This was performed in the office of the president of Kent State University. It was performed in New York and there is now research going on in California. How can this be? This violates the whole notion of the mind's relationship with nature. Nevertheless, scientists, some fifty years ago, in the quantum theory in physics, told us that the observer interferes with the system that he observes, that we must take the mind's relationship to nature into reality in any kind of science.

Now, industrialists have constantly distorted science and have said: "No this is not true. Nature is economics. Nature is strictly dead matter. Fancy theories and quantum mechanics should be ignored." The problem we have is not that the humanists are not being scientific enough, but that the people who apply and use science for power are prostituting science and totally ignoring the implications of science itself to create a kind of managerial technology that has very little to do with nature.

When people talk about solving the problem of human culture through the application of science—say, in the terms of Skinner[5] or Delgado's[6] psychocivilized society—they are continuing this abuse of true science. Science, as it has been institutionalized in the structures of an industrial managerial society, is a great threat to human culture, because for the first time in human history we're seeing an elite group of people attempting to replace human culture with management and behavioral science. This is part and parcel of industrial society.

Let me give an example: When industrial society first celebrated its own power in the great exhibition in London in 1851, there was a great crisis in the city about what to do with the trees in Hyde Park. What they decided finally was not to cut them down but to build the whole iron and glass structure around the trees. What happened in fact on an unconscious level was that human culture was saying for the first time, "Let culture surround nature." We can put nature in the park inside culture because we now control and dominate nature.

It was McLuhanism?[7]

Hegel actually. Earlier than McLuhan. McLuhan has never given Hegel the proper credit. The particular dialectic that goes on by which the sloughed-off environment becomes a work of art in a new environment is Hegel.

Now, there is research going on at Stanford Research Institute about how to deal with crisis management and how to anticipate the future. What are the forces of cultural change? How do the system of values, motivation and mythic images of man determine man's behavior and interrelationships with one another? The purpose of this is to create a larger structure, called management, and through this management science will better understand the image of man, how human culture works and then be able to take a system-analysis approach to it and draw into the structure of management everything that used to be other to it. Culture will then operate on terms dictated by behavioral science.

You are referring to Platt's[8] *work in Stanford?*

Yes, John R. Platt is a perfect example of this. He is a man of good will. This is not enough anymore because men of good will have illusions, and their illusions can generate greater problems than the ones they try to solve. Platt's approach in *What We Should Do* is that we have to have a kind of crash program on the planet. A Manhattan project. Get together all the experts who really know the problem, and they will fix the planet up for us. In many cases the experts are the very ones who create the problems we have. It is like a physician attacking the body with heart transplants and then when the body rejects these, the physician comes in and starts injecting powerful drugs and continuing the attack on the body until eventually the patient is practically at the edge of death. Never at any point does the physician turn back and say, the body is a harmonious, organic system, I am actually with my cures antagonizing the whole disease itself. Platt's is a classic example of this. I think he is definitely a prisoner of the old paradigm. (In the use of the word paradigm I am of course thinking of Thomas Kuhn's *Structures of Scientific Revolutions.*[9] There is clear evidence that there is a new paradigm emerging in which the mind's relationship to nature is different.)

Let's explain this in another way: If we had a universe that was all nature, all matter and no minds in it, it would be a sort of smoothly indifferent universe working according to mechanical laws, which is pretty much what most people think the universe is anyway. Minds on earth are the casual byproducts of dust in an insignificant planet in an insignificant corner of the universe. If we took this material universe and we introduced into its system minds that had a consciousness of nature and nature's laws through mathematics and science, the new universe could no longer be the same universe. Because now there would be a being in it conscious of it and that would radically alter and totally change the universe itself. It would become a totally new system. Minds generate feedback on nature and begin to change nature. What we call the feedback of consciousness on nature is culture. Now culture, according to the old paradigm, is emotional, is feeling, is subjective and isn't really very important; what is important is the economic, technical and material base of the culture. This constitutes the ruling notion for all the social and most of the physical sciences. The difficulty is we don't realize—or perhaps we are now only beginning to realize it now because of the ecological crisis—that the impact and feedback of culture back on nature is so powerful that it can actually change the structure of nature itself to the point of, say, nuclear energy or nuclear fusion.

We're seeing this in the planetary crisis because our culture is now visible in the polluted air. It was never visible before. When we used to talk about culture, it was located in some island or in some city. There wasn't any sense of a planetary culture. Therefore, the planetary feedback, the negative feedback of pollution, is making everyone critically aware that culture *is,* that it is intensely powerful and if we are not careful that it can actually destroy nature. In this sense human culture is a system of consciousness, of mathematics and forms of pure symbolism. We think nothing material can affect the very structure of matter itself or can change it. But this is an invasion of reality. We can almost say that the *object* of the universe is almost not as important and powerful as the *subject* of the universe, because by manipulating symbols we can imitate stars through thermonuclear fusion and can change the finite.

This should really send us back to the drawing board to say, "All right, if the mind's relationship to nature is so critically important, how do we best understand this relationship? John R. Platt would say, "We get together all the scientists because they clearly understand the manipulation of symbols and mathematics." But what do we do with those anomalies outside the scientific paradigm like the Israeli psychic who is twisting metal bars through psychic energy? I don't think the technocrats, the managerial people, see the anomalies. They reject them and say, "The old paradigms are adequate." But they are prisoners of industrial society. All they can do is have greater and greater government grants for greater and greater think tanks, for greater and greater confusion in terms of paper and xeroxing machines and the endless multiplication of data until they burn themselves out in an informational overload.

And the Skinner theory of engineering the environment?

I don't think this is going to solve the problem at all because the problem is simpler and more elegant. I don't think culture can be managed. When you have cultural engineering, you have a reduction of culture. We always seem in a sense to be talking about merely social structure. Culture is more than social structure, it is forms of consciousness and art. In many ways the truly cosmic perception that understands the relationship of mass, energy and consciousness is not really contained within the paradigm of, say, behavioral engineering.

I was talking to Carlos Castaneda,[10] recently, who has written the three very popular and significant books on the ancient Yaqui way of knowledge, of the views of the sorcerers of archaic Mexico. He is one of a number of esoteric thinkers that are introducing us into a new planetary culture, the hitherto secret techniques of small cultures. What's going on now in this planetary culture is that the old, esoteric techniques for the transformation of consciousness, the Hopi, the Indian, and now even the ancient British, are all being reintroduced into public knowledge. We now will have an understanding of things that were kept very secret. As has happened with Carlos Castaneda's books—now half a million people have read about the techniques of sorcery of a very old Indian in the north of Mexico. (He is called Don Juan.) I think it really is very significant. This Don Juan tells us that the trouble is when we die, we die with the totality of ourselves. Unfortunately we only live with a very small, insignificant fraction of ourselves. We will have to learn to live in the moment with the totality of ourselves and balance the enormity of our death with the enormity of our life.

If we take this on a planetary scale and blow it up, we can see that the planet in the next fifty years (I am quoting the Club of Rome) is dying with the totality of itself. Through Anglo-Dutch Petroleum and Standard Oil, people in villages in India and everywhere will die because the air will die. Once we go down, mankind goes down with the totality of itself. The difficulty is that at the moment we are only living with an insignificant portion of ourselves. We are living with the elite sort of industrial notions of the few technocrats and managers and experts, who are attempting to replace the vast panorama of all human culture with a single kind of vision, that of the multinational corporation.

This is not the totality of culture. Ironically, it's an illusion. It's an extension of the managerial vision, the multinational corporations are obviously going to continue to develop, to pollute and to think in industrial terms. They cannot stop. They cannot change their minds. The young scientists who are now coming up will simply shift their allegiancies to the new paradigm and begin to create a whole new revolution in science.

Young graduate students and scientists are doing precisely this. While World War II warriors like Walt W. Rostow[11] or Herman Kahn[12] are projecting simple managerial trends, the graduate students in science are shifting to Sufi'ism, Zen, yoga and psychic healing. These are the five hundred thousand people that are reading the books of Carlos Castenada. These people are trying to put nature, culture and consciousness into an entirely new relationship. There's greater promise for the future in this new blend of science and mysticism than there is in the behavorial approaches of Delgado, Skinner or John Platt.

The problem is that we have been denied our birthright in science; the tradition of science in the Western world from the seventeenth century is the great mystical tradition of men who had a truly cosmic consciousness. I am thinking of Kepler,[13] who was a mystic; of Newton,[14] who was a mystic involved with the computations of the prophecies of Daniel[15] and the measurements of the temple in Jerusalem; of Pascal;[16] of Descartes.[17] All of these men were "spaced out," in the jargon of the contemporary world. What happened is that when these charismatic visionaries passed on their birthright and their heritage, their descendants inherited the results, which routinized their charisma and created institutions where the mediocre could be trained.

Out of this entire process the greatness of science was made effective on managerial development and technology. That was very useful for a while and helped spread the scientific tradition around the world through the British empire. Yet, we have now reached the point when this has become a threat. We have to go back to our original scientific tradition of the seventeenth century, which Whitehead called the century of genius, and realize that there's more to science than just simply managerial behaviorism. The irony is that those who are spokesmen for the scientific solution of our planetary crisis are, in terms of, say, the physical sciences, very bad scientists. If you were to take the theory of science in the philosophy of Skinner and you attempted to relate it to, for instance, the philosophy of nature, you would see that the assumptions in Skinner are incredibly naive, very nineteenth-century mechanistic and have very little to do with, say, quantum mechanics or the most advanced scientific thought of today. Even nowadays there are many great scientists who are, for a lack of a better word, very *mystically* oriented.

Many of the hippy young students are rejecting science because they think it's evil. When they look at science, they think of industrial science and see Skinner, Delgado, Platt and Herman Kahn. This is a tragedy because they are moving into a groovy mindlessness as a solution to our planetary problem, getting involved in drugs and other sorts of things. If they really were properly educated about the spaced-out traditions of mystical and contemplative science, they could see that there is not really a conflict between the best of the human tradition in art and mathematics.

The aim should be to bring science and mysticism back together again. To do this we have to change totally our forms of education and move away from industrial education. This is why I have criticized MIT[18] so much. MIT is, if anything, responsible for the illusion that science is mechanistic and positivistic and has attempted to deny the creative, the imaginative and the visionary in science for the sake of making a profit. We have to gather up all these anomalies in mysticism, psychic healing and psychokinesis and build together a new image of man and a new sense of the relationship of mass, energy and consciousness. This is what is happening. It is very clearly going on in the planetary city of Auroville in India. It is going on in the community of Findhorn in the north of Scotland. We don't have to worry about it, in the sense of asking the question, Can we get a committee of experts to recharge culture? Culture is taking care of it.

This is what Soleri[19] tries to do in his Arizona experiment—

That's right. Soleri himself is attempting to take a planetary, a visionary sense of what must be done in terms of remaking the city of man—

And Illich[20] for the educational angle—

Illich is trying to change it without changing it in terms of consciousness. It is not enough to move away from schools and have experts fly down to Cuernavaca. They remain the same kind of educators. Cuernavaca turned into another think tank, a humanistic think tank. A think tank just like Herman Kahn's think tank. We have to speak in terms of the specific forms of the transformation of consciousness by which we relearn: Who we are and where we come from and where we are going.

And you feel that the East might have a very strong influence in achieving these goals in the West?

We cannot simply go back and become Indians. This is why we have to search for mysticism in our scientific tradition by rediscovering that Newton was a mystic. If we would really understand the relationship between mass, energy and consciousness, we can see three states of being in it. For most people mass is what their body is, a hunk of meat. They have no other consciousness than being reduced to mere organs. Some people regain respect for the body through yoga, and learn that the body is a field of energy and vitality. They discover a whole new system of awareness. If you continue this process and become aware of subtler and subtler forms of consciousness, then I think the individual begins to discover the feedback of consciousness on nature and that nature can be redirected through consciousness. This is very much related to the work of Paolo Soleri, who talks about the spiritualization of matter. This is also related to the ideas of Teilhard de Chardin.

There are places in the planet, spaces, where this new paradigm of nature, self and society is emerging. I myself see a greater hope for the future in Auroville in India, which is not just an Indian city. A French architect is building it. There are three hundred American students there doing the physical labor. It is a planetary city dedicated to planetary culture. I see more hope for the future coming out of Auroville than the Stanford Research Institute or John R. Platt's Manhattan Project of technocrats who are going to solve all our problems by designing the final cultural container for man—his tomb.

NOTES

[1]US psychologist of Danish origin, now professor of human development and lecturer on psychiatry at Harvard University.

[2]*Gandhi's Truth: On the Origins of Militant Nonviolence,* W. W. Norton and Company (New York, 1969), p. 51.

[3]See conversation no. 5.

[4]North American Pueblo tribe.

[5]See conversation no. 7.

[6]See conversation no. 38.

[7]See conversation no. 12.

[8]See conversation no. 9.

[9]*Toward an International Encyclopedia of Unified Sciences,* University of Chicago Press (Chicago, 1962).

[10]American author of *The Teachings of Don Juan: A Yaqui Way of Knowledge* (1968), *A Separate Reality* (1971), and *Journey to Ixtlan* (1972). These books reflect conversations between Castaneda and a mysterious old Yaqui Indian from Sonora, Mexico, called Juan Matus. As of March, 1973, *The Teachings* had sold 16,000 copies a week in the United States alone. See also *Time* magazine cover story, March 5, 1973.

[11]White House adviser to President John F. Kennedy and President Lyndon B. Johnson, closely linked to the sending of more than half a million US troops to Vietnam. Mr. Rostow told the author during a meeting at the White House in 1961, "We will not abandon one square mile of Asian territory to the Communists."

[12]See conversation no. 46.

[13]Johann Kepler (1571-1630), German astronomer.

[14]Sir Isaac Newton (1642-1727), British mathematician and philosopher who formulated and proved the law of gravity.

[15]Jewish captive and prophet living in Babylon.

[16]Blaise Pascal (1623-62), French philosopher, mathematician and physicist.

[17]René Descartes (1596-1650), French philosopher and mathematician.

[18]*At the Edge of History,* pp. 48-73.

[19]See conversation no. 10.

[20]See conversation no. 32.

69. *Joseph E. Slater*

Mr. Joseph E. Slater is president of the Aspen Institute for Humanistic Studies.

He was born in Salt Lake City, Utah, in 1922. He studied at the University of California at Berkeley, where he taught economics in 1942-43. From 1949 to 1952 he worked in the office of the high commissioner in Bonn, Germany. In 1959 he was secretary to President Dwight D. Eisenhower's Commission on Foreign Assistance (Draper Committee). President John F. Kennedy appointed Mr. Slater deputy Assistant Secretary of State for education and cultural affairs. From 1968 to 1972, Mr. Slater was trustee of the Salk Institute at La Jolla, California. Mr. Slater also is a member of the Council of Foreign Relations in New York and member of the Institute of Strategic Studies in London.

I understand that at the Aspen Institute as a follow-up of the Club of Rome efforts, a study of the planet as a whole is being initiated.

Not quite, but it's certainly a related activity. The Aspen Institute was involved with a number of the people of the Club of Rome as they were working on their report. For example, we had Jay Forrester,[1] Aurelio Peccei[2] and other people to discuss the character of planning systems and analyses of resources. We are concerned with many of the same elements and objectives as they were. I personally felt what the Club of Rome was doing was really *an introduction to the character of growth* rather than an exclusive concern on certain finite limits to growth. Growth needs to be broken down in terms of qualitative and quantitative growth, with different mixtures in different places at different stages of development. We had certain differences, but I think the Club of Rome provided enormous impetus to a debate that is imperative in the world today. It began to present a global perspective that was missing. Specifically, what the Aspen Institute has done following the Club of Rome report is as follows:

We have established a working group primarily concerned with alternative choices in the United States. We are proposing to take approximately twenty-five or thirty professionals over a period of years to work in certain key areas concerned with different sectors of the society. These experts will, with very careful and deep analyses of choices, present the choices to the government and the public which may be available to this society. They would define the primary, secondary and tertiary implications of those choices. We're concerned with alternatives and choices rather than just finite goals. We are trying to get this work done and presented so that the executive and legislative branches of government and the leadership elements in society will be forced to have more thoughtful and mindful debates about the choices that might otherwise be available to society. Most importantly we will study the implications of real choices, because we think that just stating a goal is too static and somewhat an empty exercise. To force a deeper debate and analyses of choices is a dynamic process which is essential in any state and particularly in a democratic state. We are trying to bring together those persons in diverse communities who are expert in systems analyses and disciplined scientific thinking. They will be forced to work with those leaders, politicians, communicators, sociologists, lawyers and judges and so forth, who are dealing in judgments, with intuitions, and frequently with nonrational processes. This is the area where most decisions are taken, and on this is where major things are not quantifiable and never will be.

What we are trying to do is build a closer bridge between those disciplined in scientific work and systems analyses and the community of decision makers who must know how to use and not abuse such materials. The principal problem is how to find an improvement in these materials and replace the present glaring over the fence in an adversary relationship between those people who have to make political and other decisions based on nonquantifiable insights and those dealing with quantifiable data. We need to build a national and world community of persons who can think through the implications of major decisions where more disciplined thinking is needed.

It seems to me the Club of Rome has provided a useful beginning in this area. Over the next years and decades there must be a greater perfection of systems analyses and of the disciplined scientific mind. Scientists have to be able to work more harmoniously with leaders concerned with social and human inputs. That is the first objective. The second objective is to put the results of the best analyses we can make, not in any single institution, but by orchestrating the efforts of many institutions, including leading individuals, consumer and other movements (and not just organized institutions like universities). Alternative systems should deal with major sectors such as energy, agriculture, population, education and communication, the economy and society. Alternate systems should put these analyses in a readily understood form, to enlighten public debate and force the executive and legislative branches of government to debate and examine all those aspects of choices which must be made understandable. This is certainly essential in a democratic country. I think it is essential in any society which wants to make more mindful choices and which wants to know the implications of the alternate choices. We think it is impossible to carry out such work on a state or national basis without relating the data and insights to the global setting. One cannot deal with energy or any of these subjects unless it is in a global setting. That is where we come back to the Club of Rome and the kinds of things that Tinbergen[3] and many others are pursuing. At Aspen we definitely hope to build bridges to those communities throughout the world and have their inputs available.

As I said earlier, we intend not only to involve the traditional institutions—for example, university and research institutions, government bureaucracy, and so on—but also we try to reach (not just for consultation but actual involvement) women, youth, consumers and individuals, including people like Ralph Nader[4] and others, who are becoming institutions in themselves. Many have alternatives different from those of the fixed institutions.

That is, if one would take only those alternatives that came to mind of fixed, existing, traditional institutions, one would come up with one set of alternatives. If one were to go broadly into this society, it might offer quite different alternatives. For example, some persons might break up into regions or do away with certain kinds of schooling or combine communication and education into a learning process. We don't want to be captured by the alternatives that might now be in the minds of fixed or traditional institutions; we must get out into these new movements to explore the alternatives available.

Also, we have to avoid the trap of a statesman or an elected official putting up two or three phony alternatives and one real one as a way of making sure the real one that he wants is accepted. We must ensure a tremendous integrity in such debates and in the analyses of the hard data. Our intention is to create a free-standing institution that is free of government but working with it and getting data, insights, ideas, and so forth from it. (One that is financed outside of government so that it is not beholden to any particular system or party and which tries to orchestrate the best thinking from the different sectors of the society whether quantifiable or not.) Values, priorities and attitudes and even irrationalities play an enormous part in human affairs. They must be taken into account.

* * *

Do you believe that the material that the Aspen Institute will collect would be a variable to improve the Forrester model of MIT with?

We like the idea of a consortium with maybe twenty or thirty universities, with MIT and we hope with many others. Certainly we want to stay in touch with the people who did the Club of Rome report, as well as with some of the people who criticized it. Still, I think the debate started by the Club of Rome has many times payed off, irrespective of whether one agrees with one or another aspect of its particular findings.

In other words, the Club of Rome, Aurelio Peccei, is in contact with you on the subject of this new institution?

Yes, many of its members are involved, certainly Aurelio Peccei, Meadows and other people who have our paper. We have made it as widely available as we can, because in the process of deciding whether to set up such an institute, we have to get the best thinking of which people are capable.

The Aspen Institute is not beholden to any particular sector of society. The institute has internationalized its board, staff, mentality and programs. We have picked six areas of concern that are interrelated: communications and society; education in a changing society; science, technology and humanism; justice and the individual; environment and the quality of life; and international affairs. In these six areas we are arranging workshops leading to action. The Aspen Institute brings together people from different parts of society to try to think through more mindfully the implications of alternatives and make suggestions for specific actions and results.

The United Nations is piling up millions of words in reports and documents. In what way are you hopeful that the Aspen Institute, the Club of Rome or MIT won't be adding more and more paper to this tower of Babel?

I mentioned in my previous remarks that a few of us worked for several years on the creation of an institution which is now in existence. It is the International Federation of Institutes for Advanced Study, IFIAS. We have taken approximately twenty-four very high-quality institutions from around the world, such as the Pasteur Institute, the Nils Bohr Institute of Physics, the Woods Hole Institute of Oceanography, the University Corporation for Atmospheric Research, the Aspen Institute, the Japan Economic Research Center, and have combined them into a federation which has three main functions: The first is to conduct joint research on transnational, transdisciplinary problems; the second is to exchange faculty and postdoctoral students; the third is to plan each year five years ahead, so that the institutions' plans start to conform and in time form a *de facto* university or institution (without a campus to be sure). I think with this pattern at work IFIAS can deliver quality and operationally can be related to the problems of the UN. It can work with forceful leaders like Maurice Strong[5] who is building bridges between institutions of quality (particulary existing ones of quality) which are willing to pioneer in transnational, transdisciplinary work. We can avoid a proliferation of structures within the UN and avoid many bureaucratic rigidities. IFIAS had its first meeting in Trieste in October, 1972, and its members agreed on the programs mentioned above.

No doubt the skill of Mr. Maurice Strong is due to his great managerial experience in private business. That is perhaps why we approach perhaps a more manageable world.

First, he is an effective manager. Also, he is a man who is open to ideas and new ways of doing things. He seeks out capable people, no matter where they are. He is not concerned whether a person comes from business, labor, the academic sect, the UN or wherever. He tries to orchestrate people of varied backgrounds into a team. I think his genius is his energy, devotion and willingness to have his pores open to ideas and to people. That way he gets the support of people who are loyal to what he is doing and wins their friendship and commitment to a better world order.

NOTES

[1]See conversation no. 34.
[2]See conversation no. 70.
[3]See conversation no. 3.
[4]Leader of the most controversial group of young investigators in the United States ("a citizen army nearly one thousand strong"), which has examined not only the safety of General Motors automobiles but has published its latest report, *Who Runs Congress?* Bantam (New York, 1972).
[5]See conversation no. 30.

70. Aurelio Peccei

At his request, this last and concluding conversation was reserved for Aurelio Peccei, chairman and founder of the Club of Rome.

Aurelio Peccei was born in Torino, Italy, in 1908. He received his doctorate summa cum laude at the University of Torino.

In 1930 he joined the Fiat Automobile Company. He was sent to China prior to World War II. Since 1950 he has been a member of the management committee of Fiat. He has been head of the Latin American division and chairman of the board of Fiat Concord in Argentina (one of the largest industries in Latin America).

At present he is also managing director of Italconsult, one of the foremost engineering and consulting firms in the world, with headquarters in Rome.

From 1964 to 1967 he was appointed president and chief executive of the Olivetti Company. On completing his mission he was retained in 1967 as vice-chairman. Dr. Peccei is also founder of Adela, an international investment company created to promote development and private initiative in Latin America. He is chairman of the economic committee of the Atlantic Institute in Paris.

In 1968 Aurelio Peccei founded the Club of Rome.[1]

Parts of Dr. Peccei's remarks have appeared in a special report prepared by Dr. Peccei with the collaboration of Dr. Manfred Siebker, at the request of the economic committee of the parliamentary assembly of the Council of Europe.

It must have been a sad experience for you, after the enormous effort and work put into The Limits to Growth, *to find so much criticism and abuse, especially in the beginning when the study became known.*

Not at all. Only a fool does not expect criticism and abuse when he caricatures or satirizes self-righteous mores, or exposes false values and takes a radical stand against conventional wisdom—or demystifies nothing less than the sacred goddess of growth presiding over our mercantile society. In other times, it would have been even worse—lapidation or crucifixion. It is not that the Club of Rome has the vocation of martyrdom. It is simply determined to raise the devil out of the climate of complacency and improvidence which accompanies our collective race towards ever graver crises. When it asked MIT to run this project, it believed that the time had come to bring world public opinion and decision makers face to face with the extreme alternatives of our age.

I for one welcome even the most bitter criticism as a part of the ordeal our generation has to go through to reappraise realistically the changed condition of man in his world; though I feel unhappy that only marginal, episodic or sectoral criticism has so far been leveled at the MIT report. No critic has yet disproved the existence of a fundamental mismatch between headlong human proliferation and insatiability, which are dominant traits of present-day society, and our planet's limited, vulnerable carrying capacity.

I want, moreover, to say that no criticism has in any way weakened the importance of the MIT pilot world-simulation model as a tool to break down a situation of stagnant, wishful thinking. The Club of Rome conceived this project as a commando operation, to be followed by a larger deployment of activities. Its success in this sense is undeniable. After the first shock waves, a new kind of discourse is under way in practically every part of the world; new dimensions and dynamics, inconceivable, say, one year ago, are added to our thinking. The most hope-inspiring fact—and something indeed amazing—is the serious and profound debate on the modern world *problématique* which has now seized even personalities of the highest responsibility in politics, industry and science, for instance in your own country, the Netherlands, where, as you well know, the Club of Rome study played a considerable role in the November, 1972, elections.

You mention leading politicians and ruling circles. But at the base of all societies, we find workers. The youth federation of labor unions in the Netherlands organized a special congress to discuss Limits. *They feel that while you and the Club of Rome seem to work from the top down, their task is to assist in changing the social infrastructure of society, without which they think the* problématique *you and your colleagues have brought to the attention of mankind will never be truly and effectively tackled.*

Actually, we went over the heads of the world establishment—and academic circles as well—and talked straight to the people. The tremendous popular success of the book in many languages, the hundreds and thousands of conferences, articles and public meetings which give vitality to the debate it has set off in all continents in the space of a few months, and the participation in it everywhere of ordinary citizens of different conditions and convictions, show that this is not a case of a summit exercise; and that a movement of opinion, although still confused, is in the offing.

The Club of Rome has always maintained that a change of heart and mind coming from the grass roots of the people itself, and certainly not from countries of Western culture only, is needed if mankind and the different but interdependent societies which compose it are going to extricate themselves from the present predicament and follow a new, safer and saner course. This is tantamount to a cultural and societal metamorphosis which cannot be based on other than a widespread awareness that a change of direction has become indispensable to maintain reasonable control over our destiny and so as not to preempt our children and grandchildren from having a similar chance. Let me, however, say that labor leaders and youth leaders do not always act in a way that fosters this new consciousness among the people, who look to them for inspiration, if not guidance.

Actually then, the Club of Rome might have assisted in promoting a new kind of human solidarity?

This is one of our aims. The limited spheres of solidarity which still exist today as a legacy from the past—and which have the dimensions of a city, a nation, a race, a religion—are incongruous in the technological age that has just begun. I submit that the concept of the oneness of mankind, which was initially embraced only by certain liberal spirits, thanks to the work of groups like ours is now dawning upon young and old men and women of diverse culture, language and tradition, who feel that for good or evil they are united by organic bonds with the entire texture of life on this small earth—including people of different culture, language, and tradition. All of them are beginning to grasp that "one world or no world"—the World Federalists' motto—has a ring of truth about it and is not mere rhetoric.

You have mentioned that the human condition has changed. What do you mean?

Yes, man's condition is fundamentally changed in his world. He is now called upon to fulfill a new cybernetic role in it. On the one hand, he has reached such a dominant position in the ecosystem that he is compelled to take upon himself regulative and normative functions heretofore left to the inscrutable designs of nature and providence. This requires exceptional new qualities of "ecological wisdom," both words being used in the broadest sense. On the other hand, man has created such an integrated and intricate human system that its regulation and functioning can no longer be trusted to automatic mechanisms. Man himself must manage the system, developing hitherto unimaginable qualities of "sociopolitical wisdom." "His role, whether he wants it or not," as Sir Julian Huxley[2] has said, "is to be the leader of the evolutionary process on earth, and his job is to guide and direct it in the general direction of improvement." Man has to realize his responsibility as the true "cybernete," the pilot and helmsman, governor of "Spaceship Earth"—which is at present drifting along dangerously. This is the true challenge to our generation. The longer we hesitate in recognizing it, the more reduced the options become for us and the next generations.

With respect to our environment, we must prepare for self-restraint and self-discipline, and direct our knowledge and technology rather towards protecting nature, or what is left of it, and other forms of life, instead of overexploiting them. In the social, political, and economic order, we must see the collective good take precedence. Individual initiative and profit must become subordinate.

Here you seem to approach a socialist concept of society, and perhaps even Skinner's concept[3] of reevaluating such worn-out concepts as "freedom and dignity."

Whose "freedom" and "dignity," by the way? What is the meaning of "freedom," "dignity," "democracy," "self-fulfillment," and many others, when applied to the hundreds of millions of illiterate, unemployed, hungry and bewildered "marginal" men and women who are condemned—they and their offspring—to live, breed and die without hope in this golden age of man's supremacy? If a modicum of freedom, and of opportunity for education, self-fulfillment and decent standards of life is recognized as a birthright—as I think is imperative—to all human beings, not only the values and goals of society, but also its structure, have to be radically changed.

I am afraid, however, that before this change can be engineered, the situation will become still worse, if for no other reason than the overwhelming, unrestrainable increase of the world population. No measure we can now devise and not even our newly acquired ecological or sociopolitical wisdom, supposing we achieve it, can spread the gifts of freedom and self-realization throughout human society until the growth of population is under control. During the coming decades a great deal of mankind's effort will be absorbed by the tremendous task of organizing itself into a highly megalopolized mass society, in which the problems that already baffle and defeat us today will become many times more difficult, and snowball with the new ones that appear in the meantime. Therefore, if we do not change course very soon, the situation concerning quality of life and civil liberties, too, is bound to become worse before it can be made better.

Professor Djhermen Gvishiani[4] feels that Jay W. Forrester[5] has been doing "very interesting work." He told me: "Particularly I like to refer to Forrester's studies on using management-information systems for decision making and forecasting in all fields of enterprise activities." While the Soviets translated most of Forrester's work, Gvishiani cautioned at the same time: "Unfortunately, we do not know much about results of introducing Forrester's ideas or his main concepts into practice. I would stress that when we deal with social systems, they are so complex and they need a multidisciplinary approach to explain more or less these complicated phenomena."

I think that Dr. Gvishiani is right. I have great respect for his culture, knowledge and judgment. I would like, though, to see a much greater participation of Soviet scientists, thinkers and humanists in the growth debate under way. It is a debate of truly transnational and transideological character, which has spread like wildfire everywhere else in the world. This is the time for a philosophical and intellectual effort by the entire world community, and it is sad that the powerful contribution of many socialist countries is slow in coming.

If, as you have said, our forward thinking and planning has to go beyond just the sum of singular projections into the future in a number of vitally important fields, such as the humanities, education, economy, sciences or security, how to match our rationale to their dimensions?

In order to envision and analyze not individual issues but entire clusters of systems into which human activities and expectations are channeled, we must follow a *systemic* approach. We must study the interrelationships of these activities among themselves and with the natural environment and the maze of problems which derive from their multiple cross impacts. Since many key issues have become so large as to exceed national and regional boundaries, this approach must moreover be *global*. Our "spatial horizon" cannot be narrower than the span of our problems, the consequences of our actions. Similarly, our "temporal horizon" cannot be shorter than the cycles of the phenomena we must control, and our approach *diachronic*, embracing all moments during such time continuum. And, last but not least, it should be goal-oriented, *normative*, as they say. Long-term global goals, both feasible and acceptable, have to be set for mankind. This is the most difficult challenge confronting us, but also the most vital one at this critical moment in man's evolution.

Forrester told me: "Driving an automobile is about the most complex system that the human mind can thoroughly grasp." How hopeful are you that man, in his present dismal state of underdevelopment as far as the use of his brain is concerned, will fulfill one-tenth of the program you just outlined?

Fundamentally, I am an optimist. I have faith in man. If he understands a situation, a difficulty, he is ingenious and deft enough to find a solution or a way round. As a man of industry, I always say that if the terms of a problem are clear, even a mediocre manager can passably handle it. But if the terms of the problem are not understood, even the best of managers is bound to fail. Therefore, the first step is to let and lead people to see by themselves the complicated workings of the human system and its interactions with the ecosystem, so that they can progressively grasp at least the general directions in which our collective effort should be guided. The Club of Rome project run at MIT has done a lot in this sense.

But scientists and humanists alike doubt the usefulness of the computer as any extension of the human brain. As Margaret Mead questioned whether machines can simulate human intelligence and to what extent: "I understand," she told me, "that if one gives a computer the general rules by which Beethoven constructed a sonata, it can produce a piece of music that anybody would say was Beethoven, but it cannot finish the sonata. The one thing the computer lacks is the creative process that results in a whole."

Right. Margaret Mead's computer as Forrester's automobile are just tools. And so are a TV set, a laser beam and a printing press. Man can use or misuse them; they can expand enormously his opportunities, or he can become so intoxicated by the relative power they give him as to lose control over it and apply it against other men and finally himself. This is what is occurring today. As specifically regards computers, of course they have no intelligence. If you want, they are dumb machines, but loyal ones; and they faithfully reflect the intelligence or stupidity of the people who have communion with them, instruct them and put them to task.

In your book you reflected upon the future by remarking among other things: "The crucial question will be whether and how the advanced nations of the technological age are willing and capable of organizing the world for the new kind of mass, tense society which is looming up for the '70s and '80s." We are at present racing toward the mid-seventies. How are we doing?

Badly. It is true that momentous things have happened in this beginning of the decade of the '70s that have raised our hopes. Not only has the European Community made a decisive step to become pan-European, and now tries to speak with a single voice; and the long-expected Conference on Security and Cooperation in Europe (CSCE) has finally met, grouping around one table no fewer than thirty-four nations; but in this period the two Germanies have come mutually to terms, as have the two Koreas; ceasefire at long last is within sight and the dawn of a new life can be heralded as imminent in Vietnam and the other Indochinese countries; operative links have been established with China, and the United Nations has started laboriously to absorb her into her fold; some partial agreement on nuclear-armament control has been achieved by the United States and the Soviet Union; and discussion on mutual and balanced forces reduction (MBFR) in Europe have been started.

But on the debit side of the ledger we have very grave entries to register. The powder keg of the Middle East is not yet defused, and so many people are led to despair in that area. And this is but a symptom of a deep-seated, filthy sickness. In 1971 global military spending reached a record of $216 billion, and there was a total of just over 23 million men under arms in the world. If civilians in military-related employment were included, the total would be around 60 million people. It is only slight comfort that this mad race to get ready for self-destruction will now probably slow down—when the world's nuclear stockpile is already fifteen tons of TNT equivalent for every human being. This is sheer madness. And everybody is busy anyhow increasing it, according to his best capacities: the "developed" countries making operational new nonnuclear but equally devastating armaments; and the "developing" countries bolstering their investments in conventional armaments—which between 1961 and 1971 increased by 114 percent. At the same time, the total expenditure on public education in the world is now only about 80 percent of military outlays. And yet half of the adult population is still illiterate. Disquieting signs come also from the agricultural front. While there are still between 300 and 500 million people suffering from hunger and malnutrition in our small world in 1971, the world's agricultural production is increased by a mere three percent over the previous year—and in the developing countries, where it is most needed, only between one and two percent. This is below the rate of their population increase, which is about 2.5 percent per year, and far from the strategic target set for the Second Development Decade, of four percent per year. Meanwhile, the overall gap between the rich and the poor of the world has continued to widen. A minority continues to expand its affluence, but for about two-thirds of humanity, the increase in per capita income has been less than $1 a year for the last twenty years. The current increase in per capita GNP in the United States equals in one year that expected under present conditions for India in about 100 years. Many other examples could be cited. Just one more: The long shadow of a world energy crisis is looming up very menacingly for the latter part of this decade and already some regions are in the grips of difficulties.

Let me note on another front the notable deterioration in relations among the developed nations of liberal economy—the United States, the European Community and Japan. They have continually put aside difficult problems, hoping to deal successfully with them in 1973, or 1974, or 1975. The result is that they now have to face a formidable agenda of complex, interrelated and well-nigh impossible questions. They include nothing less than the reorganization of the international monetary system, the role of the dollar and special drawing rights and perhaps of gold, essential questions of multinational trade, trade blocks, incentives, preferences, reciprocity, tariff and nontariff barriers for both industrial and agricultural products, questions of government procurement and discrimination against foreign bidders, balance of payments, international investments, capital movements, fiscal policies, burden sharing of defense costs, harmonization of antipollution standards and regulations, and the operation and future of the multinational enterprise—plus many other collateral issues, and of course the question of the overall aid needed by the less-developed nations. Unfortunately, there is no indication yet that the negotiating parties recognize the extraordinary importance and urgency attaching to the need to lay the foundations, establish the rules and create the instruments of the world community's economic life for many years to come. They seem to consider the 1973-74 negotiations as a mammoth technical exercise, which can be approached from postures of domestic relevance or expediency. They fail to grasp that the problems cramming their agenda are eminently political in a broad international sense and that as an ensemble they constitute a touchstone against which the capacity of industrial civilization to put its house in order will be measured. The lack of vision and leadership of the most powerful nations of our time is simply appalling. This is the state of the world at the time we are speaking. You, I, or anybody else can draw the consequences.

The picture you draw is impressive. Are all these problems interlinked? What may be the consequences?

The total situation, considered in depth, is alarming. Man is no longer confronted by self-contained problems, but by a tangle of highly dynamic, intermeshing problems, each of them of unprecedented complexity and dimensions. The Club of Rome calls it "the modern *problématique*." And for the first time the challenges and threats are truly global. Man is so bewildered and overwhelmed that trying to get out of the tangle, he is heading instead in the wrong direction. He hopes to win the day by increasing his ranks, or to find an escape through economic growth, and puts his faith essentially in the miracles of his technology. It is these fatal mistakes that have already set human history on a disaster course. Following this course, a succession of crises, ever more serious, is bound to occur piling up one upon the other. Their dominant traits may appear to be now ecological, now political, or economic, or military, or social, or psychological, but their profound and complex nature shows that in reality this is the crisis of a civilization. Unlike similar cases in the past, the crisis we are witnessing affects the entire human system, whose growth in size and power has the degenerative character of gigantism. If remedial action is not taken, in time, this may become a crisis of human destiny.

Is there a way out of this incredible impasse you described?

I firmly believe that there is. As I mentioned, we must first understand the changed human condition. And then make a dispassionate diagnosis of our ills, however anguishing it may be. I believe we are on the track in this sense and, if we persevere, the response of this unique and strange creature which is man will be intelligent, and save him. A profound and thorough renewal of society from inside is needed, and I think it will occur; new values attuned to the new world reality will be indispensable, and I think that they will prevail. The process, though, will be painful, and probably violent. But I think that it is so fundamentally needed and that it will have so great a regenerative power as to align behind it a vast majority of people everywhere and inspire them to carry it out in a determined but most humane way.

I am aware of your years in China, and many years in Latin America, both on assignment for Fiat. I know of your deep and sincere concern about the developing nations. When one studies Robert McNamara's figures of what the rich nations actually are doing to help the poor ones, in relation to their own GNP, then do you truly believe our part of the world will in its own wisdom decide (freely) to share its wealth with our fellow men in that vast, poor world of Afro-Asia?

Let me make a premise. Technological society needs social justice and peace more than any society of the past. In an age of exalted human power and extreme alternatives, social justice and peace not only conserve their primary and lasting ethical value, but turn out to be a matter of great political consequence, ecological concern, and existential significance. Further increases of population, economy and technology will but accentuate this interdependence. Human society will be ever more in danger unless and until the present intolerable disparities between rich and poor, between educated and illiterate, between those who have all the chances life can afford and those who haven't any are eradicated, or at least fundamentally reduced.

Once this truth is understood, the problem will be seen in different terms. It will not be the case of sharing *our* wealth with *other* people (charity or generosity), but of using it in the best way to *guarantee to us*, and others, a more secure life (spirit of community, principle of insurance against risks).

Limits to Growth *enormously stimulated public opinion, certainly in the Netherlands, and in many other nations. Did the report pressure politicians and decision makers to take these problems more seriously?*

Certainly. You are going to write a second book on growth in the near future, I understand. When you write it, I will report to you concrete steps that are now in the planning stage.

What goes for the creation of a trait d'union *between Club of Rome efforts and the lower strata of society, the labor unions, no doubt goes as well for close cooperation between rich and poor nations. Some felt, so far, that the Club of Rome has been too much a rich man's club up till now.*

The rich, the powerful, the technologically advanced are more difficult to convince, they have more to lose, and must make the greatest effort. It is only logical that action should be beamed on them first, or principally. But the Club of Rome is a microcosmic cross section of society as it is, and its purpose is to muster forces from all its parts in order to stave off degenerative involutions and change it harmoniously in all its parts.

What about future plans?

The Club of Rome is promoting a series of "second generation" studies in Europe, Japan, Latin America and the United States. Some of these will be disaggregations from the initial Forrester-Meadows world model. Others will go deeper into parts of the system, such as the population-food-agricultural interfaces or materials availability on a global scale. Others will evolve different methodologies of investigation on the overall world system.

"No single man, no group of men, no commission of prominent statesmen, scientists and technicians, no conference of leaders of commerce and industry, can brake or direct the process of history in the atomic age," Martin Heidegger[7] has said. How hopeful are you that your tire-

*less efforts and those of your collaborators and colleagues will bear fruit
before it is too late for all of us?*

I take issue with this fatalistic assessment. I think that the present
crash-bound course can be changed—by us, I mean the active segments
of the present generations upon which the main responsibility to engineer
change before it is too late rests. I have already affirmed it. Let me
affirm it again in my conclusion. Granted, all the studies and meditations
which can be made, though indispensable, are not sufficient to get mankind out of the pit into which it is more and more tumbling. Granted
as well, the higher level of understanding and vision that they permit
a wide public to reach and the transnational debate they engender about
the dimensions of the world *problématique* are developments of
paramount importance, but not in themselves capable of altering the
course of history. Something deeper and greater must occur, something
having to do with our cultural foundations, our vision of ourselves and
the world. Without the revolution of hearts and minds noted before, a
revolution capable of changing our individual and collective judgment
and behavior, and which has therefore to be rooted in a profound transformation of our entire value system, any other change will be purely
mechanistic, and may even have the adverse effect of leading eventually
to technocratic involution. I maintain, however, that the Copernican
revolution is under way. It has just started and will pick up momentum.
I give it at least a fifty-fifty chance of succeeding. In any time, values,
or the ethos, are what is considered "good" by the people according
to their own judgment, and perhaps under the influence of their leaders,
be they the healer, medicine man, astrologer, sage, prophet, king, priest,
minister, scientist, statesman, or the political class generally. The
"good," either spontaneously detected by the people or suggested to
them, is always related to real or transcendent situations they think they
understand and is invariably connected with the idea of individual or collective survival. Since the reference base which substantiated beliefs and
values in the past has been wiped out, the process of putting together
the pieces of a new reference base and correlating them with one another
is not only indispensable—but, in my view, has already started.

I maintain that at the same time, we in this generation, waking up
to face a new, harsh reality, discover that things that are fundamental
have long been forgotten or sacrificed to material values. We begin to
grasp that the sense of our humanity is indeed essential, but that it can
be derived only by the existence of nonhuman forms of life and our rela-

tions with them, while instead we are wantonly destroying them, species after species. We perceive that our sense of justice, too, is being lost right now that we can leisurely apply it with respect to our contemporaries at marginal costs only. We have the chilling feeling that the sense of danger which used to keep our forefathers always on the alert has been muffled by our arrogance and reliance on the machine, just when danger has become incommensurably greater. And we realize in dismay that even the sense of destiny has left us at the peak of our power: The future depends literally on us and we live instead on a spree of plunder and contamination which will leave a scorched earth to the yet unborn.

This is a rude awakening, but a healthy one. We must keep awake, and explore deeper around us and inside ourselves. We must feel the challenge of our time and understand the total nature of this challenge. We must know that the cost of our answer will be very dear, but that there is no way to cheat on its payment. We must above all realize that short of a profound ethical renewal and a *new humanism,* society will be in danger and our future bleak, whatever our power and capacity. However, these are not impossible things to do. We are beginning to prepare for them. The more we advance along this new road, the clearer we will, perhaps, perceive that man needs to be a much better man if he is going to live in the next century—a learning process I see under way and which shows that he is indeed a rational and spiritual creature worth saving.

NOTES

¹See also conversation no. 16.
²See conversation no. 25.
³See conversation no. 7.
⁴See also *London Financial Times,* December 29, 1972, for a concise summary of Professor Gvishiani's view that strengthening economic cooperation on an all-European basis can only enhance the chances of peaceful coexistence.
⁵See conversation no. 34.
⁶See conversation no. 4.
⁷*Discourse on Thinking,* Harper & Row (New York, 1966), p. 52.

Index